Date Due

MAY 2 4 1968		

America

in

Britain's

Place

The Leadership of the West
and Anglo-American Unity

America
in
Britain's
Place

THE LEADERSHIP OF THE WEST
AND ANGLO-AMERICAN UNITY

by Lionel Gelber

FREDERICK A. PRAEGER, *Publisher*

New York

BOOKS THAT MATTER

Published in the United States of America in 1961
by Frederick A. Praeger, Inc., Publisher
64 University Place, New York 3, N.Y.

Library of Congress Catalog Card Number: 61-11059

Printed in the United States of America

To the memory of

SARA MORRIS GELBER

*Her children arise up,
and call her blessed.*
—PROVERBS 31:28

Preface

This is a book about the leadership of the West. But it is also an analysis of Anglo-American unity. There has been a changing of the guard; Britain remains, nevertheless, the chief ally of the United States. And it is in terms of Anglo-American interaction that this work attempts to set American leadership in perspective.

A word about its general approach may be added. New York was the vantage point from which, after World War II, the writer watched the United States pick up the reins of leadership. But he lived in England from 1930 to 1938 and it was thus at firsthand that he saw how prewar Britain let those reins slip through her fingers.

Against the effect of a Nazi-Soviet pact, the writer warned in print before the fall of Austria. Between the wars, for all who cherished freedom and cared for the defense of Western society, the one element of promise was Anglo-American friendship. The writer's account of its formative years, a plea that it be brought into play at once, was published in London on the day of Munich.

World politics were conceived, however, as a contest for power and, on this side of the Atlantic that was not a popular view. In a best-seller, a year and a half after Pearl Harbor, Lin Yutang could still denounce the prospect of peace by power. It took time, among American officials and American students of international affairs, for a school of political realists to develop.

"Strength without justice is tyranny," said Pascal, "and justice without strength a mockery." The ordeal of civilization may not be the same in the 1960's and the 1970's as it was in the 1930's and the 1940's. Yet great issues do not vanish; they merely reappear in fresh guise. To show where and how they do so is the task of historians. But, such is the tempo of the age, we cannot await their findings. We must anticipate its lessons, if history is not to betray us.

No book about American leadership can restrict itself to narrow confines. For much in the future of humanity depends on the destiny of the West and much in the destiny of the West depends on the kind of leadership it receives. Some of the illustrative detail in a work of this sort may be outdated by events. Basic interests and first principles do not alter.

One circumstance attending the publication of this book should be noted. The final text was in the hands of the publisher before the writer assumed a government post. For opinions expressed in these pages, he alone is responsible.

LIONEL GELBER

Spring, 1961

CONTENTS

I

A Shift in Primacy

If you have a Hungarian as a friend, it used to be said, you don't need any enemies. To recall that harsh, Danubian gibe at a time of travail for the Magyar nation may seem ungracious. But does it not find, in the attitude of allied peoples toward the United States, a resounding Western echo? Certainly it sprang to mind as one listened to the visiting professor from across the seas who, as he finished a happy and fruitful year as guest of a famous and hospitable American university, could yet equate American forces in Europe with Soviet armies subjugating captive states; could even depict Britain and France, with American bases on their soil, as being themselves countries under foreign occupation. A renowned British scholar, with a fascinating new theory of the universe, had thus been unable to get the rudimentary facts of his own world into perspective. And if such as he can be muddled about them, what chance is there for rational understanding between lesser mortals?

The irony of events will be evident. From Versailles to Pearl Harbor it was the despair of Western democracies that, after World War I, the United States, enriched and unscathed, had retreated to an Olympian height; that she would go on reaping the benefits of victory but not share the burdens of peace. Eventually, in World War II, she joined with Britain and lesser cobelligerents to liberate Western Europe from Nazi rule; after that conflict she would do much, economically and strategically, to put non-Soviet Europe back on its feet. Since 1945, as a matter of fact, it has not been the absence of American power which some of her own Atlantic allies have deplored but its imperious outward thrust. If, nevertheless, the United States had again withdrawn from Europe, many of her critics—those, that is, who are not pro-Communist or even ultra-neutralist—would have sung quite another tune; there would have been utter consternation if the United States—in accordance with Soviet desires—had sought,

1

bag and baggage, to pull out. For to be damned if you do and damned if you don't is the price of leadership.

Peace is preserved by an East-West equilibrium, and Anglo-American solidarity has again figured in this as the mainstay of the West. But its maintenance has not been easy. Disaster loomed in 1939 because the West had renounced a policy of strength; after World War II dissension was provoked even among the English-speaking peoples by the manner in which, under an American lead, the defense of the West has had to be organized. One day a peace settlement may be attained which, requiring no enforcement, no guarantees, no alliances, is more than a reprieve from war. And when that day arrives the instrumentalities which furnished power for peace may be discarded or converted to a nobler, more creative use. Meanwhile, when absolute weapons threaten to obliterate rival camps and pollute the earth, all contestants perceive that, as President Eisenhower remarked, there is no alternative to peace. But neither, if it lacked countervailing arms, would the West have any alternative to surrender.

To its efficacy in blocking her, the best witness is Russia herself. In a ruin that were apocalyptic she would suffer as much as any; for her, too, if her aims are to be accomplished, World War III has had to be averted. Reprisals by the West, however, would be less of a menace without the North Atlantic Alliance, without American bases or missile ramps in nearby Allied lands. And by inveighing against these major vehicles of Western power, the Soviet Union would disrupt a global strategy by which she has been deterred. Anglo-American friendship is what, at rock-bottom, made feasible the coalition strategy of the West. Collective undertakings, however, have not only kept an outer peril at bay; they themselves contained an inner one. Britain's proximity to the European continent would, for instance, expose her to Soviet attack by medium bombers and intermediate-range missiles before intercontinental missiles and long-range bombers could jeopardize the safety of the United States. And among other postwar inequalities between the two allies, none has been more intractable than this. American leadership is striving to unite the Western coalition against a hostile group. But what Britain has had to ensure is that this unity, with a distant American initiative having the gravest repercussions on Western Europe and the British Isles, will not be mishandled.

England expects every American to do his duty—such, on the eve of World War II, was the isolationist version of Nelson's famous signal. No annihilation, retorted the postwar British, without representation. When Anglo-American friendship first acquired its modern shape more than six decades ago, Britain was leader of the West. Today primacy in the West has shifted from her to the United States. But it has done so in an era of bigness, when large-scale techniques at which the American giant excels at home have also transformed world politics. Western Europe remains the top prize of East-West contention. But as the chief transatlantic outpost of coalition strategy Britain may no longer be treated as a land which a conqueror, in Napoleonic vein or with Hohenzollern envy, might want to invade and subdue undespoiled; as a military target it has, in fact, been liable to wholesale devastation from the European continent ever since Hitler's day. The United States has thus not only taken Britain's place. The greater vulnerability of the latter is a constant reminder of her altered status.

Not that the postwar British, like prewar Americans, abjured wider commitments. Over counterattacks mounted from bases and launching sites on their own soil the British had the final say. But the United States controlled a global strategy by which, once set in motion, the fate of the British Isles might be sealed. Later, as the Soviet Union produced intercontinental weapons, the opposite danger was also feared: that the United States would spare her retaliatory fire in support of European allies so as to preserve her own cities and factories from a Russian onslaught. Anglo-American understanding was the key to coalition unity. Yet the far-reaching necessities of global defense fostered misunderstanding.

A shift in the primacy of the West—with the United States moving to the fore, with Britain hard-pressed to hold her own—had long been on foot. This transposition in leadership was, however, expedited by that same Anglo-American solidarity that twice saved the West; as a decisive feature of the old dispensation, it would not be outmoded in the new. At the end of the eighteenth century, Americans had broken away from the British Crown; they were destined, nevertheless, to have more contact with Britain than with any other foreign power.* A stream of ill will seethed and boiled after the War of 1812: the demarcation of Canadian-American frontiers, the quarrels of the Civil War, the Venezuelan and Alaskan boundary disputes. Another current ran deeper. The North-South conflict retarded nation-building on the

---

* *Great Britain and the United States* (New York: St Martin's Press, 1955), by H. C. Allen, is a readable and comprehensive history of Anglo-American relations from 1783 to the present day.

inside; on the outside, as Thomas Jefferson and James Madison
had been early to acknowledge, the one protective barrier was
the Royal Navy. Perhaps if the *Pax Britannica* had been less
successful, free peoples overseas would have recognized sooner
than they did what, in their self-absorption, they had owed to it.
Britain, at any rate, would look to them, among others, when
the load became too heavy for her to carry alone. England,
Palmerston declared, has no eternal friendships, only eternal
interests. His political heirs discovered, however, that this distinction could be overstressed: Britain has no more abiding interest
than some of her friendships.

Bismarck had pointed to the importance of the English
language as a bond of unity between the United States and Britain.
That an Anglo-American connection must be reckoned with, as
a new, long-term factor in diplomacy, first became plain to the
chancellories at the turn of the century. The Royal Navy, by
localizing the Spanish-American War, had staved off jealous
European powers and, in rounding out her own hemispheric
defenses, the United States could thus obtain oversea possessions;
the liquidation was begun of outstanding differences—Central
American and Canadian ones especially—between Britain and
the United States. But Jefferson's advice against entangling alliances, though now outgrown, was still deemed valid. And in
those years, as a settlement was negotiated, the Anglo-American
relationship was a very one-sided one: no *quid pro quo* was
offered for equal British rights in an isthmian canal across Central
America; the line drawn between Canada and Alaska was accepted
by Ottawa under duress. If these exactions had been those of any
other power, the British would never have submitted to them;
acquiescence, however, was in subsequent generations to pay off
handsomely. For at a juncture when Britain could no longer
operate against European cabals by herself, when Austro-German
ambitions pushed her successively into the arms of the Japanese,
the French, and the Russians, she was resolved to reinsure her
rear across the Atlantic.

In fact she did more. Theodore Roosevelt was peacemaker
between Russia and Japan. The first American President to discharge a political role at the center of world affairs, he secretly
endorsed the revision of the Anglo-Japanese Alliance. And in the
evolution of Anglo-American friendship, this move was an exceedingly significant one. For at that time Emperor William II was
not only trying to drive a wedge into the entente between France
and Britain; by mixing together the Moroccan and Far Eastern

Nothing did more to illustrate the importance of leadership than the effect of a hiatus in it. After World War I, if there had not been an interregnum in the exercise of primacy, the wind might have been taken out of Nazi sails before the Third Reich gathered force. For a productive century after Trafalgar, a free world order had arisen behind the shield of British sea power— a process that went on across vast tracts of the earth's surface where the despots of Europe and Asia could not reach and where even under the British flag the principle of self-government was seldom extended with alacrity. After World War I, however, Britain fumbled, and the United States still kept herself aloof from formal commitments. But when World War II terminated, the United States held on to reins of leadership that Pearl Harbor had thrown into her hands. Soviet antagonism towards the West was not a military danger after World War I; but Germany had scarcely been crushed in 1945 before the East-West contest began to cast shadows that were still more portentous. And yet two features of the new epoch are noteworthy. As leader of the West the United States was not only called upon to act at once. When she took Britain's place, the shift occurred within a pre-established framework of Anglo-American solidarity.

Two stages in its development have been momentous. The first was when Britain, at the turn of the century, converted her relations with the United States from a political liability into a strategic asset. The second, an outgrowth of the first, was when the leadership of the West—if there was to be a West—passed from Britain to the United States with British assent.

During the Spanish-American War the British had urged the United States to forestall European rivals and annex conquered territories overseas. With World War II, however, the tables were turned. Before 1914, Britain was reinsured by the friendlier attitude of the United States in the Western Hemisphere and across the Pacific, while the United States could rely on the benevolent disposition of British power everywhere else. Since 1945 they have each clung to their own spheres of influence— though popular American debate on the topic of imperialism would imply that the United States does not have any. Something, nevertheless, has altered drastically. Until recent years American regional interests were reinsured by general British power. Today it is British regional interests which may be reinsured by general American power.

What has not changed is the stake of the English-speaking peoples in a free world order and the extent to which this has

crises, he also attempted to lure the United States into a Russo-German grouping that would be anti-British. The test for Anglo-American friendship came in 1914. British interests were secure, as they might not have been during the nineteenth century, from American rancor or hostile American designs. The terrain had been cleared, the groundwork had been laid, for that association of the United States with the Entente Powers which was, by 1917, essential for victory.

Not that the English-speaking peoples had by then learned their lesson. If they had, there might have been no second world war and hence no sequel like the East-West contest—one whose outcome, in an era of large-scale technological warfare, could spell the doom of the human race. With the English-speaking peoples, as with others, it has been only too true that, as Santayana once wrote, those who cannot remember the past are condemned to repeat it. What should be recollected, nevertheless, is that when John Hay, as Secretary of State, responded sympathetically to British manifestations of goodwill, he did so not only because profitable deals impended, at Britain's expense; he felt that in general her influence was one for peace and civilization. The balance would be lost for ages, Hay observed, if Russia and Germany arranged things. And with so prophetic a grasp of twentieth-century issues, he put Anglo-American friendship in the context of American national interest—where it belonged.

World War I was a watershed. Anglo-American friendship had emerged before it occurred; after it men were preoccupied with Woodrow Wilson's overarching ideal of a world made safe for democracy. And while the latter was more universal in approach than the former, there was, on the whole, nothing incompatible between them. As Hay foresaw and Wilson was reluctant to admit, the power to back great objectives had to be Anglo-American power. For what, fundamentally, the English-speaking peoples have most in common is a free world order. Unrestricted German submarine warfare and other German outrages may have been the immediate cause of America's entry into World War I. The ultimate cause, as again during World War II, lay deeper.

Anglo-American guarantees to France that Congress ignored, teeth in the Covenant of the League of Nations which the Senate rejected—these were signs of the international realities with which Wilson had been constrained to grapple at Paris. Perhaps some of his program might have been salvaged if there could also have been a practical compromise between the White

House and Capitol Hill. But so lofty was his tone in Paris and Washington that an aura of perfectionism has surrounded the Wilsonian doctrine ever since. And that was a pity, for when men of principle are unrealistic, it is an unprincipled realism which supervenes. During World War II and in NATO afterwards, democracies were arrayed with dictatorships against common enemies. This, however, was not countenanced by Britain and the United States out of disregard for principle: if the great English-speaking democracies should be vanquished, democracy itself could not survive.

Nor had Wilson intended to engage in an ideological mission as such. Despite the long agony of Britain and France he had, month after month, boasted of impartiality between those embattled proponents of democracy and their Austro-German foes; there was less ambiguity in the Allied camp after Tsarist Russia collapsed, but overt acts against the United States rather than the ideological claims of Britain and France were what plunged the Americans into war at last. The facts of power then spurred Wilson on; to the preservation of a free world order, the United States devoted her fresh, unexhausted strength. But in 1945, after an isolationist relapse necessitated a repeat performance, the auguries were not so good as they had been in 1919.

Tragedy for mankind ensued when no peacetime alignment of the English-speaking peoples followed the common endeavors of World War I. Civilization, after 1914, would never be the same again. Materially, once mass technologies had been released in conflict, things were to be bigger and bigger; spiritually they would not improve. The comity of nations might in some degree be restored; the fruits of victory won at so terrible a cost would have to be digested. To accomplish all this no joint Anglo-American effort proved feasible and, as events illustrated, nothing less would suffice. Parity between them had, since the Washington Conference of 1921–22, dispelled the danger that the United States might outbuild Britain, still mistress of the seas, in capital ships. Americans, however, were no more disposed to enforce their own Washington treaties, as the Manchurian episode indicated in 1931, than they had been to subscribe to the Covenant of the League of Nations.

Manifold was the damage which came from an American isolationism protracted beyond its time. And yet would the United States have undertaken appropriate obligations to prop up a free world order without also seeking prematurely to take Britain's place? For ills might flow from a unilateral American assertion

of leadership before Britain was ready to abandon i had resigned herself to handing over the trident irrev

The United States, as it happened, celebrated of age by going into retirement. Economically and tended to destroy in peace that which she had bui As a creditor power she did not lower tariff walls; simony over war debts and reparations, bringing depression of the nineteen thirties, resulted in grief f the entire West. And then a former associate such a entitled to security, after losing the flower of her ma of help from the English-speaking peoples she reso pean policies that they were nevertheless swift to here it was not only the United States that fell sho refused to act regionally with France and so, in good the Germans from again getting out of hand. W Britain was not a lack of power but infirmity of sprang from a misreading of European tendencies no less prevalent on the other side of the Atlanti States, however, could still nourish an illusion of d price which Britain was to pay for it would be in

Memory of the German challenge faded a Soviet threat loomed on the horizon. So also We forgot that Communist efforts to bore from withir the only ones of their kind; long before Hitler, infiltrated her fifth columns in all the ranks of V As they strove to reverse the verdict of 1919, th "organizing sympathy," visibly subverted the defer world order. As brilliant as any German military Moltke to Rommel, was the psychological warfar the resumption of actual hostilities, Germans wa West. The British, quarrelling with the French a according virtual *carte blanche* even to Hitler, let of power on which their independence in Euro ever since the Middle Ages. Americans, sulking ii no good word for any power other than their would have had to comprehend the nature of tha be exerted constructively. Nor was it unforesee riage of Russian perfidy with German megalor Europe at Hitler's mercy and compel other Atlan wealth countries to resist. For the contest of pow indeed, it was redoubled when the English-speal to elude it. Misled about this in a number of re in most not led at all.

been reinforced by their friendship. Psychologically, the British could not relinquish the leadership of the West without a pang; historically, the manner in which primacy was transferred from Britain to the United States reveals how unique the Anglo-American factor has been. Seldom, if ever, can one power take another's place without their relations being warped irreparably. In the years that lay ahead there was much to vex and exacerbate; interests that the United States and Britain must defend in common have always outweighed those which might drive them apart. Wars for hegemony have plagued mankind. But the United States did not wrest her primacy from Britain. It passed to her unopposed because Britain was no longer equipped to lead the West against a bid for overweening hegemony by others.

And so a transition which a second wartime effort against Germany had begun was consummated by the peacetime exigencies of the East-West contest. Bigness made possible the new war technology and coalition strategy; but, as global deterrents were intricate and fraught with peril, they created for Anglo-American friendship and the American leadership of the West a wholly unanticipated set of problems. Nor could the allies of the United States be indifferent to the way American public opinion was formed and the American political system operated. Then, too, there was the Commonwealth—a grouping of powers in which Britain had been the focal point and whose interests, individually and collectively, would be affected when, as leader of the West, the United States took Britain's place. Never has Anglo-American interaction been so constant or ranged so far. Yet common interests might not have bound the English-speaking peoples together if there had not sprung from a common tradition a similar means of settling differences. Without it these might have been much more difficult to overcome than they were.

II

An Anglo-American Dialectic

Unity between the United States and Britain underlies the power of the West, but what underlies their unity? A free world order may be what they have most in common but a special capacity for working together, despite all that divides them, has also been exhibited. And this co-operative potential is not always to the liking of other close allies. France, for example, has long been a fountainhead of modern civilization; as a major partner of the United States and Britain, she resents any exclusion from inner Anglo-American councils. The truth is, however, that on the highest attributes of the West the English-speaking peoples exert no monopoly; they cannot arrogate to themselves a superiority, spiritual and moral, artistic and intellectual, which they do not possess. One privilege they do enjoy: generating more strength than their allies, they can also make the most of their own Anglo-American heritage. English language and literature, Magna Carta and the English Common Law, the King James Bible and the Protestant creed—held in common, these contribute to a common view of man and society and have helped expedite such collaboration as was later to be decided upon. Then, too, the experiment of the Commonwealth has revealed that much in this same background can be adopted by peoples of other tongues, races, and religions. This is significant at a time when it is incumbent upon the United States, as leader of the West, to keep in touch with them as well.

For a while, nevertheless, the character of Anglo-American friendship was misconstrued because its content was misapprehended. The myth of an ethnic tie between the English-speaking peoples died hard. Pioneers of English descent might have tried to stamp an English imprint on their rustic New World environment. But in the British Isles themselves there had been a mingling of races since before the Norman invasion; and the United States was, in a famous phrase, to be even more of a "melting-pot." From the American Revolution to the Spanish-American War a sense of Anglo-Saxon racial identity did not, after all, do much to draw the United States and Britain together; the English-speaking peoples were least in accord politically when they were most ethnically akin. The fact is that the ethnic composition of the United States was being transformed by immigrants from a variety of lands when Anglo-American friendship first became a staple factor in world politics.

As American citizens, moreover, recent newcomers may have been repelled rather than attracted by any *mystique* of race into which, because of their own ancestry, they could not enter. The Irish still had their grievances against the British while American Negroes were hewers of wood and drawers of water for all. As for German immigrants, it may be noted that German stock was deemed part of that Anglo-Saxon racialism which had its vogue during the later years of the nineteenth century and the early years of the twentieth. But in two world wars German-Americans were more split over the cause of the West than any other section of the American populace.*

Blood, then, could not be thicker than water since between English-speaking peoples there was, actually, no one blood. And that is where Joseph Chamberlain, in descanting upon a favorite late-Victorian theme, went amiss. Celebrated as an exponent of an integrated Empire and of closer Anglo-American relations, he should, on both counts, have been the first to discard the fallacy of race. From the conquest of French Canada in the eighteenth century to the multiracial Commonwealth of the twentieth, the British have been at their best when they have put at the disposal of others an incomparable legacy of law, government, and public affairs that could serve men of every color and religious belief. So also there have been great imponderables that were transmitted from the British Isles to North America and which predisposed Americans of diverse origins towards a larger unity at last. Necessity would be the catalyst. But this was preceded by modes of political action that taught the English-speaking peoples how to differ and yet combine.

Great imponderables would not by themselves bind the English-speaking peoples together. But to cherish them was to create a mutual interest in a world order where they or their offshoots might prevail. Russian and German dictatorships would

---

* The role of ethnic groupings within the American political system is discussed in Chapter V.

employ Western techniques to pervert Western values and having thus devalued man try to enslave him. The revaluation of man is, after all, the lodestar of the West.

Not that the British people were fully aware of ultimate issues when some of their statesmen began, at the turn of the century, to cultivate the goodwill of the United States. Still less were Americans properly apprised of them until, with the shift in primacy from Britain to the United States, the realities of power could no longer be disguised or evaded. For it is only when we are on the verge of losing them that we become most conscious of values that, subconsciously, we have treasured all along. On the home front, Britain and the United States did not translate these into political measures and welfare legislation at the same time or under the same circumstances; lesser democracies would do as well or better. But the English-speaking peoples have done most to withstand servile states. It is through common principles that a common resolve can be animated.

As allies, nevertheless, Britain and the United States have fitted into none of the usual categories if only because there has never been a separate formal alliance between them. At the turn of the century, when the United States rejected a British invitation to guarantee the territorial integrity of the Chinese coastline, she was not to be budged from hemispheric isolationism; by the middle years of the twentieth century, when the primacy of the West had shifted from Britain to the United States, they had numerous treaties with others but major security arrangements in which both participated were multilateral rather than bilateral. And yet the unwritten Anglo-American alliance has not only been the backbone of written ones; an order of power in which free societies might flourish could be sustained co-operatively because, through their own institutions, each of the English-speaking peoples had been schooled to co-operate. They do not have the same type of representative government and Britain has had periodic qualms over the kind of leadership the American political system provides. The forms taken among them by representative government are, however, a key to their capacity for sinking Anglo-American differences and, under global exigencies, for closing ranks.

Politically the English-speaking peoples have been nourished by values that are more than political and yet by which the public life of a free society must, in the last resort, be impelled. Not only has the franchise been widened in modern democracies; so also, with administrative controls and social services, has the function of the state. In Britain the party system emerged as a device through which, during the nineteenth century, successive Reform Bills could be implemented. In the United States, however, most of the Founding Fathers had, like the British upper classes, felt that elected representatives should be chosen from among those who by lineage or property were more patrician than plebeian; and George Washington himself visualized the Presidency as being above party. It was therefore no accident that Thomas Jefferson, who repudiated Alexander Hamilton's philosophy of a political elite, should have been the one to inaugurate the American party system; and that Andrew Jackson, symbol of rude, new popular forces, was afterwards the one to utilize it. In all free countries the game of party politics may sometimes be played at the expense of higher interests. No more equitable method of registering the national will has ever been devised.

One broad trend, never seriously questioned in Britain after the eighteenth century and after the Civil War in the United States, marked the public life of the English-speaking peoples: the party system worked because of a saving presupposition between parties that limits could be set to partisanship itself.

But, as a substitute for formal ties, there was also some such presupposition between the English-speaking peoples as a whole. For it was not only on the domestic scene that the custom grew of hearkening, below surface discords, to some deeper concord. Party differences in Britain and the United States were acute; an aptitude for transcending these could, nevertheless, be applied in a larger world arena to their mutual affairs. They had learned how the expedient must yield to principles that are beyond expediency. In the long run, what each practiced alone they might also practice together.

Self-government in the Anglo-American tradition fosters propensities out of which a common defense may be concerted. Signatories can be quite unlike each other in political methods when an alliance is a written one and contains specific terms. In an unwritten alliance, however, partners may have even more to go on when, despite institutional differences, their broad approach to politics is similar. Constitutional dissimilitudes have always been an obstacle between the English-speaking peoples; to help surmount them there have been pragmatic similitudes. It is the business of political parties in every representative democracy to diverge over how the state should be run and by whom. Only where they concur upon rooted continuities will the state itself be stable.

In all this, as a matter of fact, there is a dialectic that might be deemed a counterpart to the one which Marx borrowed from Hegel and which Lenin distorted. Nor does it merely quicken party politics. The proclivities that it engenders may be extended to a wider relationship like Anglo-American friendship. The latter has, at any rate, long exhibited a dialectical process in which the English-speaking peoples diverge and then, on a new plane, reconcile clashing interests for the sake of a still higher common interest. Their higher common interest is in the continuance of a free world order. And yet to reaffirm that is but to await another stage in a dialectical cycle which, slow or fast, shrill or muted, never ends.

Understandings achieved between the English-speaking peoples can thus be regarded as an extrapolation of understandings with which they had grown familiar at home. Not for them was the uncompromising dialectic of communist ideologues; theirs was a less rigorous one. It has been, instead, through the arts of compromise that conflicts between tradition and progress, individual and collective rights, were adjusted. Continuity meant everything to Burke, and the political philosopher who laid stress on this was also the one who uttered the most memorable of laments when the American colonists were goaded into breaking away. The British, however, had shed blood to establish the supremacy of Parliament in the seventeenth century; there would be no enduring consensus within the American Union until after the Civil War. By the close of the nineteenth century representative institutions and the party system had set the rhythm of politics among the English-speaking peoples beyond peradventure of doubt. Governing themselves by a dialectic of divergence and reconciliation, they could deal with each other in a similar vein.

In other political spheres, however, American experience still lagged behind British. Ever since the Middle Ages the English had preserved their independence by arraying themselves against monarchs who sought the domination of Europe—by trying, that is, to maintain a balance of power. And later, as leader of the West, Britain possessed world-wide interests in trade and finance, in oversea communications and a far-flung Empire, in a nascent Commonwealth association. For her the secret of statecraft lay in adaptability; she was groomed for an Anglo-American dialectic by long practice in world politics as well as parliamentary government. But the United States had, on the whole, been sheltered from international affairs by British primacy; her apprenticeship was served in her own hemisphere. What the realities of power

abroad taught the British, American public men had to learn
from sectional pressures at home. As leader of the West it was
now the duty of the United States to manifest statecraft in the
grand style. Whether the American brand of representative democracy would be as suited to this as the British was another question.

Differences in political systems might cause differences in
political behavior. Yet the unwritten alliance of Britain and the
United States was pervaded by the same political values; to
Anglo-American divergence, an Anglo-American consensus would
set limits. It is tantalizing, nonetheless, to consider how, from the
turn of the century, a written alliance between the English-speaking
peoples might have diverted history's volcanic flow. A formal
connection had been dissolved by the Declaration of Independence;
an informal one to take care of common interests—from the territorial integrity of China to the balance of power in Europe—
was, in later years, all that American opinion would countenance.
Its full import was displayed in the major crises of a free world
order; up to that point, however, it had been hard to single out—
too elusive for the English-speaking peoples themselves to pin
down or for other powers accurately to assess. Emperor William
II, detecting its potentialities, tried at first to nip it in the bud;
warmakers thought during World War I that they could achieve
victory before Anglo-American friendship was brought, if ever,
into play. And, as prior to 1917 in the days of Wilson's own
isolationism, so also in the epoch of Franklin D. Roosevelt—an
unsigned commitment upon which the American nation again
hesitated to act was not likely to restrain in time an adventurer
as rash as Adolf Hitler.

Adversaries of the West faced quite another situation,
however, after primacy shifted from Britain to the United States.
The scale on which the West might retaliate is what, in a nuclear-
missile age, deters them. But this strategic danger is the outcome
of a far-reaching political innovation: the fact that the United
States is allied to like-minded powers and committed to the common security beforehand. The exact contingencies in which coalition machinery may be used must, nevertheless, still remain
indefinite; and since it is to American chariot-wheels that her
allies are lashed, they have sloughed off one sort of uncertainty
about the United States only to encounter another. As long as
the power of the United States lay inert, her pronouncements
could soar aloft because they carried no ballast; in the era of
American primacy, what stirs misgivings is the fear that words
might be transformed into deeds all too readily. It is not the lack

of American involvement which haunts postwar Britain as the chief ally of the United States, but the specter of overinvolvement which, under American leadership, bigness in warfare now entails so remorselessly.

Two things will be apparent. In bearing the heaviest load for the peacetime defense of the West, the English-speaking peoples were linked together more closely than ever. The circumstances under which they might diverge had nevertheless altered for the worse. When, moreover, the United States took Britain's place, there were changes in outlook among influential sections of British and American opinion. British elements that might hitherto have favored Anglo-American co-operation shied away from it; American elements that formerly shunned action abroad now expounded less narrow views. The Anglo-American dialectic was modified accordingly. But it was on a note of reconciliation that the most harmful of divergences still wound up. For in the continuance of a free world order the English-speaking peoples share a common interest, and it is one that transcends all that would pull them apart.

III

Changes in Outlook

When primacy shifted across the Atlantic the British and American peoples were bound to look upon themselves, upon each other, upon world crises as a whole, from a new angle of vision. Among some in Britain it was not only strategic disparities that affected their attitude towards the United States; their general economic philosophy was enough to make them censorious. American isolationists, on the other hand, nourished a special grievance against Britain as the one power which, at the gravest turning-points, had done most to elicit American intervention; and there was a flare-up of a vestigial Anglophobia during the Korean War when they demanded that Asia be put ahead of Europe in American defense plans. The misjudgments of yesterday, moreover, dog the claims of many who today enjoy renown as men of judgment. For leadership by the United States has brought reversals, overt and covert, among some American leaders. And it is only by reassessing these that the American atmosphere since World War II can be properly gauged.

In a simpler age and in a society less complex than America's, it would have been harder than it has been to get error condoned, to live down a past which, with primacy, it is, on both the Right and the Left, expedient to jettison. A number cast into limbo because of Communist ties were mostly small fry. Others who were as culpable in misjudgment rest undisturbed in the nation's pantheon.

Nor was it only America's national interest which they misjudged. A miscalculation of Britain's world role was part of the same picture. And that not every item among historic British policies was self-regarding, that many of these arose from the exigencies of leadership itself, was what numerous Americans may have been quietly discovering. Some, at any rate, who once spurned the manner in which Britain approached global questions, have now observed that their own country cannot take Britain's place without, *ceteris paribus,* behaving somewhat as she once behaved.

And yet British critics may be indignant when the United States endeavors to comport herself on a British model. Finding fault with her, they are, as a matter of fact, also repudiating salient features of Britain's own checkered past. Most of the British people have not, however, denied the necessities of American leadership in general; what they have reacted against is the way it has been exercised in particular areas or episodes. But in at least one neutralist segment of British opinion there has been something more deep-seated than divergence over any one specific dispute—over the Far East, over the Middle East or, under an advanced war technology, over the joint defense of the British Isles.

So far as it equates East with West, that group rejects Anglo-American concepts of world order and thus demurs at the cause of the West itself. For primacy had shifted from Britain to the United States during a generation in which the clash of social ideologies has spread from domestic to world affairs, in which the global contests that rack the twentieth century have their non-military phase. When Britain was leader of the West the liberties she espoused were, from Napoleon I to William II, political and national rather than socio-economic. But since 1914 antagonists of the West have presented bids for domination, with doctrine as well as power, inimical to a free world order. When the Hohenzollern autocracy struck, it did not only breach the dikes of Western civilization. Its entire *Weltanschauung* set the tone for more hostile social ideologies which, with France and other Western allies, the English-speaking peoples would have to counteract.

Contests for power in the twentieth century have also been wars of ideas and, while these made some issues clear, they confused others. Dissidents on the Left in Britain had forgotten what, after two world wars, a number of Americans of both Left and Right were only beginning to comprehend. Public agitation by Fascists or Communists in Western countries accomplished less for adversaries of the West than undercover espionage or intrigue. Yet, from the days of British appeasement and American isolationism to those of the Soviet peace campaigns, there were many who—while devoid of ideological sympathy with them—played into enemy hands.

In two respects, however, the present situation is not the same. Before World War II the appeasers on one side of the Atlantic, the isolationists on the other, consisted of popular majorities; their critics were the ones who ran against the tide. In postwar Britain dissidents on the Left may have exerted more influence than extremists on the Right. Within the Left itself they have been a minority.

The difference is one of content as well as size. And here a shift in primacy has been all-important. Prewar appeasers were not obliged to adopt any special attitude toward the United States; postwar neutralists have no choice. Between the wars everybody in Britain was resigned to the passivity of Washington; strategically, at any rate, its offense was that it might do too little rather than too much. Today on the world stage the United States is prima donna rather than supernumerary and the limelight beats down on her accordingly. When Britain was leader of the West there existed in the United States various factions, some Irish, some German, some homebred, whose clamors were specifically Anglophobic. Now, for opposition to Anglo-American friendship, the center of gravity has moved from the United States to Britain.

Dissidents on the Left have been as wedded to democracy as their less radical colleagues. But with the United States they have had a doctrinal bone to pick. When, however, the case against American leadership of the West is overstated, the case against foes of the West is apt to be understated; the tendency is, as in the era of appeasement and isolationism, to find excuses for them. And so it is not only between East and West that lines have been drawn ideologically. On one vociferous British sector an ideological twist has been imparted to the Anglo-American dialectic itself.

At American capitalism a barrage from the Left has, nevertheless, been perfectly intelligible. The edge of the class war was blunted in Britain when a few basic industries were nationalized after World War II and additional social reforms consolidated the Welfare State; superseding the former ruling classes at home, the ruling power of the West is, for the ideologically vehement, a necessary foil. Nor is it implausible to charge that capitalists, British and American, who once egged on Hitler against Communist Russia have, in the East-West contest, been up to their old tricks. Marxian theories of the state had never made headway in Britain; the Marxian analysis of economic imperialism had, however, worked upon the British Left. As between capitalist America and anticapitalist Russia, the latter was therefore often given the benefit of the doubt.

The thesis is one which also found a haven among populist and isolationist elements of the American Midwest: the cause of war is capitalist rivalry over markets, minerals, raw materials, strategic supplies, and oversea communications. Indeed it was because they saw in its economic argument an outlet for pacifist convictions that many non-Socialists joined the British Labour Party.

But at a time of Sino-Soviet imperialism such doctrine is outdated and irrelevant. It should not therefore be mixed up with the serious problems which American leadership entails. Grounds for divergence between the United States and Britain do, unhappily, abound; yet here are fallacies that the recent course of international affairs has tragically refuted. Not that the sins of some capitalist agglomerations can be overdrawn. But in Germany, Italy, Japan, France, Britain, and the United States, they have been at their worst when they aided and abetted dictators whose ideology was anti-capitalist. In 1939 it was two anti-capitalist economies that, under the Nazi-Soviet Pact, precipitated war and set back the clock indefinitely.

For British observers who accept American leadership there has been plenty on the American scene to perturb and dismay. More particularly, American capitalism has not been as enlightened in matters of oversea trade, foreign investment, and economic assistance as it should be. And yet some of its imperfections reside in every form of industrial society. What dissidents of the Left have done is scan it from the wrong end of the political telescope. As neutralists they may not like NATO. But American loans, Marshall aid, the North Atlantic Treaty would never have been negotiated by the Truman Administration with a Labour government if Socialism in Britain had been as much of a bête noire to American capitalism as has been averred. For progressive capitalism and social democracy do, after all, have more in common than either has with any kind of totalitarian dictatorship. In the age of Nazism and communism, both have been high on the executioner's list.

Historically, moreover, the rise of Anglo-American friendship has rebutted Marxian preconceptions, for it emerged at the turn of the century just when, according to fashionable theories of economic imperialism, trade and other rivalries should have driven the English-speaking peoples apart. It was in fact when they were patching up their differences that, from behind high tariff walls, American mass production first invaded the markets of free-trade Britain and her dependent territories overseas.

From the start, nevertheless, an adversary of the West such as Emperor William II saw in Anglo-American friendship a barrier to German domination and sought to have it dissolved. So also the Kremlin, never able to explain it away ideologically, paid tribute to its power by trying to do the same. Stalin, in consonance with Communist dogma, repeatedly forecast the paralysis of the Western coalition through economic conflict; the Soviet Union might thus triumph without war. But it is the strength of the West that has ruled out military conquest, and at the heart of that strength, as the Russians appreciate, is Anglo-American solidarity. Realists, whether they like it or not, must reckon with this as a basic reality. It is the English-speaking peoples themselves who have not always realized what, in unison, their function has been.

And why was that so? Much in the history and institutions of the English-speaking peoples made for divergence. But the very effectiveness of British primacy was to obscure all that the West owed to it. Then, too, something else must be remembered. Power realities had to be understood before the Anglo-American factor could be properly rated among them. To these, with a shift in primacy, the intellectual and academic circles of the United States have lately become more alert. Before the end of World War II, however, it was somehow deemed unworthy even to call attention to them. Long practice with the balance of power had not preserved Britain from misconceiving power realities after World War I. Would the United States, less well versed in that branch of statecraft, prove any more adept after World War II?

Psychologically, the American transition to leadership was not as smooth as initial undertakings seemed to presage. After 1945, great constructive measures for the defense of the West— economic, political, military—stopped the rot in Europe. But the United States was discomfited by the fall of China to Mao Tse-tung and thwarted by the Korean stalemate; isolationists, for whom East Asian affairs came first, could now rehabilitate themselves as quasi-internationalists and thus as custodians of the national interest. Spy scares and their exploitation by demagogues soured the American temper. But the American people as a whole had never been inured by experience to setbacks overseas—and that alone may have goaded them into taking their frustration out on themselves.

Self-rending in the leader of the West was not, however, all that Allies witnessed with alarm. This has been traced by Mr. D. W. Brogan to the illusion of American omnipotence—to the belief that but for treason or knavery at home no situation abroad could be beyond the capacity of the United States to handle. Yet this was not the only illusion that had to be shed.

There was also the companion illusion of American omniscience which irked the friends of the United States: the postulate that in coalition affairs she, more than they, knew all the answers; that sagacity dawned overnight with primacy. It was true that with her strength she could do more than her principal Atlantic allies; that she always knew best what should be done "ain't," as the song goes, "necessarily so." Today, certainly, it would be imprudent for the American leader of the West to exhibit the sort of hauteur which the British, before their splendid isolation ceased to be splendid, used to display. And so the unilateral in strategic moves is not the only thing that has to be avoided. A moral unilateralism, when the United States collaborates with coalition partners as morally aware as herself, may also be repugnant.

With primacy, a new phase in the political education of the American people was inaugurated. The onus for the defense of a free world order had, but for the interlude of World War I, rested on Britain. Because of this there was a curious duality in the American outlook upon international affairs—one by which the British had often been nettled. Holding herself aloof from power politics beyond the Western Hemisphere, the United States pursued them ruthlessly within it. Americans would therefore scarcely be as impeccable in their anti-imperialism as they proclaimed. They had renounced the imperial rule of George III. By war and by threat of war, as well as by purchase and pioneering, they did in contiguous territories what the British had done on distant continents. After a vast realm had been carved out on land, moreover, the process was capped through the acquisition of key outposts overseas.

But for the expansion of the United States and the strength she could generate, a free world order would have been doomed in World War II, if not World War I. What, nevertheless, exasperated British and French allies was the notion that her power was, somehow, less equivocal, more immaculate in origin, than theirs. A habit of saying one thing and doing another was thus no monopoly of either perfidious Albion or the European chancelleries. Not that the English-speaking peoples deceived each other; the danger was when they deceived themselves. In Britain there was the collective death-wish of the Baldwin-Chamberlain period. And Americans had been taught to misjudge those contests of power which, beyond a sheltered hemisphere, the *Pax Britannica* had kept remote.

A widening of responsibility required a broader grasp of basic issues. Public orators might, as is their wont, demand that

Americans shape the present in the light of the past; but leader-' ship should also impel them to reassess the past in the light of the present. What if, for example, a somewhat different sequence of events had attended the entry of the United States into World War I? In Russia, Tsar Nicholas II had abdicated on March 15, 1917. When the United States declared war on Germany and tried to make the world safe for democracy, she did so without having had to hobnob in the Allied camp with the Tsarist autocracy. Britain and France, however, had had no such luck; it was as though, ideologically tainted from the start, they had been pouring out their lifeblood for the three most catastrophic years of the twentieth century, so that the United States, when she jumped into the fray, might remain unsullied ideologically. But after Pearl Harbor the American people could no longer opt to intervene or abstain at will. They were not only caught in the very sort of alignment—that of the West with another Russian brand of dictatorship—which they had previously managed to eschew; they had often upbraided the British for action as ambiguous as that on which they, too, were now embarking.

And as primacy has shifted from Britain to the United States, Americans have learned—though this is still never fully admitted—what the British have long perceived: that it is better to compromise ideologically and lead than not to lead at all. After World War II, moreover, it was another isolationist power, India, whose vein would be a perfectionist one—and here, too, in spite of her own regional backslidings. A high moral tone had, as a matter of fact, been apt to accompany expressions of British self-interest when Britain, supreme on the seven seas, enjoyed strategic immunity. To confound paramount power with moral superiority is, however, a luxury in which the leader of the West can no longer indulge. What the United States must do is justify the power of the West by the purpose that it serves. But so diverse are her own interests and those of her allies that this is easier said than done.

If the realities of power had not been misinterpreted before the advent of primacy, Americans would not have to reinterpret them today. The United States has taken Britain's place—and as the role of the one is elucidated, so is that of the other. But the re-education of Americans is occurring at a time when bigness, as it remolds the American economy, is also reshaping the environment in which public opinion is formed. A conformist upsurge like McCarthyism detracts from the prestige which, as leader of the West, the United States should possess in the eyes of her allies. When, however, the American economy was enlarged in scale so were pre-existing conformities.

A shift of primacy meant that the leadership of the West would be determined in a new climate of opinion. As mass living standards are raised, the tendency is for Britain and the United States to resemble each other in social organization more and more; the Welfare State is innately egalitarian. But individuality can still express itself in that British democracy the origins of which are aristocratic and relatively homogeneous; in American society, where fissiparous tendencies have to be arrested, there has been less tolerance of individuality. This may date from the Puritan era. Neither despotism nor dictatorship have, however, bound together so great a conglomeration; and for these, self-imposed uniformities may have been a substitute. Lest they be ripped apart, the American people, volatile, heterogeneous, sectionally divided, have tended to exalt a common pattern of folkways unduly.

The fact that the pace of national development was forced in the United States and unforced in Britain may, then, have had a lot to do with differing national mentalities. Vast human energies had to be summoned up before the vaster energies of the American economy could be released; nor have all scars healed—as the current segregation issue shows—from the Civil War. It is against so unquiet a recent background that the United States must grapple with the intractable in world affairs, that allies ask whether, as leaders of the West, Americans are likely to be more impatient than their British predecessors. For even when the British and American peoples are steeped in complacency, their mood is not the same. Self-satisfaction contributed to British impolicy during the nineteen-thirties; seldom does American complacency spring from an inner composure. The British people conform least, are more prone to make allowances for themselves and others, when they are most secure; apart from war periods, it is in boom times that American conformity reaches its zenith. For a psychic insecurity seems to gnaw at the American mind and it did so before the anxieties of leadership during the East-West contest arose.

When the British, at any rate, were pre-eminent in the West, they reacted with more *sang-froid* than Americans to either praise or blame. Their comedown has been drastic and a somewhat fretful demeanor is, as a consequence, scarcely astonishing. But during their halcyon days so self-assured were they that critics amused rather than angered them. At their most smug, on the other hand, Americans have never been as magisterially thick-skinned—not when spread-eaglism was at its apex, not when economic growth was steadiest. Consequently they are more sensitive, less disposed to take strictures in their stride when fault is found with the way they do things.

Nor is this to slur over countless American books, plays, cartoons, journals—middlebrow and highbrow—that, apart from the exchanges of politics, do indulge in the frankest national self-criticism. But its general tone is a somewhat humorless one. And yet, from the age of Shakespeare until the first third of the twentieth century, the British, despite strange interludes of Puritan and Victorian solemnity, always knew how to poke fun at themselves. It was indeed when they were at the pinnacle of power that they added the lilting satires of Gilbert and Sullivan to the nation's folklore; when even the raillery of George Bernard Shaw first won plaudits that his American counterparts have never had. American mass media—the radio, television, motion pictures, much of the press and theater—purport to entertain rather than edify or enlighten. Only on the rarest of occasions are shafts of the Comic Spirit ever aimed at American society as such.

Political dissent in English-speaking countries is the breath of the Anglo-American dialectic itself. Yet in the United States it is critiques of selected aspects of American life that are taken with good grace; what may not be called in question is American culture or the American economy as a whole. Elsewhere a depression like that of the nineteen-thirties might have lent point to Marxian philippics; but, with few exceptions, American Communists were intellectually mediocre and the opportunity passed. Nor did American internationalists define the insularities of isolationist America in depth; until after primacy had shifted across the Atlantic, insistence on power realities came from writers whose antecedents were not American. American democracy is scarcely alone in presenting a contrast between precept and performance. What, however, Americans seem most to resent are analyses which stir up their own hidden doubts—in which American society may be weighed and found wanting, not by alien criteria but by its own.

Concern with American traits is, of course, a reflection of America's importance. Nor was there a respite after primacy shifted from Britain to the United States; the East-West contest left no time for a gradual mellowing. When pro-Soviet attempts to plumb the inmost recesses of American strength were disclosed, old insecurities were revived and fresh ones added. Senator McCarthy, and others like him, employed lawless methods to unearth pro-Soviet endeavors among government officials. All he accomplished was to put legitimate inquiry into past misjudgment, on the Right as well as on the Left, under a cloud.

And yet until this inquiry is undertaken, the story of a shift in primacy from Britain to the United States will be incomplete. A grand inquest into past misjudgment should, moreover, be Anglo-American and not solely American. For while its British and American manifestations were not the same, there was a community of error between them.

It cut across parties on both sides of the Atlantic. Churchill was derided and Roosevelt had to tread warily until events brought the English-speaking peoples to their senses. In Britain the Right and the Center should have been intent upon upholding established institutions. Fascism and Nazism, employing Communist methods and anti-Communist slogans, constituted primarily a revolt against the West. Gulled by them, some on the Right in Britain had even aided and abetted the subversion of a free world order—had imperiled, that is, their own society. The Left, on the other hand, had grasped the nature of the threat but neither in Britain nor the United States was it disposed to forestall by force the use of force. New Dealers had been utilizing power to reform the American economy. Until the end of World War II they, nonetheless, aspersed as illiberal any who argued the case for power to achieve liberal aims abroad.

In the tight-knit world of the twentieth century, one's concept of world order is as much a test of political principle, whether liberal or conservative, as one's attitude towards domestic objectives. But most of the intellectual mentors of postwar America, rarely acknowledging past error, did not see that point until primacy had driven it home.

Where there was scant curiosity about the character of a free world order there could be no serious comprehension of the role of power in preserving it. As long as Britain was preponderant, she would be denounced by Englishmen and Americans alike for an imperfect assimilation of freedom and power. Presently, nevertheless, Americans were to learn that this defect did not, *au fond,* signify a difference in national virtue; that it was, rather, inseparable at times from the very exercise of leadership. Perhaps, too, if Americans had been taught to regard Anglo-American friendship as a unique, potent, decisive factor in modern history they would have been better prepared intellectually, and therefore politically, for world tasks. At any rate, in tomes compiled and in the academic instruction purveyed it went virtually unrecorded. After World War II there was controversy over pro-Communist influence in schools and colleges. But the political education of Americans had suffered more from what the well-meaning had neglected than from what wrongdoers may have tried to do.

Not that intellectual and academic compeers in Britain had always set a good example. Dissidents on the Left were disciples of prewar scholars and writers—some Fabian, some Marxian, some neither wholly the one nor wholly the other—who had been as sedulous as enemies of the West in disparaging the world function of the Britannic realm. And they did not only fan anti-imperialist flames among Asians who sat at their feet. American graduate students had old prejudices, dating from the American Revolution, rekindled and corroborated.

The trouble with the present generation, someone has said, is that it has not read the minutes of the last meeting. But the outlook of American intellectuals, when the United States hovered on the threshold of primacy, rendered this dictum a trifle inadequate. Who kept the minutes, it may be asked, and with what insight, when read, would they have been expounded? The realities of power, the problem of leadership, the Anglo-American factor —all these were interrelated questions of which, before primacy shifted from Britain to the United States, Americans had small inkling. From the outset, to be sure, the utmost attention had been paid in American halls of learning to cultural ties with Britain; it was as though the only bonds which the American Republic wished to sever were political ones. And yet that predilection was in itself a political fact of the first magnitude. Without it there might never have been an Anglo-American dialectic through which reconciliation became the sequel to divergence.

At the turn of the century, John Hay saw that a more definite form of unity was required. And one gifted American historian, Henry Adams, did wholeheartedly concur—though none had so valid an ancestral right as he to nourish an ancient grudge. But the view of most academic intellectuals was as provincial as the milieu to which they belonged, and Adams, deemed a trifle odd, stood with Hay nearly alone.

World War I altered that. Inspired by Woodrow Wilson, a large number of academic intellectuals thenceforth preached his ideals. Yet they often espoused brands of internationalism which would have been as impracticable as the nationalism into which the commonalty of America had relapsed. For they also evaded the facts of power—unwittingly, perhaps, because in the face of isolationist torpor they could do nothing about them. The utopian streak in their philosophy lasted, for many, through the early years of World War II, and only primacy dispelled it.

The facts of power could not, however, have been evaded if the facts of history had not been misstated. The preservation of a free world order has been the central issue of the twentieth century, and misjudgment is inevitable when this is ignored. During the first decade of American primacy, when the Soviet menace replaced the German, few cared any longer about those who had misrepresented German designs, and only those were held culpable who had duped the West about Russia. But if the West had not been self-immobilized after World War I, and if Western Europe had not been weakened by the second conflict which ensued as a result, the Russian danger might have been less acute. Isolationism was fostered when the writings and teachings of the period disregarded a special community of interest with Britain and France. When the entry of the United States into World War I was attributed to British propaganda, as well as to the influence of munitions makers and international bankers, Americans were steeled to repulse its wiles on a subsequent occasion.

They had, as it happened, merely been made more susceptible to propaganda from the other side. None could match the guile with which Germans, by depicting themselves as innocent in 1914 and therefore mistreated ever since, promoted their second bid for world mastery. And yet for complicity in a sinister campaign whose consequences we still feel, academic historians and popular writers in the West have never had to answer. For the rewriting of history did not begin with Stalin, and as the American outlook changes so are further efforts made to revise the past.

On this score, nevertheless, the British were in no position to utter reproaches. Churchill's Britain earned the gratitude of all free men. But had a firm hand been taken after World War I, the ordeal it underwent might have been avoided; appeasement had been nourished by the same sort of German propaganda as had fed American isolationism. With the fruits of a victory which cost them so little, Americans could afford to be profligate after World War I. Like their French allies, however, the British had paid a ghastly price for it and yet it left them with a debilitating sense of guilt. When told that the so-called *"Versailles Diktat"* might only be upset at their expense, the British people scoffed. But having failed to stop the rewriting of history, they could not prevent their own place in history from being remade.

For pro-German sentiment the toll has thus been prodigious. Yet its manifestations among the English-speaking peoples were not everywhere the same. After World War I it was hereditary dislike of the French together with an ingrained sympathy for Germans which prompted appeasement in Britain. When the United States and Britain backed down on their security pledges to France, the latter relied more than ever on her East European protégés. Germany paid reparations with funds which private American investors supplied. Britain and France bickered over them as well as over the Middle East. Reparations were abandoned. But the United States still wanted her French and British wartime associates to pay war debts to her. Throughout the West the upshot was economic disaster, and in Germany the Weimar Republic collapsed.

One underlying difference in British and American attitudes may be noted. Pro-German and pro-American feelings among the British were seemingly unrelated; that these two proclivities might be incompatible or mutually exclusive was a notion that never occurred to the British people. But in the composition of American isolationism, its pro-German ingredients had long been anti-British. For texts can vary when history is rewritten, and it was only in a final crisis that the same rudimentary truths appeared the same on both sides of the Atlantic.

Pearl Harbor, of course, vindicated Americans who sought to join Britain in the defense of the West. It may also have discredited those who had opposed them. A number, however, switched from one outlook to the other as though they had never been isolationists. And they did so with ease through manipulations of opinion which covered up as well as exposed. Nor was this a trivial matter. A democracy that does not hold public men to account impairs its own foundations. In private life it is right for the individual to forgive and forget; in public affairs the possible range of damage may be not only vast but irretrievable. One safeguard against the repetition of error is to pinpoint it. Another is to make sure that the credentials of those who would reveal it are untarnished.

The circumstances under which the United States went to war militated, however, against a thoroughgoing self-scrutiny. In Britain there had been a clean break with an appeasement past when Churchill took over from Chamberlain and the nation fought on alone. But in the United States President Roosevelt himself bridged the isolationist and interventionist epochs and expedited a smooth turnabout for many. A few indeed who may have been on the defensive tried to put the President there when they charged that he had invited the Japanese attack on Pearl Harbor so as to embroil his country with Hitler. Later there was controversy over concessions to Stalin at Yalta and over the conquest of China by Mao Tse-tung; the Hiss case and McCarthyism spread their blight; some who still shied away from collective measures against the Soviet Union in Europe were among those who, during the Korean War, agitated for an all-out effort against Communist China. Most preferred not to accuse lest they be accused.

The fact is that, despite the alarums and excursions of the postwar period, the American past was only raked up within narrow limits. For there were skeletons to conceal in both conservative and liberal closets. Isolationism had made strange bedmates; whatever else might be divulged, all were willing to suppress that awkward truth.

Espionage and intrigue on behalf of Russia—before and after the Nazi-Soviet Pact—were investigated by Congressional committees and came before the courts. There was more reluctance to recall that, during the Battle of Britain, when a free world order hung by a thread and Hitler had not yet turned upon erstwhile Soviet confederates, American isolationists and American Communists had been working along parallel lines. It was as though, in fellow-travelling, there might, retrospectively, be a privileged interlude. Against the defense of the West the pro-German, the pro-Russian, and the wantonly misguided could, for a critical interval, operate concurrently. But during postwar arraignments, it may have been supposed that only the pro-Soviet faction had gone astray.

Sauce for the conservative goose was, however, sauce for the liberal gander. No imputation could be made against isolationists among New Dealers that did not also apply to the American Right; care had to be taken lest they be attacked in terms that might recoil against such top Republican figures as Herbert Hoover, Arthur Vandenberg, and Robert Taft. One bizarre touch was nevertheless provided some years later. By helping to usher in the new era of American primacy, Senator Vandenberg made amends for past misjudgment. The first member of Congress honored by a memorial on Capitol Hill was, all the same, so impenitent a holdout as Senator Taft.

It is, however, not only the immunities which conservatives enjoyed and granted that should be observed. Liberals dislike being reminded that any among them have a past to live down. And yet a free world order might have been lost, there might be no liberal cause for them to champion today, if the isolationist views of some liberal spokesmen had prevailed. It may be that they did not subscribe to the evil Lindbergh fantasy that saw in Nazis and Fascists the wave of the future. But liberals were among Lindbergh's coadjutors or served America First, and even activities as sinister as these were not held against them.*

And yet what afterwards most favored those who erred, Right, Left, and Center, was the actual course of the war. Hitler, like Napoleon, could not cross the English Channel, much less the Atlantic Ocean. Unlike the French and other invaded West Europeans, the English-speaking peoples were not riven after World War II between those who had resisted the German occupation and those who had collaborated with it. In the United States, as in Britain, collaboration was never anything more than potential. What also saved liberal isolationists from impeachment by fellow liberals was that liberal attitudes in domestic affairs rather than the preservation of a free world order were still a yardstick for liberalism. But such a dichotomy was in itself a relic of a time when British predominance underwrote American independence. And with a shift in the primacy of the West to the United States it was wholly outmoded.

Illiberal trends on the home front were nevertheless what, during the era of McCarthyism, helped to make her own allies doubt the qualifications of the United States for leadership. But here, too, it would have been easier for American liberals to fight injustice if they themselves had not oversimplified the issue; if, by a misreading of recent history, they had not given self-seeking reactionaries their chance. No attention was, for instance, paid to

---

* Planning a new party, for example, Chester Bowles urged Lindbergh, in July, 1941, to run for the Senate. *See* Wayne S. Cole, *America First* (Madison, Wis.: The University of Wisconsin Press, 1953), p. 179. Was this a step, at a low point in the war, towards an American regime that would be *persona grata* to Nazi victors? According to Cole, among others who co-operated with America First were Charles Beard, William Benton, Stuart Chase, Robert Hutchins, Philip Jessup, and Norman Thomas.

Resemblances may also be mentioned here between the Lindbergh forecast and the prewar philosophy of John Foster Dulles. Lindbergh talked about waves of the future; Dulles envisaged the future as belonging to the three "dynamic" powers of the Axis who, in his opinion, would never assail the United States. (For further comment on this phase of Dulles' career, see Chapter VII.) The Dulles misjudgment went beyond the bounds of traditional isolationism. In North America, however, few grasped the kind of psychological warfare with which, between the wars, Germans and pro-Germans had undermined the West. Liberals, moreover, later had to cover up error in their own camp. They were not eager to expose conservatives on issues over which some liberal oracles had gone to an extreme.

the effect of fifth columns in wartime Europe; to the assistance proffered Hitler by French Communists when, during the period of the Nazi-Soviet Pact, the traitors who betrayed France were on the extreme Left as well as on the extreme Right. The East-West contest rendered it imperative after World War II to protect the nerve centers of American power. But American liberals, who were unacquainted with Communist machinations, pooh-poohed the danger. Demagogues and inquisitors poisoned the American atmosphere. There would have been fewer opportunities for them to appear as custodians of the national interest if liberals had been better informed.

Nor did the vogue which ex-Communists enjoyed tend to foster a more sober view. But for the irrational in their nature they might never have conspired against a free society; in the disclosures they made, in the advice they tendered, in the influence they exercised, the same irrationality was evident. An irresponsible past was exploited irresponsibly. But the liberal-minded did not only object to abuses, under Congressional auspices, of the investigative process. They decried the very idea of reassessing past irresponsibility, Left and Right.

The transition to leadership was, at any rate, attended by the political mysteries of Alger Hiss, Harry Dexter White, and J. Robert Oppenheimer, and it was out of context that all three were wrangled over. Alger Hiss may or may not have furnished Soviet agents with State Department papers, but intellectuals leapt to the conclusion that their sort of person would not do that sort of thing. That one might is written large in the history of modern times, and the sense of caste thus displayed only stirred up an anti-intellectualism which had long been endemic in American society.

As for Harry Dexter White, it was alleged that he had passed secrets from the Treasury to Russian agents. Here wartime proposals were mixed up with postwar policies. In drafting the Morgenthau Plan, did Harry Dexter White act at Moscow's behest? It may be that he did. Yet the breakup of the German Reich had first been suggested some years before, during the period of the Nazi-Soviet Pact, when the Soviet Union and Nazi Germany were jointly carving up Eastern Europe between them; Churchill was sympathetic when Roosevelt, prior to the Morgenthau Plan, broached the idea at the Teheran Conference. But McCarthyite fervors were rampant when this question was ventilated after the war; by then, moreover, the Truman Administration was endeavoring to rebuild rather than weaken Western Germany. The evidence could scarcely be analyzed without a recapitulation of the chronological facts, and this was not forthcoming.

It was, however, in the case of J. Robert Oppenheimer that lessons of recent history were ignored by some who should have respected them most. He had contributed greatly to the development of atomic weapons and to dispense unceremoniously with his services seemed outrageous. If, on the other hand, the United States had not also produced a hydrogen bomb, the free world might subsequently have been unable to maintain against Russian war technology a thermonuclear equipoise. Honest differences over the wisdom of such a step were natural enough among high-level advisers; what was disquieting in Dr. Oppenheimer's dissent was his strange ideological background. When he tried to exonerate himself, various facets of his career were divulged; it was in his own interest to make a clean breast. Nevertheless, one point, with wide implications, remained obscure. Persecution of Jews by the Nazis had, he confessed, roused him to fury and it was because Communists opposed Hitler, Dr. Oppenheimer claimed, that he backed them financially. Yet for nearly two years, as long as the Nazi-Soviet Pact lasted, the Nazis had been not combated but assisted by the Communists. The latter were given regular and substantial financial support by Dr. Oppenheimer throughout that period.

Nor did political naïveté, which was his plea in extenuation, explain matters. Dr. Oppenheimer had been conversant with the antagonism of Nazis and Communists before August 1939; the signature of a pact between them, precipitating World War II, could scarcely have escaped his notice. But this is not all that puzzles the observer. Foremost in exculpating him were sections of opinion which could least afford to wink at so basic an error; during the period of the Nazi-Soviet Pact none had more to lose than scientists, scholars, and thinkers in every field. And then, too, in Britain, where Dr. Oppenheimer was treated afterwards as a martyr to McCarthyite fears and phobias, a few unasked questions might have been apposite: what were his private commitments when the British people stood most in need of friends across the Atlantic? when the Battle of Britain raged? when a free world order was in gravest jeopardy? For anti-intellectualism darkened the American scene when the United States first became leader of the West. The misjudgment of intellectuals, alas, did little to alleviate it.

The past, however, ceased to trouble as the political education of Americans was deepened by all-absorbing contact with present-day realities. In the sphere of opinion, as in the conduct of policy, there was, nevertheless, still a lag between current exigencies and more sequestered days. Under the sheltering arms of Britain a free world order had grown up; yet Americans, who had often carped at her use of power, now assumed that in their hands it would reveal a more redemptive quality. And on the home front, too, it was still in traditional terms that most of them conceived the evolution of their own society. But an environment transformed by bigness would never be the same again. Although even conformist trends were magnified by a new, larger setting, it was only in such a setting that American resources could be mobilized for the defense of the West.

A nation is as incapable as a person of seeing itself as others see it. But primacy had come to stay and the tensions of American life were watched not because they might be academic items in a comparative study of national idiosyncrasies. The conditions of primacy had altered and all who were associated with the United States would, for good or ill, be affected by that crucial fact.

IV

The Conditions of Primacy

BIGNESS AND LEADERSHIP

During the middle years of the twentieth century, the same advances in air power that augmented the range of war also made possible the extension of deterrents against it. For in international as in domestic affairs the biggest of modern revolutions has been the revolution of bigness. Wartime coalitions had twice been organized on the largest scale; but so, when the United States took Britain's place, was a peacetime coalition. Antithetical are the uses to which bigness may be put. Techniques that enabled democracies to redistribute wealth also helped dictatorships to socialize despotism; and contending societies were not only more tightly integrated within but pitted more tautly in rival alignment against each other. Too sanguine had been the expectation that an enlarged scale of human endeavor might soon usher in One World. Technology unified the human race; strategically and ideologically it also magnified the scope of East-West differences.

Under these circumstances, moreover, the conditions of primacy had altered. The continuance of a free world order would, as ever, provide a community of interest between the United States and Britain. But there were fresh grounds for Anglo-American divergence when Britain, still a pillar of the West, strove to retain status and strength.

Much that seemed unplanned when Britannia ruled the waves could, in the new era, only be dealt with by conscious and collective efforts. A favorable balance of power in Europe, coupled with mastery of the seas, allowed Britain, except for an interlude like the Crimean War, to stay relatively uncommitted. So also there was a trend towards a free world order which its own British guarantors, with their empirical approach, never fully defined; it coincided, all the same, with the spirit of British institutions at home and with the substance of British interests abroad. Blunders in Ireland, India, and South Africa marred the effect of this salutary process; its American beneficiaries—even the British people themselves—took it as in the nature of things. And yet it was nothing of the sort. Activities that were ostensibly unrelated—from the financial role of the pound sterling and the City of London to the strategic vigil of the Royal Navy at Gibraltar, Suez, and other key points—were separate parts of a single whole. None were automatic.

When she had held the ring for the United States during the Spanish-American War, Britain hoped to win an ally or friend. But regimes antagonistic to a free world order were reared on land power and, in thus bottling them up, the British gave a classic demonstration of how sea power worked.

This was nevertheless the last gesture of its kind. After the turn of the century the West was threatened on both sea and land. In World War I it had to fight the German Navy, and in World War II there was the Japanese Navy as well as a German fleet to be subdued. Air power, moreover, had come into its own. Military changes in the task of leadership are plain. During the palmy days of British primacy, air power did not exist and even in land power, when the two German wars occurred, Britain was caught short. Today, as leader of the West, the United States must be ready to operate in all three elements.

And yet the most far-reaching change is fundamentally a political one. When world power was centered in Europe, Britain, as leader of the West, adjusted her relations with outlying countries—the United States, Japan, even Russia—so as to maintain the European balance. But now it is as a decisive counter in a global balance that the United States preserves a European equilibrium.

Of all this, however, she had few glimmerings when, after the wartime reshuffle in the leadership of the West, the postwar era began. Prime Minister Churchill and President Roosevelt had formed an epoch-making team—one shudders to think what the fate of mankind might have been at critical junctures if either of them had not been available for the highest office. But the last Roosevelt Administration, as Churchill perceived, did not want to side with Britain against the Soviet Union. To divide the German war effort and avert another Nazi-Soviet Pact, it was imperative to keep Russia in the war. At Yalta, President Roosevelt had indulged in loose talk with Stalin about the British; Churchill had dissented over the deployment of Allied troops for the invasion of Europe and wanted the Anglo-American line drawn farther to the east. Later it was Americans who, dismayed by Russian bad faith in Eastern Europe, wondered whether the British Prime Minister had not been the more perspicacious of the two. Then, also, there were elements in the Roosevelt Administration so oblivious to the historic bases of Russian power and the nature of Soviet tyranny that they hankered for a Russo-American deal at the expense of the British and French empires.

It may be, at any rate, that the prospect of Communist ascendancy throughout Europe would have been less ominous if Roosevelt, in his declining years, and Truman, when he entered the White House, had taken as seriously as Winston Churchill Poland's right, under the Yalta accords, to a freely elected government. This might have foreshortened the Soviet imperium and made it possible for all the German occupation zones to be treated as one. The United States, however, took Britain's place before her statesmen and generals had grasped the connection between military plans and political aims.* But are her estimates of ultimate interest always sound?

This, at least, was the question raised as soon as the guns fell silent in the summer of 1945 when Washington cancelled Lend-Lease. The importance of Britain to the United States had been a major item in American calculations when the Axis made its bid for supremacy. Now that victory was gained, would she be shunted aside?

Foreign policy and foreign economic policies are, nowadays, opposite sides of the same coin. Ever since the turn of the century Britain, who must export to live, has had to face an ever-stiffening competition in overseas markets; at home she abolished free trade during the nineteen-thirties and erected tariff walls. For World War I, with its aftermath of slump and unemployment, had added to her troubles. Before that ordeal, if Britain had not been economically viable, she could not have underwritten a free world order in which the United States herself had fared so well. And although income from overseas investments did much to keep her going, she had sold most of these during the Battle of Britain to pay her way when, with the Soviet Union linked to Nazi Germany, she stood alone. That what she did was done in a common cause President Roosevelt had acknowledged through the masterly expedient of Lend-Lease. But if economic support had been justified during the war itself, so was there reason for it afterwards, until Britain could catch her breath and start to recover. Lend-Lease, however, was terminated without prior notice to British

* W. W. Rostow, *The United States in the World Arena* (New York: Harper & Brothers, 1960), pp. 89-206.

or Russian wartime associates. That this blow could have been due to ineptitude rather than malice the British but not the Russians may have suspected. Yet it had hurt Britain more than Russia, not only because she was economically prostrate but because she relied in every respect on American goodwill.

The war efforts and war economies of the English-speaking peoples had, moreover, been regulated in common by an extraordinary network of joint committees—from the Combined Chiefs of Staff to boards which assigned munitions, allocated raw materials, and directed shipping adjustments. To keep it in being was a sign that in the period of postwar reconstruction the same Anglo-American unity prevailed. But at home, and in Washington, British staff work had been so effective that it seemed to have made American officials jealous.* They felt, apparently, that the United States would be leading the West in name but not in fact if the co-operative procedures of wartime were formalized and extended into the postwar period. After the demise of Lend-Lease was announced on August 21, 1945, most of this Anglo-American machinery had to be dismantled.

Lend-Lease was, as a matter of fact, terminated in strict accordance with the letter of the law, and Congress, holding the purse strings, insisted that it should be. It may not, however, have been adventitious that no preliminary arrangements had been contemplated for cushioning the shock. Some years later ex-President Truman expressed regret over an initial gaucherie, which he attributed to delegated authority, in his acceptance of advice from a Lend-Lease administrator and a State Department official before he had scrutinized the proposals they had submitted.† And it is not inconceivable that some in Washington did try to take advantage of the new incumbent's inexperience when, upon the death of Franklin Roosevelt, the onus of decision first rested upon him. The anti-British, the pro-German, lively remnants of unreconstructed isolationism within the Administration and the Congress —were there malign influences such as these which had still to be eliminated?

Britain, as Mr. Truman writes, was the "chief ally" of the United States and in the autumn of 1945 negotiations for a British

---

* Rostow, *op. cit.,* pp. 195-196. Washington's "federalist chaos" is also said to have put American officials at a disadvantage. For a comparison of the American and British political systems in the context of Western leadership, see Chapter V.

† Harry S. Truman, *Memoirs* (Garden City, N. Y.: Doubleday & Company, Inc., 1955), I, pp. 227-234; II, p. 103; and Richard N. Gardner, *Sterling-Dollar Diplomacy* (Oxford: Clarendon Press, 1956), pp. 171-187.

loan soon revealed that the former would be shored up financially. American financiers nevertheless observed how the good effect of the agreement was nullified by the stringency of its provisions. Nor could Britain, as Washington desired, liquidate the sterling area or Imperial Preference—an economic grouping which included Empire dependencies, most members of the Commonwealth, and several other smaller powers. The tariff, trade, and customs practices of the United States, against which these arrangements had been acts of economic self-defense, were not yet sufficiently liberal; the sterling area might, moreover, furnish shelter in a storm if a much-feared American depression were to occur.* But when the severity of its terms derogated from the economic value of the British loan, the United States herself did not get from it the full political satisfaction that so magnanimous a gesture warranted in principle.

It is significant, nevertheless, that of two major co-belligerents, Britain was the only one with whom the United States entered at once into a special postwar negotiation of that sort. East and West drifted rapidly apart: as so often before in the twentieth century, this merely served to weld anew the unity of the English-speaking peoples. That unity had proven tougher than Kaiser or Führer had expected it to be. And now, in trying to dispose of it, the masters of the Kremlin had, as in other features of an expansive Russian policy, harked back to Tsarist days. For during the Russo-Japanese War and before the advent of the Triple Entente, Petersburg and Potsdam had not only toyed with the idea of a wider combine but in order to associate the United States with it had sought to set her against Britain.

At that time, however, the Anglo-American factor had undergone no tests as momentous as those of 1914–18 and 1939–45. What weight did the Soviet Union attach to it after being aligned with the West against the same foes? A shift in the leadership of the West coincided with an improvement in the prospects for Russian imperialism. When Germany and Japan were vanquished, the nearest air-land barriers, one in the Occident and one in the Orient, were removed, and Russia could resume traditional pressures against weaker neighbors. Anglo-American opposition was, in the main, what stood between her and any postwar endeavor to supplant a free world order by a Communized one. If, however, a wedge could be driven between the United

---

* Truman, *op. cit.,* I, pp. 474-480, 537; Walter Millis (ed.), *The Forrestal Diaries* (New York: The Viking Press, Inc., 1951), pp. 185, 246; and Gardner, *op. cit.,* pp. 188-254.

States and Britain, even that goal might be attained without a maximum effort. Like predecessors, Teutonic and Slavonic, who mistook Anglo-American divergences for Anglo-American estrangement, the Soviet rulers adopted a dual stratagem: first, a head-on attempt to separate the United States from Britain and, second, if that tactic miscarried, an attempt to hamper the Anglo-American factor by depicting it everywhere in a sinister light.

The end, which was nothing less than the subversion of a free world order, determined the means. Given the character of the Soviet regime, its nationalistic aims intermingling with an ever wider evangel, no other end could have been chosen. As a tyranny, moreover, it projected upon international affairs its own inner tensions. It may well be that suspicion of the West by Joseph Stalin was but one symptom of a psychosis to which colleagues and comrades of every rank were subject. Yet, as early as the spring of 1945, after the Yalta Conference but before V-E Day, the British Foreign Secretary, Anthony Eden, thought that information had been withheld from the Russian Prime Minister and that Stalin's mind was being prejudiced against Britain and the United States by the Soviet Foreign Minister, Vyacheslav Molotov.

After Germany's defeat, nevertheless, what still worried so influential a Presidential emissary as Harry Hopkins was any desire by Churchill to form against Russia, and for the sake of British interests in Europe, an Anglo-American bloc. But nobody was "ganging up" on the Russians and, before the Potsdam Conference, the view was conveyed from the White House to Downing Street that this would have to be made clear. The effort failed and, some months afterwards, the existence of an Anglo-American cabal against Russia still figured among Stalin's grievances.*

A modicum of Soviet good faith would have maintained the tripartite concert of victorious great powers. But instead of Russia being excluded from postwar councils, she herself sought to exclude one of their number, Britain. For this reason American representatives had to curtail the practice of private meetings with Russian delegates at the first meeting of the General Assembly of the United Nations in January, 1946. In their attempt to establish a Soviet-American condominium, the Russians had been foiled; at the Paris Peace Conference, during the summer, they therefore re-

---

* *Forrestal Diaries*, pp. 48, 58, and 153-154; and Truman, *op. cit.*, I, pp. 260-262. The wartime conference of the Big Three at Yalta would, according to Sir Anthony Eden, have had better results if American representatives had not been afraid of any Anglo-American "ganging up." See Anthony Eden, *Full Circle* (Boston, Mass.: Houghton Mifflin Co., 1960), p. 515.

verted to the charge that, under Anglo-American auspices, an antagonistic grouping was being engineered against them. James Byrnes, then Secretary of State, has told how the Russians, with their obedient following among puppet regimes, could not believe that smaller powers like Belgium, the Netherlands, South Africa, could have independent policies. "By what right," he asked, "do those who vote ballot after ballot with the Soviet Union call those of us who do not always agree with the Soviet Union, a bloc?"*

A common front against Russia was of her own making. On March 5, 1946, President Truman attended in person when Winston Churchill, though out of office, delivered a famous speech at Fulton, Missouri. Clarifying the East-West impasse and calling upon the English-speaking peoples for joint policies of mutual security, the British statesman's prescient address marked the Great Divide between wartime collaboration with the Soviet Union and postwar rivalry. But this was strong medicine for which Americans were not yet ready. No world organization could keep the peace between great powers; it was hoped, nevertheless, that the United Nations might offer a universal rather than Anglo-American approach. In the West, moreover, wartime sympathies with Russia still lingered. Churchill's admonitions had been rejected by his own compatriots before World War II. And after that conflict the American people were displeased. These, however, were momentary hesitations and soon the exigencies of leadership took the United States along the course that Churchill had charted.

Hitler's bid for hegemony was scarcely crushed before the West had to cope with another. There was Russia's postwar breach of wartime compacts; the geographic advantages which enabled her to seize neighboring countries with impunity; the unrest fomented by Communists in Italy, France, and elsewhere; the fact that when Britain and the United States had demobilized, the Soviet Union had retained on active service more than twenty thousand aircraft and about one hundred and seventy-five divisions. Nor could so formidable a threat be countered by last-minute improvisations like those with which Germany had twice been opposed. Arrangements had to be elaborated ahead of time if the East were to be deterred or, in the event of an East-West collision, withstood. About that Britain and the United States saw eye to eye; they were in accord, too, over the absurdity of Russian attempts to lure one from the other. Policy divergences were

---

* *Forrestal Diaries*, p. 132; and James F. Byrnes, *Speaking Frankly* (New York: Harper & Brothers, 1947), p. 140.

nevertheless caused by the nature of the world-wide instrumentalities that they devised. For a mid-century war technology that made a global strategy feasible magnified as well as forestalled peril. And to that novel, ugly, unprecedented aspect of their joint affairs, the English-speaking peoples had to address themselves unremittingly.

Meanwhile, the United States had learned that in addition to the general burdens of primacy there were specific areas in which she might have to take Britain's place. President Truman announced exceptional measures of aid to Greece and Turkey before a joint session of the Congress on March 12, 1947. On a historic sphere of influence, in other words, Britain's grip was slipping. A British defensive cordon had stretched from Afghanistan across the Middle East. By its predominance in the Mediterranean, British sea power could enforce British policy in remote corners of Europe and the Levant; the commerce of all nations was protected; the safety could be ensured of what, since the Suez Canal had been opened, was a vital artery of communication for a scattered Empire and a world-wide Commonwealth. During World War II the British had sprung to the assistance of Greece and towards the same end they had, despite an American outcry, intervened again to quell a pro-Soviet insurrection—one that was still simmering in 1947.

After wartime trials and postwar tribulations, however, Britain had no choice but to retrench. Russia had been stopped from moving down into the Levant by the Crimean War; Britain had sunk differences with her prior to World War I. It was over southward Russian ambitions that the Nazi-Soviet Pact foundered and now, unless the United States buttressed Greece and Turkey, the Soviet Union might push through the Balkans and the Middle East to southern Asia and North Africa.

Domination of these regions by Germany or her allies had been prevented in two world wars. What the West had just retrieved from Hitler and Mussolini it would not yield supinely to Stalin. Stern language from Washington and London was, as a matter of fact, what induced Russia during the previous winter to carry out tripartite wartime arrangements and evacuate northern Iran. When, too, the powers discussed a revision of the Montreux Convention, Moscow would not be allowed to wrest control of the Black Sea Straits from Turkey. Such, moreover, was the growing preoccupation of the United States with this area that during August, 1946, she dispatched a naval task force to the Mediterranean.

Greek-Turkish aid was, then, a symbol of both the new and the old. What had altered was not the interests of the West but its leadership. In the Senate the chief bipartisan proponent of the Administration's program was that latter-day internationalist, Senator Arthur H. Vandenberg. Senator Robert A. Taft, however, opposed it, as he later opposed the North Atlantic Treaty; Russian expansion abroad was, in the postwar isolationist view, less of a danger than Communist penetration at home. Greek-Turkish aid was a bold innovation, and for it President Truman must get the main credit. This was the time, he recalled in his memoirs, to align the United States clearly on the side, and at the head, of the free world. When Administration proposals first came before the Cabinet, misgivings were expressed over any anti-British clamors that the United States was again pulling British chestnuts out of the fire. But these were now American as well as British— a point impressed upon legislators by Under-Secretary Acheson when Congressional spokesmen conferred at the White House with the President.*

Actually the funds allotted to Greece and Turkey, with their supervisory corollaries, amounted to less than the British loan or financial assistance to Nationalist China, less than early help given to France and Italy. But these were exercises in primacy which, as far as she wished to succor friends and restore their war-ravaged economics, the United States had taken without reference to the East-West contest. Greece and Turkey had no special claims upon her such as inspired the British loan. The locale and purpose rather than the size of Greek-Turkish aid were what made it a fresh departure. No less important was the fact that, instead of demarcating a line between American and British interests, a shift in primacy might blur it.

There would be Anglo-American unity when the United States acknowledged this truth, Anglo-American divergence when she was still impelled by outmoded impulses or pursued goals at odds with it. A few writers and thinkers had, during the previous decade, made some Americans more aware of power realities; a shift in the primacy of the West substantiated their analyses. Yet among its concomitants was the need to retain the residual power of Britain, and with that requirement Americans, bred in the pristine anticolonial heritage of the American Revolution, could not always come to terms. In his address of March 12,

---

* Joseph M. Jones, *The Fifteen Weeks* (New York: The Viking Press, Inc., 1955), pp. 138-143, 165, 174, and 193; and Truman, *op. cit.*, II, pp. 100-105.

1947, President Truman observed how Greece was but one of the world commitments which Britain was relinquishing; how, for the preservation of order in the Middle East, the national integrity of Turkey had to be maintained. Explicitly, he declared that totalitarian regimes imposed on free peoples by direct or indirect aggression undermine the foundations of international peace and hence the security of the United States. Implicitly, the Truman Doctrine suggested that at key points any breach made by a recession in British power would have to be filled by the United States.

One step, moreover, led to another. Communism in non-Soviet Europe battened on economic depression and moral despair; only with American economic assistance could war-ravaged economies be set on the road to recovery. Soon, too, Britain was again in the throes of financial crisis. Her attempt to restore multilateral trade had misfired and in August, 1947, when the British loan was nearly exhausted, convertibility had to be suspended. Under the Marshall Plan, however, more American economic aid was to tide her over.

And this got off to a flying start because a top official in Washington made certain that London knew what was afoot. On May 8, 1947, Dean Acheson, the Under-Secretary of State, gave a speech at Cleveland, Mississippi, which was the forerunner of that delivered at Harvard University on June 5 by the Secretary of State. What these two addresses were designed to convey was told in advance by Mr. Acheson to selected British journalists; through the good offices of two British editors the text of General Marshall's speech immediately reached Ernest Bevin, the British Foreign Secretary. Thus apprised, he commended the remarks of the Secretary of State with alacrity—with more, probably, than Mr. Marshall had anticipated. In London measures were taken at once to organize a combined acceptance of that joint European recovery scheme which the Truman Administration proposed, which Congress was to adopt, and which would put Western Europe back on its feet.*

But as with the Truman Doctrine, so here—leadership entailed the furtherance of concepts that were more complex in application than utterance. General Marshall disavowed ideological or political intent; however welcome in London, a plan dedicated to the existence of free institutions was nevertheless bound to be unwelcome in Moscow. "Our policy," declared the Secretary of State, "is directed not against any country or doctrine but

* Jones, *op. cit.,* pp. 36 and 199-256.

against hunger, poverty, desperation and chaos." It was, all the same, from calamities such as these that a huge pro-Soviet vote in France and Italy, followed by the seating of Communist ministers in their governments, had derived. The European section of the global balance might, moreover, be turned against the West if the Soviet Union could merge the allied zones of vanquished Germany with its own; what thwarted it were the American and British Armies of Occupation. But without fresh American assistance a depleted Exchequer could not meet the bill for the British Army of the Rhine. The United States might replace Britain as the prop of the West in Greece and Turkey, yet the defenses of the West would crumble if Britain now had to abandon her position in Western Europe.

American economic aid averted any such contingency. Unlike the Truman Doctrine, the Marshall Plan disclaimed political or strategic objectives. In the policies they expressed, they were brothers under the skin.

The Truman Doctrine enabled Britain to disencumber herself where she could. In Western Europe, on the other hand, it was a vital American interest to help her hold her ground. As leader of the West, the United States shouldered fresh burdens. Britain, however, discarded some so as to conserve the means for maintaining others.

These were, in fact, the formative years of American primacy, and Anglo-American friendship was an underlying postulate throughout. President Truman signed the European Recovery Act on April 3, 1948. Czechoslovakia, which Hitler overran before World War II, had succumbed to communism in February and a number of weeks later came the Russian blockade of Berlin. The Brussels Treaty was Western Europe's own reply to the Communist subversion of Czechoslovakia and Berlin was rescued from a Russian stranglehold by an Anglo-American airlift. Meanwhile, in June, 1948, a rupture yawned between the Soviet dictator, Joseph Stalin, and Marshal Tito; as Yugoslavia ceased to be the catspaw of Communist intrusion in Greece, the success of the Truman Doctrine was assured. But Western Europe could not stand alone, and within the next year the North Atlantic Treaty was the retort of the West to the Soviet threat— one that also brought about French acquiescence in the debut of the Bonn Republic.

Concluded on April 4, 1949, the North Atlantic Alliance had two features that may be noted. First of all, the American people, contrary to the adjurations of the Founding Fathers, enlarged strategically those responsibilities of leadership which they had undertaken in other spheres. Then, secondly, European and North American nations were not only joined together in a formal, multilateral security arrangement for the defense of Western Europe and the North Atlantic region but an informal, bilateral one, the unwritten alliance of Britain and the United States, was still its solid core.

The Senate ratified the North Atlantic Treaty in July, 1949. Late in August a nuclear explosion had been touched off in Russia.* The American monopoly on atomic weapons would, it was evident, soon be broken. During the period of American nuclear supremacy there had been brazen violations of international comity by the Soviet Union; but no preventive war was waged. For this would have been repugnant to the West's moral code; and when neutrals or pro-Soviet apologists wave that fact aside, they themselves reveal the intensity of their own bias. The first American thermonuclear tests were held in November, 1952, the second in March, 1954. The Russians have stated, however, that as early as August, 1953, they had produced a device which could be employed as a hydrogen bomb. Not until August, 1954, was the news divulged of successful thermonuclear tests by the Soviet Union. For some years, all the same, the emergence of Russia as an air-atomic power had been affecting Western diplomacy adversely.

Among the contributions of bigness to world politics none was more far-reaching, in the most exact sense of the word, than developments in this portentous domain. During World War II there had been long-range bombing; the first missiles rained on London; Nagasaki and Hiroshima were wiped out by atomic bombs. And afterwards, as East-West tension grew, the American lead in nuclear and thermonuclear weapons served to underpin a global equilibrium. It counteracted Russian superiority in conventional ground forces.

For the new totalitarian danger was not strategically the same as the one that had just been scotched. Two massive German onslaughts on twentieth-century civilization demolished the European balance of power; on the land periphery of the East, the West therefore stood impotent and virtually undefendable. What aggravated the problem was the fall of China to communism in 1949, the alliance signed on February 15, 1950, between Moscow and Peking. Hitherto, both the German and Russian agglomerations had been free to maneuver on inner geographical lines.

* Truman, *op. cit.,* II, pp. 298-304.

Sino-Soviet ones were, however, on a gargantuan scale. Only with a coalition that was world-wide could the West match the East.

Not that a single commitment has linked regional alliances. But they were to be connected by Anglo-American command of the seas; by the fact that either the United States or Britain, or both, belonged to them; and by the degree to which, though nominally distinct, they had a similar aim. The United States and Britain possessed bases of their own on home and oversea territories from which long-range bombers could fly or from which, subsequently, ballistic missiles might be launched. Through a wider coalition, and with supplementary pacts, additional facilities would be made available. From several directions the West thus strove to gain varied access for its air-atomic power to the Sino-Soviet interior—and so deter the East from major adventures. Bigness, in the era of American primacy, would establish a global balance as a mid-century substitute for that historic balance, now defunct, which had long been European.

From the start the adaptation of atomic energy to military use was Anglo-American rather than American in origin. Though the first nuclear weapons were to be manufactured in the United States, the uranium had come initially from Canada as well as the Belgian Congo; the final result was the fruit of research in which the ideas of British and Canadian scientists were pooled with those of their American colleagues and with those of European physicists who had found refuge from Nazi and Fascist terror in English-speaking countries. In August, 1945, the atomic bombing of Hiroshima and Nagasaki constituted Japan's *coup de grâce*. Two years before, when they conferred at Quebec in 1943, Roosevelt and Churchill had agreed that the United States and Britain should consult about the use of nuclear weapons and exchange information about them with each other; when, however, Harry Truman succeeded to the Presidency he could find no trace of that wartime understanding. At the White House in November, 1945, when he conferred with the Prime Ministers of Britain and Canada—Clement Attlee and Mackenzie King—they concurred that nuclear discoveries should be devoted, under the auspices of the United Nations, to peace and progress. But there were secrets of atomic production which neither President Truman nor the Congress were willing to have the United States share with her own atomic partners.*

The disclosure of pro-Soviet nuclear espionage in Canada and Britain preceded similar revelations at home. Congress de-

* Truman, *op. cit.*, I, pp. 529-544; and II, pp. 294-315.

cided in 1946 to curtail the exchange of nuclear information. There was no record of the wartime Churchill-Roosevelt understanding; Senator Brien McMahon, sponsor of the Atomic Energy Act, did not realize, therefore, that his bill clashed with it. But officials in London and Ottawa may have been unduly complaisant towards Soviet burrowings. One point is clear: fresh grounds for Anglo-American disaccord had opened up and that alone served the Russian purpose.

When Russia menaced the West, the English-speaking peoples were realigned against her. But such unison was not as thorough as it might have been. Information on the peaceful uses of atomic energy and on its application to submarines was in later years exchanged between the United States and Britain; under the Atomic Energy Law, Britain and Canada have received from the United States more weapons secrets than other allies—a matter by which the French, with avowed Communists among their scientists, have been vexed. But information acquired during the process of manufacture was not passed on to Britain; if she were to produce her own nuclear and thermonuclear weapons, she would have to obtain such information by herself. This put her in a quandary. Ever since the turn of the century the United States had always imposed her own peacetime limitations on Anglo-American friendship. But now preparedness was being delimited when an American lead called for the utmost in strategic collaboration.

Primacy in the West had shifted across the Atlantic, and while Anglo-American solidarity, long decisive in the defense of a free world order, was more complete than it had been, it was not as full as common interests might suggest. The air-atomic supremacy of the United States kept the Soviet Union at bay and set a screen behind which Western Europe could recuperate from the latest savage German onslaught; on that fundamental strategic verity, Winston Churchill, whether in office or out, tirelessly laid stress. Yet senior British officers told American defense authorities in November, 1948, that, since the requisite nuclear information had been withheld, common plans for defense between United States and Britain were "utterly unrealistic."* An atomic caveat had been entered to their partnership and the British chafed. Nuclear and thermonuclear weapons were symbols of status and by producing some of her own Britain ensured that, as principal ally of the United States, she would not fall by the wayside. But

---

* *Forrestal Diaries,* pp. 523 and 525.

this required a costly duplication of effort and it was one which, in her straitened circumstances, she could ill afford.

On its other Anglo-American sectors, however, the counter-strategy of the West did not labor under the same inhibitions. First the United States, and then Russia, built aircraft capable of mounting transoceanic sallies from home territory. Later on, Britain, too, produced heavy bombers, nuclear and thermonuclear weapons, and some missiles of her own. But a chain of bases had also been envisaged from which aircraft of the American Strategic Air Command, either stationed or refuelled overseas, could penetrate to Eurasian targets; and of those bases the chief ones were provided by Britain herself. To wipe them out, however, was now a Soviet objective; the East-West contest was thus to put the British Isles in jeopardy before most other members of the Western coalition. In 1948, during the Soviet blockade of Berlin and the Anglo-American airlift which brought succor to that city, air-atomic groups were transferred to British airfields from the United States. Church and State upheld their commitments but Washington wondered whether they would be quick to do so.*

Destruction wrought by the *Luftwaffe* and by Nazi missiles had shown how vulnerable Britain was to every kind of air assault from the neighboring European continent. And now, nearby, there were Soviet airfields in the Russian-occupied portion of divided Germany. During the blockade of Berlin, however, and during the Korean War, Russia's nuclear experiments were probably not sufficiently advanced for the Kremlin to risk a showdown with the West; nor, perhaps, had the Soviet Union produced as yet enough of the most up-to-date heavy aircraft for the delivery of atomic weapons. Eventually, too, East and West settled down to a nuclear and thermonuclear stalemate. Henceforth, nevertheless, the British were exceedingly sensitive to any step taken by the leader of either side, American as well as Russian, which might set opposing global forces in motion without due cause.

A new, vast strategic interlock was to be the countervailing tool of Western power, and the conditions under which the United States and Britain co-operated were governed by that cardinal fact. Politically the various bilateral and regional engagements of the era were unattached to each other; operationally it might be impossible, in any final emergency, to disentangle one from the other. Common interests of the most vital character were preserved by the security arrangements of the Western coalition.

---

* *Forrestal Diaries,* p. 491.

Over peripheral ones, when an air-atomic backlash might devastate allies as exposed as Britain, needless risks must not be taken.

A STRATEGIC INTERLOCK

What this strategic backlash might entail globally was first illustrated during the Korean War. There had been numerous attempts since the turn of the century to achieve Anglo-American co-operation in the Far East; President Theodore Roosevelt approved when, during a revision of the Anglo-Japanese Alliance, control of Korea itself went to Japan. The Korean peninsula is an appendage to Manchuria and it was over the rape of that Chinese province that the drift towards war in the nineteen-thirties gathered momentum. For then, when the Western powers failed to enforce either the Covenant of the League of Nations or the Washington treaties, the dream of collective security lay shattered. Under the Charter of the United Nations, however, some of it was revived. When Communist levies attacked South Korea in June, 1950, the Truman Administration offered that country its support and the world organization endorsed what it had done. This was largely an American undertaking, and other members of the United Nations who participated were those whose association with the United States has been closest.

More specific security interests were in fact also maintained when collective security was upheld. The American people might have been less disposed to honor their European obligations if Britain and other signatories of the North Atlantic Alliance had stood aloof. And such is the geographical situation of South Korea that, quite apart from the Charter, Washington could not allow it to fall into Sino-Soviet clutches.

But here the United States herself cannot be absolved from blame for what happened. For Communist appetites were whetted by the apathy that Washington displayed towards the future of the Korean Republic. At the Potsdam Conference it had been agreed that Russian troops should occupy the northern half of the Korean peninsula, above the thirty-eighth parallel, and that American troops should occupy the southern half. The Soviet Union, however, blocked United Nations endeavors to unify the country under a joint trusteeship. As Chief of Staff, General Dwight Eisenhower had thereupon advised the withdrawal of American troops from Korea and, in 1949, General Douglas MacArthur, the Far Eastern Commander in Chief, publicly excluded Korea and Formosa from the American defense perimeter in the Pacific—an Army view which Dean Acheson, the Secretary of State, was to reiterate the following January. In consonance with it, American troops had been withdrawn from Korea in 1949; Congress, in January, 1950, refused to provide South Korea with economic aid.

The atmosphere in Washington changed, however, as soon as Communists from the north tried to subjugate the entire Korean peninsula. Threatening the independence of Japan, this would have breached the American defense perimeter in the Pacific after all.

American security interests in East Asia went beyond the ambit of Allied commitments. Their effect on the Western coalition was a divisive one all the same. The United States and Britain had, as a matter of fact, tended to draw apart in the Far East before the Korean War broke out. When Chiang Kai-shek fled to Formosa, the Chinese People's Republic was recognized by London and by three Asian members of the Commonwealth—India, Pakistan, and Ceylon. If Washington had done likewise, it was afterwards argued in some British and American quarters, and if the Peking regime could have taken China's seat in the United Nations, the Chinese Communists would not have run amuck.

Meanwhile, when the Korean War flared up, the Security Council had not only assigned to the United States the main responsibility for enforcing the Charter. President Truman had dispatched the Seventh Fleet to the Formosan Straits—a precautionary measure that prevented an assault from the Chinese mainland on Formosa and on the Chinese mainland from the Nationalist island stronghold. Yet this was a unilateral act and not one for which the approbation of the United Nations had been solicited. The Charter was enforced but so was an improved version of the American defense perimeter. Only the first of these objectives had direct British support. But there, as elsewhere, would not Britain be involved if, in the midst of joint military operations, the range of conflict should be widened?

To keep the Korean War within the narrowest possible confines was the British goal. Britain was handicapped, however, by the disparity between her contribution and that of the United States. Not that hers was a negligible one. The first among the United Nations to join the United States, observed ex-President Truman in his memoirs, were the United Kingdom and other Commonwealth countries. There was to be a Commonwealth Brigade; serving under the United Nations command were air and naval units from Britain and some oversea members of the

Commonwealth. But at that time the British were busy tracking down Communist insurrectionaries in the Malayan jungles and were also, with difficulty, manning substantial forces in Western Germany and the Middle East. In the United Nations' effort to enforce the Charter, the United States inevitably bore a disproportionate share—and having paid the piper, she was bound to call the tune.

Nor was that so only on the field of battle. Later on, as the military situation deteriorated, the Allies wanted to be sure that the United States took no major step without consulting them beforehand. Washington asked for authorization to send United Nations forces beyond the thirty-eighth parallel—to carry the war, in other words, back from South Korean to North Korean territory. The consequences of that move were far-reaching. Other Charter-enforcing Powers did not seem to have had prior notice of this specific request; approval was implicit, however, in their general pronouncements. It was only after Communist China entered the struggle, as General Marshall subsequently pointed out, that concern grew in Allied capitals over American war plans.*

Korean issues did not, all the same, warrant ultimate risks, and during the autumn of 1950 the British people were apprehensive lest these were what an American lead would invite. President Truman had selected General MacArthur for the United Nations Command and met his appointee at Wake Island in October. There the United Nations Commander made light of Indian warnings that if he were to advance beyond the thirty-eighth parallel up to the Yalu River, Communist China would intervene. Within a few weeks Communist hordes did, in fact, pour down from Manchuria and his troops reeled back.

For General MacArthur's self-assurance, the cost to the United States was heavy. What frightened the British people was his desire to harry the foe, with military aircraft, across the Yalu River, in the Chinese province of Manchuria. The United States had, it is true, been pledged to consult with their British Allies over any such move. But neither in Korea nor Washington was consultation wholehearted. For the past year the Russians had been known to possess an atomic device. If the Korean War were not now localized, the Communist Chinese might invoke their mutual assistance pact with Soviet Russia. Globally, in an air-

---

* John W. Spanier, *The Truman–MacArthur Controversy and the Korean War* (Cambridge, Mass.: The Belknap Press of Harvard University Press, 1959), pp. 100-103. Also Trumbull Higgins, *Korea and the Fall of MacArthur* (New York: Oxford University Press, 1960).

atomic war, the United States might still have prevailed. Under a strategic backlash, however, the British Isles, within easy access of Russian bombers in East Germany, would have been obliterated.

Never can there have been so grim a prospect of winning battles and, in terms of world peace, losing the campaign. For American aircraft to erase Manchurian centers of supply would have been the correct military procedure, from the standpoint of General MacArthur's particular mission. Washington, however, could not permit them to do this because more than this particular mission had to be considered. Pressure against the West in the Far East did not alter the fact that Western Europe, with its human and material resources and its geographical situation, was what any major antagonist of the West must covet most. Two German wars had sapped that key region's capacity to withstand a Soviet attack; and yet with American assistance, military and economic, the ramparts of the West in Western Europe could be held. But American strength would not be available for NATO defenses if the United States were to be mired in a fathomless Chinese bog. Aggression in Korea, the British and French concurred, had to be warded off. After the Berlin blockade the West dare not lower its guard in Europe. If there were any undue diversion of American strength, the next victims of Russian blackmail might be Britain and France.

The coalition problem that haunted Anglo-American friendship was thus a dual one. The United States might, under a strategic interlock, drag Britain willy-nilly into a fight for life. Contrariwise, however, even if that did not occur, it would imperil Britain if the American leader of the West let herself be overcommitted in some outlying Asian region, if North Atlantic interests had to be neglected as a result. A free world order depends nowadays on a global rather than European equilibrium. It was nevertheless in Western Europe rather than Eastern Asia that the balance could still be turned against the West and where, therefore, it had with increasing vigilance to be maintained.

To the priority of Western Europe in Anglo-American calculations, President Truman and his advisers fully subscribed. But General MacArthur had insisted during World War II that the East Asian theatre was as important as the West European, and the British were terrified lest his Korean war plans be influenced by a personal viewpoint disavowed by his own superiors at home. Nor did the hubbub raised by Senators and newspaper proprietors with a refurbished concept of America First fortify the morale of a British ally or help the Western coalition to close ranks. The disruption of the Atlantic Alliance was, and would be, the fixed aim of Soviet world policy. In postwar America, however, Moscow had few partisans and it was self-styled patriots who did most to further the Russian objective.

That the United Nations Charter was, after all, no scrap of paper, and that the United States had taken the initiative to enforce it, appeared at the outset to augur well. Allied spirits drooped, however, when with the entry of Chinese troops a war of attrition seemed to impend; the very idea of a Western coalition, long cherished by all who cared for the common interests of the West, had turned sour overnight. And what caused anxiety was the way the Korean War might spread if it were prolonged.

In December, 1950, the new situation prompted on both sides of the Atlantic a searching reassessment of American leadership. At a White House press conference, President Truman had been queried about possible use of the atomic bomb during Korean hostilities; and though his comment was noncommittal, the British people were afraid that some all-out American reprisal against Chinese aggressors would ignite global war. Prime Minister Attlee flew posthaste to Washington, and his conversations with President Truman (as recounted by the latter in his memoirs) not only surveyed the immediate horizon but also canvassed issues by which Anglo-American friendship would be troubled in the years ahead.*

One novel element in world politics was British concern for the susceptibilities of Asian members of the Commonwealth, and this the Prime Minister displayed at the start. Communist China enlisted their sympathies on pan-Asian grounds; because of them, Mr. Attlee wanted more heed paid to Peking's views. The main enemy, however, was, as the Secretary of State explained, not Communist China but the Soviet Union; and Mr. Acheson posed the dilemma by which, as leader of the West, the United States was confronted. If the United States were overengrossed in Asia, Russia would have a free hand in Europe; and yet if Peking were to be bought off with the cession of Formosa, where Chiang Kai-shek had planted his flag, the effect on Japan and the Philippines would be serious. Korean operations were conducted from those two islands; they contained American bases upon which rested the whole American position in the Pacific. President Truman himself, moreover, reminded Mr. Attlee of British terri-

---

* Truman, *op. cit.,* II, pp. 394-413. On the eve of the Truman-Attlee conversations, false radar signals had put American aircraft on the alert and sent aloft American fighter planes stationed in Canada.

tories in Eastern Asia—Hong Kong and Malaya—that might eventually be menaced.

Loyalty to principles, friends, and treaty obligations was renewed by President Truman and Prime Minister Attlee. Upon restricting the Far Eastern war to Korea itself they were both resolved; upon the wisdom of further moves they agreed to differ. With Titoism as an example, the British government believed China might be weaned away from Russia; the United States thought otherwise and refused to enter into negotiations in which Peking would demand Formosa as well as China's seat in the United Nations. The policy presented to the American people, so Mr. Acheson argued, had to be a consistent one; if they bowed to aggression in Asia, they could not be expected to oppose it in Europe—a point which can scarcely have been lost on a British statesman. Mr. Attlee admitted that whatever was done would have to have American public backing. Approval by the United Nations was, however, also emphasized by him and, above all, the adherence of Asian countries to the West.

Changes wrought by a shift in primacy were reflected in these Anglo-American talks more than their own participants may have realized. Britain herself was now so exposed to air attack in any global conflict, to placate Commonwealth partners in Asia had become so constant a feature of her world policy, that the British would have made substantial concessions to terminate the Korean War; with Peking in control of the Chinese mainland, neither Formosa nor China's seat in the United Nations seemed worth haggling over. But Washington could not see matters in the same light as London. In the policies of both there was, as always, an intermingling of moral tenets and power considerations. The one, however, was not as vulnerable, politically and strategically, as the other and they diverged in their estimates accordingly.

The Secretary of State thus branded any proposal to transfer China's seat in the Security Council from the Nationalist to the Communist regime as a reward for aggression. American public morale, the President added, might also be hurt if a step of this kind were taken before China's misdeeds justified it. But it was the future of Formosa that concerned the top military authorities of the United States and they put their case on grounds that were also cogent from a coalition standpoint. The Secretary of Defense, General Marshall, and the Chairman of the Chiefs of Staff, General Bradley, contended that, with Formosa in hostile hands, the American chain of island outposts would be split—the Pacific sector of American global strategy might, that is, be dislocated. The British thereupon suggested a compromise of which much was to be heard later—the idea of recognizing two Chinas, that of the Communists on the mainland, that of the Nationalists on Formosa.

Meanwhile the President felt that the West would have to muster more strength—through NATO in particular. But it could not do this if the Far Eastern policies of the United States and the United Kingdom were out of tune. Britain, in other words, would have to accept coalition risks in East Asia if greater Anglo-American solidarity nearer home were to be attained.

Primacy had shifted and its conditions had altered. Unchanged, nevertheless, were the underlying dynamics of Anglo-American friendship. In a private chat, when the Democratic President and the Labour Prime Minister commiserated with each other over the domestic opposition with which each had to deal, they spoke each other's language politically as well as linguistically. Aneurin Bevan, an extreme critic of the United States and the spokesman for dissidents on the Left, was a thorn in Attlee's flesh; on Capitol Hill a group of Republican Senators had just asked for information about "secret commitments" into which the President was alleged to have entered with the Prime Minister. These were the men, remarked Mr. Truman, who saw nothing wrong in plunging headlong into an Asian war but would raise no finger for the defense of Europe; who, while they thought Chiang Kai-shek could do no wrong, believed a British Prime Minister was never to be trusted. The President and the Prime Minister talked, the former was to recollect, as only two men can talk who, having spent their lives in politics, probably understood the sources of their problems much better than they could state in a public communiqué.*

Pragmatically Mr. Truman had thus sensed a dialectical truth at which those who have occupied high office in English-speaking countries usually arrive. The manner in which divergences arose and were overcome on the domestic scene enabled them to understand each other generally even when no precise understanding could be achieved.

Reaffirming common purposes, the Truman-Attlee communiqué was frank in recording Anglo-American disagreement over the question of China's seat in the United Nations and expressed the President's hope that there would never be a call

* Truman, *op. cit.*, II, pp. 409-410.

for use of the atomic bomb.* But what was merely implicit in official pronouncements the facts of power thenceforth made explicit: in an era of bigness, the mutualities of defense did not only traverse the globe; the unsigned commitments of an unwritten alliance might be commensurately as large. NATO, other regional pacts, the United Nations Charter, may have defined and delimited; over major crises hovered the shadow of much that was to be indefinable and unlimited. To a shift in primacy the British people had accustomed themselves. But American control of a strategic interlock preserved common interests and yet kept allies on tenterhooks.

It would, as a matter of fact, be General MacArthur's public dissent from coalition necessities that precipitated his downfall. What he desired was a United Nations blockade of the Chinese coast, the employment of Chinese Nationalist troops against Chinese Communist armies in Korea, and the bombing of Chinese supply centers within China herself—proposals that would have spread a war which the American and British governments were intent upon localizing. After he conferred with Prime Minister Attlee, President Truman, in discussing American policy with his advisers, stressed the importance of working closely with Britain; only in co-operation with her, he observed, could the power of the United States make itself felt fully both in the Pacific and the Atlantic. The entire international position of the United States depended on strengthening Western Europe, and NATO armed forces were taking shape. Washington, said General Marshall, could not rush into measures for Korea and the Pacific that, by the reaction these caused in Russia, would scare away the European allies of the United States. And to divide them from each other, reported Dean Acheson, was the Russian goal.†

Mr. Truman left no stone unturned in trying, during the winter of 1951, to impress upon General MacArthur some of the broader exigencies with which, as leader of the West, the United States now had to cope. By an offer of his own, nevertheless, the Far Eastern commander forestalled a statement on a Korean cease-fire which the American and Allied governments had been drafting. And then a letter from him which seemed to favor an extension of the Korean conflict to the Chinese mainland was read to the House of Representatives; this, in General Bradley's phrase, would have been the wrong war, at the wrong time, and in the wrong place. Insubordination of that sort could not be tolerated

* Truman, *op. cit.*, II, pp. 394-413.
† Truman, *op. cit.*, II, pp. 418-421.

one moment longer. On April 11, General MacArthur's command passed to General Matthew B. Ridgway.

Discipline had to be restored. But it is noteworthy that, when he explained his course, President Truman coupled with specific responsibilities imposed upon him by the Constitution of the United States those entrusted to him by the United Nations. The strength of free nations had been united, he declared on the radio, to prevent and not to hasten a third world war.* Reassuring opinion at home, remarks such as these were addressed quite as much to Allies abroad. Certainly the recent talks between President Truman and Prime Minister Attlee would have been nullified if General MacArthur were still allowed a loose rein.

And it was in consonance with these talks that American and Allied forces persevered, that hostilities in Korea were terminated. In the spring of 1951, after the tide had turned, the Eighth Army could have advanced to the Yalu River and thus liberated North Korea as well as South Korea. But it did not do so because, had it pushed northward, it would have moved from its centers of supply while Communist invaders, as they retreated, would have come nearer to their own; Anglo-American diplomacy had, moreover, rendered Manchuria immune to chastisement from the air. Then, too, fighting in the north would have been on a broader front and must have exacted from the United States and her allies a bigger rather than smaller war effort.†

The Communist Chinese mounted their last offensive in the spring of 1951. By July, over a tenable frontier close to the thirty-eighth parallel, the truce negotiations had begun at Kaesong. The Soviet Union, said the President, could not split the United States from her Allies.‡

In the company of others, the English-speaking peoples had again stood together for the enforcement of common principles and common interests. But what the Korean War had also revealed were the political limitations of the strategically illimitable.

So as to preserve the position of the West where its defense would be decisive, the United States pulled her punches in East Asia. Thenceforth the upbuilding of NATO was accelerated; aggression by the East in the Orient steeled the West against aggression in the Occident. Soon, too, on some of the Asian borderlands of the Sino-Soviet bloc—in southeastern Asia, on

* Truman, *op. cit.,* II, pp. 432-450.

† Matthew B. Ridgway, *Soldier* (New York: Harper & Brothers, 1956), pp. 219-220.

‡ Truman, *op. cit.,* II, pp. 455-459.

the northern tier of the Middle East—there were collective attempts to build local ramparts against it. The British and other North Atlantic allies of the United States may have been panicky during the Korean War; but neither did the Kremlin want non-European conflicts to spread. Soft spots in adjacent Asian territories were probed with a certain impunity; in all that it did, from inroads in Malaya and Indochina to various forms of penetration in southern Asia and the Middle East, the Sino-Soviet bloc would try not to overreach itself. For it was as loath as its British and West European adversaries to have all-engulfing forces brought into play. And so, even for the protection of outlying regions, an over-all deterrent still had its uses.

For two years, nevertheless, no Korean armistice was signed and as long as the Chinese Communists procrastinated there was a rising clamor within the United States to jettison coalition policies and go it alone.

But that was not a course which the White House would entertain. A Republican President, Dwight D. Eisenhower, had succeeded the Democrat, Harry S. Truman, in office. Coalition policies came naturally to one who had served as commander of the Anglo-American and other Allied forces in World War II and as NATO's first military head. At the turn of the century two eminent Republicans, John Hay and Theodore Roosevelt, thwarted by popular and Congressional interdict, had foreseen wider responsibilities for the United States. But the self-regarding epoch of Lodge the Elder, Warren G. Harding, Calvin Coolidge, and Herbert Hoover, still lay ahead. A shift in primacy from Britain to the United States occurred under one Democratic President and was consolidated by another. Until then there had, but for the Wilsonian interlude, been continuity in isolationism. Continuity in leadership, when Republican and Democratic Administrations alternated at the helm, it would be Dwight Eisenhower's role to confirm.

The issue arose within his own party when the MacArthur program, as a whole or in part, was urged upon him during the winter of 1953 by Senators Taft and Knowland. It was in the name of the United Nations that the United States had taken up the cudgels; Senator Taft wished her to return this commission, to pursue the Korean War without reference to the world organization. Senator Knowland advocated a naval blockade of Communist China; Senator Taft, however, was against one if it caused a rupture with Allied cobelligerents. And that such would be its outcome was pointed out to his own staff by General Eisenhower.

We have got to have friends, exclaimed the President at a White House press conference, and he asked Republican copartisans in the Senate not to make American contributions to the budget of the United Nations contingent upon keeping Communist China out of that body. Upon termination of the Korean War, Britain might endeavor to have the Formosan regime replaced by Peking in China's seat, and the Senators wished to forestall that eventuality. Congress did no more than record its sense that the Chinese Communists should be barred. But Mr. Eisenhower doubted, though his own hands were tied politically, that such an exclusion would be wise. It was his objective to lure China away from Russia and to let Japan trade with her so that American taxpayers would no longer have to subsidize the Island Kingdom.*

After the United Nations declared Communist China an aggressor, the Truman Administration had, as a matter of fact, sponsored an embargo on trade with that country. And this ban was twice as strict as the list maintained by Western powers against traffic in strategic goods with the Soviet Union and her East European vassal states. More and more the associates of the United States sought its revision. Not only did this ban embarrass an American ward such as Japan, for whom conquest on the Chinese mainland and trade with China had once been so lucrative; its restrictions hampered Britain, who lives by foreign trade, as well as France, Belgium, and West Germany. Through infringements of the embargo they might, moreover, contravene the Battle Act of 1951—one that authorized the President to curtail foreign aid to nations which exported strategic goods to the Sino-Soviet bloc. The trade ban would be modified by agreement between the embargoing Powers. What, nevertheless, should be included in the forbidden categories and what should not? Did not items which could be shipped to Russia get to China anyway?

As leader of the West, the United States has been reluctant to repeat the fatal mistake which she and Britain had made before World War II—that of building up the military capacity of potential aggressors. The difficulty is that while strategic materials may have been prohibited, other industrial items would, nowadays, also have some strategic use. The most that could therefore be accomplished was to obstruct and slow down their sale. China does not do much shipping of her own. Goods that could not be sold to her might be purchased through Russia or European satellites for

* Robert J. Donovan, *Eisenhower: The Inside Story* (New York: Harper & Brothers, 1956), pp. 130-137.

whom, after 1954, Western trade bars were lowered. Yet that meant additional expense, and traffic over the long Eurasian railways was congested. These were questions about which the English-speaking powers would differ for years—an aspect of that Anglo-American divergence in the Far East to which Washington and London had resigned themselves.

Against the "blood trade" of Britain with Communist China, Senator Joseph McCarthy, then on his rampage, lost no opportunity to thunder. Over a Greek ship deal in March, 1953, he flouted the prerogative of the Executive to conduct foreign policy; in May, when he assailed all Western trade with Communist China, the effect on allies was anxiously scrutinized at the White House. Senator McCarthy sought, in particular, to suspend mutual assistance funds to Britain as long as the British traded with Communist China in non-strategic materials. The Korean truce was signed in July but the Senator had renewed his Anglophobic campaign in a national broadcast on November 24. On December 1, however, the Secretary of State replied with the express approval of the President; the United States, said John Foster Dulles, could not dictate the trade policies of her allies. The American capacity to retaliate against Russian atomic attack depended, moreover, on well-located bases shared with other friendly countries. To coerce allies on trade policy, added the President himself, would be the mark not of the leader but of the imperialist.*

The charge of imperialism, however, was one that the United States wanted to disclaim on quite other grounds. Not that European allies leveled it against her; it was rather their possession of oversea dependencies, many of which had helped her to round out coalition strategy, that embarrassed her ideologically. Competition between East and West for the goodwill of anti-colonial Asian neutrals mounted during the Korean War. Ever since her counsel against MacArthur's advance beyond the thirty-eighth parallel had been disregarded, India, the foremost power of free Asia, had objected to American leadership; she and Burma lined up with the Soviet bloc when the General Assembly of the United Nations voted on February 1, 1951, to condemn Communist China as an aggressor. New Delhi did, nevertheless, render service as a go-between. In May, 1953, Prime Minister Nehru was therefore told that, unless the Communist Chinese accepted an armistice, the United States would have to contemplate a

* Donovan, *op. cit.,* pp. 245-250.

resumption of the Korean War on a larger scale*—information which the Indian statesman did not, as it was hoped he would, pass on to Peking.

Stalin, moreover, had died in March, 1953, and the battle for the succession in the Kremlin made peaceful coexistence elsewhere a necessary slogan. By June an armistice was in sight. But Syngman Rhee, President of the South Korean Republic, wanted North and South Korea to be reunified first and, so as to spoil the negotiations, released prisoners of war. The armistice talks were nevertheless furthered by a strong statement which Britain and France signed with the United States on July 14th; and then all sixteen Charter-enforcing Powers announced that a breach of the truce would have consequences that could not be confined to Korea. It took courage for governments whose peoples had been full of trepidation over a strategic backlash to say that. As a peacemaker, President Truman had been hamstrung by the violence of pro-MacArthur and McCarthyite sentiment. Congress, however, would let General Eisenhower, with his military prestige, accept more lenient terms than his predecessor.† But an early truce was also desired by the allies of the United States and, having stood firm, they were entitled to consideration. The Korean armistice was signed at Panmunjom at the end of July.

More, nevertheless, could now be done to stoke the fires of Communist rebellion against French rule in Indochina. This had been a serious handicap for France at a time when she did not wish to be outmatched in Western Europe by recrudescent German power and when joint NATO defenses of that region were being organized. For her East Asian campaign she had received money and technical assistance from the United States. During the spring of 1954, as French endeavors reached a climax, American transport planes were employed to convoy French reinforcements; in nearby waters there moved, as a mute admonition to Peking, a number of American aircraft carriers. If, however, American, British, Australian, and New Zealand troops had also been sent to bolster the French, the West would have again run the risk of having its strength drained off in a marginal area. Strategic priorities had been demonstrated by the Korean War. Over Indochina, all the same, the Eisenhower Administration vacillated. In preserving the Western coalition from some irretrievable misstep, it was Britain who momentarily took the lead.

---

* Donovan, *op. cit.,* p. 118; Truman, *op. cit.,* II, pp. 361-362; and Eden, *op. cit.,* pp. 17-20.

† Donovan, *op. cit.,* pp. 117-128.

Matters came to a head when, in the spring of 1954, the French sought the relief of their beleaguered garrison at Dienbienphu. General Paul Ely, the French Chief of Staff, begged Washington for air support from the American aircraft carriers stationed in the Gulf of Tonkin. The French plea was echoed by Admiral Radford, Chairman of the Joint Chiefs of Staff; Vice-President Nixon, moreover, went so far as to favor the participation of American troops. But General Matthew Ridgway, the Army Chief of Staff, did not believe that American intervention, once it started, could be confined to a single combat element. On a primitive economy like that of Indochina, the air-atomic weapon would be wasted, while for ordinary land warfare by American troops there were no local facilities. As a professional soldier, President Eisenhower must have perceived that the proposal was an injudicious one.*

It got its quietus in London. Collective intervention was suggested to Prime Minister Churchill by the White House a month before the fall of Dienbienphu; and the Secretary of State, John Foster Dulles, after a visit to London and Paris, had supposed, but erroneously, that the British were willing to countenance some such action. By then, though, even the French had changed their minds. President Eisenhower expounded in public his domino theory: that once Indochina was knocked over other dominoes—Burma and Thailand, Malaya, and Indonesia—would also topple, while Formosa and the Philippines, with their American bases, would be jeopardized. Behind the scenes, however, President Eisenhower had stipulated that if corrective measures were undertaken, they must be executed in conjunction with the British as well as the French.†

Downing Street was less than enthusiastic. It may have felt that the Eisenhower domino thesis overdramatized the immediate threat of further Chinese expansion. Anglo-American intervention in another Chinese border zone might, after the Korean War, only provoke an aggressive China to do more than it had been doing; what had to be avoided between East and West was any air-atomic conflict of the kind which General MacArthur could have stirred up so recklessly. Before Sir Winston Churchill returned to office and General Eisenhower replaced Harry Truman in the Presidency, there had been in Anglo-American friendship a tacit scale of strategic priorities. It would not be any less valid now.

* Ridgway, *op. cit.,* pp. 276-278.
† Donovan, *op. cit.,* pp. 259-267.

From the start Anthony Eden, the British Foreign Secretary, had realized the poor effect of British diffidence on Anglo-American friendship. But New Delhi had been critical of American policy in East Asia and was eager to stay on good terms with Communist China; in plans for Western intervention and for arranging a Southeast Asian security pact, London wanted nothing done that might offend India and other Asian members of the Commonwealth. Like General Ridgway, moreover, the British Chiefs of Staff argued that little could be accomplished without major land operations. During conversations with Dulles in London, Paris, and Geneva, Eden touched upon a contingency that had been faced during the Korean War: if Communist China, entering the Indochinese conflict, invoked the Sino-Soviet Treaty, World War III would be at hand.*

Paris was informed on April 25, 1954, that London would turn down the American proposal. But on May 1, while the powers were meeting at Geneva to settle East Asian affairs, John Foster Dulles still seemed to be hankering for a blank check, for moral support by Britain of interventionist measures which the United States herself had not yet devised; and on May 15 a press leak indicated that some French-American action was contemplated.† Nineteen countries had sent their foreign ministers to confer in Geneva about East Asia and, by the armistice upon which the Vietminh and Vietnam agreed, the French were enabled to withdraw from Indochina without any greater loss of blood and treasure. While John Foster Dulles, the Secretary of State, abstained, British diplomacy under Anthony Eden had scored. During the Suez crisis of 1956 Dulles got his own back. In Far Eastern affairs, however, the less circumspect of Presidential advisers had had their guns spiked.

Divergence over the Formosan question could, all the same, still mar Anglo-American friendship. Chiang Kai-shek had been "unleashed" when President Eisenhower entered the White House, a step against which the British government protested as one whose political repercussions might have no compensating military advantage and one that, according to Prime Minister Nehru, intensified the world's fear psychosis. What it meant was that the Seventh Fleet, which had been patrolling the Formosan Straits since the outbreak of the Korean War, would go on preserving Formosa from invasion but would not stop the Nation-

---

* Eden, *op. cit.*, pp. 115 and 126-128; see also pp. 104-105, 132, and 139.

† Eden, *op. cit.*, pp. 111-120, 125-128, 133-135, and 142-144.

alists from attacking the Chinese mainland. Minor harassing operations were launched from Nationalist offshore islands and traffic was blocked to the ports of Foochow and Amoy.

After hostilities ebbed in Korea and Indochina, it looked, moreover, as if Communist China might next attempt to subdue Formosa itself. Were other scattered, offshore, Nationalist islands likely to be steppingstones to it? Would the United States also be compelled to rush to their rescue? Quemoy and Matsu came under fire from guns on the Chinese mainland in September, 1954; in December the United States retorted by signing a mutual defense treaty with Nationalist China—one, incidentally, by which Chiang Kai-shek was quietly leashed all over again. And then, in January, 1955, the Tachens, a batch of Chinese offshore islands still more distant from Formosa, were occupied by the Chinese Communists. Congress thereupon granted President Eisenhower additional authority to protect Formosa and the Pescadores—something, that is, which he could employ at his discretion.

But what if this authority were ever put to use? In July, 1955, at the Geneva Conference of the Big Four, all delegations were more concerned with the problem of the Chinese offshore islands than with danger in Europe. The Americans, it seemed to Sir Anthony Eden, knew that they had a bear by the tail. In talks with Bulganin and Khrushchev, the British Prime Minister did what he could to persuade "those present, and absent," of the peaceful intentions of the other side.* The Formosan question was, nevertheless, one over which Washington and London had diverged from the outset. For, as leader of the West, the United States could not guarantee so exposed a salient in the Far East without Atlantic allies, while technically unpledged, fearing an unlimited liability.

In the episode of the Chinese offshore islands, Admiral Radford, Chairman of the Joint Chiefs of Staff, was opposed once more by General Matthew Ridgway, Army Chief of Staff.† President Eisenhower moved with caution, however; through a formal engagement with Chiang the United States might be better able to hold him back. But whether she would do so again was a moot point in 1958 when Communist China resumed the bombardment of the Chinese offshore islands and it appeared that the Formosan regime had been allowed by the Eisenhower Administration to entrench itself upon them more deeply than ever. It was now Britain's turn to move with caution. For the British and American

---

* Eden, *op. cit.,* pp. 342-345.
† Ridgway, *op. cit.,* pp. 278-280.

governments had been acting together in the Middle East and, for the sake of unity in that theater, disunity over the Far East had to be eschewed.

Meanwhile, it had taken the Korean War and its aftermath to make the strategic pattern clear. Local adventures on the rim of the Sino-Soviet imperium might be hard to prevent. Under an American lead, nevertheless, the West had restrained the East from further conquest. And yet Britain, with other close allies, had also adjured the United States to restrain herself. Self-discipline is a condition of primacy. The American political system has not, however, always been conducive to this—a short-coming by which kindred peoples accustomed to the parliamentary form of representative democracy may still be disquieted.

With power comes a penchant for the unilateral. Britain, moreover, is the center of the Commonwealth and, in dealing with her, it behooves American statesmen to comprehend the nature of that entity. Washington, for example, disregarded Indian sensibilities when a security pact for Southeast Asia was discussed in 1954, and this exasperated the British Foreign Secretary. Not for the last time was a British ambassador instructed to notify Dulles that those in Britain who would maintain Anglo-American friend-ship were handicapped by the mounting American tendency to overlook the feelings and difficulties of allies.*

Among the English-speaking peoples, however, unilateral-ism may be curbed by inner moral brakes. The same principles of politics that impelled first Britain and then the United States to uphold a free world order can serve to induce consideration for allies. It was to Britain's interest that the United States assert her leadership. But primacy, with its shift from the one to the other, has altered in kind as well as degree. In asserting leadership the United States might tend at times to be overassertive; and when this happens, so interlaced is the defense of the West, Britain also feels a tug. Not all allies deserve to be told that, unless they are less irresolute, the United States will go it alone; all, responsive or unresponsive, are affected willy-nilly by fluctuations in Amer-ican leadership. Yet neither can the United States be indifferent to what allies do by themselves—the Suez episode and African affairs have proven that. There, however, the East-West confronta-

---

* Eden, *op. cit.,* p. 110; see also pp. 106-111 and 161-163. This acrid message contrasts ironically with the circumstances which preceded Eden's own retirement in 1957 when the Suez episode produced a *rapprochement* between Washington and New Delhi. (See Chapters VI and VII.)

tion was indirect. The incidence of an American leap into the unilateral might, on the other hand, be world-wide.

And damage could be done even if it were regional rather than global in scope. When the Korean War broke out, Secretary Acheson had been peremptory in demanding French approval for the rearmament of West Germany. It was, in fact, as a result of this same policy that his successor, John Foster Dulles, threatened the French, before they rejected the European Defense Community, with an agonizing reappraisal of the American course.

The Western European Union, through which the Bonn Republic was afterwards admitted to NATO, did not possess the supranational features that characterized the ill-fated European Defense Community. But the Secretary of State informed the British Foreign Secretary that Congress would insist upon these; without them it would be less inclined to go on backing the security of Western Europe. When Eden therefore contrived a compromise in the autumn of 1954, his aim was not only to keep the Bonn Republic fastened to the West and beyond Russian clutches; the danger of the United States falling back on a "Fortress America" policy had also to be combatted.* It may be that without the Dulles shock tactics a solution might not have been reached. More likely these reflected the capacity of co-partisans such as Senators Taft, McCarthy, and Knowland to intimidate the Eisenhower Administration—an interlude to which the midterm elections soon put an end.

The liberation of captive states in Eastern Europe had, furthermore, been a plank in the Eisenhower campaign platform over which the British people could scarcely rejoice. Not that Britain lacked sympathy; it was to her that many of the oppressed had looked during the nineteenth century when she was leader of the West. But in the era of a strategic interlock, any liberation by force which the United States undertook might jeopardize the physical existence of the British Isles themselves. And that, too, was why the theory of massive retaliation, as expounded by John Foster Dulles in January, 1954, provoked such alarm.

The deterrent strategy of the West had preserved the peace. But it was now at odds with coalition diplomacy. And for thus setting them against each other, Dean Acheson reproached John Foster Dulles.† For, as defined by him, the idea of massive

---

* Eden, *op. cit.*, pp. 32-52, 61-65, and 169-194.

† Dean Acheson, *A Democrat Looks at His Party* (New York: Harper & Brothers, 1955), pp. 98-103.

retaliation did not suggest the common defense of coalition lands but a unilateral American decision over how and where an enemy should be met. The other allies had been insistent upon localizing the Korean War. The blunder of the Eisenhower Administration was to restate coalition strategy without consulting them and when, with the Indochinese crisis impending, they were still afraid of some Far Eastern embroilment.

Within his own political family, as a matter of fact, President Eisenhower put his foot down against unilateral action. Late in 1954, moreover, the midterm Congressional elections had deprived his rasher copartisans of majority support in the legislative branch. Meanwhile hydrogen bomb tests brought to public notice the hideous potentialities of the latest war technology. The post-Stalinist rulers of the Soviet Union seemed less unamenable to some East–West accommodation; and, in 1953, Sir Winston Churchill had again proposed a summit conference of the wartime Big Four. But Washington did not then approve.

A summit conference was nevertheless held two years later after Sir Winston had retired. East and West had concurred at last on a settlement for Austria; in pending British elections Sir Anthony Eden, his successor, needed some conciliatory move; the Churchill proposal was favored, above all, by Senator Walter F. George, the new Democratic Chairman of the Senate Foreign Relations Committee. The Geneva Summit Conference of July, 1955, raised false hopes; nor was any protest lodged with Bulganin and Khrushchev over the sale of arms to Egypt by the Soviet bloc. From the outset of the East–West contest it had been plain that German reunification was unattainable on Western terms. But Western policymakers were so wedded to this goal, so eager to elicit Russian agreement, that they neglected a vital Western interest in the Middle East.

Until the Suez fiasco disrupted it in 1956, coalition diplomacy remained on a more even keel. Secretary Dulles may have boasted of his artistry in having snatched peace from the brink by threatening to use atomic weapons tactically against Communist bases in China when Korean truce negotiations were stalled; when an Indonesian settlement had to be procured; and when, over the menace to Formosa from Communist China, Congress was asked to revalidate an authority for armed action that the President already possessed. But capitals such as London, Paris, and Ottawa knew that American diplomacy under General Eisenhower had not been as unilateral as Secretary Dulles implied.

And even if it had been, a retrospective disclosure could not do as much harm as one made at the time.

It was when primacy first shifted from Britain to the United States that peace by power became the staple coalition policy of the West. What seemed curious was the delusion of Secretary Dulles that he had somehow invented a doctrine which he himself had opposed before World War II and which the Eisenhower Administration had inherited from its predecessor. To sustain it, American leadership must be co-operative rather than unilateral. It would be undermined by that separate Russo-American pact for which Moscow yearned. But in the Republican Party there were still elements which thought an outworn isolationism might be adapted to altered circumstances, which preferred, therefore, a unilateral American approach. And Dulles' pronouncements may have been a sop to them.

In coalition strategy, however, there had been a crucial change. As a nuclear, thermonuclear, and missile power, the Soviet Union, preponderant on land, would presently be able to catch up with the United States in the air; only at sea, though Russia's submarine capacity is most formidable, did the West enjoy a clear predominance. In their quandary free peoples could not exercise any real freedom of choice. The inexpugnable hazards of a coalition strategy were the one safeguard against an overweening Russian hegemony; short of surrender to the latter, they must endure the all-enveloping risks of the former. Nor did neutralism offer a way out. Neutrals themselves were sheltered, despite animadversions upon the West, by coalition deterrents.

The military stalemate between East and West had, nevertheless, deflected the East–West contest to non-military channels. Each camp was to furnish uncommitted nations with economic aid and technical assistance; rival forms of society would be propagandized. Then, too, not only was anti-imperialism fomented against Britain, and neutralism against the United States, among other peoples but these sentiments, to the detriment of Anglo-American unity, were promoted within English-speaking countries against each other. In the East–West contest, as a matter of fact, psycho-political warfare could impair or augment the military potential of either side. And behind it all there loomed that counteracting power through which alone peace might be preserved.

Never before, however, did it have to be accumulated on so big or so intricate a scale. And it underwent a qualitative change as it was enlarged quantitatively. A nightmare of coalitions, which Emperor William II finally brought about, had worried Bismarck; and yet it was not the existence of a countervailing strategy that emboldened Hitler but the imbecilic failure of the West to array itself against him. A military timetable had predetermined in 1914 how the European alliances would work; and some of their ramified fatality is what may now be feared in a strategic interlock. The preponderance of the law-abiding was perceived between the wars as the most logical basis for the organization of peace. But they have had no monopoly on techniques of bigness. With these, totalitarian regimes have built a world of their own. To enforce a rule of law against it would be to imperil civilization itself. Equilibrium rather than preponderance is what keeps the peace.

But when the peace-keeping machinery is so delicately poised, leadership is a task of infinite finesse. Anglo-American solidarity has been the backbone of the Western combine; over the continuance of a free world order the English-speaking peoples must always unite. The Korean War, with its aftermath, demonstrated, all the same, how far-reaching in extent may be a strategic backlash; how policies that are sound in themselves can yet, for coalition purposes, be unsound. With other Atlantic allies the United States and Britain must plan for joint operations. Major weapons are nevertheless so incredibly mobile that, until there is a final showdown, coalition strategy may be self-immobilized. The superiority of the East in conventional forces would, besides, induce the West to rely even for local or limited warfare on tactical nuclear weapons; but it might hesitate to employ these lest they cause all-out war. And so it is not only in corporate industry that bigness introduces rigidities. That which expedites the defense of the West can also hinder it.

There may be no alternative to peace. But there is an alternative to freedom. Submission to the East might preserve the West physically and yet destroy it in every other respect. It gambles instead on planetary deterrents. Not that this is the first time men have risked the present so as to save the future. But to enlarge the scale of things is to change much else besides. Modern weapons can pollute the earth and lay desolate all that is best upon it; today it is the future as well as the present that must be risked. The twentieth century itself is what has made the human predicament so grim. But as allies of the United States cannot rebel against that, they may tend to rebel against her. And yet when they will the end, which is the defense of the West, they will the means. These have to be accepted. There is less disposition to accept uncritically the way they are organized, managed, and controlled.

There have, to be sure, been other grounds for discontent with American leadership. The fact that British interests are still world-wide would in itself compound the chances for divergence between the United States and Britain. But the British people are not merely frustrated by a decline in status; they dread being caught in a crossfire that is not of their making. And yet the United States did not impose a coalition strategy on Britain, France, and the other Atlantic allies. They adopted it because in no other fashion could a free world order be upheld. Dangers are shared in common; on the levers of the over-all defense mechanism, only one of their number may, nevertheless, keep her hand. Disparities in power catapulted the United States to the fore; coalition strategy accentuates them. They can not be eliminated. But it is a condition of primacy that the United States assuage their effect.

V

Who Speaks for America?

Is the American political system geared for leadership? The American people are taught to revere it. But are they not pre-eminent in spite of it rather than because of it? Some Americans have long been worried by such questions; countries as close to the United States as Britain and Canada have been troubled by them even more. Anglo-American friendship may be crucial as a power factor; among the English-speaking peoples there is a common approach to public affairs and yet no real grasp of how each musters its own power and brings it politically to bear. A host of Americans are still mystified by the Commonwealth partnership and other oversea components of British strength. But what is done or left undone by the American system can, under coalition strategy, be to Britain a matter of life or death.

Is it unpredictable in its workings? Does it, as compared with the parliamentary system, tend towards irresponsibility? Not that a form of representative government which the British may deem better inevitably produces the wiser policies. Without home-grown follies between the wars, Britain's own shift from senior to junior in the Anglo-American leadership of the West might have been deferred. And yet the sudden jolts to which the American system is prone are the more distressing to an ally who not so long ago was itself ensconced in first place.

Double jeopardy may now afflict Anglo-American friendship. When Britain was in the lead, the United States could find fault with the substance of British proposals. Today differences might also be exacerbated by the procedures, constitutional and political, under which American policy is formulated and executed. Anglo-American unity was made possible dialectically by resemblances within the British and American systems. Divergence is fostered by contrasts between them.

At issue, first of all, is the locus of authority in the West.

Having donned the mantle of primacy, the United States cannot depend only on her own will and stamina; she must have the support of other free peoples. Democracy, as far as leader and led are interdependent, has thus acquired an extra dimension; the range of popular consent has expanded. Governing regimes in the East may, on the other hand, veer and tack with more rapidity. Not that the Russian dictatorship can now act in total disregard of captive nations; apart from the defection of Yugoslavia, there has been unrest in East Germany, deviation in Poland, and rebellion in Hungary. Then there is Communist China which has to be treated as an equal. Both sides in the East–West contest thus have to achieve intramural co-operation. But the American leader of the West must consider more than the minimal interests of her associates. She has to promote between free peoples unison by consent in depth.

At issue, likewise, is the locus of authority within the American system itself. And here the fact that it may be over-centralized in some respects, not sufficiently centralized in others, is what bewilders the British—an ally for whom constitutional equipoise is the very quintessence of democracy. That the American Presidency as an executive institution is overcentralized was obvious when President Eisenhower suffered his various illnesses; it is more than fortunate that neither enemies nor friends realized the gravity of the crisis into which the entire defense of the West might thereby have been plunged. The prospect of mutual extermination in the hydrogen age had, when the President was first bedridden, caused a lull in the East–West contest. The Big Four had just met at the summit in Geneva; the full consequences of Soviet perfidy in arming Egypt were yet to be discerned. But what if a still more serious challenge had impended? What if aggressors behind the Iron Curtain had thought the hour propitious for a final showdown with the West?

Strategically we can surmise how overwhelming the American riposte to an enemy onslaught would have been. But constitutionally, inasmuch as initial steps must be taken by the executive branch of the American government, little was clear. The Cabinet and the National Security Council can only advise; no one but the President may order American troops into action and, over Formosa in particular, Congress had lately reassigned that right to the President himself. Thirty-six years after Woodrow Wilson's protracted illness the American system was not equipped to cope with a contingency as dangerous for the West as for the American nation itself. Congress, which has the power to declare war, would have approved retroactively whatever had been done in the interim. But until a Vice-President supplants the President, it is not for the former to command. Legislation to anticipate a Presidential disability was discussed; none has been adopted. Nor would the American people have re-elected an ailing President in 1956 if the problem had bothered them. At the same time a constitutional amendment came into effect that debarred a third term and that could thus detract from the authority which a second-term incumbent might exert.

Under the British parliamentary system, however, there are no such built-in constitutional bottlenecks. Since a Prime Minister does not have a fixed term of office, he can, in an emergency, be replaced overnight. That was how Winston Churchill took over from Neville Chamberlain in 1940. Later on, it is true, Sir Winston stayed in office almost two years after he had undergone a stroke; but Sir Anthony Eden retired soon after the Suez fiasco of 1956 caused a further deterioration in his health. Flexibility thus distinguishes the Parliamentary from the Presidential system. In Britain, moreover, a national election can be held within a period of weeks and the country is not reduced every fourth year to a state of diplomatic semiparalysis. As long as the United States was isolationist, the character of her political system did not impinge on the well-being of others. Most Americans still do not appreciate how much it may now do so.

Would the Presidency be less of a bottleneck if there were to be a sort of Gaullist Prime Minister under it—a First Secretary who, outranking the Secretary of State, might look after foreign affairs and national security? Top executive powers are lodged inalienably in the President. A Prime Minister in the British parliamentary system has a status to which, below the President, the American political system can provide no real equivalent.

Even coalition protocol has to adjust itself to the American political system. Heads of State and friendly Prime Ministers were invited to Washington; the more allies such as Britain, Canada, France, and West Germany were to co-operate with her, the more frequent would be visits to the United States of their highest political representatives. Yet as one who is both Head of State and Chief Executive, the President cannot absent himself as easily from his own country as they can; the multiplicity of his duties, in a political system which is otherwise so decentralized, prevents him from repaying most of the high-level calls that are made on Washington. Secretaries of State might travel freely; when John

Foster Dulles did so it was to the detriment of other policy-making activities. American primacy turned Washington into a Mecca for state pilgrimages. No President can undertake as many trips in return. Nor is any likely to try after the mortifying cancellation of visits that Dwight Eisenhower was to have paid to Moscow and Tokyo.

In that American system from which its own leadership emanates all of the West has a stake. But it is the American economy that endows the American political system with strength. The interaction of these two has long been praised by Americans themselves—the equal opportunities provided by the one being a stimulus for the growth of the other. And neither Civil War nor economic depression were to set back the American economy permanently. For its natural riches have not only been abundant; the map decreed that its soil, unlike that of invaded France or Britain's air-bombed cities, should be spared the ravages of foreign war. But British primacy also had a lot to do with the success of the American economy; during formative years it could be self-engrossed because British sea power, supplemented later by Anglo-French land power, kept interlopers away. As a vehicle of leadership the American political system has not, until now, had to run the same gamut as its British counterpart. But neither is the American economy what it once was.

World contests have been enlarged in scale. Bigger also is the scale on which the American leader of the West functions internally. On two interconnected fronts, from within and from without, the traditional institutions of American democracy have thus been subjected to unprecedented strains. Not that in co-operative measures the United States since World War II has failed, as it were, to rise to the occasion. But under the conditions of primacy today it is important for the American political system to operate smoothly. And this it has not been constructed to do. Her allies have not only feared that the United States would oscillate between impetuosity and self-hobbling dissension but these two antithetical traits seemed to emerge side by side. Britain and others in the West have been anxious lest coalition strategy deprive them of control over their own destiny in the paramount field of global defense; on this topic, as on lesser ones, confidence might be sapped when controls within the web of American governance itself are hard to pin down. Leadership in an East–West contest would put on their mettle the most seasoned of peoples and the least unresponsible of systems. To neither, as it happens, can the United States lay claim.

Who speaks for America? Allies who rely on an American lead have often had to ask this question. And it is one which has stuck in British minds because in the British form of representative democracy there is seldom the same doubt over the locus of political authority. That constitutional differences might make Anglo-American cooperation more arduous had been plain since the Hay–Pauncefote isthmian treaties were negotiated at the turn of the century. And now, as leader of the West, the United States not only requires sound judgment but must have a sure capacity to follow through. A premium, however, is put on incertitude by a political system in which Presidency, Congress, and Judiciary exercise co-ordinate but separate powers—in which there is so perpetual a struggle for and against co-ordination that leadership itself may be retarded, circumscribed, or undercut.

Nor is this the only impediment. In Britain the House of Lords has been shorn of its strength; in Canada the Senate has never had much; but in the United States it is the Senate which has gained influence and prestige. Between the Senate and the House of Representatives there are jurisdictional disputes and there is a constant search for compromises that will satisfy both chambers. Then, too, action between organs of the Congress is not all that has to be co-ordinated. Some within the Executive branch itself may be publicly at loggerheads. And an internecine departmental warfare which is often so audible might be waged over foreign as well as over domestic issues.

American leadership is even affected by the congenital rift which exists between Washington and the various States of the American Union. The United Nations has, for example, adopted a Declaration of Human Rights—together with related measures against genocide, slave labor, and similar enormities. But President Eisenhower did not submit them to Congress for ratification. His own copartisan, Senator Bricker, headed a movement that, by preventing encroachments upon the legislative domain of the States and by augmenting Congressional power, would have hamstrung the President's conduct of American foreign policy. In the name of American sovereignty, what Senator Bricker opposed was social and economic reform by treaty and executive agreement.* To take the wind out of his sails and protect Executive prerogatives, the United Nations measures had to be withheld.

The latter were also anathema to the Democratic South which maintains racial discrimination by insisting upon states' rights. And any who would preserve these must reject compulsory

---

* Donovan, *op. cit.,* pp. 231-242.

jurisdiction by the International Court of Justice at The Hague. For the self-constrictive features of the American political system did not vanish when primacy shifted from Britain to the United States. Only by abjuring leadership in less decisive spheres can Washington lead in decisive ones.

The fact is that, as long ago as the 1870's, the checks and balances of the American system were seen as something to avoid rather than emulate. That, at any rate, was Canada's attitude when she drafted her constitution. As neighbors, the United States and Canada are not only like-minded; they have similar national problems to solve. Distant provinces with varying sectional interests were federated under the British North America Act of 1867; provision had to be made for the special rights of French-speaking Quebec. At the time of Confederation the din and carnage of the American Civil War was an object lesson. For union, one and indivisible, Canada would try another tack.

A federal system coupled with responsible parliamentary government on the British pattern was the constitutional framework which the Fathers of Confederation adopted. As a Commonwealth monarchy, Canada, in the years ahead, would create a synthesis of national independence with wider historic ties. But the nature of her political system also refuted the notion that, across a vast North American expanse, the American form of representative democracy would be the only feasible one.

In the American Constitution a separation of powers is not prescribed but implied. By dividing twentieth-century American power, an eighteenth-century separation of powers might serve also to hamper.

John Hay felt that it would, and his view is noteworthy. Preference voiced for British parliamentary methods by Walter Bagehot and his American disciple, the younger Woodrow Wilson, can be dismissed as that of nineteenth-century theorists. John Hay, on the other hand, testified from the practical experience of one who, at the beginning of the twentieth century, was the first Secretary of State to perceive the need for a more positive American role in the modern world. He deemed it imperative for the English-speaking peoples to proceed together in tandem; but, recalling his own mission to the Court of St. James's, he was also consumed with envy at the deftness with which, when Britain was leader of the West, his British counterparts, Salisbury and Lansdowne, could operate institutionally. Nettled and downcast, he railed against a Constitution that permitted him to negotiate but not commit, and a branch of the Congress (the Senate with its two-thirds vote on treaties) that might commit but not negotiate. What he wanted after the American war with Spain was to combine the specific new oceanic responsibilities of the United States with more general co-operative ones. What debarred these was a form of governance which, according to him, made for irresponsibility.

In the isolationist America of McKinley, as of that interventionist *manqué,* Theodore Roosevelt, gloom such as Hay's could be looked upon as an amiable eccentricity. More sanguine about Hay's accomplishments than Hay himself was his friend, that American booster by inversion, Henry Adams. And some of the neglect that has befallen so prescient an American statesman as Hay may not only be due to the fact that he was ahead of his time but that as a sceptic among true believers he had, in decrying the Constitution, violated national taboos. The age of Woodrow Wilson and the undoing of a free world order between German wars were to show how cogent his premonitions had been. When, moreover, Wilson participated in the peacemaking of 1919, he had forgotten his own early clarification of the difference between the British and American political systems; at Paris he could not play the part of a Prime Minister among his peers without derogating from what, as President, should have been a higher role. Two decades later, when primacy had shifted from Britain to the United States, Congress was willing to co-operate with the Executive. And yet neither Harry Truman nor Dwight Eisenhower could always be sure that, in so far as they represented the national will, a cumbrous machinery of government would not be interposed to thwart it.

On the whole, nevertheless, President Truman found more to admire than deprecate in the American political system. James Forrestal, his first Secretary of Defense, wished to borrow Cabinet responsibility on the British model. But this would have required a change in the American Constitution and Mr. Truman felt that the United States had done very well under it as it stood. Enough, moreover, was achieved during his years in the Department of State, and as its Secretary, for Dean Acheson to echo these views. As between the British and American systems, he pointed out that each is adapted to its own special circumstances.* Divided government is, nevertheless, a perennial problem—though the conclusions at which President Eisenhower and Secretary Dulles

---

* Truman, *op. cit.,* II, p. 60; *Forrestal Diaries,* p. 542; and Dean Acheson, *A Citizen Looks at Congress* (New York: Harper & Brothers, 1957), p. 81.

arrived were, as divulged at a White House press conference in June, 1959, much the same as those of their predecessors.

No basic alteration will, of course, be contemplated. The truth is, however, that even the powers that the Supreme Court enjoys in a tripartite system had incurred Mr. Truman's wrath. For at a moment of crisis in world affairs he was hindered by that organ when, after a Congressional default, he sought to discharge his duties as Commander-in-Chief and as Chief Executive of a nation which had become leader of the West. Pronouncing against his seizure of the steel mills in the spring of 1952, the Supreme Court ignored the fact that munitions had to be supplied to American troops still holding the line in Korea; that other "Koreas" might result from a slowdown in arms production; that, under the Mutual Defense Assistance Program, some of America's Atlantic allies had to be bolstered.* It is as it should be when an ex-President sees more to praise than to dispraise in the American system. But his own political reminiscences indicate that allies are not perturbed by bogies.

Without leadership at home there can be no leadership abroad, and what the American system needs, as Mr. Truman observed, is a strong President. But it is not often that one will arise. And for the duration of his term or terms he can be unseated only by acts of God or when convicted by impeachment. Unlike a Prime Minister of the United Kingdom, he will have won his spurs not by a superior, well-rounded performance on the highest national plane in both Parliament and Cabinet, but in some more one-sided, less qualifying sphere. Justice Brandeis, it was once recollected by Mr. Truman, used to describe the pristine American aim as liberty rather than efficiency. But in a world of bigness, where efficiency without liberty has, in totalitarian guise, made giant strides, the leader of the free must exemplify both.

The United States cannot act as One unless centrifugal tendencies are withstood. But these get leeway from a party system that is looser than any which obtains in parliamentary democracies. An Anglo-American consensus as the curb upon Anglo-American divergence may, broadly speaking, be expedited by dialectical traditions that are much the same throughout the English-speaking world; in detail the British and American party systems are as different as the constitutions under which they operate. These evolved in Britain and the United States after the latter had declared her independence. The British party system grew within an established parliamentary framework. The Amer-

* Truman, *op. cit.*, II, pp. 465-478.

ican party system was, however, superimposed upon a mode of government with which it is chronically at odds.

Divergence in policy between the United States and Britain may be overcome. Institutional differences that sometimes promote this divergence are more deep-seated. When the Executive sits in the Legislature, the party conflict comes to a focus within a single chamber and these two branches of representative government can be co-ordinated at every turn of the wheel. But when governmental organs are separated constitutionally, the political apparatus is riven throughout by an ineluctable struggle for and against co-ordination. An American President is the Head of State. He is also chief of an administration whose own party may or may not command a Congressional majority. Apart from patronage he has few reins to pull on legislative copartisans. Unless bipartisan measures can be agreed upon, all must wait until the next election year falls due—and even then similar cleavages may recur.

In Parliament, however, it is on a voting majority that Ministers depend. To diminish this, and thus precipitate another electoral bid for office, is the Opposition's main business. Not that it is a simple task to maintain a parliamentary majority or that the British party system is without blemish. But a British or Canadian Prime Minister does have recourse to a party sanction of which, under separated powers and fixed electoral terms, a President cannot avail himself. For if a parliamentary majority is unruly or tends to break up, dissolution of the House and new elections may be threatened—a prospect seldom alluring to Ministerial copartisans who, when a fresh verdict is sought at the polls, may lose their seats prematurely.

For leadership the British political system thus offers one unsurpassed advantage: Ministers, when they speak for Britain, can do so with assurance. And when there is a national or coalition government composed of more than one party the same rule applies. At Westminster an Opposition may allow the refractory among its members a latitude that supporters of the Ministry cannot be granted. In the eyes of the electors, however, it will do itself harm if it is merely fractious. The ungovernable cannot govern.

There is, however, one serious flaw in the British system. Like its American counterpart it requires party regularity; but a maverick is more likely to be penalized in Parliament than in Congress for expressing an individual viewpoint. No government would topple in Washington, as it must in London, when its legislative backing crumbles. And yet a majority at Westminster which keeps Ministers in office may be one that is disciplined unduly. To obey or not to obey—that, for members of Parliament, is the question. If a majority of them did not cast their votes with the government of the day, the nation's business could not be transacted; if all were docile, the nation might suffer. As far as it can, an administration in Washington must find legislators of its own party stripe to work with. But where governmental powers are unitary rather than separate, there will be Ministerial pressure or the party caucus to make members toe the mark.

Not that this is invariably successful. Over a particular issue dissentients may be left severely alone or may even manage to extract concessions. After the Suez episode of 1956, no reprisals were taken against a group of Right-wing backbenchers who objected to American influence on British policy; conversely, however, other members, both Labor and Conservative, were denied renomination by local constituency organizations when they pursued lines of their own. But it is the career of Winston Churchill that still furnishes the classic modern example of a parliamentary rebel who served the nation by breaking party ranks. For between the wars, when the German menace revived, he spoke the truth as he saw it. And yet, when they scouted his warnings, Stanley Baldwin and Neville Chamberlain were more representative of British opinion than he was. The fact is that parliamentary coordination between Executive and Legislature enables the world to know exactly where Britain stands—if she wishes to stand anywhere. When, as during the 1930's, no lead is given, the parliamentary system may be as indecisive as any other brand of representative democracy. When a lead is resolved upon, it is apt to fumble less.

In yet another respect, too, a British government can give a lead abroad with better assurance than an American. Legislators who support it might, as Edmund Burke hoped they would, have been elected on national rather than local issues—though national issues may be construed nowadays, both on Left and Right, in terms of class. More than in Britain, at any rate, members of Congress or the Canadian Parliament tend to be deputies for local interests. And here North American sectionalism does tend to cut across other differences in the American and Canadian political systems.

The fact is that, as representative democracies, neither Britain nor the United States lives up functionally to its prospectus. And for both this could be a serious matter. Constituencies in Britain may be so carved out that the party which takes office will have received fewer votes than those which opposed it. A similar defect in the United States is the device of the Electoral College—one through which a President is elected not by direct popular vote but through the votes of each State registered as a single unit. A candidate who may have won a State by the barest of pluralities is credited with all of its votes in the Electoral College. And so when electoral minorities are scattered across the nation, the votes of individuals who belong to them are not added up but annulled. When, on the other hand, electoral minorities are concentrated in particular regions like the Solid South or the Middle West, they carry more weight than is democratically their due.

Nor is Congress itself as representative as it purports to be. And by institutional deformities the character of American leadership may be deformed. In the Upper House, under a rule by which sovereign states first joined the Union, Senators from sparsely populated states have the same vote as those from more populous ones; the bulk of the American people are thus deprived of a voice commensurate with their numbers. For members of the Lower House, with its two-year term, there is too brief an interval between election campaigns; Senators with their six-year terms enjoy greater latitude. But wherever the ballots of rural electors are worth more than those of urban ones, there is a permanent gerrymander which favors the isolationist mentality.

Not that this will entail pressure for an about-face in the over-all obligations of primacy. It is too late in the day for that. But it does encourage propitiation of the farm bloc; the accumulation of agricultural surpluses that, when dumped abroad, may spoil markets for Commonwealth allies like Canada, Australia, or New Zealand and compel Asian neutrals to make commercial deals with the East. Until recently, moreover, isolationism was centered in the Middle West. With industrialization, the South has acquired a more protectionist, less internationalist outlook. In the Lower House, Southern Democrats tend now to be as averse as Midwest Republicans to economic aid for underdeveloped countries—and at a time also when, in competition with the East, such funds must be increased rather than curtailed. The special position that sectional blocs—Midwest Republican, Southern Democratic—can occupy is therefore of more than academic interest.

It is, however, not merely political abuse of representative institutions that aggravates the disabilities under which an American lead must labor. These institutions, with their struggle for and against co-ordination, are designed to obstruct. The way they operate will be further examined presently. But first some attention must be paid to bipartisanship, a procedural innovation that the exigencies of primacy have evoked.

A very different sort of effort to cut across party lines had preceded it. For some years Democrats from the South and Southwest and the Right wing of the Republican Party had backed each other—the latter obtaining support for its fiscal and economic views while, in return, Civil Rights bills, through which southern Negroes might benefit, were postponed. But under this arrangement the Executive can be by-passed; bipartisanship in foreign affairs is a co-operative endeavor. A regrouping within parties to achieve a legislative majority, it is also one that denotes an *ad hoc* co-ordination between the Executive and the Congress. Not that bipartisan consultations are complete: under the Truman Administration the Far East had been excluded from them; and then there was a famous remark by Senator Vandenberg, their foremost Republican exponent, that he and his colleagues wanted to be in on the take-offs as well as the crash landings. But this was not a complaint that the Democrats were to reiterate during the Eisenhower Administration when they controlled the Senate. Bipartisan majorities were still provided. A free hand to amend and even oppose would also be retained.

Separated powers are what call for such an expedient, and under a parliamentary system it is not necessary to devise one. British Ministers would not be in office if there were no organized majority in the House of Commons on which they could rely—and that is so even when a coalition or a national government has had to be formed. Nor did Mr. John Diefenbaker's recent Conservative experiment in minority governance at Ottawa last long; within less than a year the Canadian electorate converted it into a parliamentary majority—one indeed that left the Liberal and other parties numerically weaker than an effective Opposition should be. At Westminster the party leaders may consult during national emergencies. But a Conservative Opposition in 1949 and a Labor Opposition in 1958 rejected the idea of a bipartisan committee to discuss defense matters in secret with the government. Parliament would have been stultified if confidential information imparted to the Opposition precluded it from speaking out and thus from doing its job.

Without bipartisanship, however, the American political system cannot meet the demands of primacy. But unlike a pre-existing parliamentary majority, it has no life of its own; it must be renewed item by item. And while the Roosevelt, Truman, and Eisenhower administrations fostered it, they did not all do so in precisely the same manner. The Democratic administrations of Presidents Roosevelt and Truman solidified Republican backing by giving senior Cabinet posts to distinguished Republicans; and it was under them that major responsibilities were initially assigned to General Eisenhower and John Foster Dulles. Yet when these two were in the saddle no comparable Democratic appointments were made. There was less reason for making them. Democrats in Congress had no choice but to approve of the staple internationalist policies which their own party had first espoused. It was between a Republican Administration and its own legislative copartisans that co-ordination was needed most; the problem could not be solved by offering high Cabinet positions to eminent Democrats. This is not to suggest that the Democratic Party is any less split than the Republican. But its main fissures are over such domestic issues as civil rights—though today liberal Republicans may be more warmly disposed than Southern Democrats towards lower tariffs and foreign aid.

Normally, under the British system, a lead in foreign affairs does not have to have a legislative support that is bipartisan. Under the American system there could have been none without one.

Nor has faction been the sole problem. During the Eisenhower Presidency, it was the party officers charged with the task of effecting co-ordination between the Senate and the White House who were among the most contumacious. Bipartisanship, ever since Senator Vandenberg belatedly saw the light, had provided internationalist majorities. Yet now it was not the usual encounter between isolationist and internationalist which nonplussed allies, nor even that between two species of internationalists. Over great coalition issues Senator William F. Knowland, Republican floor leader in the Senate and the Administration's legislative spokesman, was often the Administration's chief critic.

In any representative assembly there is procedural chaos when a government spokesman may, as he pleases, be more opposed than the official Opposition. But Senator Knowland was not asked to resign from his party post. Another President might have lashed out against so irregular a state of affairs; only in a loose party system where there are separated powers could it arise at all. An isolationist society might commend that kind of free-wheeling; with the United States as prime power of the West, it could be disastrous. In 1954, when control of the Senate passed from the Republicans to the Democrats, Senator Knowland ceased to be majority leader. But even as minority leader, on important foreign questions he acted less as a co-ordinator between his own party and an Administration that belonged to it and more as a party insurgent.

In advocating extreme steps against Communist China he assailed one of the Executive's principal coalition policies—that which forbade a rupture with Britain, Canada, and other allies over the Chinese issue. The American capacity to lead the West against the East might have been crippled by the Bricker Amendment; Senator Knowland, voting for a modified version, would have curtailed the prerogatives of a President to whom, ostensibly, he had special party duties. As late as the summer of 1958, Senator Knowland, in company with Senator Styles Bridges, Chairman of the Republican Policy Committee, opposed the Eisenhower Administration's desire to use the foreign aid program for weaning other Communist countries from economic dependence on the Soviet Union and to extend the reciprocal trade agreement from three to five years.

Responsible government, in the British parliamentary sense, was far to seek. When there is no likelihood of concurrent power, a Democratic Executive may, as in 1947–48, have to rely on a Republican Congress to put through epoch-making initiatives; and, conversely, it may be a Democratic Congress which, as after the midterm elections of the first Eisenhower Presidency, delivers a Republican Administration from reliance, in the Legislature, on mutinous copartisans. *Quis custodiet ipsos custodes?* Not until majority control had passed from his own party to the other side was President Eisenhower the master of his political household. Nor is it inconceivable, as Southern Democrats veer towards isolationism, that a Democratic President will, one day, again have to rely on Republican internationalists. Unity between allies will be imperative. But the United States did not encourage the others when her own political system functioned so erratically.

Under President John F. Kennedy a Democratic Administration will have in Congress a party majority of its own political complexion. Whatever coordination is reached between the Executive and the Legislature cannot, under the American system, last long. And divided government will, in other respects, still obtain.

There are, however, two traditional links between the Executive and Legislative branches—one that is nominal and another that supplements such loose co-ordination as political parties themselves may supply. The first of these is the post of Vice-President; the second is the role of Congressional committees. The Vice-President is, with the President, not only one of two nationally elected officeholders; presiding over the Senate and empowered to break a tie vote, he also sits with the Administration as a member of the National Security Council. But in discharging its legislative role, the Congress, unlike Parliament, lays more stress on inquiry than debate. Sifting measures proposed by the Executive, it does its principal work in committee. In the select and other committees of Parliament, the decisions of either House may be improved upon; in Congress, the two chambers tend merely to ratify what its own committees have decided. Nothing in Parliament will compare therefore with the power of Congressional standing committees. And it is through these that some procedural nexus between separate branches is obtained.

Committee transactions furnish, at any rate, a substitute for that face-to-face debate between members of the Cabinet and of the House of Commons which are so notable a feature of parliamentary life at Westminster. Messages to Congress, like a Speech from the Throne by a reigning monarch, can be delivered at a joint session of the Congress by the President in person. But as Head of the State as well as Prime Minister, the President could not properly take part in the rough-and-tumble of a representative assembly. Cabinet officers and other Executive officials may, however, be summoned to appear before Congressional committees in private or public sessions.

Not that this custom is a satisfactory alternative to parliamentary debate. In the latter there may be a fair exchange between participants; all that the former allows is a one-sided cross-examination of the non-elected by the elected. Legislators best qualified for a particular committee may, besides, not have been assigned to it. Nor is cross-examination of permanent officials always sound practice. They are expected to uphold departmental views. But, as administrations change, they may be chary of giving offense and might even be in touch with committee chairmen behind the backs of their political superiors.

Then, too, the President's own confidential advisers will be exempt, by the separation of powers, from committee appearances. Celebrated among these were Colonel Edward M. House in the Wilson Administration and Harry Hopkins in the four Administrations of Franklin D. Roosevelt. In 1958, however, it was revealed that Sherman Adams, General Eisenhower's Presidential Assistant, had misused his influence. When a Congressional committee called him on the carpet, the usual plea of Executive privilege sounded hollow and he proceeded to testify.

What, as between Executive and Legislature, the American system lacks is conjoint responsibility. In Britain, an elected Minister would have to answer to fellow legislators for action taken by non-elected government servants. In the United States, non-elected government servants answer to legislators for themselves and for the Administration if they can. Such a procedural nexus as there may be between the Executive and the Congress is, at best, an awkward one.

Separated powers are not exercised, however, in wholly separate compartments. In that sphere of Western leadership which is foreign affairs, Congress has a jurisdiction that impinges upon Executive prerogatives. The chief example of powers that are separate but shared is, of course, the Senate's two-thirds vote on treaties—with its Committee on Foreign Relations being correspondingly important. As an exception to this, nevertheless, there are Executive agreements—informal accords into which an Administration may enter with other countries and upon which the Senate does not have to stamp its approval. Nor is the Senate the only branch of the Congress whose special legislative powers give it a voice in the conduct of foreign policy. Money bills originate in the House of Representatives; indeed, contrary to the practice of Parliament, committees of that organ, by proposing to withhold or add funds, will even rewrite an Executive's budget. And when items such as foreign aid, mutual security, or defense expenditures are instruments of primacy, the manner in which the two Houses operate can be of as much concern to allies of the United States as to Americans themselves.

A British government may, at any rate, generally be sure of the authority with which it negotiates. But with no Cabinet rule in either chamber and with slack party reins all round, an American administration cannot always tell how bills will fare in the committee stage. Nor is their acceptance by one committee any guarantee of their fate in another; a foreign affairs committee might have its recommendations pared by an appropriations committee. Furthermore, the two chambers may differ over what the legislative end product should be. When, as in Britain, the Lower House is supreme, there can be no similar struggle for and against co-ordination. But in Congress both chambers possess rights that neither will yield to the other. And so an Executive-Legislative conflict is not the only one that is embedded in the American political system. Additional compromises will have to be achieved between the two Houses of Congress if any sort of co-ordinated lead is to be attained.

As a procedural nexus between the Executive and the Legislature, Congressional committees suffer, moreover, from the discretionary power enjoyed by their chairmen. It was fortunate that, when primacy shifted from Britain to the United States, the chairmanship of the Senate Committee on Foreign Relations fell—as majority control alternated between Republicans and Democrats—to legislators with broad, imaginative coalition views. But the McCarthy saga is significant not only because of harm done by the Senator in the realm of opinion and co-operation with allies; as a committee chairman he was even able to make the Administration knuckle under.

Seniority is no longer all that determines the assignment of members to Congressional committees, although committee chairmanships are still invariably awarded according to seniority rather than according to merit or distributed by rotation. And, as it happens, senior members of Congress are often those with safe seats from the Solid South or from unenlightened rural areas under the sway of a single party. Liberals were successful in the Congressional elections of 1958 but that made little impression on Senate majority leader Lyndon Johnson; so also in the House of Representatives, the Chairman of the Rules Committee, a Southerner, could decide what measures should get to the floor and be put to a vote. Rotten boroughs were eliminated from Britain more than a century ago. Upon such, nevertheless, repose about half the seats of Congress today.

It is in those large, populous, urban states which are the heart of the American economy that there is a genuine two-party system. And that being so, they are the ones where the turnover in elected personnel is greatest. But newcomers do not possess seniority in Congress; states that are democratically the most robust are thus the ones that, under seniority rules, may be penalized in the main legislative work of the nation. It is conjectural whether the United States could have done more as leader of the West under another form of representative government. But given the American system as it stands, some of the best intelligence and energy of the American people has been and will be underrepresented.

One other procedural nexus between Executive and Congress has frequently been suggested. In Parliament the two branches of government have official access to each other through set debates; at Question Time, moreover, Ministers may also be interrogated on the day-to-day conduct of departmental affairs. Would it be practicable for Congress to adopt the custom of Question Time? Through it a British Foreign Secretary and other members of the Cabinet can, with Junior Ministers, keep in touch with fellow parliamentarians and yet not, like their American counterparts, be diverted by committee hearings from other duties. Still, even the British procedure may groan and creak. In 1960, after the Earl of Home, a member of the House of Lords, was appointed Foreign Secretary, another Minister had to answer for him in the House of Commons.

Question Time seems ill-suited to the American system for two reasons. The first is that nowadays only one house of Parliament enjoys a major role, while in Congress the principal Cabinet officers would have to be at the disposal of both chambers. The second is that there would still be none of the other co-ordinating processes between Executive and Legislature that are the essence of responsible government under a parliamentary system.

It is noteworthy, moreover, that Dean Acheson, from the vantage ground of top-level experience in the era of American primacy, differs from predecessors such as Henry L. Stimson about the desirability of a question period. He admitted that, considering the amount of time consumed by meetings of a Secretary of State with committees and subcommittees of Congress, the moments of positive accomplishment were disappointingly few. But a question period cannot, in his opinion, be grafted upon the American system. Cabinet officers who participate in Congressional debate might be deemed rivals by Committee chairmen; they might also forget that, unlike British Ministers, they have no electoral status of their own but only such political footing as the President himself confers upon them. Then, too, Westminster has disciplines of House and Party and under them the Speaker can, in a manner that is not possible on Capitol Hill, make all stick to the point under discussion.* In the parliamentary system, commanding figures have had to have talent for both debate and administration. But Mr. Acheson doubts that an amalgam of these qualities is necessary—a view that typifies the separation of powers by which he himself had been schooled.

As Secretary of Defense, however, James Forrestal was among the first to wrestle with the problems of American primacy, and he looked with envy upon the allies of the United States who had the parliamentary system as their form of governance. In

---

* Acheson, *A Citizen Looks at Congress*, pp. 65-80.

1948, after a meeting in Ottawa with the Defense Committee of the Canadian Cabinet, he jotted down some rueful meditations on the way he and his colleagues were, by contrast, constrained to conduct their affairs. If Canadian Ministers could not speak for Canada, they would not be in office. But officers of the American Cabinet, while responsible to the President, still had as their main job, Forrestal observed,

> to sell Congress. They do not speak for the government in the sense of reflecting party control of the Legislative branch. Therefore, the decisions they take are decisions only in the sense of an effort to merchandise a particular idea to the really controlling power, the power of the purse. In the formation of our military budget, for example, the power of the Secretary of Defense is really one of recommending to the President what he thinks should be spent in what proportions between the various Services. After he has made such a recommendation, it is a free-for-all before the appropriations Committees . . . who, if they are of an opposite political control, are quite apt to take particular delight in altering the budgets sent up by the Executive.*

Nor is that the only outcome of separated powers. A procedural nexus between the Executive and the Legislature that is centered in the committee process may, if witnesses are treated unfairly, bring government service into disrepute. Not that this occurs whenever spokesmen for the Executive are cross-examined. Within Congressional committees, however, the accent is so much more on the investigative than the deliberative that, even when Cabinet Secretaries testify, they are not always accorded the respect due those who frame and administer departmental policies for the prime power of the West. Others may have a worse gauntlet to run.

One flagrant illustration of that occurred in 1954 when General Zwicker was browbeaten by Senator McCarthy during a notorious committee hearing about espionage at Fort Monmouth. This, moreover, was an ordeal to which, in Britain or Canada, an officer like General Zwicker could not have been exposed at all. Under the unitary system a departmental head assumes full responsibility for whatever subordinates do in his name; and behind his own Cabinet colleague stands the head of the government himself. Separated powers, however, permitted Secretary Stevens to waver over General Zwicker, and President Eisenhower to waver over

* *Forrestal Diaries*, pp. 474-475.

Secretary Stevens.* Not until McCarthy's fangs had been drawn was the Administration willing to back up those who were entitled to its support.

There might, accordingly, be a sudden assault on the morale of the Civil Service and the Armed Forces—on that of their middle and upper echelons, at any rate. The plain fact is that under separate powers a constitutional and administrative irresponsibility may be interrelated. American citizens can thus feel on their own home territory what allies feel abroad—the bewilderment that wells up whenever there is uncertainty over where, within the American political system, responsibility lies.

It is true, nevertheless, that where legitimate inquiry should precede legislation, the Congress does render service. All the great constructive measures of leadership that, with a shift in primacy from Britain to the United States, have marked the American course, were subjected to the fine-comb of committee investigation. Not that this is their sole job; committees also supervise the work of administrative agencies that Congress has established. The danger arises when, as the career of Senator McCarthy and others like him demonstrated, the accidents of party control and committee seniority allow the investigative power to be abused; when the function of the police and the courts is usurped. Nor was it merely the rights of fellow Americans that the Radical Right treated with scorn. By his Anglophobe outbursts the Senator also showed his contempt for wider American interests.

Unfortunate, too, was the fact that excesses by Congressional committees obscured the need for smoking out Communist spies from Executive departments. In Canada a similar task had been discharged after World War II by a Royal Commission— a method of investigation employed by parliamentary countries and one that removes any partisan taint from full-scale inquiries. Liberty of the subject was indubitably violated, and injustice done, by Congressional probes. But the amount of atomic and other pro-Soviet espionage that still went undetected in Britain would seem to suggest that a better mode of inquiry is futile unless it is promptly and effectively used. Lax British security arrangements were a matter of concern to more than the British people when nuclear scientists fled from Britain to Russia or when two Foreign Office officials, Burgess and MacLean, decamped. For the information which these renegades possessed in the fields of science and diplomacy were, thanks to Anglo-American interaction, not solely British property. And in this sphere, as in others,

* Donovan, *op. cit.,* p. 251.

divergence results when allies quarrel over the degree to which domestic and coalition affairs impinge upon each other.

In 1957, at any rate, when the Norman case aroused a storm, the Communist issue was not all that figured in it. There had been disclosures by an Internal Security subcommittee about the Canadian diplomatist Herbert Norman, and Canadians protested that the license accorded Congressional investigators had driven him to take his own life. Accustomed to a well-coordinated parliamentary process, they stood aghast at the irresponsibility that a Senate subcommittee could exhibit under the separate powers of the American system. But how prudent had Ottawa itself been? Herbert Norman may have been innocent; and yet had it been wise to send him to Cairo where, at a time of Soviet penetration in the Middle East, it was also essential for the allies of Canada to have confidence in him? No doubt, as an arm of the Executive, the State Department deplored a tragic legislative foray into a coalition domain. But was it, under the circumstances, as fortuitous as it appeared?

Canadian and British observers are, nevertheless, not the ones who, from the standpoint of coalition leadership as well as comparative government, have been the severest critics of Congressional probes. The most authoritative inside view has been that furnished by ex-President Truman himself. And while Congressional committees denounced the Truman Administration for negligence in the province of internal security, the legislative branch was charged by him with derelictions that, in a leader of the West, are no less grave.

At Westminster, during World War II, a number of secret sessions were held by the House of Commons. But when members of an American Cabinet or high Presidential advisers testify *in camera* before Congressional committees on matters of vital import to the United States and her allies, there is no assurance that confidences will be kept.

In his memoirs, at any rate, Mr. Truman told how secret information given a Congressional committee by one top military figure was often on the news ticker before he had returned to his office. In Mr. Truman's opinion, it must have been Soviet leaders who procured satisfaction from the Senate hearings on the dismissal of General Douglas MacArthur: "The committee Republicans (with few exceptions) made this an occasion to spread on the record almost every detail of our strategic planning." Some time was spent by President Truman in discussing with the National Security Council how "security leaks through congressional channels" might be prevented. No practical solution could be found.

The problem was traced back by Mr. Truman to the public's right to know government business as published not only in newspapers but in the *Congressional Record* and the hearings and reports of Congressional committees. "We worry a lot about the chance that some employee of the government might give away secrets, and we fire and humiliate people because of a mere suspicion that they might perhaps some day be indiscreet. Yet for the price of a good clipping service an enemy of the United States can acquire untold items of information about our plans and intentions and even about our installations and our equipment. . . .

"Since no two people are likely to agree where the security needs end and the public interest begins, all an enemy of the United States has to do is to stir up a good fuss that will lead to a congressional probe. Then he will probably receive at no extra charge all the information he wants."*

That is a bitter indictment. Such adversaries of the West as Soviet Russia and Communist China cannot be similarly embarrassed; in totalitarian states there is, by definition, no right to know. Not that this is a drawback which inheres unavoidably in representative democracy. English-speaking countries with a parliamentary system were caught napping by Soviet agents but have managed otherwise to keep their own defense secrets to themselves; the question for them has been whether those that they share with their American leader would also be safe. During the MacArthur hearings, General Omar Bradley, as chairman of the Joint Chiefs of Staff, had declined to reveal to the combined Committees on Armed Services and Foreign Relations the substance of a conversation with the President; and this refusal, reasserting the separation of the Executive and Legislative branches, Mr. Truman again commended in his memoirs.† Yet the "security leaks" by which he and his advisers were harassed flowed from the very tripartite separation of powers that he admired; from a struggle for and against co-ordination that is innate in the American system.

The "strategic planning" of the United States is, moreover, interlocked globally with that of her allies, and breaches of security by legislators, for whom the Executive could not account, also worried them. The problem is a perennial one. In June, 1956, towards the end of the first Eisenhower Administration, alarm was

---

* Truman, *op. cit.*, II, pp. 451-452; see also p. 292.
† Truman, *op. cit.*, II, pp. 452-454.

spread throughout allied lands by testimony that nuclear bombing of Russia would result in several hundred million deaths which, according to wind direction, might as well be those of friends as of foes. A secret forecast that may have been exaggerated, its gratuitous release was politically stupid. For publishing it, however, both the Defense Department and the Senate's Special Subcommittee on Airpower dodged responsibility. Though buckpassing is an occupational disease in all government and every collective undertaking, separate powers make it peculiarly virulent.

Policy divergences may thus be engendered by divergences whose origin is institutional. The American and British publics, pillars both of a free world order, are entitled to the same kind of governmental information; but as the means of obtaining this vary, so does the temper, even the ethics, of political discussion. Where powers are unitary rather than divided, the onus of party dialectic falls, on the Ministerial side, to members of the Cabinet. Within the American system, however, committee hearings are the only procedural nexus between Executive and Legislature. But there are press conferences with the President and Cabinet officers. Incapable of correlating separate branches, these serve as a sounding board for the views of the Executive.

So important a role does not have to be filled in a parliamentary democracy by that sort of makeshift. Woodrow Wilson was the first President to hold press conferences regularly; nowadays these are broadcast and televised. But where there are no written questions, there cannot, as there can in Parliament at Westminster, be well-considered written answers. Except for a President's corrected transcripts and an occasional prepared statement, American governmental press conferences are extemporaneous. And in 1956, as the Suez crisis boiled up, the French Foreign Minister complained about a coalition diplomacy that off-the-cuff pronouncements rendered imprecise. This, however, is not the only political defect which American press conferences exhibit. Ostensibly an expedient to democratize the workings of the Executive branch, they are democratically anomalous. For no electoral mandate bestows upon reporters and commentators the political privilege that they exercise: one of semiformalized public exchanges on a nation-wide scale with the chief officeholders of the nation.

And it is this fact that makes the American governmental press conference so unsatisfactory a device for the enlightenment of the American public. Though it has a wide compass, it seldom gets below the surface. For reporters and commentators have no constitutionally sanctioned footing within the electoral process. They therefore can be evaded, as fellow parliamentarians at Question Time or in a full-dress parliamentary debate cannot be. Routinized and yet elusive, what the high-level press conference does is to accentuate rather than mitigate the unco-ordinated nature of the American system. For it by-passes a function that belongs in parliamentary countries to elected representatives.

It is, however, when American governmental information has been improperly rather than properly extracted that allied chancelleries have most reason for dismay. And it is not only through Congressional committees that security leaks occur. Mass media have news channels of their own. They may oscillate between manipulation of public opinion and the defense of popular liberties; in the quest for circulation and profits they also compete with each other. And a freedom of the press that may impair the nation's freedom as these ill-assorted objectives are pursued would not be deemed a legitimate freedom in other walks of democratic life. In this regard, at any rate, the new period of American leadership did not begin well. On the eve of Pearl Harbor, the United States had broken Japanese secret codes, and advantage could be reaped only as long as Tokyo was unaware of that American feat. The *Chicago Tribune,* which had already published an American war plan, proceeded, nevertheless, to divulge what American intelligence had accomplished.

There have, moreover, been "inspired leaks" from within the Executive branch itself. In a tightly co-ordinated political system, the misuse of classified security information would be less easy. But the Armed Services have sought thereby to influence the attitude of Congress toward departmental budgets or to overshadow each other; there has been "Potomac Fever," an itch for publicity by members of the Administration. Secretary Forrestal, for one, had to deal with this problem soon after the United States became leader of the West. But when he asked publishers to censor themselves voluntarily, they told him that the Executive branch should first clamp down on some of its own officials. This was done. "Certain publishers," Mr. Truman was nevertheless to write in his memoirs, "seem to forget that the responsibility belongs to them as well as to the government, and the destruction of the country would destroy them also."*

That is true enough. And yet a democracy is only as free as its press. Classified security information can also be a shelter behind which misguided officials and bureaucrats may entrench

---

* Truman, *op. cit.,* II, pp. 291-293.

themselves; it is through unauthorized disclosures of government secrets that error might be likewise scotched. For here, as elsewhere, the conflict between security and freedom is what makes freedom secure. Some midpoint between extremes is the obvious goal, but under the American system this is hard to find.

What also disquiets allies are statements of strategic import made by officers of the Armed Services that should be made, if at all, by civilian superiors. Little or no blame can be attached to them when these are elicited at committee hearings; there is, however, much bold talk on other occasions. Is this done under orders or against them? Sometimes one department can thus say what another would leave unsaid; sometimes Washington as a whole might thus say what, for the sake of harmony with a divergent Britain or other anxious allies, it can attribute to an unruly general. The fact is that where co-ordination is loose, a good deal will be tolerated that, in a well co-ordinated democracy, would be quite intolerable.*

And so a change in strategic conditions is not all that coincides with a shift in primacy from Britain to the United States. Changed also are the political conditions under which policies of leadership are debated and hammered out. Understanding between the English-speaking peoples is sustained by a similar tradition of political dialectic. In Britain, however, the dialectic of democracy has a single parliamentary forum as its center; under the American system of separated powers the debate is not concentrated but diffused. A Congress from which the Executive is dissociated and in which it may not have a party majority, the rule of Congress by committee, the extra-constitutional function of the high-level press conference, the information role of the press in general—where such various mechanisms for political activity operate, there is no one focus for political dialectic. American democracy must thus make up its mind in a forum that is, as it were, a forum beyond the forum—one in which two branches of government are also poised for debate but cannot institutionally debate with each other.

For leadership at home and abroad, so unco-ordinated a system as the American raises other problems that will be noted. But in the particular sphere of political parties and Executive–Legislative relations, there is for the United States, as for Britain, one saving grace: limits are set to divergence; a sense of continuity in an accepted order of things is deep-seated. This furnishes the dialectical basis of Anglo-American friendship; and what each of

* The new position of the Armed Services is discussed on p. 121 ff.

the English-speaking peoples owes to a common political heritage, the plight of France has underscored. For in that country, between Left and Right, liberal and reactionary, clerical and anticlerical, little common ground is presupposed. France is still torn over the French Revolution, and even if she had no Communist masses she would still be riven to the marrow. Enemies without, enemies within, have, over the tragic years, sapped and mined. But the position of France is now a disjointed one because, while the French belong to the West, they do not belong to each other. She is the keystone of NATO defenses on the European continent. All who are committed to that have, therefore, a special interest in her political well-being.

Tumult in North Africa brought matters to a head. A more repressive policy was sought by the French Army on the spot, and weak governments in Paris could not always control it. For ever since Napoleon III had resurrected the Bonapartist legend, the Third and Fourth Republics had been palsied by their own special brand of divided powers. Marshal MacMahon and General Boulanger may have wanted to convert a Marshal's baton into the dictator's rod that Marshal Pétain wielded at Vichy; rather than let a Cabinet acquire a necessary authority, the National Assembly tried to keep too much. In Britain a Prime Minister can have Parliament dissolved and new elections called when his majority in the House dwindles. This disciplinary expedient is one that may not be feasible under the separate powers of the American system; it could have been made more freely available to French Premiers —but was not. The upshot was a series of group bargains within the Chamber itself rather than adequate majorities established by popular vote—a tendency enhanced by electoral lists that nourished small parties and splinter groups within them. Indeed, what France demonstrated was how a multiplicity of parties and party fragments can be so overrepresentative that a representative democracy may stifle itself.

A free world order would have succumbed long ago if the English-speaking peoples had not learned how to do better than that. But in 1958, when General Charles de Gaulle preserved the shell of French democracy, he preferred divided rather than unitary powers. Under the Fifth Republic, as in the United States, these require a strong President; and in France there will not always be a de Gaulle. Before the American and French Revolutions of the eighteenth century Montesquieu wrote that the English eluded tyranny by separating executive and legislative powers; his misreading of English trends was incorporated into the American Constitution by the Founding Fathers. It was, nevertheless, from them that Montesquieu's own Gaullist compatriots borrowed, and when they did so they ignored those quirks of geography and history by which the United States had been favored.

But whatever the favoring circumstances, the American people share with the British one contrasting truth. Their forms of representative government differ; so do their party systems. And yet these divergences are institutional rather than conceptual. For each of the English-speaking democracies is unified by the same underlying postulates of politics, and what serves each nationally would enable them internationally to overcome divergences and work together.

Differing political systems are not, however, all that differentiate the American and British party systems from each other. That which is practicable in a small, compact economy may be impracticable in one that stretches across a continent. On a national scale, third parties, for example, have not flourished in the United States. The Know Nothings, the Free Soil Party, the Populists, the Socialists, the Bull Moose Progressives under Theodore Roosevelt, the Progressive-Socialist grouping under Robert LaFollette, the fellow-traveling Progressives under Henry Wallace —these movements, with the notable exception of the one that marched under Theodore Roosevelt's banner, appealed to class or sectional interests. But when so vast a national area must be covered, it is the task of national parties to rise above them, to conciliate and not sow discord. Rather than sponsor third parties, powerful economic blocs—agriculture, labor, business—have tried to assert themselves within the two existing major parties.

Even politicians can, moreover, switch their support from their own party to another and yet retain their former allegiance. In the 1952 elections the Republican candidate, General Eisenhower, was backed by conservative Southern Democrats. The latter were not punished by their colleagues in the Senate for what they did, and in the 1956 election they returned to the Democratic fold. Another defection from their own party might, however, entail the loss of that party seniority on which Committee chairmanships depend. And Southern control of these is what has helped to give Congress its unrepresentative character. Such, then, is the paradox of American politics that, in this case, a sectional breakaway may not only rid the system of minority rule but can make the Democratic Party more genuinely national.

In other respects, nevertheless, if the two major parties are to remain vehicles of national unity, they must recognize, tolerate, and condone their own inner disunity. Each may endeavor to be more all-inclusive than the other; one yardstick of success is when incongruities do not result in an open breach. And it is this same national imperative that precludes a doctrinal realignment—one that would allow the political philosophy of Republicans to be uniformly conservative and that of Democrats to be uniformly liberal. Franklin Roosevelt and Wendell Willkie liked the idea of such a realignment; and so, apparently, did Dwight Eisenhower soon after he arrived at the White House. The latter, however, denied that he had ever cherished the notion of organizing a third party; his aim was to rejuvenate the Republican Party itself. It is significant, nevertheless, that Mr. Eisenhower felt the need for an internationalist outlook in his own party at a time when fellow-Republicans, eager to reduce Congressional appropriations for mutual security with allies of the United States, might have impaired the American leadership of the West.*

There are, at any rate, still some older inwrought national cleavages to which the demands of primacy cannot be accommodated. Among these, the difference within the Democratic Party over civil rights for Negro citizens not only divides it over United Nations projects that might invade the legislative domain of the states but the nation as a whole is put at a disadvantage among the colored multitudes of Africa and Asia. Yet so variegated in both parties are the blends of liberalism and conservatism, isolationism and internationalism, that consistent party programs are not feasible.

And in Canada, with its parliamentary system, the party situation is much the same. For there, too, third parties make no headway; there, too, across a vast continental expanse, national parties must find room for varied sectional interests. A certain doctrinal opacity in the party politics of North America might ensue. But even from the standpoint of America's coalition leadership, this would not be entirely bad. A bleak vista for third parties may be what ultimately routed Senator McCarthy. Once he had shot his bolt within the Republican Party, he had nowhere else to go.

Britain, on the other hand, being geographically smaller and nationally more homogeneous than the United States, can afford doctrinal alignments that are comparatively less vague. The highest common denominator between particular interests is what her political parties must likewise seek. But each will determine this in the light of its own special tenets. One of Britain's two

* Donovan, *op. cit.,* pp. 142-153.

chief parties was but a new third party a generation ago; crushed between Right and Left, the Liberal Party has been supplanted in the main by the Labour Party. So that a majority in Parliament can be achieved, the emergence of a third party or the exigencies of a major crisis may necessitate a two-party, or national, government. Yet unlike the old French custom of multifaceted Ministries, this is seldom more than a passing phase; at Westminster, as at Ottawa, the tendency is for a reversion to one-party majorities. Parliament functions best under a two-party system and, on the whole, the electorate appreciates that fact.

But just as the stress in North America is on a harmonization of sectional interests, so is it on ideological elements in British party combat. Before the Labour Party took hold, the impetus for reform had, with some upper-class leavening, come from the middle class; the initial objective was to liberalize politically rather than recast economically a society in which the Conservative Party stood for privilege. But then, under the prodding of Socialist intellectuals, an emancipated working class resolved upon the transformation of the entire British economy. And yet, after a milder version of the Welfare State had been accepted by the Conservative Party, there was less for the Left to thunder against.

Nor, despite anti-American outcries among the Left's own dissidents, did economic experimentation in Britain set the English-speaking peoples apart. For one thing, while American social reform shunned ideological labels, it had been substantial. Most Democrats today are the heirs of the New and Fair Deals; solicitude for the rights of property and corporate business has been attributed to Republicans. Differing party and sectional emphases could, all the same, not disguise the degree to which, in general economic principles, there had been an approximation between them. But that was not the only approximation of its kind. Britain had created her welfare state. And as American parties adopted their own quota of economic and social reform, British measures looked, from across the Atlantic, somewhat less reprehensible.

The realignment of American politics along class lines may nevertheless still be possible. The goal of a third party has been eschewed in the United States by organized labor; a recent merger of craft and industrial unions could, however, provide a foundation for it. A severe depression would be its catalyst. But the progressive capitalism of mid-century America is regulated by government and collectivized by itself; in such an economy neither of the established parties can let a depression get out of control.

A nation-wide Labor Party would no longer be the sole advocate of ameliorative action. And that, too, is why there may be less room for one than ever before on the American scene.

There is, however, yet another feature of American party politics that distinguishes them from those of Britain and that has caused Anglo-American misunderstanding. The British have never understood the influence that ethnic groupings of non-British origin exert within the urban party machines and in rural areas. These minorities possess the same rights as other American citizens to agitate and protest. Yet when it is British policies against which they club together, the British are taken aback. That the element of race binds together the English-speaking peoples has been an illusion long nourished in Britain. But the unit rule of the Electoral College gives a casting vote in populous States to voters whose ancestry is not early American. And, among other sectional interests, candidates and parties will vie for that vote. Not that a more pro-British outlook can always be expected from Americans of impeccably British descent. Anglo-American relations were least tranquil when they were predominant.

National interest rather than racial antecedents has, of course, been the basic determinant of Anglo-American friendship. Socially and ethnically, moreover, Anglophobe diehards have formed a curious hotchpotch. Racial groupings may have expressed at the polls their special grievances against Britain—German-Americans, Irish-Americans, even, during World War II, Italian-Americans. And yet many of the unreconstructed isolationists with whom they collaborated were of an older American vintage. But that, too, is far from being the whole story. In particular neighborhoods, urban districts, and state-wide groups, Anglophobe elements may have voted en bloc; kinsmen who moved elsewhere and were absorbed in other communities tended to follow their own bent. And then, when the time came for the United States to don the mantle of primacy, most ethnic minorities were as responsive as any major racial element in the land to the demands of leadership. The ethnic composition of the American people has been a mixed one. It was, all the same, at the turn of the century, when this became more mixed than ever, that the Anglo-American factor emerged in international affairs. Underpinning a free world order, it transcended, by the very nature of its task, the usual differences of race and creed.

As leader of the West, the United States is today the one who must do the most to keep her allies well-disposed. But for Britain it was only yesterday that the shoe was on the other foot.

And the more the British sought American goodwill, the more the road for aggrieved Anglophobic minorities passed through Washington. Between the wars, fortunately, an Irish settlement had robbed of its sting the most serious anti-British group-agitation in America. A later generation in Britain must wonder at stiff-necked forebears who would not grant Ireland the sort of home rule that Canadians—English-speaking and French-speaking, Protestant and Roman Catholic, together—had been able to extract; if what was done after World War I by David Lloyd George had been conceded in Gladstone's day, the good accomplished might have been felt at once on both sides of the Atlantic. Ulster, nevertheless, is still a bone of contention. Ireland wants to annex it and the British are blamed when the majority of Ulstermen wish to remain part of the United Kingdom. During World War II the Allies could not use neutral Irish ports and that hampered them in their command of the seas; a free world order in which alone Ireland could be free was thus ill-served by the Irish people. Between London and Washington, Ireland has otherwise ceased to trouble.

The Anglophobia of German-American voting groups was, however, in quite another category. For here the anti-British grievance had been a general rather than a specific one; only by abandoning her world status and betraying her global responsibilities could Britain do much to mollify it. The British and French had interposed themselves since Bismarck's era between Western society and a pan-Germanic hegemony. The downfall of Britain would, that is, have subverted a free world order in which the United States herself had so great a stake. No such aim was entertained by other American ethnic minorities; their dissents from particular British policies were often the same as those voiced in the British Parliament by a Loyal Opposition. But, short of a Germanic world order, there was no redress for the Anglophobia of German-Americans. Its exponents could exercise their franchise within the American political system; they might wrap themselves up in the Stars and Stripes. So far as a free world order had to be preserved, they could not be overtly anti-British without also being covertly anti-American.

It was, moreover, Nazi genocide in Europe that accelerated the postwar rebirth of Israel and that thereby injected yet another ethnic issue into American party politics and Anglo-American friendship. Before the establishment of the Irish Free State, sympathy for the cause of Ireland had not been restricted to American voters of Irish ancestry; so also, in British public life, the claims of Zionism had been endorsed by Conservatives like Balfour and Churchill as well as by their Liberal antagonists. Yet when Ernest Bevin, a Labour Foreign Secretary, mishandled this problem, he attributed the backing received by Israel from the United States to local party politics, to Jewish voting strength in some of the key metropolitan areas of the United States.

That, no doubt, was the oversimplification of a guilty conscience. And President Truman had been riled by the innuendo that he was not being guided by national ideals or national interests but solely by party politics.* The Irish question had furnished the classic instance of American domestic pressure seeking, through the complicated machinery of American party politics, to influence the conduct of American foreign policy. But it was a more statesmanlike approach at Westminster that erased this disruptive item from the Anglo-American agenda. In no other fashion could any Anglo-American divergence over Israel have been avoided.

To this episode, moreover, there clung, in terms of both the recent past and the immediate future, a strange irony. Before Pearl Harbor and during the Battle of Britain, when the British most needed friends in the United States, the pro-British attitude of so anti-Nazi a group as the American Jews had provoked Charles Lindbergh, the German-American Bund, and other militant isolationists into purveying some of Hitler's murderous anti-Semitism. In the field of international affairs, nevertheless, the next encounter of American Jews with anti-Semitism was that which Ernest Bevin, with his departmental and military advisers, provided. And then, in 1956, the American Presidential election coincided with the Sinai campaign and the Suez venture. There is no evidence that, when President Eisenhower tried to stop Israel, he forfeited Jewish votes.

It is other ethnic minorities that may henceforth be most heard from. Unrest in Eastern Europe and the problems of European settlement are of special concern to the American kinsfolk of nations groaning under a Soviet yoke. And while that includes East Germans, the Bonn Republic holds a watching brief for them. From 1919 to the age of appeasement, it had been Britain and France who decided the attitude of the West towards Central and Eastern Europe; what either of them did, or did not do, registered, in turn, through organized ethnic voting groups, on American party politics. But today the initiative in the West rests with the United States herself. New, smaller racial elements had

* Truman, *op. cit.,* II, pp. 149, 153-154, and 168-169.

fresh complaints to utter; before the 1956 Presidential election, when the question of Cyprus envenomed relations between three NATO allies—Britain, Greece, and Turkey—American policy-makers were influenced by the fact that there were more Greek-American than Turkish-American voters to be wooed—a matter that embarrassed the British and angered the Turks.* By their oversea policies, nevertheless, the British had, on the whole, reme-died the grievances of anti-British ethnic minorities in the United States. And others, when the United States took Britain's place, were to come within Washington's own purview.

But the party mechanism is, with Executive-Congress ten-sion, not all that must be considered in estimating the effect of the American political system on American leadership. There is the manner in which the Executive branch itself operates; there is the augmented role of the Armed Forces; and there is the func-tion of other large-scale governmental agencies, old and new. Before these additional topics are dealt with, however, it might be well to consider a related subject that affects the Executive and Congress alike—and one by which, in the era of American primacy, allies are often bothered: to what extent, in both the elective and administrative spheres, is the best American talent attracted to national affairs or used in them to the best advantage?

POLITICAL POTENTIAL VERSUS POLITICAL SYSTEM

American leadership must suffer if the nation's own po-litical potential is not developed to the utmost. There is, to be sure, no guarantee that this could be done if the American po-litical system were less unwieldy; and the more representative a mass democracy, the harder it will be for the exceptional rather than the average to come forth. But, among those who legislate or administer, a parliamentary democracy like Britain may know how to put to better use such talent as is still available. From the standpoint of American primacy, there will, at any rate, be a direct correlation between the quality of American efforts and the caliber of those who must plan and execute them. The United States would not be where she is today if her economy were not one in which there have been myriad opportunities for the gifted and ambitious. But much in the American system has made public service less than a magnet for the most qualified. And are even those who may still be drawn to it properly utilized?

Nor is the question merely one of what happens to men

_____
* Eden, *op. cit.,* p. 463; see also pp. 448-449 and 453-456.

of ability in Washington. It might be difficult for many to go there under more favorable political circumstances. British public life is distinguished by the fact that Britain's greatest city is also her political capital. The one-sided character of Washington as a capital handicaps American public life. For in the United States, as in Canada, there is a geographical hurdle to surmount. Political figures, if they are to make the long trek to Washington, may have to abandon local vocations; the full time given to politics, as much as their growing intricacy, is what has served to professionalize them. There is, to be sure, the same trend across the Atlantic, but in London it has been possible, until recently, to combine a political career with some more lucrative pursuit.

Then, too, there is the Civil Service which a number of well-trained Americans entered during the days of the New Deal and which the spirit of McCarthyism rendered less alluring. Incentives within it are far from satisfactory. There is permanency on the lower rungs, but on the higher ones there is still appointment by patronage. A political appointment will, moreover, be withheld if, under a rule of Senatorial courtesy, a nominee from the Senator's own state has incurred his displeasure. The upshot is that men of promise, as either legislators or officials, skirt national affairs and, staying at home, tend to be de-politicized.

Noblesse oblige was a leisure class virtue that enriched Britain's epoch of primacy—one that the two Roosevelts, the first for the Republicans, the second for the Democrats, as patricians in American politics, had exemplified. In the United States, however, most prestige still accrues to prominence in business; to notables with whom corporate and public interest has not always fused as felicitously as public relations counsel would have them aver. From the start, moreover, human energies were widely dispersed as the American wilderness was subdued, as populous new urban centers sprang up almost everywhere. On the American scene a separation of powers is, then, not merely constitutional; the sheer length and breadth of the United States renders everything less compact than in Britain or France. Physically as well as intellectually centrifugal, the North American environment, by itself, opens a rift between the world of thought and the world of action.

Bearing witness to this, Henry James fled to England while, at home, Henry Adams dwelt morosely in a kind of exile from exile. The British and French provinces have been drained of their strength by an overconcentration of industry in the capital and a few selected regions. But America's creative life has been impoverished by the fact that, unlike Britain or France, the United States has two capitals—New York City being her capital for all save politics, and Washington her capital for politics alone. London and Paris have been crucibles for an intermingling by which the national being is refreshed and replenished. For the kind of cross-fertilization that they provide, the United States has no full equivalent. Washington, on the one hand, is overspecialized and parochial as a result; New York, on the other, is politically more parochial than major political capitals. The advent of the United Nations headquarters to New York has broadened some of its horizons. The main currents of American endeavor flow through that metropolis rather than Washington. The conduct of national affairs is somewhat removed from them and they, by the same token, are removed somewhat from it.

But most of this is in the domain of intangibles. Other dampers on political careers in the national field are more concrete. The costs of participation, when mass publicity must be employed in a mass democracy, are prohibitive. Candidates may be able to finance their election to the House of Representatives; in the larger, populous states few can afford state-wide campaigns for a governorship or a seat in the Senate. A private fortune may be needed; to get support, dubious political bargains might be struck. Under the British system, a parliamentary candidate is severely limited by law on what he can spend in his own constituency. And to ensure any further ascent up the political ladder, no additional expenses have to be met.

Electorally, in the United States, the affluent thus have the edge over the non-affluent. But, contrariwise, the possession of wealth may hinder non-elected officials of the Executive branch. Under a conflict-of-interest statute, Cabinet officers must sell stock holdings in corporations with which their departments do business. Senators and Representatives legislate on cognate matters but they are exempt—and so are Presidents and Vice-Presidents. In the face of such discrimination, some men of means may decline Cabinet and similar non-elective appointments. From service in one branch of government, they are discouraged; for service in another, they enjoy a substantial advantage. On neither count does American democracy operate as well as it should.

Talent, at any rate, is harder to tap under the American than the British political system for yet another set of reasons. Even when Americans are in a position to run for the House of Representatives they can be elected only from the locality in which they live or, if their goal is the Senate, from the state in which they are domiciled. And that residence rule might alone induce them, once they arrive in Washington, to devote themselves to the furtherance of sectional rather than national interests. Few legislators nurture the hope, moreover, that they can work themselves up, by the excellence of their congressional performance, to Cabinet rank. A member may get himself promoted from the Lower to the Upper House; seldom can the Presidency or Vice-Presidency beckon farther. Parliament is a testing-ground for higher office. Congress is usually a blind alley.

The fact is that few modern Presidents have been recruited from the Legislative branch—though Harry Truman showed how valuable to a Chief Executive a prior sojourn in the Senate can be. Experience of national affairs has been as likely to disqualify as qualify for nomination; the battles that have won a Senator eminence will also have gained him enemies. But that situation, as the nomination of Nixon and Kennedy demonstrated in 1960, may change; more and more a President will have to possess familiarity with world politics. Until World War II, favored candidates were those who had been governors of key states in the Electoral College. Nor are Cabinet posts (unless Taft and Hoover furnish good examples) regarded as steppingstones to the Presidency—although, in the early days of the Republic, five of the first seven Presidents had served as Secretary of State. Congress is apt to show a Secretary of State goodwill if he has been one of their number—a member, as it were, of the club. But where powers are separate, he may be appointed from quite another sphere.

And that is why Cabinet officers in the United States do not, as in Britain, aspire to the highest office. As Presidential advisers they are recruited mostly from non-political pursuits; they have not had to win spurs as legislators or junior Ministers. And when they transact government business with Cabinet officers from parliamentary countries, they do not shine politically by comparison.

The truth is that twentieth-century America has done more to conserve its national than its political resources. Not that the British system gives free play to parliamentary talent; local party organizations and the party caucus nowadays put too much of a premium on the party hack. But it still allows merit and experience to enrich each other and unfold together. In the American system, with its separated powers, no such conjunction is necessary; its chief prize, as the Eisenhower Presidency has illustrated, might indeed lie entirely outside the representative process. And when this happens, political life is downgraded. For other spheres take precedence when the top political reward falls to someone who has not served an apprenticeship within it. Nor, on lower planes, will public service beckon to the best unless whatever is best within it can be equitably deployed.

Under the American system, there is, in fact, at most levels of policymaking and representation, an institutional wastage of accumulated experience. After he has been Chief Executive, an ex-President cannot, for example, like any former Prime Minister in Britain or Canada, ensconce himself on the Opposition front bench against the day when he and his party may return to office. Perhaps American legislators would not be edified by the presence of one who has held so august a post; precluded from administrative experience themselves, they do not want to be overawed by it within their own assembly. Then, too, the principle of separate powers might be contravened if a former President were accorded a non-voting seat in the Senate.

Nor is it only an ex-President who is thus debarred. There is no niche in the American political system for a defeated Presidential candidate. Tens of millions of his compatriots might, as they did for Adlai Stevenson, vote for him; but his own elected copartisans in the Congress would not, as under the parliamentary system, have welcomed him as Leader of the Opposition. So, too, after the 1960 race for the Presidency there was no room among the minority Republicans in Congress for the defeated candidate; and yet the former Vice-President, Richard Nixon, had polled against Senator John Kennedy nearly half the popular vote. Senators and Representatives are spokesmen for the majority and minority parties in the committees and on the floor of the two Houses—and that is a privilege they will not willingly relinquish.

There is, moreover, yet another objection—one which arises from American primacy—to seating a defeated Presidential candidate on the floor of the House. His party may be the majority one; a President who belonged to the minority party might thus be dependent for the passage of bipartisan measures on his late rival. In London or Ottawa, a contingency of that kind would cause a change of government. But to do that there must be a degree of co-ordination between branches, and this the American system, with its divided powers and Presidential fixed term, forbids.

Similar dichotomies exert, furthermore, a similarly wasteful effect on the Ministerial plane. Cabinet appointments must be confirmed by the Senate; and when that body rejected the nomination of Admiral Lewis Strauss in 1959, it demonstrated that even an architect of national defense may not, with impunity, step on august Senatorial toes. Such incidents have been rare; but a deracinated type of politics has been characteristic of Cabinet tenure in the unco-ordinated American system. So feeble is the governmental bent of Cabinet officers that, on retiring from office, they seldom stand for a seat in Congress. A rich store of official experience has been acquired; unlike their counterparts in other representative democracies, they are not afterwards expected to contribute from it to legislative deliberations. Nowhere in the American political system is there a well-tutored cadre that is departmentally proficient and politically mature—and one from which, as in parliamentary countries, a new Cabinet can, with a swing of the party pendulum, be recruited. Separate powers require that most Administrations start wholly afresh.

So, too, experience is squandered rather than conserved among junior ranks. Senior Civil Service posts are occupied in Britain, Canada, and other parliamentary democracies by permanent Under-Secretaries; they carry on from Ministry to Ministry and may act on behalf of their political chiefs. But American Under-Secretaries and Assistant Secretaries have usually been political appointees. Such, however, are the demands of primacy that these posts ought to be filled by professional experts. At a key department like Defense, at any rate, a rapid turnover in Assistant Secretaries has meant a string of novices taking hold and a wastage in experience when, after a brief interval, they quickly depart. Perhaps appointees cannot adjust themselves to the struggle for and against co-ordination that permeates their branch as well as the entire American system. Many officeholders cannot afford a prolonged sojourn in Washington. But maybe, too, political responsibilities have often been assigned to men whose hearts were never in politics.

On still lower levels, moreover, the United States has been sending many abroad on errands of mercy, postwar reconstruction, mutual defense, economic assistance. Some of these officials are technical specialists; others get types of experience which should be, but frequently are not, put to further public use. Nor is this merely a domestic loss. The Western coalition might have done better if allies had not had to negotiate with a succession of tyros who, upon mastering their jobs, vanished from the official American scene.

There is, however, a permanent repository of specialized experience in the State Department and Foreign Service. Do American party politics, does the struggle for and against co-ordination in the American system, permit them to function as well as they should? Postwar Congressional investigations, the period of the Hiss case and McCarthyism, may have disheartened a devoted band of government servants. But they have never had a satisfactory footing among their own compatriots.

A shift in primacy from Britain to the United States had scarcely been consummated when, with the Hiss case, a staff problem in American diplomacy burst upon the American people and stunned the Western coalition. Nothing seemed more alien to the State Department or Foreign Service than Communist sympathies; not until Burgess and MacLean defected did the British people realize that what had happened in Britain might have happened in America. Meanwhile the Secretary of State, Dean Acheson, impaired his own usefulness to the Truman Administration by remarking that he would not turn his back on Alger Hiss; his successor, John Foster Dulles, was less than staunch in protecting subordinates from false McCarthyite accusations. Loyalty-security probes, if conducted fairly, should have cleared the air. The Foreign Service and the Department of State were demoralized when these were bungled by Democrats and Republicans alike. A number of officials resigned and others played it safe. The Korean War, the deepening of the East-West contest, the growing intricacy of the West's countervailing defenses called for fresh, independent thought among professional advisers. The governmental process militated against this.

Diplomacy, as a profession, has never rated high in American popular esteem. Non-career men are the ones who have shed most luster on it—historic figures who undertook special missions at particular junctures. To be preoccupied with foreign or non-hemispheric affairs was, in an isolationist nation, to abstract oneself from the main stream of American life. Americans, moreover, were imbued with the belief that their statesmen and diplomatists had invariably been outwitted by British counterparts—this, despite steady American expansion by land and sea and the hard bargains driven in the protracted settlement of Anglo-American disputes. The *savoir-faire* and intellectual attainments of some British professionals had, nevertheless, given Americans an inferiority complex. But that may be changing. Among the social reforms of postwar Britain has been one that opens the Diplomatic Service and Foreign Office to less privileged candidates. A merit system had been adopted before that by the Foreign Service of the United States. Top diplomatic posts can, however, still be assigned under patronage rules.

Until the United States became leader of the West, anybody could represent her abroad—and very often did. Nowadays the qualifications of political appointees are examined with more care. But patronage is a practice that party managers are reluctant to have abolished; it helps pay off election debts. And Congress maintains it by failing to provide career diplomatists with adequate entertainment allowances. For the upkeep of embassies in capitals such as London, Paris, Rome, Bonn, Madrid, and New Delhi, a private fortune has been necessary; prior to the Kennedy Administration career diplomatists could afford only the so-called hardship posts. As Chairman of the Senate Foreign Relations Committee, Senator J. William Fulbright sought to have confirmation withheld from unqualified political appointees. But Congress would have had a more cogent case against selections made by the Executive if it had been less parsimonious itself.

A niggardly attitude toward State Department budgets must be seen in a wider context. Diplomacy used to be an aristocratic pursuit; it may now be as suspect to the conformists of a mass democracy as it once was to the egalitarians of the frontier. A tool of the Executive branch, the Foreign Service is the one whose activities are traditionally the most occult. The Armed Forces and new, large-scale undertakings in war technology and government intelligence also move in mysterious ways. But defense needs speak for themselves; diplomacy is an art which by its nature cannot do so. Behind it there is no sectional or organized interest. To keep the Foreign Service on strict rations is, moreover, for the Congress to hold a tighter rein on the Executive.

American diplomacy is an instrument of American leadership. But with it the separate powers of the American system may, here as elsewhere, be at odds. At any rate, when top posts are earmarked for men of wealth, men of ability will either shun the profession or retire from it as soon as pension rights permit. To American diplomacy neither the equal opportunities of American democracy nor the much-lauded incentives of American enterprise have fully applied.

Not that the Foreign Service should monopolize American representation abroad. The ample allowances that Britain gives professional diplomatists enable them to serve her at Washington, Paris, and other major capitals. Non-career ambassadors have sometimes done as well, but such appointees have generally made their name on the upper levels of British public life beforehand; in some contingencies their qualifications may be superior to those of career diplomatists. Occasionally, too, the American Embassy at London has been occupied by men of ripe public experience.

On the whole, nevertheless, American appointees have neither been of that type nor of career officials who have earned promotion.

The merit system is not flouted; there may even be an advantage, when men who have distinguished themselves in other sectors of public affairs are chosen at intervals for key posts. They will have more of a flair than most of their subordinates for policy questions; from the prejudices of Service or departmental coteries they may stand aloof. Such, too, is the American political system that their views will carry more weight in Congress or at the White House than those of non-partisan professionals. Having access to the President, they might, it is true, by-pass the Secretary of State and thus deprive the State Department of information it should have; under John Foster Dulles, it was the Secretary of State himself who often kept his assistants in the dark. Primacy suggests how to proceed. When there is so much to be done, the objective must be to make the best use of those who are qualified; while top posts should be open to career officials, non-career appointees cannot be debarred. But what will first have to be improved are the political practices out of which inequities may arise.

There are, moreover, still other agencies of government that touch upon the conduct of foreign affairs and upon which the imprint of separate powers is stamped. Elsewhere, too, the modern state has endowed semiautonomous organs with executive, legislative and judicial authority to regulate its economic life; with the three other branches of the American system, these are often regarded as a fourth. But in some of them a crisis of personnel has mounted—one of ensuring that there will be commissioners who, at once impartial, incorruptible, and expert, can protect the rights of all, public and private, individual and corporate, who are entitled to protection.

Democratic and Republican administrations alike have, at any rate, nominated either party wheelhorses or commissioners chosen from the industries they are empowered to regulate. Legislators as well as members of the Executive branch have, at the same time, trafficked in backstairs influence and tried to sway decisions. Not that parliamentary countries are exempt from that sort of venality. Protests are frequently heard against arbitrary rulings by British appointees to comparable bodies. A more responsible system of government has, nevertheless, instilled in them a more solid tradition of public responsibility. American regulatory agencies are supposed to be independent of both the Executive and the Legislature. Against unpalatable decisions appeal can be made to the courts. Yet Congress had long shirked any thorough investigation of these agencies lest it wind up investigating itself. They were therefore, like so much else in an unco-ordinated system, largely unaccountable.

Most of their terrain is domestic. A few, nevertheless, hand down decisions that can affect American leadership abroad. The Federal Maritime Board might, for example, approve shipping routes in a manner that the State Department would oppose. Despite an Anglo-American agreement that allows British Overseas Airways to fly between Tokyo and San Francisco, the Civil Aeronautics Board long hesitated to grant permission; albeit the British themselves did not allow Northwest Airlines to pick up a second American franchise for serving Hong Kong. Allies or neutrals can take offense when the Immigration Service fails to administer justly immigration laws that are themselves discriminatory. However, should the United States Tariff Commission recommend that tariffs be raised, or differentiate between imports from one ally and another, it is the Executive branch that has the final say. The fact that rulings are made by a number of authorities may not be understood in other countries. The effect is the same.

THE DEMANDS OF PRIMACY

Within the American system there is an incessant struggle for and against co ordination. But does the Executive branch itself speak on national and international affairs with a single voice? A strong President is necessary not only to make the system function; co-ordinated action among his own coadjutors also requires a firm hand. Agreed Cabinet policies are drawn from a variety of differing views in every representative democracy; in Britain, however, Ministers are collectively responsible for each other and, so as to maintain that majority support on which office rests, must face Parliament as a unit. Cabinet officers and other high officials in Washington are banded together by no such procedural compulsion. They are beholden to the President but neither to Congress nor one another. And in an overcentralized Presidency, its incumbent has more to do than stand watch over his own subordinates.

That the latter will, as a result, tend to get out of step did not matter very much before the United States took Britain's place. Until the advent of the New Deal, her administrative machinery was relatively small; few Cabinet officers were officially preoccupied with the outside world; there were no allies to be frightened by audible dissensions in a capital from which a well-articulated lead is now essential. Harry Truman, under whose Presidency the classic postwar measures of American primacy took shape, had the temperament to grapple with this problem. But President Eisenhower, though a professional soldier, was more easygoing. Governmental unison, among the English-speaking allies of the United States, is a prerequisite of responsible government. Would the United States herself be able to lead without this?

Less indiscipline among Cabinet officers was a condition of primacy, but some holdovers from the Roosevelt period did not realize that old habits had to be dropped. And they were probably emboldened by Mr. Truman's own initial lack of administrative experience. Not many months elapsed before the direction of American foreign policy had to be retrieved from James Byrnes, the Secretary of State. Harold Ickes, the Secretary of the Interior, was let go when, in testifying before a Congressional committee, he torpedoed an appointment that the President had made. And Henry Wallace had to be dismissed when the Secretary of Commerce, despite Allied demobilization and the Eurasian preponderance of the Soviet Union, publicly assailed a modicum of preparedness. "Well, now he's out," wrote the President, "and the crackpots are having conniption fits."*

And then during the Korean War, when the allies of the United States feared that General MacArthur or Congressional exponents of his operational viewpoint would force the hand of the Administration, fresh dangers might have attended Cabinet indiscipline. Four years earlier, before the American atomic monopoly was broken, Henry Wallace had charged that some, in the higher echelons of the Armed Services, favored a "preventive war." Influenced by them, the Secretary of the Navy, Francis Matthews, openly advocated one, and was duly reprimanded.† It was not, however, because of any such public indiscretion that Louis Johnson, successor as Secretary of Defense to James Forrestal, had been dismissed. He had erred by talking to legislators on Capitol Hill against the Administration of which he was a member.

The Eisenhower regime was a more permissive one. But the effect of this on American coalition leadership, after a truce had been signed in Korea and control of the Senate passed from the President's own rambunctious copartisans, was not as adverse, at first, as it might have been. In 1957, however, the missile age

---

* Truman, *op. cit.*, I, pp. 545-561.
† *Ibid.*, II, p. 383.

dawned, and the sound of divided counsels among Cabinet officers and other high Executive officials was not a good omen. The President might harp on the teamwork that characterized his two Administrations. The more he did so, the more frequent were the backslidings of senior colleagues.

He himself, moreover, invited disobedience by assigning to key posts officials who did not sympathize, in coalition and other matters, with his aims. Mr. Eisenhower agreed with Downing Street, for example, that trade with Communist China should be embargoed no more severely than trade with Soviet Russia. Nevertheless, Walter Robertson, Assistant Secretary of State, enforced a stiffer policy. So, also, Admiral Arthur W. Radford held office as Chairman of the Chiefs of Staff even though anxiety was rife in Allied capitals when he differed from the President by his advocacy of a forward course in East Asia; by toying with a plan for the withdrawal of American troops from Western Europe; and by treating sceptically the Administration's disarmament efforts. His ties had been with the extremist faction among the President's own fellow Republicans. Against them in Congress there were bipartisan measures to preserve American leadership. But this might also be crippled by palace turbulence, by friction within the Executive branch itself.

A Presidential attempt to be all things to all men must, at any rate, produce less governmental co-ordination than obtains among parliamentary Cabinets. One after another the major figures of the Eisenhower Presidency collided with each other and even with the President himself over leadership issues. In 1956, when neutrals were being cultivated, Mr. Eisenhower spoke in soft accents about neutralism, and the Secretary of State, John Foster Dulles, denounced it harshly. Both of them, however, had their differences with Charles E. Wilson, the Secretary of Defense. In 1957, when the President allowed his Secretary of the Treasury, George Humphrey, to sabotage the budget, the Secretary of State had to fight back lest foreign aid items be cut ruinously. Harold Stassen went on serving as Presidential disarmament adviser after he had opposed the renomination of Vice-President Nixon. There was a clash between him and Admiral Lewis Strauss, Chairman of the Atomic Energy Commission, and John Foster Dulles. Over East–West disarmament proposals, nevertheless, Strauss and Dulles were at loggerheads with each other.

So, also, in 1958 when Vice-President Nixon paid an untimely visit to Latin America, he called for a stand against dictatorship, but Secretary Dulles insisted that non-interventionist principles forbade this. Later that year, President Eisenhower and Secretary Dulles excluded foreign policy from partisan debate in the Congressional elections and then publicly accepted the view of Vice-President Nixon that it should be debated. Briefing a Senatorial subcommittee on Russian missile striking capacity, Allen W. Dulles, Director of the Central Intelligence Agency, gave a much grimmer estimate, early in 1960, than Defense Secretary Thomas S. Gates, Jr. An intradepartmental dispute was, moreover, one of the matters that brought Prime Minister Macmillan to Washington in March, 1960, so that an Anglo-American front could be restored in the conference at Geneva with the Soviet Union over a nuclear test ban. Then, in May, 1960, came a resounding series of contradictory statements about American air-reconnaissance over Russian territory; yet another departmental muddle had been revealed. A kaleidoscopic picture—and for the American and allied peoples alike, a disconcerting one.

On a lower departmental level, moreover, primacy stretches intra-Administration feuds beyond the water's edge. And these are felt by allied and neutral countries in the political-economic as well as the military-diplomatic spheres. Soviet Russia and Communist China have been endeavoring to augment their influence through economic aid and foreign commerce. But there is not only a rising chorus of complaint from Japan to Canada and from Britain to Latin America over the import-export policies of the West's own leader. In the execution of these, the Executive branch itself is frequently at sixes and sevens.

Presidents Truman and Eisenhower were both aware of the extent to which the leadership of the West requires the United States to be more liberal-minded on matters of foreign trade, ship subsidies, customs regulations and practices, than any bipartisan majority in Congress would endorse. Domestic industries are protected by escape clauses in trade agreements and the Buy-American Act: sometimes quotas, like those against metal imports, are applied impartially; sometimes Japanese textiles are favored at the expense of British; sometimes "security reasons" are adduced when lower British bids for heavy electrical equipment are rejected. But friends and allies are not restricted in access only to American markets. Other markets are spoiled for them when various fragments of an unco-ordinated Executive branch espouse conflicting interests.

Allies such as Canada and New Zealand, neutrals such as Burma and the Sudan, for instance, protested when subsidized agricultural surpluses were unloaded by the Department of Agriculture. Behind this lay protectionist deals into which the Congressional farm bloc entered with the mining and textile blocs. Yet that sort of dumping would never have been permitted if the State Department, whose duty it is to put the national interest before sectional interests, had not been overruled.

Not that the national interest is always simple to ascertain. It may, at any rate, have been special interests that lurked behind a Cabinet dispute over a State Department proposal to return German and Japanese properties seized during World War II. When the Department of Justice, the Treasury, and the Bureau of the Budget objected, they were the ones who, in this case, upheld the wartime obligations of the United States to her allies and to American taxpayers.

Still another public display of intra-Administration differences was provided in 1959 when Senator Fulbright failed to get a five-year budgetary allotment to the Development Loan Fund. President Eisenhower, with the advice of the Treasury and the Budget Bureau, preferred an annual appropriation; but the State Department made no secret of its view that leadership required a more imaginative approach. No one section of the Executive is, in other words, invariably the best judge of the national interest. And here the President must furnish guidance at every stage. Unless he does, the struggle for and against co-ordination within the Executive branch will duplicate that which rages between it and the Legislature.

Even space programs openly competed. In March, 1959, when one agency failed to keep another properly informed, a satellite went undetected. So, too, the Atomic Energy Commission objected to inspection methods after the State Department had completed negotiations for American aid to the European Atomic Energy Community.

And a similar question was raised in September, 1959, on the floor of the Senate when Laos, harassed by pro-Communist infiltration from North Vietnam, appealed to the United Nations. Had American policy in that country, asked Senator Mansfield, been laid down by the President and Secretary of State or did it consist of an accommodation among various Executive agencies, with the State Department trying to guide the boat but unable to control the rudder? It is a story, as a matter of fact, with which the allies of the United States are now familiar. For they have been embarrassed more than once, in organs of the United Nations and other international bodies, by American intragovernmental tiffs.

And so a leadership that has preserved the West is also one in which its right hand may not know what its left hand is doing. A struggle for and against co-ordination is not only waged on the Executive-Legislative plane but the more departmental powers extend, the more refractory they become. What Americans may not comprehend is how much allies such as Britain and Canada fret over American governmental disarray. For the closer the bonds with the United States, the more worrisome this will become.

But it is also in the light of the American disarray that American goals must be understood. The activities of American business abroad are, for instance, occasionally depicted as being part of a premeditated scheme, one that would reduce non-Soviet lands to American economic dominance. This is a danger of which Latin American countries are cognizant; Canada will do what she can to avert it. And yet it is more the result of accident than design; anything else would not come naturally to a people who think in terms of a struggle for and against co-ordination rather than of unavowed, deep-laid plots. Exploitation has occurred here and there; neglect by private American corporations, as well as official economic agencies, is now charged as often. Across the board these antithetical grievances would seem to cancel each other; at various junctures they have both been valid. What they do suggest is that, apart from wartime contingencies, there has never been a single co-ordinated plan, economic and political, for the projection of America. To devise one would go against the American grain. For while American endeavors are overorganized in some respects, they are underorganized in others. The fact is that, in keeping with the American system and American history, American leadership has been leadership by inadvertence.

This does not mean that its impact in economic affairs, as in political, is any less heavy. Behind official and unofficial American operations abroad there may be no ulterior motive—beyond, at any rate, specific objectives; their cumulative effect is, all the same, what leaves an impress. From above the Canadian border, from across the Atlantic and Pacific Oceans, from below the Rio Grande, there is one sadly discordant refrain. It will be their own great achievements, since the shift in primacy from Britain to the United States, that Americans are apt to recall. They will wonder whether allies are ungrateful. Yet allies are perplexed by a leadership that is at once politically constructive and institutionally haphazard, steady in some vital categories, wavering in others.

But leadership not only projects these alternate trends on a larger global screen. It lends an unwonted importance to the Armed Services and to a new war technology. With a shift in primacy from Britain to the United States, the American political system has had to accept and manage fresh modalities of power. Will the supremacy of the civil authority always be acknowledged without demur? Anglo-American divergences during and after the Korean War demonstrated that this was not simply a problem of domestic American concern.

Not that in the parliamentary democracy of twentieth-century Britain the Armed Services have always been models of political decorum. But insurrectionary rumblings in Ulster before World War I were those of party politicians playing the soldier, rather than those of soldiers themselves meddling in politics; while the General Strike of 1926, like similar more recent unrest in the United States, emanated after World War I from quite another sector of society. American governmental authority is, however, not only more widely dispersed than British; never before has it had to cope on a large scale with permanent standing forces and with peacetime forces in training. Civil jurisdiction has been upheld. But allies are not likely to forget how, under the authority of the President, it is the American Armed Services whose hands are kept on the levers of a strategic interlock with which their own security is enmeshed so inextricably.

Has the United States been less militaristic than other great powers? Embedded deep in the American mind is the conviction that when she declared her independence from Britain she not only isolated herself from the quarrels of Europe but from modes of behavior by which these were provoked. And from this belief had stemmed an outlook that affected Anglo-American co-operation until primacy in the West shifted across the Atlantic. A divided form of representative government could, nevertheless, evolve as freely as it did because it never had to tackle questions of national defense in a world-wide setting. Not only were European invaders warded off when the British were predominant at sea. When she expanded through conquest, when hemispheric power politics enabled her to cull the fruits of war without going to war, the United States could still avoid protracted military efforts that might have subjected nascent political institutions to external strain.

The American Civil War had indicated that the American nation packed an awesome potential for violence. Turned inward, vented by Americans upon Americans, it did to the United States what the English had done to each other in the days of Cromwell, what Catholics and Protestants had done to Europe in the wars of religion, and what was done to France by the Revolutionary terror. But after the Union had been reforged on the battlefield and the war with Spain had been won, only some minor provisions had to be made for the governance of distant territories. The same order of power that permitted the American people to be both pacifist and warlike, imperialist in fact and anti-imperialist in utterance, saved the American political system from the test of events.

That test British parliamentary institutions had passed with flying colors. For a century they had kept watch over a free world order; and it was the special nature of Britain's primacy abroad that enabled the British to maintain at home the post-Cromwellian subordination of military authority to civil. Domestic upheavals in which the sword was arbiter had been outgrown—though the graver sort of economic injustice in an industrial society had, as the masses were enfranchised, still to be rectified. As a sea power, imperial Britain could eschew the absolutism that has been synonymous with empire among land powers. There had been domestic reaction after the Napoleonic cycle, campaigns on colonial frontiers, wars waged in the Crimea and South Africa. No mass levies were raised in the British Isles, no headstrong military caste arose to lord it over the nation.

Later on, if the English-speaking peoples had not shared ultimate principles of politics, a free world order would never have survived. And for it, the French, too, have made great sacrifices. But it is as a land power that France has, in the main, had to carry on and defend herself; between the extreme Left and the extreme Right, in the political obtrusions of the army, a conflict between absolutism and democracy still divides her. It was, after all, the English-speaking peoples who sowed the seeds of freedom in far corners of the earth. Unlike land power, sea power worked at a distance, and with it parliamentary democracy has been more at ease.

To sea power, the American political system was also indebted. A British shield not only fended off the ill-disposed; behind it American life could be set in non-military molds before the need arose for a huge permanent military establishment. And yet the burdens of preparedness were less manifold when Britain was leader of the West. Prior to 1914 the British did not muster giant strength in more than one element at a time; the United States has had to maintain varying degrees of strength, on land, at sea, and in the air, simultaneously. Then, too, the Armed Services differed over how this should be done and, when they engaged in polemics, other issues also cropped up. There have been similar tussles in Britain. But where political self-discipline is lax, exalted brands of military indiscipline have more leeway.

Occupation duties were one aspect of a new political role that the Armed Services had to perform. After World War II, zones were allotted in Germany and Austria to the principal victors; the United States had done most, however, to subdue Japan, and that country became an American ward. Proconsulates under the British flag were by comparison rather humdrum. The French had had Marshal Lyautey, and, after the United States conquered the Philippines, General Leonard Wood took charge. But not since the turn of the century, when Cromer in Egypt, Curzon in India, and Milner in South Africa marked her imperial climacteric, had Britain picked for overseas missions figures equally outstanding as MacArthur in Japan and Clay in Germany.

Of these five, moreover, only the Americans were soldiers. Nor had Washington ever previously handled an overseas problem like that posed by the guidance of major American proconsulates. Sometimes it gave them direction; sometimes, in default of clear direction, military government pursued local policies of its own. The experiment did not last long; as the East–West contest wore on, such proconsulates were liquidated. A politico-military constellation of semiautonomous power had, nevertheless, with a shift in primacy from Britain to the United States, entered the American public orbit.

Nor did its advent merely add fresh tension to the American political system. Occupation duties in Europe and Asia touched the interests of allies; over these there were administrative differences between Washington and London. But when the Korean War broke out, it was American politico-military authority in nearby Japan that enabled the United States to enforce the United Nations Charter. General MacArthur's downfall may have been due to a *hubris* which antedated his command; when President Truman reasserted his own prerogatives, he solved a coalition crisis as well as one within the American political system. It was frightening enough for Britain and other allies to be committed under American leadership to a strategic interlock in whose use, against some deadly overriding peril, they might, on short notice, have to acquiesce. It would be intolerable if the die were to be cast globally by politico-military elements over which, in an unco-ordinated system, civil controls might not always be firm.

Was NATO susceptible to proclivities as high-flown as these? Washington selected American commanders—Eisenhower, Ridgway, Gruenther, Norstad, and naval counterparts—who furthered its co-operative purpose. Dissension among the Armed Services was, all the same, endemic on the home front. This had to be handled by a civil authority which is itself constitutionally divided.

What aggravated matters was that a shift in primacy from Britain to the United States had coincided with a transformation in war technology. When the Army, Navy, and Marine Corps were unified in 1947 under the Department of Defense, the Air Force was given an independent status. But such are the circumstances of the time that the youngest American Service now outranks its elders in strategic priority. What roles and missions will be assigned to each? In combined operations, when functional distinctions are hard to draw, which Service will have the command? To which weapons, both for offense and defense, should the larger budgetary allocations be made? To which Service do particular weapons more properly belong? So as to justify claims, they vie with each other in research and in developing new devices.

Has inter-Service competition acted as a stimulus or as a hindrance? When Russia forged ahead in the production of ballistic missiles, it was felt that there had been wasteful duplication. But for any American lag, Service jealousies are not alone to blame. In the Department of Defense there is a congeries of committees, civilian officials, and political appointees that impedes the best use of human resources, military and scientific. Nor have administrations, in their budgetary and military policies, steered a clear, steady course.

Inter-Service rivalries have, moreover, borne profoundly upon the relations of the United States, as leader of the West, with her allies. The Army, averse to overemphasis on long-range bombing, has insisted upon a less unsymmetrical preparedness in the air, at sea, and on land. Has the Air Force accumulated more than it needs in the form of nuclear and thermonuclear weapons, aircraft, and missiles to do its job? Is there, conversely, a perilous gap in intercontinental ballistic missiles between the United States and Russia? On the borders of Eurasia and the Middle East, the Russians are equipped to wage either a nuclear or conventional war. As a counterbalance to Russian preponderance in conventional forces, American, British, and NATO plans have envisaged the adoption of tactical nuclear weapons. But Russia may react against these with all-out nuclear and thermonuclear warfare. The West will, at any rate, be self-immobilized if it is not equipped with conventional forces to keep limited wars limited. For incidents which would not warrant counteraction with nuclear weapons, large or small, may also have to be dealt with. European allies might be demoralized in advance if there is no chance of local defense without risking total destruction.

Coalition issues are, in fact, affected by American planning at virtually every point. Increased firepower might compensate for the smaller size of American and British divisions stationed on the European continent. But this would leave the West German Army, with the French preoccupied in North Africa, as the largest single element on the NATO front lines—a contingency about which there could be misgivings.

Meanwhile, air and missile bases might, for political or strategic reasons, not always be as available overseas as they are at present. As substitutes for them, the American Navy has launched supercarriers. These, however, the Air Force considers vulnerable. So, also, the Navy has built atomic-powered submarines that carry missiles. But the Air Force contends that there must be a single retaliatory command for strategic weapons; it therefore seeks control over those that submarines can mount. Russia, moreover, outnumbers the West in the possession of submarines. Does the Navy devote enough of its budget to anti-submarine endeavors in European waters as well as nearer home? If the sea lanes were cut, European allies could not be supplied, and Anglo-American landpower on the European continent could not be sustained for long.

Some of these jurisdictional disputes may be settled by the Secretary of Defense; others require Congressional action. And it is here that a system of separate powers fosters political assertiveness between competing Services. While the President is Commander in Chief, Congress is enjoined under the Constitution to provide and maintain the national military establishment; yet no exact boundary between the domain of the Executive and the Legislature is demarcated. As the Armed Services wrangle, they may try to play off one branch of the government against the other. In the Soviet, as in the Nazi dictatorship, the regime needs its own military backing; under the British parliamentary system the armed services are, on the whole, kept within bounds. But where powers are separate, there may yet be another struggle for and against co-ordination—one between brothers-in-arms who are rivals, and rivals who are brothers-in-arms.

Prior to the MacArthur episode, the first dramatic example of high-level disobedience in the era of primacy was the so-called admirals' revolt. The Navy doubted the combat value of heavy bombers that the Air Force wished to purchase and, in the spring of 1949, sought, through opinion media, to disparage them. President Truman would not tolerate that sort of indiscipline. Heads rolled. Under President Eisenhower, however, a former Navy rebel did attain high rank: Admiral Radford became Chairman of the Chiefs of Staff and Admiral Arleigh Burke was appointed the Navy member. But Admiral Radford was Senator Taft's candidate, the favorite of radicals of the Right who were willing to spread the Korean War, copartisans whom Mr. Eisenhower strove to placate.* The Radford appointment verged on a politicization of the Services that, as an eminent soldier, the President would otherwise have deplored. The sphere was one, though, in which he himself had the professional *expertise* to hold his own. Nor did he reappoint Admiral Carney, the Navy Chief of Staff, after the latter published views that fomented a war scare throughout the West.

It may, in fact, seem proper that, as paymaster and overseer, Congress should have a voice in determining Service missions. What legitimizes a certain politicization of the Armed Services is the way in which that legislature operates. A subcommittee may, for example, approve a larger appropriation than the President requests or desires—and do so with the blessing not only of a Cabinet officer but of Service witnesses as well. Yet civilians who give testimony are not under military discipline and do not have the same kind of duty to observe towards the Commander in Chief. Military officers must respond to interrogation; and they may or may not be penalized for volunteering their own opinions. As Army Chief of Staff, General Ridgway was dropped by President Eisenhower after his dissent over Army cuts had been elicited in Committee hearings. General Maxwell Taylor, however, did not have to retire from the Chiefs of Staff, but when he did so he called for a strategy of flexible response to supplant the self-constricting program of massive retaliation.† Then, too, there was the idea of a permanent airborne alert—one that his Commander in Chief had rejected but for which the chief of the Strategic Air Command, General Thomas S. Power, pleaded with Congressional committees.

---

* Truman, *op. cit.,* II, p. 53; and Donovan, *op. cit.,* p. 325.
  † Ridgway, *op. cit.,* pp. 274-332; and Maxwell D. Taylor, *The Uncertain Trumpet* (New York: Harper & Brothers, 1960).

Prompting witnesses to walk a disciplinary tightrope, Congress does what it can to protect them from punishment. Under the National Security Act, a Service Secretary or Chief of Staff may ask to be heard by a Congressional committee—a right which, among his reforms of the Defense Department, President Eisenhower tried in vain to have abolished. Legalized insubordination was how he described the practice. But a system of separate powers is what invites that.

And so the politico-military upshot of a constitutional division is divided loyalties. Nevertheless, when Service witnesses speak out, they can attempt, at least, to have shortcomings in policy corrected. If heed had been paid to the committee testimony of professional critics, military and scientific, the United States might never have let herself fall behind the Soviet Union in some features of war technology. But inflated claims accompany Service rivalries; much that is said tends therefore to be discounted by the Executive and Congress alike. The two branches have, moreover, been economy-minded—though, typically, not over the same questions at the same time. Perhaps a mammoth Defense Department can be reorganized for a decision-making process that is more expeditious; indecisiveness, where powers are divided, is inwrought.

Not that defense problems are solved without difficulty under a parliamentary system. Senior British officers went beyond the fixed chain of military and civilian command when, during the disasters of World War I, there was need for better generalship at Westminster as well as in the field. And then the Armed Services were restive over the military reforms with which Harold Macmillan, as Prime Minister, and Duncan Sandys, as Defense Minister, ushered in the missile age. A bigger role for manned bombers was wanted by the Royal Air Force; the three services argued against an undue stress on nuclear weapons. But on such occasions there is less latitude in a system of unitary powers than of separate powers for public evidence of service lobbying or rivalry. The same battles rage in London, as in Washington, between Cabinet members, service officers, and the higher civil servants. Though sound and smoke escape, they are fought out mostly behind the scenes.

With a tenure resting on majority support in Parliament, Ministers accept full collective responsibility for the decisions that are reached. A government that sits in the House may be persuaded during the course of debate to modify defense or other policies; there is no intimation, item by contentious item, of what professional advice it has had. The procedure is one that restricts the extent to which military officers and higher civil servants can, even when they feel duty-bound to do so, dabble in politics. It has been suggested that the Opposition and public should not have to wait until final Ministerial conclusions are reached before defense issues are officially ventilated. But against the unco-ordinated practices of the American system, Parliament will protect itself.

From the standpoint of American leadership, nevertheless, it is noteworthy that the military fame which elevated General Eisenhower to the Presidency was coupled with a genuinely civilian demeanor. Generals Washington and Grant, who rode the same wave, had displayed the same qualities; but General MacArthur did not, and it was this which disqualified him politically in the end. Perhaps if the United States had fared less well in World War I, a military hero, rather than a Harding, a Coolidge, or a Hoover might, even at that juncture, have personified the postwar American mood. In an era when the United States has taken Britain's place, her Armed Services tend to be politicized; and yet it was under a soldier-President that, in comparative East–West preparedness, the United States lost ground. It is noteworthy, too, that after the Napoleonic Wars, when Britain's great century still lay before her, she also turned to a famous general, and one so civilian in fibre as the Duke of Wellington. It was not merely what he had done in World War II, but what he might do to stave off World War III, that gave Dwight Eisenhower the votes of fellow Americans, that made them entrust to an architect of victory their hopes of peace.

Before this, however, the United States had acquired, as instruments of primacy, four new institutional adjuncts: the National Security Council, the Joint Chiefs of Staff, the Central Intelligence Agency, and the Atomic Energy Commission. Serving a coalition strategy, all reflected the magnitude of an East–West contest in which rival technologies were ultimate tools of power. Bigness, as productivity grew and living standards were raised, had long been transforming the American economy; in the days of the New Deal the scope of governance was enlarged. And now, not only preparedness was being furthered on an elephantine scale but traditional organs of American democracy had to make commensurate adjustments.

Through the National Security Council and the Joint Chiefs of Staff, it was intended to improve policy-making procedures within the Executive branch. To them the American political system could accustom itself; the Atomic Energy Commission and the Central Intelligence Agency did not fit in as well. Over the latter, Congress held a watching brief. But such was the nature of their function that these two governmental entities were exempt from the sort of legislative scrutiny to which most others could be subjected.

Similar innovations have been made by Britain for similar purposes. But she has less need for an advisory body like the National Security Council where, with the President in the chair, top officials of specialized Executive agencies and Cabinet officers of selected Departments can ponder together the issues of leadership. In a parliamentary system, tasks of co-ordination are discharged by the Cabinet itself. Inalienably, in American governance, it is the President who decides, and Mr. Truman disagreed when Defense Secretary Forrestal argued that the National Security Council should be converted into "an operating super-Cabinet on the British model."*

But under President Eisenhower, the Council outranked the Cabinet. More important than Cabinet members who attended only Cabinet meetings were Cabinet officers and heads of Executive agencies who attended meetings of both groups. And sometimes a President consulted neither. Before the National Security Council had been established the preliminary statement of the European Recovery Program, as enunciated by Dean Acheson at Cleveland, Mississippi, was not shown by President Truman to his colleagues.† Ten years later, Secretary Dulles propounded the Eisenhower Doctrine without submitting it first to the National Security Council. Not that the problem of policy-making can always be solved by this sort of mechanism. General Eisenhower wanted the Council to iron out disputes between warring departments and agencies before questions were put before him. Yet under the American system, it is for the President to impose his will upon them.

It was, at any rate, disquieting to learn from Senator Jackson that "research and development in Defense are proceeding without any foreign policy guidance and without any consideration of the foreign policy implications of weapons developments. At the same time, foreign policy is being conducted without knowledge of scientific and technological developments that might have an important bearing on our position in the world. The failure to launch a satellite ahead of the Russians and the lag in the development of the intercontinental ballistic missile provide classic

---

* Truman, *op. cit.,* I, pp. 59-60.
† Jones, *op. cit.,* p. 211.

examples." And it was further observed that "the policy-making processes of the National Security Council are not now closely related to the budgetary process. This means that policy decisions, presumably made through N.S.C. channels, are, in fact, made in the complicated bargaining that occurs in the preparation of the budget."* The fault here may be one of men as well as measures. But its constitutional roots are apparent.

Perhaps the National Security Council could do more by looking ahead and thereby obviating last-minute *ad hoc* improvisations. Defects in the procedures of the Chiefs of Staff may have to be rectified.† But in a coalition strategy there are also allies that will constantly have to be considered; and all-inclusive plans would be more feasible in an Executive branch where loci of responsibility are less hard to fix. National policies that are effectively co-ordinated may be among the desiderata of primacy. The policy-making process will, however, always run up against that struggle for and against co-ordination by which the entire American political process is pervaded.

Then, too, there is the Central Intelligence Agency, which is the espionage arm of the National Security Council. The United States had no need for any such undertaking before primacy shifted to her from Britain; like British Intelligence, its activities are secret—though, with an inveterate American penchant for publicity, not as secret as its vocation might require. Various Congressional subcommittees pass upon the sums spent by the Central Intelligence Agency. But, as with British Intelligence, its funds are concealed in departmental budgets; here, that is, are appropriations of whose size neither Parliament nor Congress, as a whole, is cognizant. Elected assemblies are unwilling to modify the power of the purse. The East–West contest, like those in which Britain previously bore the brunt, leaves no choice.

Unlike British Intelligence, the Central Intelligence Agency is a statutory body. Unlike the Atomic Energy Commission, it has had no special Congressional committee to supervise it. There is, however, a more significant difference between the Central Intelligence Agency and the Atomic Energy Commission. What the latter hides from the adversaries of the United States, what it does not wish divulged through Congress or allies, is how it does things rather than what it does. From start to finish nothing done by the Central Intelligence Agency can safely be disclosed.

* Henry M. Jackson, in *Foreign Affairs,* April, 1960, pp. 452-454.
† Taylor, *op. cit.,* pp. 80-129.

And the ensuing dilemma is one that concerns not only American democracy but the well-being of the entire Western coalition. In ferreting out intelligence abroad that may be strategically meaningful, the Central Intelligence Agency renders vital service. Yet when, as is generally believed, it engages in more positive operations, there is danger of wider involvements from which the United States and her allies cannot extricate themselves. It did not adequately underline warnings, which came also through other channels, about Communist China's entry into the Korean War, General MacArthur was allowed, therefore, to disregard them. What has perturbed many since then are allegations that the Central Intelligence Agency was behind a contingent of Chinese Nationalist guerrillas on the Burmese-Thailand frontiers of Communist China; that it backed plots which toppled King Farouk from the throne of Egypt in 1952 and dislodged Premier Mossadegh of Iran in 1953; that in 1954 it sponsored the coup that overthrew Guatemala's Communist government; that it supported abortive attempts to deliver Syria from pro-Communist elements. Some of these objectives were more in the interest of the West than others. The question is whether entanglements have been incurred of which the American people and their allies are unaware.

In episodes of that kind, there had been, of course, little that was novel. Such is the nature of power-politics that Britain, too, was long rumored to have played the same game. In her more co-ordinated political system, however, there is less chance of undercover interventions being politically unco-ordinated. To some of these, a few officials in the State Department might lend themselves; of others, the White House itself may not be fully apprised. British Ministers have also winked at clandestine adventures for which they did not wish to be held responsible. But as they are politically accountable to Parliament they have more reason to ensure that all governmental entities should be administratively accountable to them.

And this point was highlighted in May, 1960, when an American photoreconnaissance plane was brought down in the Urals, deep within the Russian interior. Such activities were justified by President Eisenhower and Christian Herter, the Secretary of State, on the ground that, as a closed society, the Soviet Union was better able than its Western antagonists to keep military secrets—even to prepare for mounting a nuclear surprise attack on the West, in the style of Pearl Harbor. It was reported that the Royal Air Force had also reconnoitered Russian territory. When a furore arose, the White House first disclaimed knowledge of the overflight whose failure at that particular juncture hampered American diplomacy and put the West at a disadvantage in an ill-starred East–West conference at the summit in Paris. Did this unhappy sequel have its origin in a lack of co-ordination between Washington departments?

Certainly it was a farce of cosmic proportions when Nikita Khrushchev, as head of that Soviet regime which rested on tight dictatorial control, could jeer at the absence of proper controls within American democracy. It ceased to be funny when the Russian Premier, gainsaying himself, gave the Russian Defense Minister authority to bomb Western bases from which overflights might come. President Eisenhower afterwards assumed responsibility for what had been done. He and his official advisers may have been at fault; and yet also to blame for Executive anarchy was the nature of the American political system. In 1961 President Kennedy had had poor intelligence reports when he endorsed a fruitless landing by Cuban exiles against Castro's Cuba.

It is, however, the Atomic Energy Commission that best exemplifies the institutional effect of primacy. Britain's own strategic vulnerability was what had influenced her attitude towards the United States during the Korean War. But another kind of fear, as Russian attempts to filch weapons secrets were revealed, swept over the United States and, poisoning the American atmosphere, raised doubts about American leadership among her allies. Her nuclear and thermonuclear capacity, together with the Strategic Air Command, were the governing sanctions of the West's countervailing defense; but as the largest single American industrial undertaking, the Atomic Energy Commission had also become the epitome of bigness in domestic affairs. A stupendous new center of organized power has, as a matter of fact, been planted by war technology at the heart of the American economy—one that the government owns and directs but into whose arcana few can penetrate.

Some exceptions in theory and practice resulted. The Chairman of the Atomic Energy Commission often found himself in Congressional hot water. The management of that body, like that of the Central Intelligence Agency, must, all the same, be largely taken by Congress on faith—treatment which the Executive branch itself cannot expect to receive. In addition, contrary to the vaunted tenets of American free enterprise, a major energy resource has had to be developed as a government monopoly. Private enterprise may share its benefits. It is public endeavors, like the Tennessee Valley Authority, that can be adapted more smoothly to the American system.

As leadership and bigness coincided the consequences were felt throughout the American economy. Washington had to enforce laws against private monopoly; monopoly was fostered, nevertheless, by the technological demands of primacy. In some sectors of the American economy, as over the Tennessee Valley Authority, bigness in government vied with bigness in business; in that of defense industry these elements ministered to each other. Bigness in preparedness favors the big industry over the small; it is therefore the corporate vested interests of American capitalism that have gained most. In big private corporations the control that shareholders exercise is a perfunctory one. But neither is political control simple to enforce in that indeterminate zone of the American economy where the Armed Services and large-scale industry must collaborate.

Not that the industrial demands of primacy are all that have quickened the drift toward bigness. Tax laws do more to stimulate mergers. But the Armed Services have, for example, become the principal customers of aircraft manufacturers. Defense industries are financed by the taxpayer and provided with plant and equipment at little or no cost to themselves; the nation must always have access to their productive facilities. They employ retired senior officers who have expert knowledge and useful contacts in Washington; a gray market in governmental influence appears. It is thus not only on the highest echelons of the Armed Services that politicizing tendencies are discerned. An equivocal relationship between government and business has long been a feature of large-scale economies. Defense industries in the era of primacy do not dispel it.

Such, too, are the demands of primacy that military beach-heads have also been established in the groves of Academe. But that could not be done without important issues, intellectual and political, being raised. Research under government subsidy by university staffs and scientific laboratories has necessarily been a quest for practical solutions to pending defense problems. But in the long run pure science is the pathfinder—something that the Russians, evidently, have understood. Will more ample funds for it be provided?

Meanwhile, scientists working under official auspices on defense projects have had to undergo loyalty-security examinations. A government that did not take precautions would be inexcusably negligent. When, however, loyalty-security programs were mishandled, a pall was cast over many fields of research and spread to other related quarters. Scientists who had regarded themselves as private persons now discovered immediate public responsibilities in the pursuits they embraced; some never learned that, as professionals, they could not be as free as they liked if a free society were to retain its freedom. Less injustice was done by the security procedures that other English-speaking peoples had adopted; but these also had to be tightened after spy trials and the escape of suspects behind the Iron Curtain. Furthermore, where preparedness efforts were smaller, there could be a smaller dragnet—one which was not as prone to abuse.

It was, moreover, the play of giant new forces under the strategic demands of primacy that the Oppenheimer case dramatized. For here, unlike the period's other ideological *causes célèbres,* there was no question of espionage or disloyalty; Dr. Oppenheimer's early Communist associations were followed, in the wartime production of the first atomic bombs,· by scientific and technical services of great moment. Yet, for subsequent policy-making in a society of bigness, at what stage did past misjudgment disqualify? The West might have labored under an irretrievable handicap if, when Russia tested hers, the United States had not also produced a hydrogen bomb. But when Dr. Oppenheimer advised against this step, it was asked not only whether he had fully lived down his past but whether the physical scientist should give counsel in a political sphere for which, by his own confession, he had no training and showed no gifts. Is it possible to tell what, though technically enlightened, is also politically self-willed? For in a society of bigness, the scientifically indispensable enjoy a vast organizational power and thus, though ostensibly non-political, can have far-reaching political repercussions.

Undue influence by the military-industrial complex, research dominated by the government, the capture of public policy by a scientific-technological élite were, at any rate, three dangers against which President Eisenhower was to warn in his farewell address to the nation. But leadership had subjected the entire American system to stress and strain.

The United States may speak through traditional institutions with a certain or uncertain voice. There are also new untraditional instrumentalities through which policy has been shaped and reshaped. Postwar generals and admirals, the weapons scientists, the political appointees who administer large government authorities—all wage their struggle for or against co-ordination within an apparatus and on a scale which the classic philosophers of American democracy could not have fathomed, much less illumined. The fact is that in a society of bigness everywhere the old simplicities wane, new sophistications take hold. And a shift in primacy from Britain to the United States has accelerated this trend. Policy is expounded and votes garnered through traditional vehicles. Untraditional ones are also required for leadership.

Nor is it only new governmental forces that are in play. Opinion industries affect American public life on the same enlarged scale. And the more concentrated these become, the less traditional are the lines on which they operate. None of them can exercise a nation-wide monopoly; there is still multiplicity in manipulation. Bigness, however, abridges freedom of expression in fact, though not in law. For while it amplifies the physical range of political debate, it also reduces comparatively the number of those who can participate on equal terms. Senator McCarthy's influence was built up and demolished through mass media. Critics who lacked access to them had no adequate means of crossing swords with him.

Governmental powers were, nevertheless, what gave him his chance to wield extragovernmental power—and in a parliamentary system he would not have had those. Never before had a major American demagogue possessed this dual capacity to intimidate. Senator McCarthy was, moreover, the first of his kind after primacy had shifted from Britain to the United States; when, that is, the East–West equilibrium could not be stabilized if the West's own American leader were politically unstable. The totalitarian State emerged where, as large-scale techniques were adopted, there were few of the inner correctives provided by a heritage of freedom. McCarthyism, like early Italian Fascism, had no program; unlike German National Socialism or Russian and Chinese Communism, there was no organized impetus behind it. But the investigative procedures of Congress furnished it with an official base that it would not have had in other democracies. That separation of powers which Americans deem the secret of their liberties can, when mass outlets are also employed, be turned against them.

It would, nevertheless, be argued that the decline of McCarthyism illustrated the resiliency of the American political system. No bold adventurer could, after all, master it. As far as that is so, however, the risks run in the meantime, the damage inflicted not only on American democracy at home but on its standing abroad, cannot be omitted from the reckoning. What saved the American political system from a more serious bout with McCarthyism was the localization of the Korean War; affinities between the McCarthy and MacArthur schools, their common disdain for coalition policies, were no accident. The storm was weathered. But localization of the Korean War owed much to the insistence of Britain and other allies. The well-being of the United States as a representative democracy was intertwined with her interests as leader of the West.

In the long run, then, American leadership can be no steadier than the political system by which it is sustained. And as multifarious as its burdens is the catalogue of complaints from allies and neutrals. Not that these are always warranted or come from those who have earned the right to sit in judgment. Often, too, the United States is blamed for fumbling with problems that are inherently intractable. There is a point, nevertheless, at which American leadership may be ill-served on the domestic front. For the magnitude of her general response to the challenge of primacy, the United States deserves praise; and yet ceaselessly in train is the self-disabling nature of her own governmental processes. For these tend to be flexible when they should be rigid and rigid when, for the sake of leadership, they should be flexible. The upshot has been a pattern of checks that may hinder as well as safeguard, political balances that are upset by vast national imbalances, disproportions that bigness enhances.

One gauge of democratic virtue is the extent to which, in every representative system, the locus of responsibiilty may be ascertained and pinned down. But in American governance as the small scale and large scale, the traditional and newfangled, combine and intermingle, this becomes more rather than less elusive.

Nor is the issue thus raised merely one of organization and procedure. It goes to the very heart of American leadership. Is the political potential of the American people evoked, conserved, and brought into focus as fully as it might be? Not that parliamentary government in Britain has been an infallible fount of superior wisdom. If it had, the self-crippling follies of appeasement days would have been averted. But even these were due to misjudgments which most of the nation shared; institutionally there was nothing to hamper the formulation and execution of sounder policies. The proposals of an American administration may be well-conceived. Until the inwrought struggle for and against co-ordination within and between separate branches has been overcome, it cannot speak for America irrefutably.

And whatever mars an American lead gratifies the foes

of the United States. It is her friends who are dismayed. The American people have been taught to attribute much of what they have done as a nation to the character of their political system; and this identification is sanctified by the war they fought among themselves to preserve it. Yet leadership in a world contest prescribes the most effective use of American strength and some other type of representative democracy may be better for that.

Primacy abroad derives from vitality at home. To unite a nation which is at once so outspread, so vigorous, and so free has, nevertheless, been no easy task; a struggle for and against co-ordination does not, after all, run merely through American public affairs but through the whole of American society. A political system that should alleviate centrifugal pressures tends, rather, to be their mirror. And it may also be to offset these that Americans have conformed.

The fact is that a good deal that unifies the American people did not grow up unbidden but, like their Constitution, had to be contrived in advance. The idea of separate powers was an attempt to devise an order of liberty through counterpoise; the American system has had to regulate that disorder which stemmed from pioneer life on an expanding frontier, from diverse sectional interests, and from cultural differences between recent and less recent immigrants. That a more perfect Union had yet to ripen and mature was demonstrated by the Civil War and America's still unfinished business over the enforcement of civil rights. The nation has not had those deeper roots which, as in Britain, might bind together naturally and in the fullness of time. But above its cleavages there has been a veneer of conformity and that has served as a kind of cement.

Bigness, moreover, has accentuated conformity. When livelihoods must be earned and careers pursued in large-scale units, the habit is to ride with the herd. Americans may have been more receptive to the McCarthyite upsurge because of this added, prior socio-economic conditioning. Yet long before that, there had been a need for symbols around which all might cluster and which other peoples mistook for mere vulgar flag-waving. Even mass media serve a double purpose. They foster conformities, but they can also broaden horizons and thus unify in a good sense as well as a bad.

Such, at any rate, were the molds in which American governance evolved and that, with primacy, would have an ever-widening effect. The American people still exhibit many of the same political traits as the kindred British; divergences in policy were nevertheless sharpened by differences in the framework of politics. Both have had to deal with the inner tensions of a mass democracy. In Britain the party dialectic over social reform was fierce; the necessary adjustments could at least be made without the further complications that assail the American political system. And yet there has been a struggle for and against coordination with which British statecraft has also had to cope. Its setting, however, is not at home but overseas.

The fact that British power has been oceanic and American power continental remains a major cause of Anglo-American divergence. Britain might have been little more than an overpopulated, impoverished island in the North Sea if she had not become the suzerain of a dependent empire and the pivot, later on, of a voluntary commonwealth. A structure of power in which not all were free, it had nevertheless upheld a free world order. Centrifugal pressures that operate within the American political system may impede America's leadership of the West; those with which Britain has had to contend can affect the important part that she still has to play.

The nature of the ties between the English-speaking peoples determines the interest each must have in the other's political potential. Disaster awaits a free world order in which the United States does not assert primacy. And yet the United States took Britain's place without the place she formerly occupied being taken by Britain; as second in the West, Britain can neither be isolationist nor rest on wilted laurels. The manner in which they work together has, as a result, been altered; Anglo-American friendship no longer consists of two associates, one active and one relatively inert, but of two allies constantly engaged side by side. The divergences they must overcome so that a free world order can be upheld conjointly are institutional as well as political. The way in which the American political system functions is a matter of abiding concern to all the allies of the United States. Among them Britain is still foremost. But there have been changes in the British power structure, and to these, as leader of the West, the United States has also had to adapt herself.

VI

The Commonwealth in the Era of American Leadership

From the First to the Second Commonwealth

In the global contests of the twentieth century, Britain has drawn strength from a web of oversea connections that are easier to describe than define. To what extent does she still do so? What advantages are obtained from this historic grouping by its other members? Trends within it must be watched by the United States not only because Britain is her principal ally. Today, in the well-being of various other Commonwealth members and of some British dependencies, the United States has particular interests of her own.

And that, too, denotes a shift in primacy. From the turn of the century, at any rate, formal assessments of British oversea interests included an American element; reference was made to it, after Anglo-American friendship started to take shape, whenever the Foreign Office surveyed a darkening scene or whenever a tour of the horizon was conducted at Imperial Conferences by statesmen of the period. But now, British oversea interests must also be included in global assessments of American policies.

In evaluating these, however, Americans are affected by their own anticolonial tradition. Nor is that all. Even the Commonwealth segment of British oversea interests lends itself to no simple explanation. For members of the Commonwealth have always found it less difficult to see where that aggregation was going than to say what it was. The view they took of it might be an inexplicit one; this did not matter so long as they all subscribed to the same world view. But they did not do so after World War II and that was a change with which, as leader of the West, the United States has also had to reckon.

Centrifugal pressures within the Commonwealth have been incessant. And yet against these must be set the one plain counter-

vailing fact that, since the era of Emperor William II, has so con-
founded adversaries of the West: a potential for unity in the
absence of which the Commonwealth would have disintegrated
long ago. Outwardly it is a complex of peoples who are either
British by derivation or who, as British rule has been removed,
still converge upon each other. But why do they do so and how?
The question to be solved during earlier formative years was
whether the national units of which the group is now comprised
could fulfill themselves individually within a collective Britannic
fold. That First, or British, Commonwealth was, however, super-
seded after World War II. What has supplanted it is a Second
Commonwealth, one from whose title the prefix British may be
discarded. A stage has been reached in which major processes
that refashion the character of the group lie beyond its own
control. The play upon it of outer global, rather than inner constitutional, forces is what distinguishes the Second Commonwealth
from the First.

A new phase, it had begun prior to the shift in primacy
from Britain to the United States and before East–West antagonism had become acute. The latter, however, aggravated a
number of intramural problems by which the Commonwealth had
been plagued for a generation. Trends such as neutralism and
anticolonialism are not, as Commonwealth phenomena, entirely
novel; Ireland, during World War II and before she seceded, was
a non-belligerent, while many in India and South Africa were
disaffected. But these tendencies could, under postwar circumstances, be more disruptive; and what yesterday were unofficial
emotions can today be reiterated officially. Nor is anticolonialism
the same as the classic demand for full self-government which
Canada was the first to enunciate. That had been attained. The
sovereign rank of newly emancipated Commonwealth members
has, however, been utilized on behalf of peoples who are still
dependent—a campaign pursued beyond the confines of the Commonwealth but one that has had some of its main objectives
within the Commonwealth itself.

Asian powers of the Commonwealth had achieved independence during the East–West contest and that compelled them
to make crucial decisions at once. A few refrained from taking
sides. When they did the query was raised whether, within a
single Commonwealth, interventionism and abstentionism may
coexist.

Between the wars, in the days of Locarno and Geneva,

partners of the First Commonwealth did not always see eye to eye. Their differences, however, never touched the fundamentals of world order; even the neutrality of the Irish, after they seceded, stemmed from a specific quarrel with the United Kingdom over Northern Ireland rather than over the cause of the West in general. Apart from Western alliances, most contemporary groupings—Sino-Soviet, Afro-Asian, Arab, African, West European, Latin and inter-American, the Atlantic community—belong, more or less, to a geographic area of their own. But a Commonwealth scattered to the four corners of the earth cannot have a regional outlook.

Flexibility in procedure has been its knack. Dissension over the issues of world order is, however, in quite another category. Other great human undertakings may or may not survive an East–West conflict; a Commonwealth that contains interventionist and abstentionist members might be among its early casualties. Members of the Commonwealth disagree over how to maintain peace. And yet peace gains when so variegated a partnership can exist at all.

The paradox of the Commonwealth is that while diverse in action, as an historic entity it still perseveres. Two changes, an internal and an external, have altered it since World War II. Internally what transformed the First Commonwealth was the admission to equal status of India, Pakistan, and Ceylon. Ireland and Burma have departed from it—and in 1961 South Africa, on becoming a republic, also withdrew. But after World War II the upsurge of Asian nationalism could no longer be repressed: exhausted, penniless, battle-scarred, Britain had to grant what, in Salisbury's late-Victorian phrase, were "graceful concessions." And it was as a consequence of these that the Commonwealth circle has, by common consent, been enlarged.

Constitutionally this has allowed for independence without separatism; voluntary ties that vary from the tenuous to the strong. India, when she proclaimed herself a republic in 1950, renounced allegiance to the King and yet accepted him as Head of the Commonwealth. A formula that others could adopt, it is one under which Commonwealth republics may stay on as members by recognizing in the Crown—though they forswear a limited monarchy for themselves—a kind of limited presidency for the entire partnership. Britain, Canada, Australia, and New Zealand are content with their status as Commonwealth monarchies. Nor could Britain become a republic so long as she wished to preserve her own world rank. For the Throne is no mere relic of outworn feudalism. Around it, in several degrees of loose association or historic loyalty, a midcentury Commonwealth revolves.

Most Asian and African partners of the Commonwealth are likely to prefer its republican form. Nor is this all that unites them. Pakistan's boundary dispute with India prompted her to renounce neutralism. They were, all the same, still thrown together by anticolonialism and by a pan-Asian doctrine that served the East against the West.

The Second Commonwealth, divided and yet undissolved, has thus been bisected into two wings—one that had Atlantic-Pacific origins, the other whose locale is Afro-Asian. But the Union of South Africa could fit into neither branch. For the Afro-Asian wing was alienated by her racism; Atlantic-Pacific members by the undemocratic behavior that ensued. And American policymakers have had to take these cleavages into account.

In Commonwealth economics the differences are not the same as in Commonwealth politics. There is a measure of economic unity that cuts across political disunities. And this regrouping is important since the Commonwealth, amounting with dependencies to one quarter of the earth's populace, does a large fraction of the world's trade. Britain, for one, having jettisoned foreign investments before Lend-Lease came to the rescue, has been hampered since World War II by a dearth of fresh capital and strained by the endeavor to hold wages and prices at noninflationary levels. A nation which lives by exports, she has, as a result, been getting less than her share of world markets. American and Canadian loans plus Marshall aid have helped tide her over; from day to day, it is Commonwealth economic arrangements that do much to keep her going. With the exception of Canada, every member of the Commonwealth adheres to the sterling monetary area—of which Britain is the central banker and to which a handful of non-Commonwealth countries also belongs. And then there is the system of Imperial Preference in which, under the General Agreement on Tariffs and Trade, barriers vary from low to high and to which, as pivot of the Commonwealth, Britain clings for political as well as economic reasons.

Britain did not want to have her exports shut out from the six-nation European Economic Community. She had therefore proposed a seventeen-nation free trade zone that would not only give her partial entry to the European Common Market but would also be compatible with prior Commonwealth economic commitments. France blocked that solution and Britain fell back instead on a less satisfactory project for a smaller free trade zone, one of the Outer Seven, with European countries outside the European Economic Community. In the British attitude there has been preoccupation with the interests of Commonwealth partners as well as with those of Britain herself. The United States, however, tends to diverge from it. For the Common Market is a step towards a West European federation, an undertaking she has sought to promote.

Meanwhile, as a gesture towards Commonwealth unity, there has been the Colombo Plan. This scheme was launched by the Atlantic-Pacific wing so as to furnish Asian members of the Commonwealth with economic aid and technical assistance. A Commonwealth replica of American Point Four Aid, it is an enterprise that the United States has joined and backs substantially.

On Commonwealth economics, as a matter of fact, American influence has alternated between the positive and the negative. It had been to protect herself against American protectionism that Britain, concurring at last with other members of the Commonwealth, adopted Imperial Preference three decades ago. And after 1947, when the American Loan was so rapidly exhausted by an abortive attempt to make the pound convertible, Britain would long be wary of suggestions to abolish exchange control. As banker of the sterling area, she faces serious risks: independent members of the Commonwealth are not subject to regulation. British solvency may therefore be endangered when, like India, they withdraw sterling balances from London. It is important for the West that India find the means to finance her Five-Year Plans; the exchange burden must, however, be spread more widely. The amount of dollars and gold that Britain possesses is one-eighth of American reserves, but with it she finances forty to fifty per cent of world trade; that this is too narrow a margin on which to operate, periodic runs on the pound have indicated. For while the United States has taken Britain's place in diplomacy and defense, she has not done so in high finance.

It does not, in other words, suffice to spark recovery abroad and try to improve the economies of underdeveloped countries. As leader of the West, the United States must pursue investment, credit, and tariff policies that are commensurate with the exigencies of leadership. And West Germany, too, now that she has accumulated gold reserves that are twice as large as Britain's, will have to do more and more as an exporter of capital.

Not that Britain can hand over major banking services to others. For her to manage an international payments system like the sterling area is salutary in a number of ways. When oversea countries funnel through London a considerable portion of their monetary wealth, they remain associated with her in a vital sphere. The financial, the political, and the strategic are intermixed when dollars have been earned for the sterling area by the rubber and tin of Malaya, by cocoa from Ghana, by Rhodesian copper and Australian wool. So, too, apart from meeting home demands, there is income from the sale of Middle Eastern oil and the investment in London of non-British oil profits. To divert the flow of such proceeds from the sterling area may be the aim of forces antagonistic to the West—ultra-nationalist, pan-Arab, pro-Soviet. But as long as the resources of outlying territories are available, it is not only Britain and producing countries that stand to benefit. A structure of power that is a prop of the West will also be sustained.

Together with Anglo-American friendship and the security of Western Europe, the Commonwealth figures as one of three major factors in British calculations. But how do oversea units themselves look upon the Commonwealth? What, indeed, is it? When statesmen have tried to define the Commonwealth they have pointed to a common purpose, to the symbol of a common Crown, to the habit of consultation between member governments. Yet rifts over colonialism and neutralism, and the aberrant role of the South African Union, have detracted from the notion of a common purpose; not all the partners accept the Crown or acknowledge it in the same manner. That leaves consultation. And that does provide a clue. By means of consultation, members of the Commonwealth—Asian, African, Atlantic-Pacific—stick together even though their grounds for doing so may vary.

Lacking rigid bonds, the Commonwealth is likewise devoid of absolute criteria. There is no one drive that impels all who adhere. But while their motivations are not identical, much has been predetermined by history. Among some, the momentum of the past is renewed by sentiment and common antecedents. Although, as with Anglo-American friendship, ethnic ties can do less and less to unite a multiracial Commonwealth, yet public life in each Commonwealth country is shaped by time-honored British institutions and practices. Not all other members have maintained the British judicial system, the English Common Law, and the British form of parliamentary democracy as faithfully as it was hoped they might. But even as norms these have set standards and thus have served to bind.

The range of things that Commonwealth members have

in common—from reciprocal privileges over citizenship and nationality to transactions in the domain of sterling and preferential trade—may be uneven. Averse since the days of Joseph Chamberlain to any semblance of a recentralizing hand, oversea partners have never permitted a permanent Commonwealth secretariat to be established in London—though the Colombo Plan has its own administrative machinery and so would any Commonwealth bank. One unifying element is the use of the English language as a lingua franca not only between polyglot units of the Commonwealth but within them. French-Canadians enjoy their ancient linguistic rights; in South Africa, Afrikaans has long vied with English. But Asian and African members are riven by a babel of tongues and tribal dialects. Britain, however, has endowed them with a language as well as a framework of governance that are both a means to independence and, even among Afro-Asian neutrals, a tie with the West.

In the end, though the Commonwealth, with its Britannic origins, is supposed to defy logic, it actually does have a logic all its own. It may be that just as the struggle for and against co-ordination in the American political system frequently baffles the British people, so also, to Americans, an unco-ordinated Commonwealth is often inexplicable. But the Commonwealth might be less inexplicable if an analogy were drawn between the way it works and the way Anglo-American friendship itself has operated. Britain and the United States do not have the same constitutional forms; a political dialectic to which they have been accustomed in domestic affairs enables them to diverge when they will and yet unite when they must over the continuance of a free world order. In the Atlantic-Pacific wing of the Commonwealth such modes of behavior are inbred; among Afro-Asian partners they go less deep. Their recent institutional conditioning was, nevertheless, under Britannic auspices and that gave Commonwealth politics a common stamp. Will similar influences foster similar understandings between them and the American leader of the West?

To procure unity the Commonwealth foregoes uniformity. In no two members do tangible and intangible interests coincide precisely; yet between members, as among themselves, some of these interests overlap. And it is because enough of them do overlap that the Commonwealth endures. The common denominator of an overlapping Commonwealth is the desire or willingness of its partners to perpetuate their affiliation.

The Commonwealth is, in fact, not even organized as a

single entity for joint defense. Today, moreover, it is American rather than British leadership that is the touchstone of strategic alignments. In the two world wars of the twentieth century, fellow Commonwealth nations served at Britain's side; during the dark months when Britain held out against Hitler, and before either Russia or the United States had been embroiled, they lent support. Members of the Atlantic-Pacific wing could do that of their own volition and Canada postponed her declaration of war to make this clear; other countries under the Crown had to do whatever Britain did. But nowhere in the Second Commonwealth do fully self-governing units, Atlantic-Pacific or Afro-Asian, now incur an automatic liability of that sort.

Within the Commonwealth, nevertheless, a few powers have undertaken local commitments voluntarily. South Africa and Britain had arranged for the defense of the sea routes around the Cape and for the land defense of southern Africa. With her consent, British, Australian, and New Zealand forces are stationed in Malaya to assist in her defense, in that of nearby British colonies and protectorates, and in that of Australasia itself. As among NATO Powers, there is co-operation between the Armed Forces of the Commonwealth over training, weapons, equipment. There is, however, no single all-inclusive scheme of Commonwealth preparedness.

And yet there is an instance in which Western defense interests could prevent a future member of the Commonwealth from attaining one of its sovereign rights. But here it is the United States rather than Britain that creates a problem. Since the turn of the century it had been the Monroe Doctrine and not the Royal Navy which had sheltered that Caribbean region where the Federated West Indies aspires to a higher status. Its best site for a federal capital at Chaguaramas, near Port-of-Spain, Trinidad, is occupied, however, by a strategically important American naval base; one that was leased from Britain in the Anglo-American "destroyers for bases" deal of World War II. Over this state of affairs the West Indian Federation may be far from happy. But it would scarcely be more secure if American defenses were impaired—though, during a period of seventeen years, the matter is to be reconsidered.

Some members of the Commonwealth have, of course, joined major regional combinations, but none to which the United States does not also belong. And in terms of Commonwealth defense, this is a sign of the times. It is as signatories of the North Atlantic Alliance that Britain and Canada are formally allied; and in the South Pacific it is again the United States which does most, through the Anzus Treaty, to underpin the regional security of Australia and New Zealand. Britain, Australia, New Zealand, and Pakistan adhere to the Southeast Asia Security Pact, but so does the United States; and then there is the Central Treaty Organization, the former Baghdad Pact, that Britain and Pakistan have joined and in which the United States, though she eschews full obligation, participates to the full. For defense purposes Pakistan may, at the moment, be regarded as a member of the Commonwealth's Atlantic-Pacific wing; yet that, in turn, is bound together by something more potent than a Commonwealth defense commitment. Through a common heritage, Britain, Canada, Australia, and New Zealand are similarly oriented in international affairs. There may be no defense prearrangements of a general character between them. The same concept of world order impelled them to band together in past emergencies and might do so again.

Members of the Commonwealth that do not share this concept will not be predisposed to collaborate on its behalf. For the Commonwealth has not only been revamped by an inner constitutional revolution; a shift in the primacy of the West has had upon it almost as revolutionary an impact. Equality of status was not wrung from Britain without conflict. Afro-Asian members of the Commonwealth have, however, had few direct ties with the United States. The educated among them may have sensed some of those imponderables of politics that vivify Anglo-American friendship. But these carry over into international affairs, and here the two branches of the Commonwealth part company. For it is only Afro-Asian members that have expounded a theory of peace calling for non-involvement between East and West. The defense of the West is, moreover, the *raison d'être* for American leadership. Accepted by one wing of the Commonwealth, it is rejected by the other.

Over this question the Commonwealth could be split irretrievably. The auguries are, nevertheless, that, short of an East–West showdown, it will not be. During the Suez crisis of 1956, Anglo-American divergence was accompanied by yet another regrouping within the Commonwealth itself. And an empirical approach to politics, one that is in both the Commonwealth and Anglo-American vein, was a clue to that.

But it is as an inseparable part of the West that Atlantic-Pacific members of the Commonwealth maintain their national independence, contribute to the preservation of civilized society, and uphold the Commonwealth's own unity. The prospect of defense and counteroffensive by the West is what has warded off the East, what has lessened the likelihood of an attack by the East on the West. The idea of peace by power, was, however, branded by India and her followers within the Commonwealth as a wicked fallacy. And when they inveighed against the West's global strategy they also decried the security foundations upon which older members of the Second Commonwealth had each staked their future—by which, indeed, the life of the Commonwealth itself can alone be prolonged.

Changes in the Commonwealth and in Anglo-American friendship are interrelated. Nor is it surprising that they should be. There has, after all, been interaction for a century and a half between an emergent America and the British power structure. As long as Britannia ruled the waves and no one country ruled Europe, the expansion of the United States could proceed unmolested. Before World War I, over the abandonment of British rights in an isthmian canal across Central America and over the settlement of the Alaskan boundary, she had gotten her own way; but when rivals threatened Britain in Europe and elsewhere, the defense of Canada and of other British interests in the Western Hemisphere had been reinsured. Boers might fight the British, and Indians spill blood; but if Imperial Germany had enlarged her African foothold or if Tsarist Russia had conquered India, they would not have brought freedom with them. The experiences of the Irish, the Boers, and the Indians were not of a kind that might endear the British power structure to them. But others, despite grievances, could realize what they owed to it.

A strategic postulate that British power would be commensurate with British responsibilities was implicit in the First British Commonwealth. In the Second Commonwealth, though Britain is still its pivot, this can no longer be predicated. The United States has taken Britain's place, and it is from Washington rather than London that the West's chief impetus must emanate. But when that happens a basic premise in the national security of other Commonwealth members has been modified.

Then, too, there are those in the Afro-Asian branch of the Commonwealth who have kept strategically aloof from the West—who preen themselves on standing between East and West, uncommitted to either. No preconcerted master-plan for the defense of the Commonwealth as a single entity has anyhow ever been feasible; the differing regional interests of its Atlantic-Pacific members precluded this. As long, however, as they subscribed to the same kind of world order, it was not conceptually impracticable. Today it is in their concepts of world order that the two wings of the Commonwealth differ most.

Commonwealth neutrals do, nevertheless, have a stake in a free world order. If they did not, they would hardly perpetuate their membership in a Commonwealth that is one of its pillars. But coalition strategy entails risks; most Afro-Asian countries have all they can do at home. Here, then, some resemblance may be discerned between a neutralist outlook and that isolationist viewpoint which the United States, after she achieved independence, had espoused. On this ground, too, Americans are loath to find fault with those who do what they themselves once did.

One cardinal distinction must, all the same, be noted. The United States and the Britannic realm overseas may have had British maritime supremacy as their bulwark. Britain was predominant, however, before contests of power were bipolarized, before bigness had maximized the scale of international rivalry and rendered it all-enveloping. Safety for neutrals resides more than ever in the strength of the West. Will it, now led by the United States, be handicapped by the non-alignment of Commonwealth neutrals? Will they, at least, be genuinely neutral?

To assess the role of the Commonwealth when primacy has shifted from Britain to the United States, the position of each member must be analyzed. But that of Britain is still the most intricate, and various facets of her power structure, in Europe and overseas, will be treated first. When these have been reviewed, some further reflections on the nature of the Commonwealth can be essayed. Other members of the Atlantic-Pacific branch, such as Canada, Australia, New Zealand, have individual positions that will be sketched next. British interests in Africa will be dealt with when trends among Commonwealth members on that continent are scrutinized. Consideration will finally be given to those that Asian members of the Commonwealth reveal—though such is Malaya's regional problem that it will have been examined in another context. And as a backdrop throughout remains the fact of American leadership. There was a serious Commonwealth crisis in 1956 when the United States and Britain diverged over the coercion of Egypt—an episode to which some attention will lastly be paid.

THE FOUNDATIONS OF BRITISH POWER

What should first be recalled in analyzing Britain's position is that the Anglo-American factor, though recast, endures as the tacit core of the West. The part that she plays under the new dispensation must therefore still be an effective one—something that will scarcely be possible if her oversea connections melt away. The United States has not only had to conjure with the endeavors of her principal ally to revise and retain these. Oversea connections have made the British reluctant to join unreservedly in the movement towards a federalized Europe that the Suez crisis of 1956 speeded up and American statesmen have encouraged. Britain has participated in the Council of Europe at Strasbourg, in the Organization for European Economic Co-operation, and in the European Payments Union; a working relationship was established with the European coal-steel pool. She may join this as well as the European Atomic Community. But the problem of co-operation with the European Economic Community raises issues that might affect her world status.

The supranational features of recent European undertakings are what the British must shun. These may be held in abeyance as long as General de Gaulle is at the helm in France; the European communities will nevertheless be thwarted if their original aim, that of a federalized Europe, is not eventually resumed. The plain fact is that Britain cannot subordinate her own sovereignty to what, on an eighteenth-century American model, would be a semicontinental European sovereignty. When she abstains, there is Anglo-American divergence over the nature of the British power structure. And yet even from the American standpoint the British case may be a cogent one.

Certainly the United States of America would exhibit less enthusiasm for a United States of Europe if such a union sought to operate between East and West as a Third Force. Not that it could do so without detriment to itself. Transatlantic power as well as its own is the basis of Western Europe's security; it is neither self-contained economically, nor, when a global equilibrium safeguards the peace, strategically self-supporting. Yet that same global equilibrium would be impaired if a federated Europe, in an illusive spirit of collective detachment, toyed with neutralist ideas. From tendencies such as these, at any rate, Britain must steer clear; and if she does not, other members of the Atlantic-Pacific branch will oppose them. For it is not only the defense of Britain that is hinged regionally by treaty and globally by concept upon collaboration with the United States. So in the Commonwealth is that of her non-neutralist partners.

South Africa's military commitments were made with the United Kingdom alone. But it is with the United States rather than Britain that the local defense of Canada, Australia, and New Zealand is chiefly interwoven.

And that is why the Commonwealth itself could never be converted into a global Third Force—an objective with which some postwar British politicians expressed sympathy and one that most of its Asian capitals might not have discountenanced. Friendship between the United States and Britain has long been a prerequisite for unity between Britain and other Atlantic-Pacific members of the Commonwealth. Americans themselves may advocate British participation in a European federal union. This, nevertheless, is a step that might detract from American leadership. And in so far as it also detracted from Anglo-American friendship, it would further attenuate Commonwealth bonds.

Within limits, Britain must collaborate with the European communities, and other members of the Atlantic-Pacific branch urge her to do so. What they cannot recommend is an unlimited federal merger, one that would strip Britain of a sovereign independence that is the political, economic, and moral hub of their own historic grouping.

Moreover, what such a merger must also presuppose is that, as leader of the West, the United States can afford to dispense everywhere with the individual exercise of British power. For constitutionally a federal union is all-absorbing; its constituent states cannot maintain external connections of their own. Apart from those with European allies, Britain has one set of special ties with the United States, another with Commonwealth partners, and yet another with oversea dependencies. Most of these, in a fully integrated European union, she would have to discard.

The circumstances that spur on federalizing projects are precisely those that, because British power is world-wide in structure, compel Britain to keep a free hand. Atlantic policy-making has sought to divert resurgent German energies from East to West; so as to counterbalance these, however, Britain (as the French once desired) cannot amalgamate with her neighbors. Not that an enlargement of European markets would be unwelcome to her; but access to them might be purchased at too high a price. The harmonization of global with regional interests must, for her own sake and for that of a free world order, be considered by Britain at every point of advance. And this cannot be done, the regional will have consumed the global, if by joining a Western European federation Britain were cut off from all exterior ties of her own—if she had to forfeit oceanic bonds with her own dependencies, with equal partners of the Commonwealth, with the United States herself.

In the coalition defense of Western Europe, British capacity must still rate high. But before her strength can be brought to bear, it has to be conserved. The weight Britain exerts in the European theater is governed by the degree to which she functions as the center of an oversea structure that is varied in its attributes and complex in its make-up. As a European Power, as an Atlantic ally, as a pillar of the Franco-British entente, it is Commonwealth and Anglo-American global affinities that nourish her regional vigor and of which, in any European federation, she would necessarily be deprived.

Britain's status rests, then, on multiple props, and failure to comprehend that basic fact has invalidated much postwar discussion on both sides of the Atlantic. Differences between the British and American systems of representative democracy have evoked a kind of pre-established divergence; more important still is an organic contrast between the foundations of American and British power. One sort of struggle for and against co-ordination may rage within the American continental land mass. It is yet another sort with which Britain, as she banks on an oversea power structure, must contend as uninterruptedly.

As far, moreover, as can be foreseen, no Administration or Congress in Washington is likely to favor any wholesale surrender of American federal sovereignty to a higher—Atlantic or universal—supranational authority. A similar British diffidence springs from the global character of British power. And its very nature must rebut the charge of a parochial or particularist motivation. It is on behalf of a power structure that is transnational rather than national in composition that the British demur.

But what may occasionally be suspected in British quarters is that, with Western Europe successfully federalized, the United States herself intends to curtail her own armed vigil on European soil against the East. In American quarters it is conversely suspected that when Britain drags her feet over federalist proposals she is trying to retard any such American withdrawal. The truth is that, over these questions, neither the United States nor Britain enjoys much latitude. As long as the East–West contest lasts, both must maintain the diverse interests to which each is committed at present.

Inconsistent objectives may be furthered, nevertheless, by oversimplified assessments. The problem of a more co-ordinated exercise of power is one that neither the American system at home nor the British structure overseas has resolved; and the English-speaking peoples have to accept each other's imperfections if, in an imperfect world, common tasks are to be discharged in common. The federal principle may well be a secret of American national unity; the United States herself would shrink from applying it to Anglo-American friendship or the North Atlantic community. Some Commonwealth countries have borrowed it for their own political systems; from it, as a means of unifying the Commonwealth as a whole, they have shied away. When she solidifies ties with West European neighbors, Britain must eschew any all-out integration. As the linchpin of a global power structure, she can adopt no other course.

American leadership benefits, even if American political philosophy is rejected, when the status of a British ally is thus upheld and a world-wide Commonwealth kept together. For centuries Britain has had one foot planted in Europe and one outstretched across the seas. The amputation of a limb rather than a change of stance is therefore what entry into a supranational European union would entail—with a corresponding drain in total vitality. In the American continental union, federating states gained a larger scope; in any comparable European scheme, Britain, and all of which she is a focus, would be diminished. In the era of American primacy, Britain still has a special place. And a multiplicity of attachments is what enables her to maintain it.

TROUBLED OUTPOSTS

There is, however, another angle from which Washington has been concerned with British oversea interests. Some members of the Commonwealth acknowledge an American lead, while others stand aloof. But one segment of the British power structure still consists of dependent territories, and over the ensuing colonial problem the Afro-Asian wing of the Commonwealth has had less to divide it from the United States than from Britain herself. Serious divergence over this question has been avoided. Yet the United States, though the butt of neutralists, has been torn between obligations to allies who possess dependencies and her desire, as leader of the West, to stop anticolonial neutrals from going over to the other side. In courting the latter, moreover, she can always remind them of that colonial revolution against Britain through which her own independence was won. Yet leadership and anticolonialism do not always go well together.

When, as a matter of fact, the North Atlantic Alliance was signed, the United States did not refuse outright to support the colonial policies of her principal allies. The Senate Foreign Relations Committee observed in 1949 that the United States would evaluate each on its merits.

There might be less misunderstanding of the British power

structure as a buttress of a free world order if Americans had a better grasp of their own. Oversea possessions were essentials of primacy in the West before this shifted to the United States; they are still its adjuncts. But these are realities that the American mind, shaped in a matrix whose initial expansion was continental rather than oceanic, has been slow to accept. Patting herself on the back over the liberal treatment given Cuba, the Philippines, and Puerto Rico (as though there were no similar prior examples in the British record), the United States relegates to a *soi-disant,* non-colonial category her own more permanent lapses from grace.

It is fortunate for the West that Alaska was purchased from Russia and that the United States took Hawaii. Both territories have become states of the Union. All the same, by her presence there and in other distant lands (the Panama Canal and its approaches, Samoa, Okinawa, Pacific isles acquired during World War II) the United States still exerts sway over a vast imperial realm—and one that, as a lever of primacy, she dare not yield. What Britain did the United States has had to do. About the right of dependent peoples to rule themselves they are in accord; it would be contrary to the genius of their own free institutions for them to diverge over that. But they are both confronted with borderline cases. And the worst of these are those in which local claims and larger common interests tend to be at variance.

Isolationism could not be outmoded without some reexamination of companion principles being called for. For it was the United States herself who first mixed together the neutralist and anticolonial evangels; maxims against entangling alliances and colonial fetters were coined by the Founding Fathers simultaneously. The British Empire, nevertheless, embodied a structure of power that stood between the infant republic and any more predatory imperialism. Nor had bigness furnished mass tyrannies with the tools of global domination; the earth was not polarized as yet between those who would preserve and those who would subvert a free world order. But it is not only neutralism that these adverse developments put under a cloud; the more headlong species of anticolonialism may now also have to be treated with caution. Local grants of freedom will, at any rate, have to be considered in the light of global forces; a wider frame of reference must likewise be employed. That self-government is better than good government was once sound liberal doctrine. It may be this no longer, the consequences can be illiberal, if bad government in exposed areas hampers the defense of the West.

It so happens that, before Moscow or Peking could pose as kindly paladins of Afro-Asian nationalism, lines of advance within the Commonwealth had been set and major concessions registered. There were differences over colonial issues as well as over the East–West contest; between neutralism and anticolonialism there have, in fact, been numerous points of contact. And the dependencies that Britain still possesses makes her even now an anticolonial target. But for some of these the yardsticks of viability are not what they once were. For dependencies may be so situated on the map that, by any misuse of freedom, the entire free world would suffer.

Most of the British power structure is, of course, voluntary in character. But unless avenues of communication between its scattered units are kept open, its future will be precarious. For it is not only on land and in the air that the West must plan to defend itself. A free world order and particular groupings within it have oceanic links to preserve. The United States may have taken Britain's place as mistress of the seas; control that the British still exercise from outlying bases, despite the loss of Suez, Bombay, and Trincomalee, remains a boon for the West. Watch is kept from these points over economic lifelines along which pass the oil supplies of the Middle East, the raw materials of Southeastern Asia, the trade of the Orient. In this manner the administration of colonial dependencies is expedited; traffic between Britain and members of the Commonwealth in the Indian Ocean and the South Pacific is likewise safeguarded. Some oversea holdings are important because of where they are situated on the British communications system. And it is as victims of geography that they have proceeded towards full self-government at a slower pace than more primitive communities.

The East–West contest is what impels the United States to assert her primacy. It is also what has made Britain reluctant to abandon strategic outposts.

There has, at any rate, been a colonial problem along the communications sector of the British oversea power structure that is distinct from the one with which she has had to grapple elsewhere. Matters will be complicated wherever dependencies are multiracial in composition. But in Africa the conflict is between indigenous peoples and British settler minorities. It is a quite different one in strategic outposts where racial majorities have ties of kinship with powers inimical to the West. For then grants of independence may serve interests other than those of either grantor or grantees.

Not that such issues arise at every strategic outpost. At

Gibraltar, for instance, the difficulty is not one of internal governance but of foreign policy. Agitation against British rule has not
come from within but from across the frontier, from Spain.

So also, at Malta, the Mediterranean headquarters of the
Royal Navy, there may be clamor against Britain and the NATO
facilities that she provides. As a European base with no hinterland, the island is particularly exposed to nuclear or thermonuclear
attack; cuts in official British expenditures at the local dockyards
fomented unrest. Complete independence for the self-governing
Maltese would be economically impracticable. And as an alternative to that they asked for a tighter union with the British
Parliament, but one in which commensurate tax burdens would
not have to be borne. The upshot has been less rather than more
autonomy. Athwart a vital route, Malta also lies close to Italy
and North Africa; before breaking away from Britain, she would
have to accept a neutral status. But as this must spell bankruptcy,
she might even look to Cairo or Moscow for economic support.
The British do not wish to hold on to Malta as a dependency.
As long as they do, however, the West will still have her naval
base at its disposal.

Then, too, it was as a coalition rather than colonial
problem that the question of Cyprus had to be tackled. The last
site of its kind for British land and air forces in the eastern
Mediterranean, Cyprus furnishes access to southeastern Europe
and to Arab lands whose neutralism may have a pro-Soviet
flavor; obligations under both NATO and the Central Treaty
Organization can be implemented from that island. The Anglo-
French expedition against the Suez Canal Zone in 1956 showed
that Cyprus has small value as a naval base; the island proved
useful otherwise, however, when the United States and Britain
intervened during the summer of 1958 in Lebanon and Jordan.
Not that its utility in this regard would have justified a British
refusal to relinquish Cyprus. It would have been morally wrong
and economically wasteful to hold the island against the will of
a hostile populace if wider considerations did not supervene.

Self-determination for a people as developed as the Cypriotes is a legitimate aim if national independence is what they
genuinely seek. It had in fact been envisaged as merely a prelude
to the annexation of the island by Greece. In a union of Greek-
speaking Cypriotes with their Greek brethren, a Turkish minority
would be transferred from the British to the Greek flag; and
rather than accept this, Ankara proposed a partition of Cyprus
between Greece and Turkey. Both powers are signatories of

NATO, but Turkey is also a member of CENTO; as keystone of Western defenses in the Middle East, her objections could not be ignored. And what troubled her was the desire of Greece to acquire an island which is six hundred miles from the Greek mainland but only forty miles from the shores of Anatolia. Cyprus commands the approaches to Iskenderun, a port which is the anchor of NATO's supply line to its Turkish bastion; one which might some day become a Mediterranean outlet for a pipeline from Iraqi oil fields. With Cyprus in neutralist hands Turkey could not feel safe; if Communists, who are strong locally, should dominate that island, she would be menaced. Greece already possesses three steppingstones—Mytilene, Chios, and the Dodecanese—to the Turkish coast. If so volatile a nation were to be penetrated by Communism and desert NATO, the ring around Turkey might be sealed.

Old animosities between Greek and Turk were rekindled. But that could not be helped when, with Russia looming in the north, pro-Soviet machinations might presently also be expected from the south—from the Syrian province of Nasserist Egypt. In anything that now rendered their Mediterranean frontier insecure, the Turks would not acquiesce supinely.

What the Cyprus problem illustrated was the degree to which disputes within the British power structure could affect the West's defensive power. Nor was this merely a matter of whether to keep or let go a well-situated vantage point. The demands of the Cypriote majority could not be conceded without inviting a Turkish military occupation; and as far as that put Greece and Turkey at each other's throats, Western strategy in the eastern Mediterranean would be seriously disrupted. An outcome that might please Moscow and Cairo, it was scarcely one over which Washington could rejoice.

And yet the United States had to tread warily. She could not favor the Greek idea of a United Nations regime for Cyprus; that would give Russia a voice and exclude the island from NATO plans. London and Ankara knew, however, that there was a Greek rather than Turkish lobby in Washington, that there were more American voters of Greek than of Turkish extraction.* Anticolonial sympathies might, in any case, have ranged the United States on the side of the Cypriote majority; Athens had been annoyed when they did not do so. But to the British power structure, as to the American oversea realm itself, the old anticolonial shibboleths were no longer germane.

---

* Eden, *op. cit.,* p. 463; see also pp. 448-449 and 453-456.

There could, at any rate, have been little sorrow in Washington when Britain stood out against them. She had vetoed annexation and partition alike; both were excluded from the settlement upon which, at American prompting, Athens and Ankara finally agreed in 1959. So as to enforce its terms, Britain, Greece, and Turkey have the right to intervene conjointly or individually; as these three NATO powers guarantee the independence of Cyprus, the control of that island by foes of the West is also precluded. A Greek-Turkish garrison may be stationed on it. Britain, moreover, retains sovereignty over two military bases that she can use on behalf of NATO or on her own if circumstances in the Middle East so require; and she might avail herself of defense facilities elsewhere on Cyprus. It would pay the Cypriote Republic to remain within the sterling area and, so as to get a tariff preference in Britain for her agricultural produce, to become a member of the Commonwealth. When she entered its councils in 1961, one further fact was evident. Cyprus has not been eliminated from the British power structure and to that extent the security interests of the West have been preserved.

In Aden, however, unrest does not set NATO Allies apart. But there also the Western coalition would be ill-served if Britain were to forfeit her authority gratuitously. Situated at an entrance to the Red Sea and the Indian Ocean, Aden is the one well-equipped harbor of which the British communications structure disposes between the Indian subcontinent and Mediterranean ports. The Suez artery was blocked during the Anglo-French expedition against Egypt in 1956; yet a closure of the canal did not rob Aden of all its value in the defense of the West. There are other avenues of communication to be safeguarded, and, as headquarters for British forces in the Middle East, Aden exerts a broad jurisdiction. Surveillance is maintained from there over those territories in the Persian Gulf whose oil is so essential to the British economy. Americans and Australians as well as the British would have a local junction in Aden if a roundabout approach to the Middle East, across the Pacific and Indian Oceans or up from the tip of Africa, should ever be necessary.

To replace the one lost at Abadan when Iran evicted British oil companies, Britain has erected a big oil refinery at Aden. The bunkering activities of that port make it the third busiest—surpassed only by London and Liverpool—under the Union Jack.

But Arab nationalism stirred up the populace against

British rule. There were the Cairo radio and agents from Nasserist Egypt to foment trouble. Preliminary steps toward self-government have been taken in the colony itself; in the neighboring protectorates some of the principalities have been federated by their British patron. It is nevertheless idle to suppose that so backward a country will soon be ready or inclined to enjoy an autonomous status within the Commonwealth.

Yemen, moreover, covets all of Aden, and there have been border skirmishes with her. Back of that Arab despotism stands Egypt; through their association in the United Arab States, Cairo hopes to wrest from Britain mastery of the Strait of Bab el Mandeb and the approaches to Suez. After Russia and Egypt first became cordial, Yemen took arms and aid from the Sino-Soviet bloc: an airfield was built and a submarine base constructed on the Red Sea. But Yemen tried to patch up differences with Britain when, after the overthrow of the monarchy in 1958, the new Iraqi regime looked to Moscow rather than Cairo; some American aid has also been accepted. The fact is that the British presence in southern Arabia bolsters one set of Arab interests against another; it preserves both the princelings of the protectorates and the pan-Arab nationalists of the colony against Yemeni subjugation. And it prevents the doctrine of self-determination from being misapplied.

Nor is it only in the West that the retention of Aden as a strategic outpost should be favored. Neutral as well as allied members of the Commonwealth's Afro-Asian branch are served by the communications sector of the British oversea power structure.

At Singapore, however, the colonial problem has been complicated by pro-Communist influences which emanate not from Cairo or Moscow but from Peking. And while that island state enjoys a large measure of autonomy, it is restricted in the fields of defense, foreign policy, and internal security. Overseas Chinese, whose sympathies are preponderantly with Communist China, outnumber its Malay inhabitants by four to one. Full self-government would allow them to remove Singapore, the last strategic outpost of the British oversea power structure in the Far East, from the sway of the West. Not that this can be done without inviting economic ruin. The comparatively high living standards and social welfare regulations that British colonial governance provided were financed by income derived from entrepôt trade and naval-military expenditures. A union between Singapore and Malaya might, all the same, convert the Communist objectives into practical politics. But Malaya's own reluctance to merge with her neighbor would first have to be overcome.

Upon Singapore, so pivotal is it in the defense of Southeast Asia, the Royal Navy has based a fleet. From that island the British expect to discharge commitments under the Manila Pact and even, perhaps, under CENTO; it is a center for patrols on the sea routes to Hong Kong and other British dependencies of the region. In enemy hands, moreover, Singapore might be a dagger thrust at Australia and New Zealand; from it there is a line of communication with four Asian members of the Commonwealth that has to be protected. As a British strategic outpost Singapore could be outflanked by a pro-Communist regime in nearby Indonesia. In other respects she is kept out of China's grasp by the brakes that have been imposed on her own self-determination.

Nor are these maintained by Britain alone. Shared with the Federation of Malaya, they can scarcely be attributed by Afro-Asian or American opinion to a vestigial colonialism in Whitehall. On the council that supervises internal security in Singapore, there are three local representatives, three British and one appointed by Malaya. If the latter should be dissatisfied with the way Singapore is governed, he can withdraw his casting vote and—apart from the reserve powers that Britain herself may exercise—the state would revert to a colonial status.

About the adjacent island, Malaya must, it is plain, be exceedingly cautious. A substantial percentage of Malayan exports are shipped abroad through the port of Singapore; overtures for amalgamation between the two neighbors are, for ethnic and ideological reasons, treated coolly. The indigenous Malay element would be submerged throughout the Malay Peninsula if the Federation's own Chinese residents were to combine with Singapore's huge Chinese majority. As a member of the Commonwealth, Malaya is today an independent country; as a client state of Communist China she would cease to be one—though that is the goal of her own Communist Party. It would be safer for Malaya to unite with oil-rich British colonies in nearby Borneo. Wider arrangements with some of the other countries of Southeast Asia are being undertaken.

An elective five-year monarchy, the Malayan Federation, like its Republican associates, recognizes the Queen of England only as head of the Commonwealth. British forces have, however, done much to quell Communist guerrillas; with Malaya's express permission, a contingent of British, Australian, and New Zealand troops is stationed on Malayan soil. Through this section of her strategic reserve, Britain plans to fulfill Commonwealth and international obligations. But the fact that the Malayans enable her to do so reveals the extent to which, within a Commonwealth divided between Atlantic-Pacific and Afro-Asian concepts of world order, there are countervailing unities. Malaya may not have signed the Southeast Asia Security Pact. But her regional interests overlap with those of three other Commonwealth members, and she co-operates with them accordingly.

An outlying Asian position might thus still be held—one whose importance in the East-West contest is economic as well as strategic. Nearly one-half of the world's rubber and one-third of its tin is produced by the Malayan Federation; it is essential that these precious raw materials be kept at the disposal of the West and denied the East. Britain and the sterling area have relied financially on dollar earnings from the sale of Malayan tin and rubber; for Malaya, with a standard of living that is relatively high for Asia, the bargain is no one-sided one. In their portion of Vietnam the Chinese Communists are but a few hundred miles to the north, while to the south, across the Straits of Malacca, lies Indonesia where rebels still defy the Army and where, despite a dispute with Communist China, close ties exist with the Soviet Union.

A submarine base established by Russia on the Banda Sea, cutting the route between Australia and Singapore, can threaten lines of communication within the Commonwealth and the Southeast Asian Security Pact. Certainly Malaya and Singapore would be encircled if the anarchic Indonesian archipelago, with its enormous natural riches, were to move closer to the Soviet bloc. It is on the British structure of oversea power that the Malayan Federation depends for its defense. But this in turn is a major segment of a Western coalition in which the United States takes the lead. Strategically the interrelationship may be somewhat remote. It is significant, nevertheless, that Malaya has adhered to no militant doctrine of neutralism and anticolonialism by which, in preserving her national independence, she might hamstring herself ideologically.

There is, moreover, one other East Asian point whose position under British rule has had to be reassayed: Hong Kong. After Pearl Harbor it fell to Japan, and if Communist China should ever be embroiled with Britain's chief ally, the United States, it would succumb again; it has therefore been written off as a British strategic outpost. Warships based on Singapore may be stationed nearby; Hong Kong's own naval dockyards have been closed down. For the West, nevertheless, it is now an outpost of another kind. But such is Anglo-American interaction that it could not be this without American activities in the vicinity—support of the Formosan regime by the United States, her alliance with the Philippines—that enable the Crown Colony to live on borrowed time. Hong Kong's own demeanor has, besides, been studiously inoffensive; where other offshore islands had been fortified for assault on the Chinese mainland, the Crown Colony remained as circumspect as possible. Communist China has, at intervals, threatened to annex it. For a number of years, however, the *status quo* was as convenient to her as to Britain and the United States.

Can Communist China alter it without a frontal attack? She might starve Hong Kong into submission—provided, that is, that a clash with the West, when it brought succor, could be risked. What purported to be a legal basis for doing that was pegged out by Communist China in September, 1958, when she proclaimed twelve-mile sea and air limits for her territory. Encompassing Hong Kong, such a doctrine could also embarrass the British if applied to so vitally strategic an outpost as Gibraltar. The Crown Colony must get its foodstuffs from the Chinese mainland and their supply could be stopped; it is a free port and local manufacturers might be undersold by Chinese imports. The reasons for leaving Hong Kong unscathed were, as a matter of fact, economic as well as military. Communist China has needed Western industrial products, and hard currency with which to purchase them is obtained through sales on the Hong Kong market or through the Crown Colony's re-export trade. And from that adjacent island, Communist agents, posing as refugees, can fan out to other Asian countries.

Hong Kong's value, even to the anticapitalist Chinese, was thus a capitalistic one—something the Crown Colony would lose when it passed from British hands to their own. For its British suzerain, its main utility as port and entrepôt was the degree to which, in its affluence, it contributed to the sterling area. Since World War II and the trade embargo after the Korean War, it has done little business with China. But infractions of the trade embargo by Hong Kong rather than by Japan or West Germany were what aroused American ire. And Washington blamed London for permitting these.

Not that the United States could still be sorry over Britain's retention of Hong Kong. The entire sterling area gained from the boom in the Crown Colony; it has, moreover, also been a haven for refugees from the Maoist terror. But the freedom that its Chinese inhabitants enjoyed did not include the freedom which representative democracy would have furnished—that of delivering Hong Kong to the Peking regime.

Situated on the outer rim of the Chinese mainland, Hong Kong, like Portuguese Macao, became a window through which a watch on developments behind the Bamboo Curtain might be mounted. The lease on its mainland strip would not expire until 1997; during World War II, however, President Roosevelt had urged that, as an anticolonial gesture, Hong Kong be given as a gift to General Chiang Kai-shek. This was not done and, after the Communists subjugated China, Washington must have been glad that its advice had not been taken. The lesson was clear. Yet it was not one which the United States, torn between a pristine anticolonialism and the responsibilities of leadership, could digest ungrudgingly.

Nor have these issues arisen only along the communications sector of the British power structure. They occurred elsewhere in the Britannic realm and whenever they did so they were apt to affect Anglo-American as well as Commonwealth relationships. And yet within the Commonwealth itself Britain has never been wholly estranged from anticolonial neutrals like India and Ceylon or from an anticolonial ally like Pakistan. At the United Nations, apart from the permanent seat occupied by Britain in the Security Council, a nonpermanent seat rotates between other Commonwealth members; joint consultations within the Commonwealth group are customary. In colonial questions, nevertheless, her own anticolonial partners have raked Britain over the coals almost as severely as any mouthpiece for the Soviet bloc. It was, in fact, from latter-day British colonial practice that the mandates and trusteeship systems acquired the principle of accountability for dependent peoples. But to make their case against British imperialism, Afro-Asian partners consorted with regimes that did much to flout this very principle.

Strange, too, was the company in which, at times, the anticolonial campaign put the United States. Members of the United Nations are forbidden under Article II of the Charter to pry into the domestic affairs of other states. Colonial powers that are allied with the United States have stood upon the letter of this ban when their American leader tended to be less than adamant. In its maintenance, all the same, the United States has had a particular interest of her own. It would scarcely be with her consent that the topic of racial segregation in the American South might be inscribed on the agenda of some United Nations organ. Yet she cannot keep it off if she herself helps establish precedents that may be invoked against her.

SEMANTICS OF THE COMMONWEALTH

It is, however, not only the colonial problem as such that has been an awkward one in Anglo-American friendship. The Commonwealth sprang from the British Empire, but in British usage there are semantic anomalies that deepen confusion about them.

The British power structure derives strength from the dependencies of the British Crown and from Britain's free association with Commonwealth partners. London, nevertheless, has been loath to treat the first of these groupings apart from the second. One example of its reluctance was furnished in 1953 when, lest that colony be communized, the constitution of British Guiana had to be suspended. This could not have been done if Westminster had granted full self-government. Its retention of imperial authority was, moreover, in the American interest; the anticolonial sympathies of the United States are apt to be muted when there is danger, whether it be in British Guiana or Guatemala, of a pro-Soviet regime on the approaches to the Panama Canal. A step wholly within the ambit of colonial governance, it was, all the same, taken not in the name of the Empire but of the Commonwealth.

So also "Commonwealth and Empire" is a double-barrelled Churchillian phrase that the British employ and that, with a nostalgic hint of faded glories, covers more ground than it should. For there is no single body of that sort. And sovereignties cannot be coupled with dependencies without the character of the Commonwealth itself being blurred.

The tie between the Commonwealth and the British Empire has been organic. As separate entities, however, they are not interchangeable. For where Britain formerly had one function to discharge, she now has two: as a member of the Commonwealth, even as bellwether of the flock, she is an equal among equals; in her own Empire, over forty colonies, protectorates, protected states, and trust territories are still subject only to her. Australia and New Zealand also possess dependencies of their own. The Commonwealth, by embracing its members, includes their holdings. "Autonomous communities within the British Empire" was how they depicted themselves after World War I; they do so no longer.

Today it is within the Commonwealth rather than the other way round that the British Empire operates.

For entities that are so incommensurable, can a single omnibus term be devised? It is improbable that the anticolonial wing of the Commonwealth would bracket them together. But neither would it do to employ "Commonwealth" as a substitute for "Empire." In Britain, all the same, that is done frequently— the "Empire" term is discarded and "Commonwealth" used as a synonym for it. In an anticolonial epoch a better gloss can thereby be put on Britain's management of her own colonial affairs. And yet this might (as Nkrumah of Ghana pointed out in 1960 to the British Prime Minister, Harold Macmillan) conceal existing realities. The term "Dominion" was set aside by self-governing partners when, implying a status inferior to Britain's, it tended to become obsolete; in the British structure of overseas power there is, nevertheless, still a cluster of dependencies on which the Commonwealth label cannot be accurately pinned. For the Commonwealth has not, despite talk to the contrary, supplanted the British Empire. Through Britain these two entities may intersect and, as they do so, bolster her global rank. There is for each a sphere of its own.

Inestimable is the service that the British power structure can still render a free world order. Never has so great a role been performed on so narrow a margin. And that explains the British *penchant* for lumping together Commonwealth affinities and Empire possessions, for regarding them as one big undifferentiated whole. At a time when primacy has shifted across the Atlantic, the British people might thus impress outsiders and, above all, reassure themselves.

But this tendency is also a holdover from their own more spacious days. In contrast to the United States, Britain forged to the front with an unwritten constitution, with a political system that was correspondingly flexible. And semantic imprecision comes just as naturally to the British people when they adapt themselves to new trends in an oversea power structure.

Their various political hats are, moreover, not worn consecutively, but simultaneously. Commonwealth and imperial functions blend, for instance, when a British dependency attains independence and is raised to the Commonwealth circle. For here the imperial origins of the Commonwealth leave Britain with a prerogative that is virtually innate. In theory, any member of the Commonwealth might sponsor a colonial ward for election; that is an attribute of equality of status. Candidates under the tutelage of the United Kingdom are, in fact, the only ones who may presently make a bid. But what if an adverse vote should be cast? It is for an imperial suzerain to confer self-government. Dependencies cannot, however, be admitted to the Commonwealth table by Britain alone. There has been no blackball as yet. But if there were one, how serious would be the repercussions in a colony thus rebuffed, in an Afro-Asian wing which is so passionately anti-colonial?

South Africa, before she herself forsook the Commonwealth, may, with her racism, have been tempted to veto recent candidates. But over their eligibility the well-disposed might also have suffered qualms. It was hoped that law and Parliament in the British tradition would be among the interests that overlapped between all members of the Commonwealth. Few in the Afro-Asian branch have, however, shown themselves as ready for representative democracy as for national independence. Undue haste in conceding full autonomy along the communications sector of the British oversea power structure would detract from the defense of a free world order; and elsewhere, too, when dependencies have been upgraded prematurely, the battle for freedom is far from won. India will be the test case. Nor is this only a crisis of democracy. A crisis for the Commonwealth itself is latent within it. Members of the two branches have agreed to differ over concepts of world order. But if the great imponderables of public life also cease to bind, what will?

A clear-cut answer to that question is, in the nature of the Commonwealth itself, unlikely. Then, too, some common ideological ground remains between true Commonwealth democracies and Commonwealth countries where democracy is suspended in practice but not repudiated in principle. Steadily at work is the unifying influence of economics and finance. And here overlapping interests also extend to Britain's own dependencies.

Colonial territories augment substantially the sterling area's flow of trade and payments—a monetary grouping to which anti-colonial members of the Commonwealth also belong. As its banker and clearinghouse, London gains when sterling balances pile up; in leaner times these can be reinvested by a suzerain power within the colonies themselves. And that dependencies should thus fit into the largest of multilateral trade schemes may be deemed anachronistic by Americans who have urged both the liquidation of empires and an ampler freedom of trade. Such, however, have been the tariff schedules of the United States herself that under no other arrangement could British colonies have done as well.

But here, also, the less there is exploitation in the classic,

Marxian, sense of economic imperialism, the more prone have the British been to drift from an Empire to a Commonwealth nomenclature. The fact is that colonial territories, as they advance toward self-government, can regulate imports in their own domestic markets. Nor, with the growth of secondary industries, do they have to concentrate quite so much on raw-material exports to supply the factories of the United Kingdom and other industrialized countries. Considerable amounts have, besides, been allocated by the British Parliament to Colonial Welfare and Development Funds —in addition to what is obtained by loans and local revenues. That was done at a time when British industry needed capital for its own renovation. And Americans who recall the origins of the American Revolution might wonder whether sums thus earmarked would not make even Lord North turn over in his grave: though her colonies pay no taxes to Britain, Britain taxes herself on behalf of her colonies. But this is not merely Empire progress in the spirit of Commonwealth evolution. When dividing-lines are imprecise, the British people are all the more apt to forget where the one begins and the other ends.

Even defense is still considered by many in Britain as a sphere of unity rather than disunity. And this is a remnant of the notable contribution made by oversea countries of the Britannic realm in two world wars. Canada, for example, is the one senior member of the Commonwealth who dwells far from strategic theaters where Britain must either safeguard her communications system or operate regionally as an imperial power; and while another global conflict might again put her at Britain's side, it will be as NATO allies as well as Commonwealth partners that they will stand together. The Commonwealth itself has no all-encompassing defense plan; some members are neutralist in bent and others have undertaken local obligations with the United States. Yet each of them, whatever the commitments they accept or reject, profits strategically from the existence of the British power structure. Britain may think therefore of Empire dependencies and Commonwealth partners not as individual strands but as one interwoven fabric of global defense. She might be inexact semantically. Politically, a free world order is reinforced.

CANADA, AUSTRALIA, AND NEW ZEALAND

Overlapping interests may be what keep the Commonwealth going—what help Britain sustain a place next to that of the United States. But it is in oversea members of the Atlantic-Pacific branch that Britain finds her closest Commonwealth collaborators, and among these, in world affairs, Canada plays the larger part. For Australia and New Zealand, when the primacy of the West shifted across the Atlantic, an entirely new relationship with the United States opened up. Canada, however, was in a quite different category. Like Britain, she had to cope with an established relationship, one to which she would now have to adapt herself afresh.

The American impact on the growth of Canada has, ever since the American Revolution, been unremitting. Before and after World War I, it was Canada who pioneered the quest for equality of status—a constitutional reform that enabled the Commonwealth to survive. Against her giant American neighbor she needs a counterpoise; her national interest is served when the Commonwealth is perpetuated. Each geographic region of Canada has had to withstand economic suction from corresponding regions across the border; American pressure welded together what it might have disrupted. But national independence has also been reinsured by that equipoise between Commonwealth association and American alliance that is the key to Canadian policy.

With fewer encounters between the two North American countries there might have been less friction. Canada, however, does not fill American horizons as the United States fills Canadian. She has come into the news only when specific disputes arise— and usually, if settled, these have had to be settled on Washington's terms. Yet when the United States took Britain's place and arrayed the West against the East, Canada was to shoulder some of the burdens of world order and not augment them.

Evidence of a new stature, its meaning would, in crucial respects, be overlooked by most Americans. Canada participated with Britain and the United States in the wartime atomic energy program; she had from the start been a donor and not a recipient of mutual and other brands of aid; in NATO and the United Nations she carries weight. She has, moreover, been surging forward economically. Though the American Middle West will also benefit from the St. Lawrence Seaway, Canada did not only take the initiative against an entrenched American lobby but bore most of the cost. The development of the Columbia River Basin is to be a joint one. Her economic vigor is indeed what emboldened Canada to assert herself as a Middle Power. Of the Canadian attitude toward general questions, Washington made note. To Canada's own grievances against the United States, it was less attentive.

One difficulty is the size of American investments in Canada. She offers lucrative opportunities in a congenial political climate; American branch factories can also export, under preferential tariff arrangements, to other Commonwealth countries. But the more the Canadian economy is thus nourished by private American investment, the less control Canada can exert over her own economic destiny.

Her trade deficit with the United States is huge, and this has been redressed by the influx of American capital. The result is, however, that sixty per cent of her manufacturing industries is owned by Americans; that large sections of her own petroleum, chemical, automobile, and pulp and paper industries do not belong to her. Only a fourth of these undertakings sell stock to Canadians, and to few senior posts are Canadians appointed. Over trade with Communist China, American subsidiaries were at one time expected by Washington to observe American rather than Canadian rulings. Resented, too, were efforts by Washington to make them obey American antitrust laws. To the infringement of Canadian sovereignty, the intimacy of Canadian-American contacts is a standing invitation.

The problem is to protect the Canadian economy without retarding its expansion. But the tariff and trade practices of the United States have also been an irritant. As a wheat exporter, Canada protested against the dumping of American wheat on world markets —though similar complaints were registered against her by the United States, with New Zealand and Britain chiming in. There have been American restrictions on the import of lead and zinc. Quotas against Canadian oil did not, however, last long.

What makes such questions so prickly is the way they take shape. Over them Congress often ties the hands of the Executive. For in a political system pervaded by a struggle for and against co-ordination, Washington cannot always deal with Ottawa along lines which the Administration itself deems proper. Differences may be examined by a joint committee of American and Canadian legislators. But its American members can only speak, under the separation of powers, for one branch of their own government.

Canada tries to offset the local effect of American ascendancy by widening her scope. Through the Commonwealth grouping she has not only been brought into touch with Australia and New Zealand; special bonds are forged as well with Commonwealth members in Asia and Africa. British investments in Canada may now be comparatively small. But Canada is Britain's third largest export market and attempts will be made to increase trade between them.

Meanwhile, as a constituent part of Anglo-American friendship, as a NATO ally, and as a Commonwealth partner,

Canada has a variety of interests to harmonize. Membership in the inter-American system could mean additional subjection to hemispheric American influence; this Canada has avoided. As a going concern with an identity of her own, she exemplifies the triumph of politics over economics; the dynamics of American culture are, however, hard for her to resist. For the governance of a semi-continental domain, Canada adopted the British form of representative democracy; saturated by American mass media, the English-speaking half of the country has the same tastes as Americans and about the same living standards. It is, in fact, the resemblance between these two North American peoples that deceives Americans; for Canadian expressions of national individuality, they are unprepared. And it is by leaning toward others that Canada balances herself.

Her own experience as neighbor of the United States must, at any rate, color her adjustment to American leadership on the world stage. During the Korean War and its aftermath she deferred to American susceptibilities and yet urged restraint upon Washington. Unlike Britain, she had not recognized Communist China; but, like her, she had sought to modify Western embargoes on trade with that country. She proposed that the United Nations resolution condemning Communist China as an aggressor be toned down. She disagreed with the American view when disputes have flared up over the Chinese offshore islands, regarding them as the property of mainland China rather than Formosa.

On these items of policy Canada was more in accord with Britain than with the United States. Yet both of them tried to bring together Asian partners and their American ally. Through the Colombo Plan, Canadian aid to underdeveloped countries has remained within the Commonwealth—most of it going to India, Pakistan, and Ceylon, with Ghana and the West Indies getting a little. During the Suez crisis of 1956, Canada found herself closer to Asian partners and the United States than to Britain.

Her record is not one that displeases Afro-Asian members of the Commonwealth—and that is an asset that she has put to good use. Unlike Britain, Canada has never been a colonial power, nor, like South Africa, a racist state; when barriers have been raised against Japanese or other Asian immigrants, these have been less severe than Australia's. But the esteem that Canada enjoys among Commonwealth neutrals is important because her own roots are planted so deep within the West.

And it is this fact that must finally be decisive. At the United Nations, where her prestige is high, Canada may go her own way; she is less able to do so when the United States and Britain act together, as they did over Lebanon and Jordan in 1958, upon a salient issue. For geography and history ordain that, among national desiderata, Anglo-American solidarity heads the list. Post-Suez trends may have been such as to eliminate any need for Canada to perform as an "honest broker" between her chief English-speaking associates. As the nineteen-sixties were ushered in, she was casting about for some new, untrammelled role.

Her freedom of maneuver may, however, be less than had lately been assumed. With the advent of long-range weapons, question marks are raised over interrelated aspects of Canadian policy, domestic and external. During two world wars, Canada moved on the perimeter of world contests; in the East-West contest she lies between the two major contestants. When Sino-Soviet designs are so far-reaching, a land as geographically accessible and bountifully endowed as hers could not be left undefended. Neutrality was not only the antithesis of all that she stood for in two world wars; it would not be respected if it debarred some conclusive stroke by Russia or the United States—and if she lacked strength to enforce it against either or both. Canada chose sides as a matter of principle. But had she wanted to hold herself neutrally aloof, the map would in any case have compelled her to make a choice.

NATO has the virtue of combining for Canada three historic connections—those with Britain, with France, and with the United States. Her troops and fighter aircraft are stationed in Western Europe; her Navy helps police North Atlantic and North Pacific sealanes. Linked, too, with the common defense is the Arctic vigil that the United States and Canada maintain.

This joint northern endeavor has not, however, been as reassuring for Canada as she thought it would be. Against Russian aircraft and guided missiles three Canadian-American radar warning lines have been strung across Canadian soil; Canadian personnel have, at some points, had to supplant American, lest Canadian sovereignty over the vast Canadian northland be queried. There are islands in the Arctic archipelago that possess rich natural resources and in which Canada has not made her occupation effective. American submarines traverse waters below the polar ice pack, and its air space may be useful commercially as well as strategically. Over Canadian claims in that area discord may also arise.

For the United States, on the other hand, it is fortunate that the Soviet menace loomed from the north rather than the south. With Canada she has made strategic arrangements that would have been feasible with no other power in the Western Hemisphere. And the attention of the United States, as leader of the West, is thus less likely to be distracted from other East-West theaters.

The nature of the North American Air Defense Command illustrates the state of Canadian-American amity—the operational unity that propinquity imposes, the degree of detachment that Canada still preserves. At headquarters in Colorado, a Canadian air marshal is deputy to an American general—though Canadian governments were reluctant in pre-NATO days to hand their forces over to any but the highest wartime British or allied generalissimo. The North American Air Defense Command is responsible, however, to both Washington and Ottawa—not just to Washington.

It is, besides, the only American command that has been authorized to fire nuclear weapons without prior approval by the White House—a prerogative, world-shaking in its potential effect, that, during the absence of the American commander, might be exercised by a Canadian deputy. Canada, like Britain, has been worried since the Korean War by hazards that lurk in American direction of the strategic interlock; but as far as she is involved by an attack on North America, she will have a voice in its use. Washington and Ottawa have, in addition, established a number of governmental boards for Canadian-American co-operation, and there is a supervisory Cabinet Committee on Joint Defense.

A familiar note may be detected throughout. Canada's insistence upon equality of status had made her an architect of the First Commonwealth. Britain, however, no longer leads the West and it is largely in concert with the United States that measures of preparedness must be taken. What, then, a shift in primacy will signify for Canada is a change of venue rather than attitude.

A status that is protected in the sphere of operational commitments can, all the same, be jeopardized by other circumstances. The main target of any Russian air assault on North America will, of course, be the United States; it is proper, therefore, that for repelling one, the latter should pay most of the cost. But Canadian skies are not merely the first line of North American defense. The home bases of the Strategic Air Command and the North American launching sites of the intercontinental missile are repositories of the West's over-all deterrent; when Canada helps to safeguard these, she discharges wider obligations. A proportionate contribution to every phase of Canadian-American defense has, however, proven too expensive. In the European theater, Canadian land

and ancillary air forces are equipped to carry out NATO engagements. But Canada's own home theater in North America must also be held.

Offense is still the best defense, and long-range offense in the age of nuclear-missile warfare would be beyond her means. Though Canada shared in the early development of the first atomic bombs she has since devoted herself to the civil uses of nuclear energy. Major weapons would be futile without vehicles for delivery—without heavy and medium bombers or long-range missiles; Canada has, all the same, bolstered the defense of North America with fighter aircraft. Neither the United States nor other NATO allies would, however, purchase a new fighter that she wished to manufacture, and she could not afford to produce it solely for her own defense. In 1959, Canada decided to rely mostly on the latest devices and interceptor missiles of the ground control radar scheme that she and the United States had been building.

Her interceptor-missile scheme should be effective as long as key points in North America can be threatened by long-range Soviet bombers. An early warning system against ballistic missiles is also being constructed by the United States. It was argued that an active continental defense might still be useful. Canada has had to adopt a more static one.

After the outbreak of World War II, Canada prided herself on the rank of Middle Power. But a varied armament is required to uphold her new status, and in that crucial sphere a heavier load than anticipated may have to be borne.

There is as close co-operation in space and defense sciences between Canada and the United States as between the United States and Britain. Yet such is the nexus between preparedness and status that Britain has made a special effort in the field of war technology; over this very issue France was to fall out with her chief English-speaking allies. Canada, however, has been overtaken by that revolution of bigness, by those changes in war technology, through which rank in international affairs may finally be determined. Her status as a Middle Power, her capacity to mediate within the Commonwealth, between the United States and Britain, or at the United Nations, were not only governed by historic ties; a relative strategic invulnerability also gave her a certain political leeway. But she is no longer as secure as she once was and that can affect her role.

As for a more potent American influence, this is not only felt by Commonwealth countries such as Britain and Canada. Australia and New Zealand, as members of the Commonwealth's

Atlantic-Pacific wing, have also had to adjust themselves to it. They do not, however, have the same geographic locale as Canada; and so American leadership does not impinge on them in quite the same way. All three welcome it. But Canada preserves her national identity by establishing inner and outer counterweights to the continental supremacy of the United States. The regional presence of American power is, conversely, what Australia and New Zealand have first had to ensure.

This has been for them a wholly new departure. Unlike Canada, they have not had to develop under the shadow of a nation outside the Britannic realm; and from that realm, until the primacy of the West shifted across the Atlantic, there had been little to divert their gaze. After World War I, as a matter of fact, Australia and Canada disagreed over whether or not the Anglo-Japanese Alliance should be renewed. When Ottawa persuaded London to drop it, Anglo-American friendship was upheld and Canada extricated from a painful dilemma. But two decades later, when Australia was saved from Japanese invasion at the Battle of the Coral Sea, American and Australian forces fought side by side.

Nor will Australians soon forget lessons taught by World War II. Their loyalty to the Crown, their positive attitude toward the Commonwealth, are still governed by ties of kinship with the people of the British Isles—and while other European immigrants do not possess the latter, they can accept the former. What has to be considered is the growth of hostile Chinese air power bordering the western Pacific; the wartime danger of Russian submarines in nearby waters; the prospect that, in any emergency, traffic between the Antipodes and Europe will have to ply routes longer than the old British lifeline through Suez. In some outlying phases of regional defense, it is with Britain that Australia and New Zealand still principally co-operate. Their basic security, as that power retrenches strategically, has had to be underwritten by the United States.

A number of current issues illustrate the new trends. Elsewhere in the Commonwealth, American support of the Formosan regime has been regarded as a stumbling block between Communist China and the West; for the defense of Australia, Canberra wishes Formosa kept out of Peking's grasp. So, also, it wants Britain to cling to Singapore, a naval base whence Japan threatened Australia during World War II. Singapore might be rendered useless by a pro-Soviet Indonesia. Australia and New Zealand joined with

Britain to suppress Communist insurrectionaries in Malaya and to protect the Malayan Peninsula.

The United States entered the picture through the Southeast Asian Security Treaty and the Anzus Pact. Canberra and Wellington waited to sign the first of these agreements until Washington had done so; by means of the second, the United States has guaranteed the *status quo* in the Antipodes. Australia and New Zealand had to be reassured about defense arrangements between Tokyo and Washington. But what the Anzus Pact has really done is fortify English-speaking allies in the South Pacific against the fresh menace of Communist China.

Willingly or unwillingly, Britain did not participate—though she had substantial interests of her own in the region, and though it vexed her to see three of her closest associates combine without her. Formerly, before key bastions of British oversea power had crumbled, Antipodean members of the Commonwealth could help Britain fend off enemies at a distance—hence their war efforts in the Middle East. During the Suez crisis of 1956, when Ottawa as well as Washington opposed the Anglo-French expedition, Australia backed the British. The West's grip on the Middle East had, however, long been relaxing. The dangers with which Australia has chiefly been preoccupied since Pearl Harbor have lain nearer home.

One of these, the possibility that Communist China might win over Indonesia, has receded of late. But that feckless archipelago is situated across the Timor Sea from Australia and contends that it is the rightful heir to all Dutch colonies in the vicinity. The Netherlands has not relinquished Western New Guinea, and, as Australia is entrenched in the eastern half of New Guinea, she desires her Dutch neighbors to stay where they are. In Eastern New Guinea is the Australian dependency of Papua and a United Nations trust territory that Australia administers. And if the Dutch should tire of their thankless task, it will no doubt pass to Canberra rather than Jakarta. For Australia cannot permit an extension of Indonesian misrule to an adjacent island that is a buffer between her and the troubles by which East Asia is beset.

Washington and London are embarrassed, nevertheless, by differences between Jakarta and Canberra. On this issue Russia has come out for neutralist Indonesia. Nor can the United States uphold her two allies, the Netherlands and Australia, without incurring the ill will of anticolonial friends. After World War II, when Washington, London, and Canberra favored Indonesian independence, The Hague was angered; now Washington is chided by anticolonial elements for not demanding that Dutch New Guinea be ceded to Indonesia. Racially, the inhabitants of New Guinea are not the same as the people of Indonesia. But in Asia, when imperialism is of Asian or Eurasian origin, it is, somehow, not always deemed imperialism.

Moreover, it is not merely the goodwill of the Netherlands and the security of Australia that American policymakers have to maintain. There is a direct American interest. The Dutch offer naval facilities in New Guinea; this colony is one of a chain of allied bases that stretches up the western Pacific from Australia, through the Philippines, Formosa, Okinawa, and Japan, to the Aleutian Islands. And as the West loses East Asian footholds, these island outposts bulk large in its global strategy.

Then, too, the sphere of weapons and logistics is a mirror of circumstances by which Australian policy has been reshaped. At Woomera, Australia provided Britain with her principal testing range for guided and ballistic missiles. But communications through Suez would probably be choked off during wartime; it will be safer for Australia to depend on a supply line to the United States. Standardization with American weapons and aircraft has therefore been adopted.

Not that perfect concord reigns between Australia and the United States. As in Canada, corporate American capital has not allowed Australians to share in the control and earnings of American branch companies. The old Commonwealth attachment to Britain is still cherished. But intermingled with it is a new, decisive tie-up with the United States.

And the same dual commitment prevails in New Zealand. Her troops are stationed with British and Australian forces in Malaya. Under the SEATO and Anzus treaties she must also act with the United States in defense of the South Pacific and Southeast Asia. As an exporter of wool, meat, and dairy produce, she turns largely to the British market. It was, however, by a loan from Wall Street that she tided over the economic recession of 1957–58. In Western Samoa, New Zealand had administered a United Nations trusteeship, while the United States was still ensconced in eastern Samoa. Here it is New Zealand rather than the United States which has been liquidating a benevolent colonial rule.

The American attitude toward the future of Antarctica has, moreover, been of concern to both New Zealand and Australia. For that inhospitable continent lies close to the Antipodes. Russia has established a base for scientific exploration in a sector of Antarctica that Australia claims; Canberra has been anxious about Soviet encroachments. Antarctica can furnish valuable weather information; in the space age it is particularly well located for scanning the skies and for monitoring weapons tests. Air routes across Antarctica could, as a matter of fact, be important in both peace and war. It would be dangerous if hostile air, missile, or submarine bases were built there. The Suez Canal could be blocked by political or enemy action, while air-atomic weapons might even rob the Panama Canal of its immunity. The West must therefore protect the use of Antarctic waters for traffic between the Pacific and Atlantic and the Atlantic and Indian Oceans.

Agreement over the question of Antarctica would, nevertheless, be difficult to achieve. Britain has long disputed the claims of Chile and Argentina at the South Pole; no special rights, whether of Britain, Chile, and Argentina, France and Norway, Australia and New Zealand, have been recognized by either the United States or Russia. Existing claims were left as they were and new ones precluded; international administrative arrangements had to be adopted. Ports and airfields in New Zealand are used by the United States as jumping-off ground for Antarctica. Canberra and Wellington looked to Washington in this matter rather than London. For here, as in other major aspects of policy, it is from the United States that Australia and New Zealand must now also take their cue.

THE PROBLEM OF AFRICA

The Atlantic-Pacific wing of the Commonwealth is, however, not the only one to be affected by the East-West contest and the shift from Britain to the United States in the leadership of the West. In Asia and Africa other Commonwealth powers breed differences that govern their reaction to these epoch-making changes. Though India and Pakistan have much in common, they are ready to leap at each other's throats; between Ghana, Nigeria, and South Africa, the chasm could not be bridged. South Africa's doctrine of white supremacy is, moreover, at variance with progressive colonial policies that Britain has been pursuing elsewhere on the African continent. Hated by the Afro-Asian wing of the Commonwealth, frowned on by its other former partners, the South African Republic is an Ishmaelite whose main adversary is, *au fond*, the twentieth century.

Once Asian and African countries were admitted as sovereign equals to the councils of the Commonwealth and thus to membership in the United Nations, they were bound to emphasize African questions. Yet when they do so the English-speaking peoples—the Atlantic-Pacific branch of the Commonwealth as well as the United States—must proceed with caution. The defense of Africa is essential to the defense of the West. On the one hand, Africans, with their newly-awakened race-consciousness, must not be driven into the arms of Russia; on the other hand, the Republic of South Africa is the most westernized state on the African continent, and to its security her contribution is important. Commonwealth relations below the Sahara are sorely vexed. For Britain as a colonial power has one set of interests there, South Africa as an African power has another, while anticolonial partners have been a goad to both. Nor, as leader of the West and ally of Britain, can the United States be indifferent to the way Commonwealth issues in Africa unfold.

Under the doctrine of white supremacy, those in South Africa itself whose hue is black, brown, or mixed have been segregated and disfranchised. Britain's own African territories are, however, administered with solicitude for the welfare of dependent peoples. Harm is still done, all the same, when color bars are raised in the British Isles against resident minorities from the West Indies and British Africa or against Afro-Asian members of the Commonwealth. Britain's role as center of a multiracial Commonwealth did not permit her to restrict the immigration of colonial or Commonwealth subjects after the unfortunate race riots of 1958. As a matter of fact when immigration laws, local ordinances, or social customs anywhere in the Commonwealth have discriminated against the citizens of its non-white partners, their faith in the entire Commonwealth association has been shaken.

Nor in this respect is the British connection with the United States an unalloyed boon. The latter gets credit in African eyes as a power that has diverged from Britain and other Atlantic allies on colonial issues. Praise from Africa and Asia alike will be more wholehearted when the racial inequities of American life are less flagrant.

Africa, above the Sahara, is part of the Mediterranean and Middle Eastern zone of world politics. Increasingly, nevertheless, the rest of the African continent has been influenced by what goes on there. The United Nations Economic Commission for Africa treats it as a single whole. But Africa, below the Sahara, is regarded as a separate region in itself by the Commission for Technical Co-operation that has been established by the colonial and independent powers of the area. In South Africa, as Lord Hailey has argued, the doctrine of white supremacy may spring from the desire to maintain high living standards; among the indigenous peoples of British Africa, the problem may well be one of a political advance that is faster than economic conditions warrant. It is complicated, moreover, by white settlements. For then the appeal of native Africans is not against London but to London against the newcomers.

And this is in contrast to the situation that obtains in strategic outposts of the British power structure. For these are multiracial societies in which majorities clamor for a self-determination that might, instead, serve alien interests. So far, in the multiracial societies of British Africa, the goal has been one of Africa for Africans.

Orderly progress under British tutelage is, however, the last thing which Russia and Egypt, as foes of the West, have wanted for British Africa. Pan-Arab propaganda has not only been beamed by the Cairo radio to North Africa and the Middle East; Swahili has been employed for broadcasts against Britain in her East African dependencies. These endeavors, moreover, dovetail with those of the Soviet Union which, as it penetrates African territories, preens itself on being their champion against colonial masters. In Africa, as in Latin America, the Communist Chinese are also busy. And such ferment may have one dire outcome which, by paralyzing the defense of Africa, could impair the over-all defense of the West—as a counter to white dominance a pan-African racism might be set ablaze. Not that patronage by Russia or China portends a lighter yoke: in the long run the destructive furies of African racism may likewise be vented upon it. But even in the short run Africans themselves must take care lest, by an indiscriminate anticolonialism, the interests furthered are not their own.

Will they have statesmen who perceive this danger? A longer acquaintance with modern technology, a populace that is not multiracial in composition—these have allowed the West Coast of British Africa to move more rapidly than the East Coast towards independence. By the elevation of Ghana and Nigeria to equality of status and to membership in the Commonwealth, Britain herself scored a debating point not only against Soviet tyranny but against her own anticolonial partners and allies. Much in the cause of African self-government hangs on the capacity of these two new Commonwealth countries to meet the needs of their own people. The manner in which they hew a path between East and West will be no less significant.

Dr. Kwame Nkrumah, the founder of Ghana, has collaborated with other independent African states to project a distinctive African personality. Yet there are hurdles to surmount at home before wider objectives can be accomplished.

Ghana's domestic problem is that of reconciling the Ashanti of the interior and her northern territories to a centralized political system. Tribal chiefs have been shorn of their ancient rights. But cocoa exports from Ashanti districts are what have permitted the country to prosper and enabled it to contribute substantially to the sterling area's dollar pool. The aim is to diversify a one-crop economy. Ghana may produce aluminum from her bauxite deposits when, with private assistance from British, Canadian, and American companies, a big dam is built across the Volta River. Yet how safe, in a politically radical environment, will private non-African investment always be? Does Ghana, do other newly independent African countries, have enough citizens with skill and probity to run a modern state? Does the Soviet bloc have the means to slip in wherever the West is bashful?

Ghana has not, as a matter of fact, been oblivious to the spirit of goodwill in which, towards the last, she was shepherded by Britain towards democracy and nationhood. The experiment of parliamentary institutions and civil liberties may falter; Ghana must not only retain the confidence of British and American friends but of others in Africa who aspire to freedom. Becoming a Commonwealth republic, she has, in constitutional and external affairs, taken Nehru's India as her mentor. She may do business with the Soviet bloc. When the former Belgian Congo was reduced to chaos in 1960, it looked as though Ghana would do more to further Russian ambitions in Africa than her own. But against the sterile pan-Asian rancors of the Bandung Powers, Ghana has taken assistance from Israel. To the chagrin of Cairo, the emphasis has been on a pan-African rather than Afro-Asian grouping.

And yet the loose union with Guinea and Mali into which Ghana has entered could make things awkward for fellow members of the Commonwealth. Guinea and Mali had seceded from the new Franco-African community. The French, bickering with Britain over the Common Market and nourishing other grievances against both of her principal English-speaking allies, suspected at first a plot to enlarge the Commonwealth at their expense.

Failing to consult Commonwealth associates, Ghana had actually contravened Commonwealth procedures. Her own future in any Ghana-Guinea-Mali union is rendered economically difficult by the fact that she relies on Imperial Preference for oversea markets and adheres to the sterling area, while Guinea and Mali have belonged to the franc zone. Guinea, moreover, groomed for independence in the French political tradition, toys with Marxist ideas, has numerous contacts with the Soviet bloc, and is a one-party state; Ghana, though authoritarian, is more moderate. What Kwame Nkrumah, President of Ghana, has been seeking is a West African federation as a first step towards all-African unity. But as Nigeria emerges his country may take a back seat. He therefore made his move before Nigerian rivals could do so.

The alignment of African states with the East would not merely be contrary to the general interests of the West. For specific geographical reasons of her own, the United States would dislike an anti-Western orientation on the West Coast of Africa. Countries situated on the hump of Africa, or just below it, face that oceanic expanse of the South Atlantic over which Anglo-American naval power has long been predominant. This would be hampered by a Russian submarine base and radio installation in Guinea. Soviet footholds in North Africa could menace the Mediterranean route and turn Europe's Mediterranean flank. So, too, when the peoples of the West African coastline are slanted towards the West rather than the East, Latin America and the United States will be strategically more secure.

And here the position of Nigeria is noteworthy. For she is not only the most populous of African states; she conceives of Commonwealth membership in pro-Western terms. Ghana achieved independence before she did because Nigerians could not agree among themselves. Nigeria is divided politically, ethnically, and religiously into three main districts—all of which depend upon each other economically and are watered by the same Niger river system.

Ghana is a unitary state. Nigeria must necessarily be a federation. As a representative democracy, Ghana may leave much to be desired; Nigerians have incorporated safeguards in their federal constitution: parliamentary forms and the rule of law can only be abridged with the consent of regional components. Then, too, there are the tribal chiefs who retain a traditional, if not an institutional, influence. Two-thirds of Nigeria lives, however, in the semifeudal north and fears subordination to the more westernized southerners. As a poor, backward Moslem region, it tends to turn to Cairo for guidance. And yet no section of the country is more disposed to perpetuate Nigeria's stance as a Commonwealth monarchy.

But the first question that independence and Commonwealth membership must pose is not how changes in status will be utilized externally. It is whether, with British suzerainty removed, Nigeria can be kept as a single unified state from falling entirely to pieces. Will Dr. Nkrumah's relatively strong hand at home enable Ghana to vie with a larger, disunited Nigerian state in setting goals for African nationalism? Nigeria, if she holds together, may have her own ideas of how to organize a West African or even a pan-African union. Nor is it only in regard to this that Lagos may be disinclined to give heed to Accra. Nigeria is less neutralist in outlook. Communist trends in the Cameroons, next door, may prove disquieting. A defense treaty with Britain reveals, at any rate, that on foreign policy Nigeria will not let Ghana do her thinking for her.

With some exceptions the Commonwealth may be split between members that are neutralist and powers that are committed, under an American lead, to the defense of the West. But Nigeria's attitude, like that of Malaya, demonstrates how Commonwealth affiliation can, in itself, be a bond with the West.

Elsewhere on the West Coast there is a former British dependency—the colony and protectorate of Sierra Leone—on which independence has also been bestowed. With her mineral resources, among them diamonds and iron ore, she might attain economic viability. But illicit mining and smuggling of diamonds deprives the government of its revenue. Will Sierra Leone's Commonwealth membership preclude union with Guinea and Liberia?

Racially homogeneous, British dependencies on the West Coast of Africa have thus moved more rapidly than others toward independence within the Commonwealth. Tribalism is an obstacle, however, which African nationalism in all parts of sub-Saharan Africa has yet to surmount. A pan-African racism might incite Africans against the West. Would a deep-seated parochialism turn Africans against each other? The road to independence may be less smooth in dependencies whose population is multiracial. Yet self-governing institutions might break down, ambitious schemes of larger unity will be unworkable, if tribal heterogeneity among Africans themselves is not overcome.

When Belgium failed to train Congolese for self-government, the new Congo republic collapsed. But in that tragic episode there was a lesson for African nationalists as well as for their friends in the West.

Meanwhile it is not merely the multiracial character of East Coast dependencies that keeps them in turmoil and harasses their British suzerain. There is the proximity of Nasserist Egypt and all that her agents have done to foment unrest against Britain and the West. The Cairo radio broadcasts in African dialects; messages beamed by Peking to eastern and central Africa are in English. And what actuates Egypt is regional as well as general policy.

It is through the construction of the Aswan Dam that she plans to improve her economy. The headwaters of the Nile run, however, through the Sudan and for these that country also has uses of its own. The Sudan, a mixture of Arab and Negro elements, is no longer ruled by an Anglo-Egyptian condominium but by a military dictatorship. And it is in the British interest to have her withstand Egyptian pressure; an independent Sudan provides a barrier between Egypt and such British territories in East Africa as Kenya, Uganda, and Tanganyika—lands that also possess one of the sources of the Nile. During and after the summer of 1956 the project of the Aswan Dam figured in Egypt's rupture with the West and in consequent Soviet efforts to penetrate the Nile basin. Then, too, on the coastal fringe of the area, on the Red Sea and the Gulf of Aden, the West has strategic interests which also have to be considered.

The advent of independence to Italian Somaliland had, for instance, compelled Britain to grant British Somaliland a degree of self-government to which other dependencies were more entitled. And union with Somali neighbors has followed. The former protectorate may have thought it would benefit a greater Somalia to join the Commonwealth. Somalia, however, is an impoverished land which Egypt has brought under pan-Arab influence and which Russia might assist economically. The outer edge of the Horn of Africa jutting forth into the Gulf of Aden and the Indian Ocean may thus pass from the jurisdiction of the West. It is from Aden that Britain has watched over transit through the Suez Canal, controlled the Persian Gulf with its oil riches, and kept an eye on the oceanic communications of the region. The Yemeni neighbor of that strategic outpost enrolled in the United Arab States. Now Aden may be checkmated across narrow waters by an Egyptian or pro-Soviet foothold on the Somali promontory.

Somali turbulence is a danger also to Ethiopia. Somalia

wants to annex portions of French Somaliland, Ethiopia, and Kenya in which fellow Somalis dwell. When, at any rate, the Emperor Haile Selassie dies, it may be difficult to hold together the Coptic Christian Kingdom. Russian interest in the region was revealed during 1959 when Moscow granted Ethiopia a larger loan than she could use. Ethiopia's Lake Tana is, moreover, the main source of the Blue Nile. It is therefore a constant temptation for Egypt to meddle in the affairs of that country.

The United States, however, has an interest of her own in the sovereign independence and territorial integrity of the Amharic kingdom. She may do less than the Soviet bloc to assist it with loans and investments. But when she furnished Haile Selassie with arms, he permitted her to install an Air Force radio station at Asmara and to use docking and naval facilities at the port of Massawa on the Red Sea. For the East–West contest carries the United States far afield, and now she has even acquired a toehold on the African ledge of the Middle East.

This particular area is, as a matter of fact, one where two species of African self-determination are typically in conflict. Ethiopia seeks to preserve her nationhood; Somalis, with instigation from Egypt, may endeavor to undermine it. The prototypes for British dependencies are Ghana and Nigeria. Will Britain be able to repeat her experience with them?

The situation with which she has had to cope elsewhere is a much more complicated one. The apparatus of self-government that evolved on the West Coast rested on a substratum of racial equality; racial inequality retarded a similar development on the East Coast. The cool highlands of Kenya had, for example, invited European settlement; and to that, the Mau Mau outrages were an extreme African reaction. Spokesmen for six million indigenous Kenyans have spurned multiracial constitutions that under British auspices might have preserved the privileges of some sixty thousand Europeans and two hundred thousand Asians.

Whether paper safeguards were worth much, British settlers themselves came to doubt. But on the West Coast there are not only greater natural resources; there are also more qualified Africans for private business and public administration. Non-African minorities are the ones in Kenya that have training and enterprise; if these are uprooted or submerged the country will be set back. Social progress is a nationalist aim. And yet as the economy deteriorates, a black dictatorship, Communist or non-Communist, may be what supplants white supremacy.

In the end the British have had little choice. As a state will Kenya be viable when a fuller emancipation is accorded? There can be no democracy when that is withheld; and it can scarcely be withheld when neighbors as close as Uganda and Tanganyika march towards it. Self-government is, moreover, a prerequisite for independence within the Commonwealth—a status for Kenya that African nationalists have envisaged.

It is, as a matter of fact, three sub-Saharan countries with which Britain is deeply concerned—Kenya, Central Africa and the South African Republic—where a question raised in the former Belgian Congo recurs. Can non-Africans, even in economies that they have built up, maintain a residuum of their racial prerogatives? The South African Republic and the Central African Federation, though their attitudes are not the same, believe that they can. Britain, on the other hand, has, as a colonial power, been trying to coach rather than curtail African nationalism. But in Kenya she has not only had multiracial circumstances to ponder. There is a defense item to be considered and one which her American ally cannot belittle.

Now that Egypt, as master of Suez, might cut the British lifeline, Kenya has also become a strategic outpost. On one side of that Egyptianized artery are Malta and Cyprus; on the other, Aden, which can be supplemented through air transport by troops of the British strategic reserve stationed in Kenya for operations in the Middle East. The port of Mombasa, lying along the Indian Ocean, is part of a Kenya Protectorate for which Britain pays rent to the Sultan of Zanzibar. With the departure of the Royal Navy from Bombay in India and from Trincomalee in Ceylon, it may serve as a regional base in the British oversea power structure. But the territory is one that a self-governing Kenya would probably want to annex. Nationalist politicians have objected to the strategic reconversion of Mombasa on neutralist grounds. Guarantees like those that Cyprus has accepted may be sought. And yet the British dilemma has a certain bearing on the responsibilities of the United States as leader of the West. Americans have encouraged the cry of indigenous Kenyans for independence. But when its accents are neutralist, the defense of the West may be hampered.

Less serious in effect is the communal clash on the two islands of the Zanzibar Protectorate farther down the coast. Here there is a population of three hundred thousand which mainland nationalists, together with the Cairo and Peking radios, have stirred up against Britain. But differences between a large Arab minority and the African majority tend to delay grants of self-government and prolong British rule.

Uganda, a British protectorate, presents another tangled skein of affairs. In Uganda, there is a relatively small number of Europeans and Asians; Ugandans are divided, however, among themselves. The kingdom of Buganda is more advanced than the other three provinces which fear domination by it; it has sought independence, and now, if British authority is maintained, may want a federal rather than a unitary constitution for the country as a whole. When Uganda obtains self-government, Buganda will have to bow to majority rule. Without Buganda the country cannot exist as an economic and political entity. Meanwhile, there is propaganda by Peking, and, as Russia tries to establish footholds in Ethiopia and the Congo, Uganda could serve as a conduit between them.

In Tanganyika, a former United Nations trust territory, African nationalism has been able to progress without violence. It has few Europeans and Asians; a multiracial constitution would therefore point the way to independence with Commonwealth rank as its concomitant. In Tanganyika, as elsewhere, tribal chiefs might not yield prerogatives readily. But her future may be decided by what happens in neighboring countries. Nyasaland and parts of Northern Rhodesia are eager to secede from the Central African Federation and might wish to join her. As African nationalism presses onward, the map of Africa may be redrawn.

For administrative and strategic reasons, the British themselves had favored a sectional unification of African dependencies. Cape-to-Cairo and *Mittelafrika* were the forgotten dreams of rival empire builders; later on, nevertheless, common necessities evoked a similar approach. There has, in fact, been an East African High Commission through which the governors of separate British dependencies can act together. As long as white settlers enjoy special privileges in Kenya, it is unlikely that the African nationalists of Uganda and Tanganyika will agree to an outright merger. These three countries nevertheless border upon Lake Victoria, by which the White Nile is fed. It is vital for Egypt that the flow through the Sudan of the White as well as of the Blue Nile should be maintained. But Kenya, Tanganyika, and Uganda must also utilize the waters of their own lake for the purposes of irrigation and electrification. And when treaty rights with Egypt are renegotiated, a single view will have to be presented on their behalf.

Will a closer union eventuate as they fend for themselves?

Separately or together would they, like Ghana and Nigeria, opt for membership in the Commonwealth? Tribal animosities might fade, differences in custom and tenure might decline, where industrialism is introduced, if an urbanized Negro proletariat were cut from traditional moorings. Moreover, local independence movements get a unifying stimulus from the West Coast. But it is only half the story to say that colonial powers and white settlers can no longer turn back the clock. How well equipped are the indigenous peoples of the East Coast to keep the clock going?

In Central Africa, Britain has to cope with a still more baffling problem. For there the question is not that of linking together separate political entities but of preserving a union that already exists. Far ahead of East African countries as a modern autonomous state, the Central African Federation of Rhodesia and Nyasaland is a patchwork of inequalities, constitutional, ethnic, and economic. And these are what have debarred it from full membership in the Commonwealth circle. Of its three sections, Southern Rhodesia has been a self-governing colony, while Northern Rhodesia and Nyasaland are British protectorates. The latter have their own legislative councils but the Colonial Office in London watches over native rights.

Southern Rhodesia, with a population of 225,000 Europeans and 2,600,000 Africans, dominates the Federation. There are 2,250,000 Africans and more than 70,000 Europeans in Northern Rhodesia; in Nyasaland, which has between 5,000 and 10,000 Europeans, there are 3,000,000 Africans. What the Central African Federation has sought is some middle way between the Boer racism of its South African neighbor and the slogan of "one man, one vote" that African nationalism disseminates. Equal rights for all "civilized" men was the famous dictum of Cecil Rhodes. A recipe for racial partnership, it is one under which few Africans seem to qualify and, despite concessions, a white settler minority is still on top.

The Nyasaland Protectorate never wanted to enter the Central African Federation, and Northern Rhodesia also seethes with discontent. Between its three components there has, all the same, been a real community of interest. It took the Europeans of Southern Rhodesia to tap the natural resources of Northern Rhodesia; furnishing migrant labor, Nyasaland badly needs the subventions that the Federation provides. Economically, the Protectorate would not fare as well if it seceded and joined Tanganyika. But what would happen to Southern Rhodesia if the Federation were thus split asunder? Together with the Northern

Rhodesian copper belt—other parts of Northern Rhodesia accompanying Nyasaland—she might still flourish as a wholly independent state. And yet to annex or carve up Northern Rhodesia would be to flout British authority in the Protectorate. Will Southern Rhodesia unite with South Africa? To such an augmented union the British will not lightly relinquish the Africans of Northern Rhodesia.

Not that the Boers would rejoice over an increase in the size of South Africa's English-speaking population. But the Rhodesias, as a whole or in part, do not only offer vast resources; rather than let hostile forces get control, South Africa will have to move in. Yet that must also mean the subjection of resident Africans to Boer racism. Britain conceived of the Central African Federation as a dike against this. British policy, if the Federation disintegrates, will have miscarried. Differences over the doctrine of white supremacy impelled South Africa to withdraw from the Commonwealth. Equal status within the Commonwealth is what the Central African Federation has demanded. Its own breakup may ensue.

Between two adjacent sectors of the Britannic realm there are thus contrasting disparities. On the one hand, in East African dependencies, economic growth does not match political developments; in the Central African Federation, on the other, political developments have been accelerated but are outpaced by economic progress. And in this, the United States has a substantial interest. Private American capital did much to develop Northern Rhodesia's copper belt; there have also been loans by the American government. African unrest and political uncertainty may, as in the case of South Africa, frighten away British and American investors. But the Federation's mineral wealth is of military as well as economic value to the West.

The copper mines of Northern Rhodesia are inferior to those of the United States and Chile in the amounts produced but in quality of ore are second to none. The Federation also has coking coal, asbestos, and chromite in abundance. Territorially extensive, the country has a mild climate; one hydroelectric project, that of the Kariba Gorge on the Zambesi River between Northern and Southern Rhodesia, promises a degree of further industrialization as great as any on the African continent. The land could, moreover, be a brace of regional defense for the British oversea power structure. The armed forces of Britain and the Central African Federation co-operate closely.

Politically, nevertheless, European settlers are in a cleft

stick: they cherish their loyalty to the Crown; yet the racial inequities that they uphold have prevented the Federation from attaining the same Commonwealth rank as such all-African countries as Ghana and Nigeria. It was, in fact, the insistence of white settlers upon equality of status that fanned the flame of rebellion in Nyasaland. Not that African nationalists dislike the Commonwealth idea. But when the Central African Federation achieves a fully independent status, Britain must forfeit the reserve powers that she has exercised on behalf of protectorate Africans. The upshot for them might be a permanent servitude, and that is what they will not stomach. Their quarrel is with Salisbury rather than London. From its repercussions neither Britain nor the rest of the Commonwealth can escape.

Afro-Asian members will, at any rate, now have to approve before the Central African Federation may be elevated to Commonwealth rank. Shorn of Nyasaland, it would still have an African majority that labors under political, social, and economic disabilities. Formed at the time of the Second Commonwealth, it came upon the scene too late. When Britain granted self-government to the South African Union after the Boer War, this was deemed a liberal gesture. More recently, liberal principles were what caused independence to be withheld from the Central African Federation.

Ambivalence is the word for Africa. This is not only illustrated by the political zigzags that Britain has had to follow within her own sphere of responsibility; the position of the South African Republic also makes it difficult for Britain, for other members of the Commonwealth, and for the United States as leader of the West to pursue a straight course. The more progressive policies adopted in sub-Saharan Africa by the British and the French may be a foil to South Africa's ethnic absolutism. It is a serious matter, nevertheless, when 10,000,000 Africans, 1,300,000 of mixed ancestry, and 500,000 Asians are enslaved by 3,000,000 whites—in the name of Western civilization. South Africans may speak solely for themselves. But do enough Africans—and Asians—elsewhere know it?

Racism should be repugnant to the West on grounds of principle. Yet even as a question of expediency, this is hard to condone. For Communism may always present itself as an alternative. It is, nevertheless, because of the East–West contest that the West has hesitated to break with South Africa. The natural resources and geographic situation of the African subcontinent are major counters; least neutralist among the powers of the region, South Africa is militarily the strongest. Aligned with the West, her only specific commitments are with Britain; ill at ease in the dual Commonwealth, the Union did not wish to depart from it. In 1960, after native Africans were shot down at Sharpeville by South African police, many demanded the expulsion of South Africa from the Commonwealth. But while Britain had been outraged by South Africa's racism, the British were reluctant to show her the door. For while the Republic has been a moral liability, it is also a strategic asset.

On one colonial issue that affects them both Britain has been unambiguous. Three British dependencies—the Bechuanaland and Swaziland protectorates and the colony of Basutoland—lie within South African territory or adjacent to it, and she would like to annex them. A million and a quarter Africans live there, however, and they have no desire to exchange British rule for the Republic's doctrine of white supremacy. Imperial authority is maintained, and this is done not to deny but to further human rights.

At the United Nations, however, Britain and the Union have not been as far apart over related issues that come legally within South Africa's own purview. The United Kingdom did not vote against her when South Africa refused to convert a League of Nations mandate for South-West Africa into a United Nations trusteeship. Nor was Britain so outspoken as the United States when South Africa discriminated against Indian residents and oppressed her non-white majority. Under the Charter, the United Nations is forbidden to interfere in the domestic affairs of member states. This prohibition was construed more loosely after 1960 when the Security Council called upon the South African Union to abolish its racist policies. But in the preservation of that ban it is not only the colonial powers of the Commonwealth and NATO which have had an interest.

Upon this topic, their American ally, with her own problem of racial segregation, is also sensitive. In South Africa, it is true, racism is a national policy, while in the United States only the governments of southern states discriminate officially. It would, however, be awkward for American representatives to explain a system of democracy in which constituent states possess rights whereby democracy itself may be mocked. Any lead on this issue by the United States is tempered by her own moral vulnerability.

But here, too, India may be in for a rude awakening. The Asian population of sub-Saharan Africa numbers one million, and, as these resident Asians have been accused of exploiting natives, African mobs have attacked Asian business properties. The mistreatment of migrant Indians by South Africans was what first gave Mahatma Gandhi a sense of mission; in accordance with anticolonial precepts, Delhi assumed that the Asian and African cause is everywhere the same. Yet in Kenya, in Uganda, in the Central African Federation, and in the South African Republic, the Asian minority feels caught between two fires. It cannot do much to protect its own interests. But in a choice between Europeans and Africans, it may yet have to opt for the former.

Their compatriots are supported, however, by home governments. With South Africa, India and Pakistan have had no diplomatic relations; in 1960, other Afro-Asian members of the Commonwealth enlarged India's economic boycott of the Union. During 1956–57, nevertheless, when the Suez Canal was blocked, rerouted Indian vessels used South African ports. The British oversea communications structure had been dislocated. A common interest between Commonwealth powers, antagonistic to each other but dependent upon it, thereupon overrode other differences.

Within the Union, moreover, the Commonwealth has been a bone of contention between South Africans themselves. The European community comprises over 1,700,000 Afrikanders of Dutch stock whose language is Afrikaans, and over 1,200,000 South Africans of British or other Caucasian descent; with few exceptions, its two branches are unanimous about white supremacy. Yet, there is disagreement over the severity with which this should be imposed. English-speaking South Africans and Boer moderates would, besides, respect constitutional processes. To Afrikander nationalists, white supremacy comes before the supremacy of Parliament.

Constitutional processes are identified with Commonwealth traditions, and these are cherished by that English-speaking segment of the European populace which is a minority within a minority. Communal antipathies that date from the South African War, when the British conquered the Boers, have thus been rekindled. And yet Europeans will lose their dominance if they do not stick together. A gerrymandered Parliament may not be fatal. A deeper rift between two sections of the European community might well be.

Not that English-speaking South Africans are likely to join with the native African majority in a multiracial front against Boer racism. A less repressive brand of white supremacy would, for the indigenous African population, still be too repressive. But if the two segments of the European community are completely estranged, the African majority, with support from independent African peoples, may get out of hand. And what might make the breach irreparable is South Africa's withdrawal from the Commonwealth. For external reasons it is not in the national interest to sunder all historic ties. On domestic grounds, too, this has been impolitic.

That is why South Africa voted to become a republic within the Commonwealth rather than secede from it. Other countries which have assumed such status have been able, however, to reconstitute themselves more readily; not so large a fraction of their populace treasures allegiance to the Crown itself. The race-conscious Boers thus subscribed to a formula that India, their chief critic, was the first to adopt. Under it they could have worked off a hereditary grudge against Britain and English-speaking opponents without sacrificing such concrete advantages, at home and abroad, as the Commonwealth association provides. But her racist policies made South Africa unacceptable when she reapplied, as a republic, for Commonwealth membership.

Afrikanders yearn to go it alone. Nevertheless, for the ruling whites (inferior in numbers though superior in techniques) to sever South Africa's connections with the West would be to seal their own doom. Isolated morally and politically, the Republic is not therefore isolationist strategically. For the defense of Africa below the Sahara the South African government has wanted to co-operate with Britain and the United States. But the only American commitment of that sort has been an agreement with Liberia, a West Coast republic founded by Negro freedmen from the United States, early in the nineteenth century.

A treaty with South Africa might indicate acquiescence in Boer racism. Here, with an eye to African and Asian sentiment, the United States has refrained from giving a lead. Other members of the First Commonwealth adjusted themselves to a shift in the primacy of the West. South Africa, as a corollary to American diffidence, did not do so.

The West must, all the same, rely on South Africa for any concerted defense of the African continent. She is the one power with the technological capacity to serve as a regional fulcrum. British strength in the Middle East had long barred a Russian thrust towards Africa. But as that dwindled, pan-Arabism furthered Soviet designs. Now, every indigenous African state that values its independence may also be imperiled. With South Africa they are utterly at odds. Nevertheless, measures taken for continental defense are in their interest as well.

Meanwhile, through commitments with Britain, South Africa aligns herself bilaterally with the West. These envisage a joint land defense of that African continent whose gateway is the Middle East; the security of the sea routes around the Cape must also be ensured. Simonstown, a historic British naval base at the tip of Africa, has been handed over to the Union but it can be used by Britain in peace or war—even, significantly, should South Africa itself be neutral. During World War II, when traffic had to be diverted from the Mediterranean, the control of the shortest alternative route between Europe and the Orient centered on Simonstown; Britain could thus keep in touch oceanically with distant Antipodean units of the Commonwealth, with great Asian dependencies verging on independence, and with numerous outlying portions of the British colonial empire. The importance of South African ports was, moreover, again demonstrated in 1956–57 when Nasser's Egypt blocked the Suez Canal and oil tankers sailing between the Persian Gulf and Western Europe had to circumnavigate the African continent.

With the loss of Bombay and Trincomalee, the Royal Navy has at its disposal fewer suitable ports from which to patrol the Indian Ocean sector of the British communications structure. But there is access to it from Simonstown. Australia and New Zealand have, besides, an interest in this arrangement. Antarctica may be demilitarized. All the same, it is essential for Australia and New Zealand that the Royal Navy keep watch on the passage round the Cape of Good Hope.

Britain and South Africa may have been uneasy in their Commonwealth relationship. But this facilitated a strategic tie-up from which the West as a whole stands to gain. For a gap in Western defenses has been plugged that American leadership itself might never have filled. It is as a signatory of NATO that Canada sits in the councils of the West. Geography decrees that for Australia and New Zealand the Anzus Treaty with the United States should be the formal link. Afrikanders may not be ecstatic about their association with Britain, and yet it is through her that the main contact between the Republic and the West is sustained.

Then, too, South Africa and the Western powers need each other economically. Like the Congo Republic and the Central African Federation, South Africa is endowed with great natural wealth and many strategic minerals. She is renowned for her diamonds; her output of uranium, a by-product of gold mining, has been next to that of Canada and the United States. Britain and most other members of the Commonwealth benefit when the largest gold producer belongs to the sterling area. In trade and finance, South Africa has always looked to the City of London. British and American capital have helped her to grow industrially.

But African labor has also been employed to speed up that expansion—a fact that might upset Boer schemes to separate the races geographically. Less than half of the African population lives in the reserves out of which eight quasi-autonomous Bantustans may be created; the remainder is divided between white settlements, rural and urban. The secondary industries of South Africa cannot develop without an increasing supply of non-white workers; to a project for apartheid that makes fewer rather than more of these available, even Boer employers might object. Africans are excluded from white universities; they may not have trade unions and they cannot strike. But with urbanization and industrial skill comes the ability to organize, to boycott, to withhold labor, to engage in civil disobedience. A pan-African movement has been catching on that is more impatient with multiracial solutions than the African National Congress used to be. For just when Boers try to pen up Africans, the economic progress of the country works against their containment.

Misgivings about South Africa's future have, as in the Central African Federation, already discouraged British and American capital. Nor will an increase in European immigration enable South African industry to dispense with African helots; Boers would only be satisfied with newcomers who are non-Catholic, devoted to white supremacy, and willing to let the Afrikaans culture absorb them. Economic doubts are aggravated, moreover, by fissures within the European community itself. Its English-speaking segment has been the one which runs South African commerce and industry; the agrarian Boers feel, however, that without economic ascendancy their political domination will be incomplete. Yet, they cannot dislodge English-speaking elements financially without wrecking the Republic's prosperity—something in which they likewise share.

Apartheid is, therefore, only one of two items in a dour, Calvinistic gospel, which may not be pushed to a logical conclusion. To dispossess English-speaking South Africans would also be impracticable. And when these retain influence, so does that Commonwealth bond to which they are wedded.

But what might also have perpetuated that bond is the solitary position of South Africa in a world where few can stand alone. Britain differs with her over the issue of race; they agree, nevertheless, that the African continent must be kept within the ambit of the West. Moreover, when these two Commonwealth powers co-operated for defense, their Afro-Asian partners did not demur. South Africa, ostracizing and ostracized, is in a class of her own. But a Commonwealth that includes interventionism and neutralism, parliamentary democracy and authoritarian variants, might have been elastic enough to include her.

There was, as it happened, no room in a multiracial Commonwealth for the South African brand of racism and, on becoming a republic in 1961, South Africa withdrew. Did the refusal of most Commonwealth members to tolerate apartheid mean that henceforth they might sit in judgment on each other's behavior and interfere in each other's domestic affairs? This they could never allow. But did not apartheid have repercussions that made it more than a domestic matter? Most Commonwealth countries seemed, at any rate, to feel that, as a principle of nationhood, racism was an absolute evil; that, in comparison, other violations of democratic practice were relatively venial—if only because, unlike ethnic differences, these were subject to change. The multiracial character of the Second Commonwealth had been confirmed and on its well-being, as on world politics as a whole, the effect might yet be far-reaching.

INDIA, PAKISTAN, AND CEYLON

It is, however, developments in southern Asia rather than sub-Saharan Africa that have done most to shape Commonwealth trends, that have accelerated the transition from the First to the Second Commonwealth. And by these a fresh twist was given to the Anglo-American dialectic. For it was not only Britain which had to work out a new relationship with such Asian members of the Commonwealth as India, Pakistan, Ceylon; so, with a shift in the primacy of the West, did the United States. During the early years of the twentieth century, as the First Commonwealth evolved, it was no simple task to keep Commonwealth partners in agreement on world issues. But, since then, the co-ordination of external policies has been rendered still more arduous by the neutralism which pervades most Afro-Asian capitals of the Commonwealth, and the anticolonialism which pervades them all.

Something else, in addition, influences India and Pakistan.

An invariable touchstone for them has been the undeclared war they have waged against each other.*

The United States, moreover, has vacillated in her attitude towards neutralism and anticolonialism. And this has magnified the range of Anglo-American divergence, actual or potential. Swallowing her own qualms over headstrong American generalship, Britain, during the Korean War, tried to dispel anxiety in Asian capitals of the Commonwealth about an American lead. Nevertheless, after Egypt nationalized the Suez Canal, the United States lined up against Britain, accompanied by forces, Commonwealth and non-Commonwealth, that had also been anti-American.

Suzerain powers could not have withheld independence from greater Asian peoples even if, after the trials and tribulations of World War II, they had so desired. But when free Asian countries slurred over their debt to it, a free world order did not profit as much as might have been anticipated. And this was a contingency the Sino-Soviet camp was to exploit. If Asian neutrals would not enter it, they could at least be dissuaded from going over to the other side. India, above all, was to be the chief Asian prize of the East–West contest. Willy-nilly, and despite her relative military impotence, she thus became, as it were, a global make-weight.

A member of the Commonwealth, India established her independence in the image of British parliamentary democracy. Could she maintain it? Communism on the Left might operate through representative institutions so as to suppress them; reaction on the Right would, if it could, suppress them so as to refashion the government on a more illiberal model. When a Communist regime took office in Kerala the problem it presented was not merely one of provincial misrule. If a ministry that had been lawfully elected were ousted by unconstitutional methods, Communists might employ them in other states and in a bid for office at the center.

In a neutralist vein Indians were loath to admit that these domestic issues were bound up with external ones. But even if Indian Communists did not act at the behest of Moscow and Peking, the questions raised were clear. India is foremost among non-Communist lands requiring economic development, and others will follow suit if dictatorship rather than democracy shows her

---

* The position of Malaya, another Asian member of the Commonwealth, has already been dealt with in this chapter.

the way. A race in social reconstruction between India and China will, then, determine more than the future of India alone; if she is left far behind, the global equilibrium might also be altered.

External policies that embarrassed the West, internal ones that it had every reason to back—such has been the record of India. Economic aid from the United States and Britain and, under the Colombo Plan, from her other Commonwealth partners, may be given with no strings attached; when so much depends on the success of the Indian experiment in social democracy, this is self-justifying democratically. Russia gets more credit for doing less. But the defense of India can be no stronger than her economic strength. The West has been told that in assisting India it must disclaim motivations that arise from the East–West contest. Yet its motivations, and those by which India herself is impelled, are not so far apart as reprimands like these would imply.

A nation of four hundred millions, she is weighed down by a multiplicity of evils. Among these are the most abysmal poverty, mass illiteracy, a caste system that dies hard, a dominant Hindu religion many practices of which are primitive and socially degrading. There are denominational, sectional, and linguistic feuds that, but for a firm hand in New Delhi, could rip the Union asunder; even Gandhi's philosophy of civil disobedience has been transmuted from non-violence into a creed of mob violence. India's food supply is overtaken, moreover, by population growth. To overcome this deficit, Prime Minister Jawaharlal Nehru favored a series of farm co-operatives; elsewhere, however, collectivization of the land has not brought an increase in the production of foodstuffs. Socialism may be India's goal. Her economy is, in the main, still capitalistic.

It was no malicious foreign critic but the revered organizer of Indian nationhood, Jawaharlal Nehru, who once depicted India as a country suffering from a split personality. And sympathetic observers must often have wondered at the degree to which unplumbed emotions have diverted him and his compatriots from what would appear to be a rational calculation of national interest. A coalition strategy that underpins a free world order is, for example, what reinsures India's own defense. She has, nevertheless, impugned this constantly. And she has done the same in her dispute with Pakistan over Kashmir; her ban on a United Nations plebiscite in that northern territory has had the approval of the East rather than the West. Though she castigates the West for its power politics, it is by the use of force that her segment of Kashmir is held.

Patent inconsistencies, they have made her prickly to deal with. The question of abandoning the Commonwealth was raised whenever Britain, like the United States, backed Pakistan over Kashmir in the Security Council. Pakistan averred that India had been handled with kid gloves. Yet her inclusion in SEATO and the Baghdad Pact (now CENTO) was regarded by New Delhi as further evidence that London and Washington have been ranged on the side of its Pakistani antagonist.

Irritating also to New Delhi was the American refusal to endorse India's title to Goa, a Portuguese enclave on the Indian subcontinent. Portugal furnished NATO bases and Washington's reluctance hardened Indian prejudice against coalition strategy. But after the Kennedy Administration approved of an inquiry by the United Nations into the affairs of Portuguese Angola, the Indian claim to Goa was less likely to be disapproved. On the Indian subcontinent itself, moreover, anticolonial India has pursued policies that have not been unequivocally anti-imperialist.

On an intermingling of the rational with the irrational in the conduct of external affairs, India, to be sure, enjoys no monopoly. What bewilders some of her Commonwealth and American friends is the vehemence with which she has railed at others for doing what she also has done. But only on sea frontiers where Anglo-American power still predominates is she secure. Her insecurity is the clue to attitudes that seem mutually inconsonant.

Soviet Russia is within reach and China is next door. Geography would ordain that India be more circumspect towards the East than the West even if there had been no anticolonial doctrine and no coalition strategy to account for a sedulously unneutral rancor. For, at bottom, Indian policymakers have not been worried by the West's contracting imperialism but by the expanding imperialism of their Sino-Soviet neighbors. As Russia penetrates Afghanistan, the entire Indian subcontinent, and not merely Pakistan, might be affected; cold shivers must run down Indian spines at the notion of a tunnel, blasted by Soviet atomic energy, beneath the Himalayan barrier. The fact, moreover, that Kashmir is situated at a northerly junction of Pakistan, Afghanistan, Russia, and China would alone suffice for India's insistence upon the retention of that key province.

Perils that lurked beyond the Himalayan mountain barrier were brought home to India soon after independence had been achieved. China was inert when Britain ruled India, and during the nineteenth century any menace came from Tsarist Russia; today it is a Chinese hegemony that free Asia fears. Communist China had undertaken to respect the autonomy of Tibet, and India was alarmed when she broke her pledge in 1950. Four years later, however, Peking and New Delhi subscribed to *Panch Shila,* the much-touted five principles of Asian coexistence. What these were worth was revealed after Tibet was again suppressed in 1959. For Chinese troops had also crossed Indian frontiers, and India learned she must meet a threat to the integrity of border states such as Bhutan and Sikkim, while Nepal was subject to infiltration.

The Chinese had, moreover, built a highway through a corner of Ladakh, a province in the Indian section of Kashmir. They also laid claim to territory that the Pakistanis hold. The route through Ladakh is the shortest one between western Tibet and southwestern Singkiang—a Chinese area on which Russia has long had her eye. Kashmiri territory might thus figure in Sino-Soviet rivalry for the control of Central Asia. To a better demarcation of this boundary line with Tibet, New Delhi could agree. But when the quadruple forces in play bear so directly on the defense of the Indian subcontinent, India would scarcely be willing to relinquish sovereignty over a disputed Himalayan zone to her weaker Pakistani neighbor.

Scorning the rights and religion of an ancient Buddhist people, Communist China had again put the screws on Tibet and free Asia was aghast. Would New Delhi, after an exchange of asperities with Peking, now bury the hatchet with Pakistan and even sign a pact for the joint defense of the Indian subcontinent? New Delhi was not disposed to alter neutralist policies. Pakistan was aligned with the West, and her alliance with India would infuriate Moscow as well as Peking just when fresh grounds for avoiding Sino-Soviet animus had been revealed. As long, too, as danger from the north underlies India's retention of Kashmir, she would want to keep on it a tighter grip than ever.

Other reasons for New Delhi's recalcitrance may be rooted in differences that first caused the partition of the Indian subcontinent. Under the best of circumstances it was improbable that India could entrust the defense of a strategic province to a Pakistani neighbor whose life expectancy as a viable state might be somewhat dubious. And yet, whatever protracts controversy between India and Pakistan will tend to protract Indian grievances against Washington and London.

There is, for instance, the extent to which Pakistan, as a signatory of SEATO and CENTO, has been equipped with American arms. She promised not to use these against India. But the latter has had a fixed ratio of military superiority over Pakistan. And this cannot be sustained unless India devotes, to an increased arms expenditure of her own, funds earmarked for more fruitful endeavors—some of which the West itself has provided.

What Indians may yet realize is that they have sent their complaints to the wrong address. They have argued that, by its ties with Pakistan, the West introduced the East–West contest to the Indian subcontinent. But, after the subjugation of Tibet in 1959, many perceived that the Sino-Soviet hazards that they face in southern Asia are the same as those confronting the West elsewhere. And Pakistan, which has long known this, will commit national suicide if she attempts to employ American arms against India; any such adventure would only give Moscow and Peking the opportunity they await to intervene and to start whittling down the independence of Pakistan and India alike. An arms race on a subcontinent that is crying out for every sort of social amelioration is indubitably a tragic waste. And yet extra arms are not what the West foisted upon either Pakistan or India but what both must have if, as they bicker with each other, Sino-Soviet designs are to be withstood.

Not that a threat from behind the Himalayas is all that may account for India's quarrel with Pakistan over Kashmir. She has had to consider the future of that Indian democracy which her friends in the West have hoped she would preserve. But for hatred between Moslem and Hindu there might have been no Pakistan; while the latter is Islamic in character, it was as a secular state rather than a Hindu theocracy that the Indian political system was devised. And over 40,000,000 Moslems still live in India among more than 320,000,000 Hindus. As long as nothing is done to stir up the Hindu Right, a repetition of the large-scale horrors that debased the severance of Pakistan from India can be prevented.

But communal antipathies may again burst forth when the Moslems of Kashmir are permitted to decide by plebiscite whether or not to join coreligionists in Pakistan. A holy war proclaimed by the fanatics of Islam in Pakistan would goad Hindu bigots into retaliation against India's Moslem minority. Apart from the question of subcontinental defense, India may therefore rebuff her Moslem neighbor so as to protect the lives, property, and civil rights of her own Moslem citizens.

And if that is so, inconsistency in her treatment of the Kashmir question would be more apparent than real. Liberal procedures might have the most illiberal consequences for a representative democracy that can only progress through national unity and that, without a modicum of communal toleration, cannot stay united.

Pakistan, moreover, may yet exert another kind of influence on the future of Indian democracy. In a number of Asian countries, so as to stop political corruption and forestall Communist inroads, the army had seized the reins of office; when that occurred in Pakistan during the autumn of 1958, New Delhi was afraid that a Pakistani military dictatorship would then try to settle the Kashmir issue by war. This it did not dare to do. But what still perplexes India is the example that Pakistan has set. The Indian Army also enjoys prestige; for a military coup, there might be wide popular support after Jawaharlal Nehru vanishes from the scene. Pointing to the speed with which Communist China modernizes her economy, Indian Communists have been furthering the idea of totalitarian short cuts. If only to head them off, there will be a temptation to jettison Parliament and let the Indian Army, like its Pakistani counterpart, take over.

India may, however, meet threats of dictatorship, Communist or Army, by strengthening her own democracy. Peasant self-government in the villages might be extended; public officials and the Indian middle class can improve their political behavior; more must be done to establish a legitimate Opposition to the Congress Party, one out of which an alternate Ministry could be formed. Can underdeveloped countries build up their economies through representative institutions? Among the free nations of the Orient, India is the most important, and there the test may well be decisive. Strategic commitments are eschewed. Democracy is nevertheless a bond with the West, and here the connection with Britain, renewed nowadays through the Commonwealth tie, has left its mark.

At first, all the same, India seemed inconsistent about this, too. On the one hand her economic aims and constitutional principles stemmed from the West; on the other, measures taken by the West to defend a free world order evoked more censure than what the East did to subvert it. Some of this discrepancy was prompted, no doubt, by the need to placate formidable anti-Western neighbors; some of it, however, did not derive from practical necessities but from impulses whose springs lay deeper. A blend of Gandhi and Machiavelli might be rational enough. It tended to become irrational when a pan-Asian element was added to it.

When India achieved independence, she clung to Western institutions while rebelling against the West emotionally. In the British raj there had been a racist streak and India recoiled from that with her own brand of racism. A call of the blood, not un-mixed with *Schadenfreude,* may have thrilled Asia when imperial Japan routed imperial Russia in 1904–05; when Japan, during World War II, occupied the East Asian and Southeast Asian ter-ritories of European empires; when Communist China held non-Asian powers at bay in Korea. A political consciousness that is pan-Asian might, nevertheless, have spelled danger for an experi-ment in freedom as vast and precarious as India's.

Social democracy is rational in its origins. It evolves within a political framework that the English, French, and American Revolutions of the seventeenth and eighteenth centuries had estab-lished. But against the authentic revolutionary tradition of the West, there is a counterrevolutionary one that the modern totali-tarian state, Right and Left, embodies. The West is never happy about its own manifestations of racism. The degree to which racism is at home in a counterrevolutionary evangel the Germans under Hitler were to exemplify. Counterrevolution is the antithesis of what the Gandhi-Nehru school had visualized. But tendencies that could have been self-defeating were uppermost for a time.

In India, at any rate, the Soviet Union gleaned a propa-ganda windfall from the Afro-Asian fallacy that imperialism can only be equated with color—with the rule of non-whites by whites. For Russia's more publicized or more recent conquests have been in Europe rather than Asia; and during the autumn of 1956 it took weeks for the outraged opinion of the West to elicit from Prime Minister Nehru some belated expression of sympathy with the Hungarian uprising. So far as Indian statesmen let Russia pose as an anticolonial power, they facilitated the Communist penetration of their own country. They thus obtained important backing for the Afro-Asian stand on colonial issues at the United Nations. But they could not put Western powers in the dock with-out suffering on other fronts some loss of their own.

It was, moreover, not only Moscow that reaped where New Delhi had sown, but Peking as well. *Panch Shila,* the five principles of coexistence, were re-enunciated when Nehru and Chou En-lai fraternized during the pan-Asian conclave at Ban-dung. Its luster faded, however, after Communist China wiped out Tibetan autonomy in 1959. In Eastern Europe it was not the

West but the Soviet Union which had extinguished the liberties of other peoples. And then, when imperialism at its most ruthless returned to Asia, an Asian power had been the one to bring it back.

India may have purveyed a pan-Asian doctrine with more zeal than her strategic vulnerability called for. Yet in pro-Chinese endeavors she was not inspired by a general sentiment alone. She did most to urge that the Chinese seat in the Security Council be assigned to Communist China; such a step might make an eruptive neighbor less eruptive. Perhaps, too, behind its separate propitiation of Moscow, New Delhi nurtured the hope—one which some quarters in the West have also shared—that Moscow and Peking can be pried loose from each other. For the Indian subcontinent might be crushed between the jaws of a Sino-Soviet pincers that stretch from the Khyber Pass to Burma. Towards the East, India has had her somersaults to perform; her pan-Asian doctrine may, in its overtones, have been anti-Western as well as anticolonial. And yet, significant also were the undertones of Indian adherence to that Commonwealth of which Britain, with her own oversea holdings, is still the pivot.

For a policy that is footloose but not fancy-free, Jawaharlal Nehru was to repudiate neutralist labels. But an *ad hoc* diplomacy, an active Indian role as spokesman for various Afro-Asian groupings and regroupings, could not mask its essentially isolationist character. Like the United States before she became leader of the West, India would shun entangling alliances; so, too, as far as a free world order must be preserved, she leaves the onus to others. In Victorian days, however, it was possible to escape involvement. Involvement despite isolationism is today what neutralist India must apprehend.

For the idea of peace by power India denounced the West and its American leader. But the Hyderabad and Kashmir episodes revealed that—high-minded disclaimers notwithstanding—India is not entirely averse to the use of force. The East–West contest is, however, on an all-encompassing scale of power. And what India really abhors is the nuclear-missile age, that adaptation of bigness to a war technology upon which the global equipoise reposes. For she has achieved independence only to discover that, with an underdeveloped economy, she can decide her own destiny less than ever.

Sino-Soviet expansion may be what caused the West to band itself together and devise a countervailing strategy. But as none in the East could be admonished as safely for the predicament in which India finds herself, the West had to bear the burden of her wrath. She would be imperiled if a free world order collapsed; she, like others, might not survive the means taken to maintain it. And anticolonialism, even when valid politically and morally, is, by comparison, a secondary issue.

Moreover, what may again be noted is that the coalition strategy that India spurns is not only one over which the United States presides. A number of Commonwealth partners also participate in it. Dissent from them about strategic or colonial matters does not, however, compel India to secede from the Commonwealth. Jawaharlal Nehru had, to be sure, once thought that she should withdraw. But his own predilections were pro-British and he felt that it would be better for India to stay than to depart.*

In the concluding stage of India's bid for independence Britain had, after all, displayed goodwill. It was, in addition, through a British frame of governance that she hoped to further social democracy; a bequest from the British oversea power structure, it was one in which Indians themselves took pride. Self-determination, though first advocated as a liberal ideal, has, in the Occident and Orient alike, often assumed an ugly illiberal guise. And as far as India eludes this, she may do so because educated Indians were schooled to conceive of freedom from Britain in British terms.

The British raj may have laid the groundwork for Indian nationhood by imposing on the Indian mosaic up-to-date communications, a certain administrative unity, and an efficient civil service. But it did more than that. When Indian intellectuals imbibed socialist ideas at Oxford, Cambridge, or London, these were more often Fabian than Marxian. And wherever emancipated Indians were trained in parliamentary arts, a window to the West was opened that they would not willingly shut.

Their use of the English language is, furthermore, something else that must predispose them towards the West. Mass education may tend to supplant this with Hindi; it cannot do so entirely so long as India will have to borrow tools and techniques from others for the modernization of her economy. For the moment, at any rate, a linguistic bond expedites official and unofficial contacts between her and the English-speaking peoples. Another product of the British raj, it is also one for which Russia and China can offer no equivalent.

---

* Frank Moraes, *Jawaharlal Nehru* (New York: The Macmillan Co., 1956), pp. 331 and 414-417; and Michael Brecher, *Nehru* (London: Oxford University Press, 1959), pp. 413-418 and 579-581.

Time may erode these affinities and, if India ever re-
nounces principles of democracy that she acquired from Britain,
an interrelated Commonwealth tie might also be dropped. To
Britain, all the same, it has been gratifying that India, the greatest
of former oriental dependencies, should thus bear witness to the
fact that the British oversea power structure has not served the
interests of Britain alone. It is more disconcerting when Britain
cannot do so much as the United States or Russia to help India
economically.

Britain had been hard pressed when India, a member of
the sterling area, drew on London reserves in financing five-year
plans. And the British have been unable to make substantial new
investments in a land where they are still the largest foreign investors. There is, however, the Colombo Plan to which the United
States contributes heavily and under which Britain has been joined
by Canada, Australia, and New Zealand in giving assistance to
their Asian partners.

But intra-Commonwealth influences such as these may not
be all that keep India within the Commonwealth fold. It offers the
kind of association she needs without demanding the sort of alignment she rejects. The transition from the First to the Second Commonwealth was signalized by India's acceptance of membership
as a Commonwealth republic. And yet India might soon have
withdrawn from it if there had not been a shift in the primacy of
the West. For a coalition strategy at which New Delhi looked
askance was then emerging. The British are also bound by it;
but they are not its propulsive element. Neutralism and the Commonwealth tie, according to India and her followers, are not incompatible; if they had been, if London rather than Washington
were the one that did most to array the West against the East,
India might have had to cut herself off. For the Commonwealth
commits her to nothing diplomatically and strategically. Bonds are
perpetuated through it, all the same, that form a bridge to the
West.

Here, as elsewhere in the Commonwealth, there is an overlap of interests. India is fortified by every contact that enables
her, ideologically and economically, to withstand pressure from
the Sino-Soviet bloc; the more she holds her own, the better it is
for the West. India may abjure the game of power; she is no more
exempt from it than others. Unlike her Russian and Chinese
neighbors, the West has no designs against which India must be
on guard; her own sovereign independence would have evaporated
if, under an American lead, the West had not organized a counter-

poise to the East. That may have been obstructed by an interplay of the anticolonial with the neutralist, the pan-Asian with the anti-Western. But there are countervailing trends among Indians, and to these their Commonwealth affiliation attests.

Neutralism and interventionism have, as a result, co-existed within the same Commonwealth. Members of the Commonwealth may disagree over how a free world order should be preserved. A joint and abiding interest in its preservation is implied.

Pakistan's approach to issues with which India has been grappling is, however, a different one. During the autumn of 1958 the reverberations were wide when, after the constitution had been annulled, General Mohammed Ayub Khan imposed a military dictatorship. The shortcomings of Pakistani officials and politicians invited this drastic step; India is trying to prove otherwise, but representative institutions may yet be unworkable in newly independent countries where the mass is illiterate and impoverished. It is, at any rate, under army rule that Pakistan must now endeavor to reform land tenure so that she might produce more foodstuffs, absorb Moslem refugees, and accumulate foreign-exchange reserves. There is little chance that Pakistan can be converted into a viable state by her own unaided efforts.

Concern for her future is felt by London and Washington on a number of grounds. She is aligned with the West and, as its leader, the United States has provided her with large amounts of economic assistance. Then, too, Pakistan is a member of the Commonwealth. But when she renounced democracy on the British parliamentary model and envisaged a revision of British law, she turned her back on a governmental process by which Commonwealth bonds are renewed. Pakistanis have supposed that they would do better with a presidential style of representative democracy, as in the United States or Gaullist France; yet this is to overlook the extent to which, in the absence of a strong President, a system of divided powers is even more subject to deadlock. In Pakistan, as in other underdeveloped countries, the immediate intent of the army was, nevertheless, to seize office before the machinery of government broke down; and, as Communism might batten on misery and chaos, it served as an alternative to that. But if no advance is made in the sphere of economic alleviation, one type of authoritarian rule may merely pave the way for another.

As the most effective arm of the state, the Pakistani Army owes much to Anglo-American influence. Its tradition and training were inherited from the old British Indian Army; the stress in American assistance to a South Asian ally had been on the military rather than economic side of things. This, together with a military overemphasis in domestic budgets, aggravated economic crisis and hastened the advent of army rule. None of it was likely to please India. In Pakistan, as a matter of fact, there is often no line between external and internal affairs. For she herself had to be bisected territorially when the Indian subcontinent was partitioned.

The problem of Pakistan is to unify politically and economically that which geography sets apart. A thousand miles of Indian territory stretches between her two halves. In West Pakistan, moreover, the main language is Urdu while in East Pakistan it is Bengali—one segment being Middle Eastern in mentality, the other South or Southeast Asian. Parties in Parliament were, accordingly, sectional rather than nation-wide. In West Pakistan the tendency was to splinter into four or five subprovinces; in East Pakistan, to seek more regional autonomy. What the latter has wanted is a fair proportion of the national revenue to which its jute and tea exports contribute.

And now that there is a military regime it will have a fresh grievance. For the Army is recruited mostly from West Pakistan, though East Pakistan has a fuller representation in the Navy and Air Force. East Pakistanis are, in any case, more politically-minded; less amenable, therefore, to authoritarian rule. Economic progress might arrest separatist trends. These are, however, in the very nature of the state.

Nor has Pakistan been overjoyed about her ties with the West. As in India, where there are also many tongues and dialects, official business is transacted in English; without economic support from the United States, and from Atlantic-Pacific partners of the Commonwealth, her plight would be desperate. But she cannot always find Western markets for her jute crop and, as allies, her Western associates have disappointed her.

Pakistan belongs to CENTO, the former Baghdad Pact, and in SEATO she is aligned with the United States, France, and such Commonwealth powers as Britain, Australia, and New Zealand. It is on behalf of these obligations that she is supplied with American arms. But she herself has had another objective in mind; she would have liked to employ them in a showdown with India over Kashmir. Washington, however, made her promise that American arms would be employed solely to combat Sino-Soviet aggression. India, with her British arms, is nettled at Pakistan's broad commitment to the coalition strategy of the West. Pakistan, armed by the United States, has chafed at the American ban on the use of American weapons against India.

Besides, the West's refusal to alienate India is not all that irks Pakistan. She also resents the fact that an Asian neutral should be furnished with more economic assistance than an Asian ally.

A community of interest between Pakistan and the West is, all the same, what prevails. As a neutral she could not have afforded to build up a large arms establishment, and without one she would lie at the mercy of hostile neighbors. Nor can Moscow support Pakistan over Kashmir in exchange for a Pakistani realignment with the East; the Russian aim is to keep India out of the Western camp and not push her into it. Peking's rift with New Delhi could, however, drive Pakistan and Communist China together. Meanwhile, with one foot in the Middle East and the other in Southeastern Asia, Pakistan might be a link between SEATO and CENTO. Not that either of these instruments can be rated high. But as long as they are maintained, it is useful to fill a gap between them.

Here, in the regional counterstrategy of the West, Afghanistan might drive a wedge. For that secluded, mountainous country juts down from the Soviet Union between the Indian subcontinent and the Middle East; upon it, however, Russia will have less of a stranglehold if Pakistan gives Afghanistan an outlet at Karachi to the Arabian Sea. With Soviet backing, Kabul has claimed Pathan areas—the so-called Pashtunistan—in Pakistan's own Northwest frontier province or demanded independence for them. Subsidized by Russia, Afghanistan also gets economic aid from the United States. Washington has tried, moreover, to settle a quarrel from which Moscow alone would profit. And so in 1958, when Afghanistan and Pakistan conceded to each other reciprocal transit rights, the United States agreed to finance a railway between them. The Afghans may still endeavor to dismember Pakistan. But Russia is the one that can exploit any breach in Pakistani defenses, something that may be done by first occupying Afghanistan herself.

It is, as a matter of fact, by protecting home soil that Pakistan best serves the Western coalition. She might synchronize action with her allies; but neutral Burma impedes her support of Thailand under SEATO, and her vigil against Afghanistan will not allow her to move far under the CENTO pact. West Pakistan lies athwart the historic invasion routes of the Indian subcontinent from Russia in the north, and East Pakistan might help block any

Chinese attack from the southeast. When Britain was leader of
the West she waged three Afghan wars to check Russian expansion
above the Oxus River. But in the era of American leadership, it
is only through her alignment with the West that Pakistan gets
strength to hold fast.

And that she should do so is a vital interest of India's.
The latter now has a watch of her own to keep against a resurgent
China. But as long as Pakistan is allied with the West, neutralist
India may shy away from any treaty for the common defense;
nor can they combine to withstand Sino-Soviet designs when these
further tighten India's grip on Kashmir. The upshot is a diversion
of military resources from the natural frontiers of the Indian subcontinent to artificial ones within it. And yet the atmosphere might
be improved when other border disputes are settled.

The dispute over the control of great rivers has at least
been moderated. When boundaries were first drawn between
Pakistan and India, the farmlands of West Pakistan had to rely
on irrigation waters whose sources remained in Indian Kashmir
or the Indian half of the Punjab. Pakistan not only suspected that
their flow might be manipulated by New Delhi as a means of
political and military pressure; India has had on foot mammoth
irrigation projects of her own for which some of these waters from
the basin of the Indus River have been tapped. American en
gineers helped to construct them. And it was Pakistan's complaint
that Washington and London did not withhold economic assistance
from India until that country accepted an equitable accommodation.

The International Bank for Reconstruction and Development, a United Nations specialized agency, has finally brought one
about. Engineering works through which India is to compensate
Pakistan will, moreover, be financed by five Western members of
the Colombo Plan—the United States, Britain, Canada, Australia,
and New Zealand—together with West Germany and the World
Bank. A group of English-speaking and Commonwealth powers
has thus shown once more that the relief of economic distress
on the Indian subcontinent is a major Western interest.

Nor is this the only territorial issue over which India and
Pakistan may yet concur. Border disputes have poisoned their
relations; but India would be in gravest jeopardy if the existing
frontiers of Pakistan could not be maintained or if the Pakistani
Union were to disintegrate. The Indian Republic might annex East
Pakistan; that acquisition would not be worth much if, with the
breakup of Pakistan as a whole, the northern ramparts of the

Indian subcontinent could be pierced more easily. India and Pakistan may be at variance over Kashmir. Nowhere on the Indian
subcontinent can New Delhi afford to have the *status quo* upset.

At an early juncture Pakistan may have expected that her
commitments with the West would give her a counter for negotiations with her neutralist neighbor: New Delhi's consent for a plebiscite in Kashmir might be exchanged for a Pakistani withdrawal
from SEATO and the former Baghdad Pact. No solution so neat
as that has proved feasible. A modus vivendi can be envisaged.
But it would be one that leaves India in possession of Kashmir,
and Pakistan aligned with the West.

Not that any formal acknowledgment of this is likely.
Together with ten million Hindus, Pakistan has a population of
seventy-five million Moslems; and in a country where there is a
constant tussle between the theocratic and secularist, a holy war
to redeem Kashmiri coreligionists might always flare up. None has
been started. It is with social democracy as a national objective
that communal antipathies are damped down in India. In Pakistan
it may be her Western orientation that restrains and stabilizes.

Pan-Islamic sympathies were, it is true, soured during the
Suez crisis of 1956 by the influence that India enjoyed at Cairo.
Yet India's own pan-Asian proclivities did not compel her at that
time to sever the Commonwealth tie. If Pakistan had done so, she
would, logically, have had to renounce collaboration with Britain
in SEATO and the Baghdad Pact—to pursue, unrewarded, the
neutralist policy that her Indian adversary recommends. Two years
later, as a matter of fact, when Pakistan backed the Turkish and
Iranian signatories of the Baghdad Pact, she even urged Anglo-
American intervention in Lebanon and Jordan. For over the exercise of Western power in the Orient she has not taken the same
view as India. But on this topic India herself may now differ less
from Pakistan than she deems it expedient to say: if Western power
were unavailable, neither of them would be safe.

Nor are they the only ones that it renders, explicitly or
implicitly, more secure. On this theme, however, Ceylon presents
yet another set of variations. A Commonwealth neutral, she leaned
at first towards the West. But under S.W.R.D. Bandaranaike her
outlook changed; after 1956 Ceylon turned to New Delhi rather
than London for inspiration. She may try to keep herself aloof
from the East-West contest. It does not leave her alone.

Across Palk Strait and the Gulf of Manar, the Indian subcontinent stands between Ceylon and any nearby menace. Yet she
herself could pose a danger to the mainland if, through ideological

penetration, she were converted into an adjunct of the East. For then there might not only be northern frontiers from which to exercise pressure on India and Pakistan; with Ceylon under the control of the East, the Sino-Soviet encirclement of the Indian subcontinent would be complete. Naval and air bases may now be withheld by that Commonwealth neutral from the communications sector of the British oversea power structure; a regime in Ceylon that subserved the East might damage the West's oceanic interests regionally. But it is the adjacent mainland that would suffer most.

And what will decide all this is the degree of success with which Ceylon tackles serious domestic problems. She can become a Commonwealth republic without difficulty. The question is whether a parliamentary system that she also inherited from Britain will be preserved.

A people as easygoing as the Ceylonese has been fair game for ideological militants. The broad trend may, as in India, be towards social democracy; there is, however, a proliferation of Marxist parties that control labor unions and attempt, through them, to paralyze key industries. Among these it is not Communists of the orthodox Stalinist school that are the more numerous but a Trotskyite heresy peculiar to Ceylon. Yet in a land that is chiefly Buddhist, the local Communists have, with the co-operation of the Russian Embassy, been infiltrating the Buddhist priesthood —though here the desecration of Buddhist Tibet by Communist China may be a handicap. In Pakistan an authoritarian regime was set up before there had been a general drift towards the extreme Left; after the assassination of Prime Minister Bandaranaike in 1959, the future of Ceylon seemed more obscure than ever. The crisis of democracy affects, moreover, every aspect of public affairs.

Economically, Ceylon needs outside help for capital investment so that there might be an increase in food productivity and a rise in living standards. But this is discouraged by the prevalence of anticapitalist doctrine, by the clamor for nationalization, by the tendency for nationalism to turn into xenophobia. The Ceylonese sell rubber to Communist China and buy rice from her; they have received more economic assistance from the East than the West. The United States was late in entering the field. As their economy deteriorated, the Ceylonese thought a pro-Western attitude had been ill-requited.

The Colombo Plan, which pioneered economic aid by one branch of the Commonwealth to another, took its name from Ceylon's own capital city. Though it has done much, its resources have had to be spread thin. And now, if tea and rubber plantations should ever be nationalized, British investors and planters would be hardest hit. Instead of moving into Ceylon, foreign capital has been moving out. Nor do communal riots advertise her as a land in which it is prudent to invest.

What does most to mar Ceylon's political landscape is the feud between a Singhalese majority and the Tamil minority. The latter, numbering two million, amounts to a quarter of the island's total population; a dispute over language rights and over the unobstructed exercise of the franchise has been further envenomed by the fact that the Singhalese are Buddhists while the Tamils are Hindus. For Tamils, whether migrant workers or long-settled inhabitants, are of Indian origin. Some zealots would combine Tamil regions in northern and eastern Ceylon with comparable Tamil areas in southern India. The solution that Colombo prefers but New Delhi rejects is to send all Tamils back to India.

What they themselves propose is that Ceylon be reconstituted as a federal union, one in which they would possess an autonomous province of their own. The Singhalese tongue still ranked ahead of Tamil after the disturbances of 1958, but more official recognition has been accorded Tamil. And while there is, in part, an Indian background to these communal hatreds, New Delhi will not willingly intervene. It tries to allay antipathies that simmer at home or impinge on relations with Pakistan. But unrest in Ceylon has not as yet been of direct concern to India. And it may bother her only when the defense of the Indian mainland has to be considered.

To assuage local differences there has, moreover, been the further fact that both countries have endorsed the same view of world order. At the outset, to be sure, Ceylon interpreted neutralism in a somewhat pro-Western fashion. She engaged in trade with Communist China but also discussed with SEATO the protection of Southeast Asia from Communist propaganda. And in 1955, at that Bandung Conference where pan-Asian sentiment was crystallized, no Asian ally of the West impeached Soviet imperialism and Communist dictatorship with more vigor than Kotelawala of Ceylon. But Indian influence preponderated under his successors. Ceylon swung away from the West and defense arrangements were modified accordingly.

For a century and a half Trincomalee had been a British naval base from which maritime invaders of Ceylon could be thrown back and, in more recent years, the Royal Air Force had established a station at Katunayake. That island and the east coast of India were saved from conquest by Japan when, after the fall of Singapore during World War II, the Royal Navy routed the Japanese in nearby waters—a defeat that also prevented Japan from joining up, through the Middle East, with the Italo-German sections of the tripartite Axis. Then, too, some in Ceylon feared Indian domination and regarded British bases as reassurance against that. As a Commonwealth neutral, India had withdrawn Bombay from the British oversea power structure; but when Ceylon first achieved independence, she signed an agreement with Britain for collaboration in defense. The presence of British bases on her soil would, however, be incompatible with a less pro-Western concept of neutralism.

The argument revolved about the position of the United States as leader of the West. Prime Minister Bandaranaike made the point that, as long as Britain possessed bases in Ceylon, they would be at the disposal of Britain's American ally; the objection was to their use as instruments of coalition strategy. But what actually speeded up the transference of Trincomalee and Katunayake to Ceylonese sovereignty was the Suez crisis of 1956— when Asian members of the Commonwealth were in tune with the United States and out of tune with Britain.

There might, however, be a partial substitute for the relinquished bases. Watch had been kept from Ceylon over a segment of a communications structure that stretched from Aden to East Africa, across the Indian Ocean to Pakistan and India, thence either to Australia and New Zealand or around the Malayan Peninsula to Singapore and up to Hong Kong. But a footing might also be maintained in the vicinity from the Maldive Islands, a British protectorate three hundred miles below India in the Indian Ocean and about four hundred miles southward from Ceylon. A staging post had been built on the island of Gan by the Royal Air Force during World War II and, after their departure from Ceylon, the British started to rebuild it.

Foreign interests that were anti-British and anti-Western might have gotten at the Maldivian government. Negotiations were suspended. But southern atolls, where the staging post has been constructed, welcomed it, and were stung into revolt against the sultanate.

What made this project feasible was the development of long-range aircraft. By use of its staging post at Gan, the Royal Air Force could by-pass the Middle East, whose crossing depends upon refuelling rights at Calcutta and Karachi that have to be renewed annually—a region that is full of political uncertainties. It will be fortunate if an alternative to that arterial Commonwealth route can be found within the Empire-Commonwealth nexus.

The idea is to have air traffic diverted by way of Nairobi or Mombasa in Kenya to the Maldive Islands, and thence on to its final destination—either to Singapore and Hong Kong in East Asia or, via the Australian base in the Cocos Islands, to Australia and New Zealand. Not that such a detour will rest on solid political foundations; Kenya, for instance, may be unavailable when her nationalist African majority rules the roost. For, within the Commonwealth, it is not merely on the plane of high policy that neutralist tendencies leave their impress. No less palpable is their effect on the communications sector of the British oversea power structure.

Contact by air with Australia and New Zealand may, in the end, have to be maintained across Canada and her American neighbor. Members of the Atlantic-Pacific branch of the Commonwealth have separate ties with the United States. A collective one in the sphere of communications is not inconceivable.

DIPLOMACY AND THE COMMONWEALTH

When the United States leads the West it is, above all, the impact of American primacy that may determine the course followed by members of the Commonwealth, neutralist and interventionist alike. Special intra-Commonwealth problems were created by the Korean War and the Suez venture of Britain and France against Egypt; negatively or positively, American policy was, on both occasions, a crucial element. New grounds for Anglo-American divergence had appeared during the enforcement of the Charter in Korea. Yet to be explored, after the United States had taken Britain's place, were the limits of Commonwealth co-ordination.*

London and Ottawa toiled for a localization of the Korean War lest, on a peripheral issue, the strategic interlock prove to be a Western boomerang. But India deplored the sort of coalition machinery through which, in alliance with the United States, the other branch of the Commonwealth planned the defense of the West. She had also relayed information from Peking that warned

---

* Only the Commonwealth aspects of recent major crises are touched upon in this particular context. Anglo-American divergences arising out of the Korean War were dealt with in Chapter IV. Other, later episodes are analyzed more generally in the next two chapters.

that China would intervene if MacArthur advanced to the Yalu River and was incensed when, despite her efforts, the specter of global war had been raised.* New Delhi did not condone North Korea's attack on South Korea; afterwards, however, she was loath to condemn China as an aggressor. An Indian hospital unit but no Indian contingent went to join the Commonwealth Brigade in Korea; and Pakistan, fearing some adverse move by India in the Kashmir dispute, was compelled to keep her own troops at home. Universal ideals of human brotherhood were proclaimed from New Delhi. But when non-Asians were smitten by Asians there was, in the midst of a pan-Asian upsurge, some ill-concealed satisfaction over that.

A knotty point in Commonwealth co-ordination thus came to the fore. One group of Commonwealth members had to perform the feat of marching with Washington, but at a pace that did not leave others, India more than Pakistan or Ceylon, too far behind. For the Korean War revealed what Middle Eastern developments were to corroborate: that non-Asian intervention in Asia to preserve common interests was still more obnoxious than a lawlessness whose springs were Asian or Eurasian. Not many years before, it was the United States which had called upon Britain to grant India her independence. Now the strictures of their neutralist Indian partner underscored pleas for restraint that London and Ottawa were, in any case, addressing to Washington.

Nor did this chapter of intra-Commonwealth–Anglo-American diplomacy terminate with the Korean armistice. Both wings of the Commonwealth, the Asian and the Atlantic-Pacific, tended to huddle together whenever there were signs that, over the further crises of Indochina and the Chinese offshore islands, Washington's stock of patience might wear thin. So, also, there was broad concurrence between Commonwealth members when they differed with the United States over such questions as the seating of the Peking regime in the Security Council or over the rigors of the trade embargo against Communist China.

The latter had been recognized by Britain, India, Pakistan, and Ceylon before the Korean War broke out. Since then, on matters that could still be negotiated with Communist China, Britain had represented the United States; between East and West, moreover, neutralist India served as intermediary. Soon after the Korean War began, Britain had broached the idea of recognizing two Chinese governments—one for the Chinese mainland, the other for Formosa. But the United States had borne the brunt

* Truman, *op. cit.*, II, pp. 361-362.

and, rather than offend her, most Commonwealth members marked time on the recognition issue.

India, however, did not let it lapse. She had hugged the East-West sidelines; nevertheless, when she advocated the replacement of the Formosan by the Communist regime in the United Nations, she often said out loud what Commonwealth partners, which voted against her, really felt. The Western coalition had, under American leadership, been exerting power for peace. Yet the United States also propped up Premier Syngman Rhee and President Chiang Kai-shek, two rulers who might seek to achieve their objectives through a general war. A conflict precipitated by them would drag in their American patron and, under the strategic interlock, could set the world aflame. But with a Far Eastern settlement, their last chance might pass. And when India sought to forestall them, the plaudits she earned did not emanate solely from pan-Asian galleries or neutralist friends.

The brute fact was that on the Chinese mainland, from which Chiang Kai-shek had fled, the Chinese Communists alone held sway. The United States insisted, nevertheless, that they could not qualify for China's seat in the United Nations until they had loosened their grip upon North Korea and North Vietnam, agreed to elections under which Korea might be reunified, released American political hostages, and renounced threats of force against Formosa.

Not having been retroceded to China after World War II, that island bastion had, as a matter of fact, been converted into an important outpost in the defense perimeter of the United States. But many in the West who still sympathized with the Far Eastern policy of the United States could do so no longer when she winked at Chiang Kai-shek's military build-up on the Chinese offshore islands; when his use of counterforce from them might have reignited the Chinese civil war and, through American involvement, spread it irreparably. In 1958, during the second crisis over Quemoy and Matsu, Commonwealth allies as well as Commonwealth neutrals deemed the Eisenhower Administration almost as reckless as the MacArthur school had ever wanted to be. Britain, nursing a post-Suez *rapprochement* with the United States and with troops in Jordan, could not afford to diverge from Washington publicly. Interventionist and neutralist powers of the Commonwealth differed about the Middle East. Over gratuitous risks that the United States might take in the Far East these same powers were again ranged together.

Nor was that the only aspect of American policy about

which Commonwealth powers tended to agree with each other and to disagree with the United States. The embargo on trade with the Sino-Soviet bloc was a long-standing irritant. Nations violating it might, under the Battle Act, be deprived of American economic assistance. None, as it happened, did more to contravene the regulations than such American wards as Japan, the Chinese Nationalists on Formosa, or the Bonn Republic. And it was only when Congress had been reminded of this that outcries against Britain were muffled.

The British, however, did not merely want to increase their own exports. They had oversea interests about whose maintenance the United States, as leader of the West, could not be unconcerned. Ceylon was an independent member of the Commonwealth when she sold rubber to Communist China, but in 1956, when she did the same, Malaya had not yet achieved that status; the sterling area and the economy of a strategically important country benefited when, on the latter's behalf, London resorted to an "exceptions procedure." Against Russia and her European satellites, a somewhat less stringent list had been adopted by the embargoing powers in 1954, and the application of the milder one to Communist China as well was urged thereafter by the Commonwealth and NATO associates of the United States. That differential was eliminated, first by Britain and then by the others, in 1957; in 1958 trade barriers were again modified. But while this had been done with American consent, the United States still upheld her own embargo on trade with Communist China, North Korea, and North Vietnam. The amount of business that any in the West could do with Communist China was, for the moment, to be small.

Then, during the Suez episode of 1956, a drastic reassortment of attitudes occurred. Members of the Commonwealth that had frowned upon American policy in the Far East now endorsed it in the Middle East. Nor was Anglo-American friendship all that suffered. New trends in the Commonwealth were being put to the test.

Through it ran no simple cleavage—the Asian wing against the Atlantic-Pacific. There was, instead, a compound fracture. Britain had support from Australia and New Zealand, but India and Ceylon, with Pakistan trailing uncomfortably along, were in the van of her critics. As for South Africa and Canada, the former sat on the fence while the latter, objecting to the British course, served, within and without the Commonwealth, as a conciliator. In Korean and Far Eastern affairs it was the nature of American leadership that had presented Britain with a problem of Commonwealth co-ordination. Commonwealth as well as Anglo-American divergence marked the crisis of 1956.

Britain had long been the guardian of Western interests in the Middle East. Tsarist Russia had once been held at a distance; and after oil was discovered in the Persian Gulf, its transit from that region through the Mediterranean had to be maintained. As she plied a celebrated lifeline, Britain could supervise her imperial domains in Asia, Africa, and the Antipodes; then, too, most of those that achieved independence within the Commonwealth were still dependent on the British oversea communications structure. But on the Mediterranean-Indian Ocean route the Suez artery had always been a political bottleneck. Disraeli had purchased shares of the French operating company for Britain; these, nevertheless, were of no avail after Britain relinquished her large military base in the Suez Canal Zone. For an Egyptian dictator who banked on Moscow could now expropriate the property and exert a monopoly over it. But this was a danger that Asian members of the Commonwealth, rather than let Britain and France reoccupy the international waterway, were willing to risk. And when the United States censured her British and French allies, she was prompted by the desire to win Asian goodwill.

Among Commonwealth powers, the neutralists had the easier time. Having no formal commitments, they could oscillate between East and West and between various exponents of dissonant views within the West itself. Canada, Australia, and New Zealand were in more of a quandary. The contingency they always sought to avoid, that of having to make a choice between their senior Commonwealth partner and the West's American leader, was the very one that stared them in the face.

Canberra and Wellington, at any rate, backed the British. Nor was it merely on grounds of sentiment that they resolved to do so. At that moment one set of practical considerations outweighed another. Through the Anzus Pact it was the United States which had underwritten the security of Australia and New Zealand —while in SEATO, to which Britain adheres, these two were guarantors rather than guaranteed. But the Middle Eastern sector of the British communications structure also had to be upheld. To keep the area out of hostile hands, Australia and New Zealand fought alongside Britain in two world wars before the United States had entered either. An endeavor to curb pan-Arab or pro-Soviet influences was therefore sure to elicit their sympathy. In regional defense, they relied on their alliance with the United States. On the Suez question, they stood with Britain.

American policy, however, evoked praise from Asian members of the Commonwealth. For Britain and France had not only resorted to force but resorted to it in Asia; they had not only indulged in what Washington regarded as outmoded colonialism but they had done it in the wake of that pan-Arab *bête noire,* Israel.

The political attitude of Asian powers was at variance with their own economic interests. Sixty per cent of India's export trade, for example, and over seventy per cent of her imports are still carried in British bottoms through the Red Sea-Mediterranean route. When the Suez Canal was nationalized, New Delhi opposed efforts to extract adequate international safeguards. And yet its closure in 1956–57 was a clear demonstration of what, as Cairo wishes, can occur again. For this did harm not only to the economies of Western Europe; India's own second Five-Year Plan lost time and incurred extra expense when imports of capital goods had had to be shipped around the African continent.

Strategically, also, India is less secure as a result of the changeover at Suez. For this impaired the communications sector of the British oversea power structure, and that might still expedite her territorial defense. Neutralism does not abolish a moral lien on assistance from other Commonwealth partners. A bar at Suez on seaborne help from the West would, however, render India less capable of resisting Sino-Soviet pressure on her own northern frontiers. Nuclear weapons delivered by air or from a submarine might, in an East–West conflict, demolish so narrow a passageway at once. But India must be prepared for hazards that are less total and more local in extent. In meeting these she might be hamstrung by a regime at Cairo that is pro-Soviet or anti-Western. Yet it was such a regime that India befriended.

She was not, all the same, carried away by an inveterate anticolonialism. Prime Minister Nehru did not let India come to an open breach with Britain or, despite popular clamor, secede from the Commonwealth. Nor was this the only illustration of a faculty for alternating reason with emotion in the conduct of foreign policy. About other trouble-spots on the communications sector of the British power structure, India had been discreetly reticent: no prolonged fuss was made about Cyprus, which is not in Asia, or about Singapore, which is. But the Suez controversy touched a still more sensitive nerve. For here the pan-Asian, with its anti-Western drive, was accentuated by a neighborhood quarrel, one that sprang from fears and desires of Asian origin.

Kashmir shapes the attitude of India and Pakistan towards questions far removed from it. The Baghdad Pact was designed to fortify a northern tier of Moslem states—Turkey, Iran, Iraq, Pakistan—against Russian mastery of the Middle Eastern crossroads. But its one Arab member, Iraq, refused to treat Egypt as kingpin of the Arab world. India, moreover, had been trying to head off any pan-Islamic solidarity that, in their Kashmir dispute, would bolster Pakistan against her. When, too, Hindu India espoused the cause of Egypt, she could not be accused by her own Moslem populace, or by Moslem peoples elsewhere, of being anti-Moslem. During the Suez episode the four Moslem signatories of the Baghdad Pact had to support Colonel Nasser on pan-Islamic grounds. But India had stolen a march on them at Cairo. The military grouping to which her Pakistani rival belonged was, besides, an instrument of Western strategy. Anything done against it by New Delhi would therefore please the Kremlin.

American and Indian policies seemed to converge. From the standpoint of American leadership they could, in the long run, seldom have been further apart. There was not only the Asian phase of coalition strategy that New Delhi, like Moscow and Cairo, wanted to undermine; not even when they denounced the use of force against Egypt were the United States and India in genuine accord. Britain, France, and Israel accepted the United Nations as a vehicle for liquidating the Sinai and Suez episodes. Yet when Russian tanks mowed down Hungarians, India abstained from condemnation of Russia in the world body. Moscow had to be propitiated. Nor was that all. Whatever would be done under international auspices to mitigate Soviet tyranny in Eastern Europe might furnish a precedent that could be invoked against India in Kashmir.

Ceylon, on the other hand, had no axe to grind in the Middle East, but her policy and India's were now exactly the same. Like other Asian members of the Commonwealth, she ought to have favored international safeguards for transit through the Suez Canal; yet she also was against these when the waterway was first nationalized. Such, too, was her concept of neutralism that only when New Delhi had been shamed into an expression of dissent from Russian infamy in Hungary did Colombo speak up.

Pakistan, however, followed a path of her own. Unlike India and Ceylon, she had her Western commitments; like theirs, the larger proportion of her export-import trade—seventy-six per cent—is conveyed through the Suez Canal under British and other flags. As an ally of the West, she relies on the communications sector of the British oversea power structure for the passage of American economic aid and American military supplies; treaty assistance from abroad, with the Suez artery closed, might arrive too late. But public opinion in Pakistan was not preoccupied with international safeguards for the Middle Eastern waterway; the coercion of a fellow Moslem country by Britain and France, as well as Israel, was what concerned it. And yet solicitude for Egypt cooled off as Pakistan's own rival, India, acted at the United Nations as a mouthpiece for Cairo. Together with the Arab states, India and Ceylon equivocated on the Hungarian issue; Pakistan voted with the West. She had, in fact, accepted an American lead on the two major questions of a critical autumn.

Soon afterwards, moreover, when London and Washington were about to settle their differences, Pakistan and Turkey persuaded Iraq and Iran to overlook Britain's attack on a Moslem nation so that the Baghdad Pact could be reanimated. Mass impulses might be anticolonial and pan-Islamic. Pakistan, still pro-Western in orientation, turned not only to the United States but to her old British partner.

Among Commonwealth powers, South Africa was the one that had least to say, pro or con, about the Suez expedition. She did not use the canal; its closure by Colonel Nasser was, however, to increase the traffic that made the long voyage around the Cape and touched at her ports. Sixty per cent of the Union's petrol and oil requirements moved, moreover, down through the Indian Ocean from the Persian Gulf; it would be catastrophic for South Africa's booming economy if pro-Soviet–anti-Western influences were to dominate the oilfields of the Middle East. Then, too, Egypt herself was situated in North Africa. And she did not only exploit African nationalism against the West. She provided Russia with a foothold for penetration below the Sahara.

To the African continent, the Middle East was a gateway upon whose joint defense the British and South African governments had concurred in 1955. And for South Africa to have supported the United States against Britain would have been for her to vote with her own chief Asian detractors. Yet neither could she go along with Britain on such an issue; recalling their own past, Afrikanders may not have been insensible to the charge that the Suez expedition heralded a revival of old-fashioned British imperialism. A middle path might have been pursued if, like Canada, South Africa had had the sort of standing at the United Nations and in the Commonwealth that would have permitted her to moderate and pacify. But, at the time, her own representation in the world body was only a token one. Neither able to take sides or intercede, she kept her own counsel.

Canada, however, was now to perform a mediatory role. And she did not only do so at the United Nations; her parallel efforts within the Commonwealth itself are the best index to the crisis which that association underwent. During the summer of 1956, Ottawa had advised London against the use of force and thought well of an Indian plan by which international participation in the management of the Suez artery would have been meager.* When the coercion of Egypt began, rather than vote against Britain, France, and Israel, Canada, like South Africa, abstained. But Prime Minister St. Laurent remonstrated with Sir Anthony Eden in a message which its sender deemed frank, and its recipient as more than frank.

Some of this may have been due to the influence exerted upon St. Laurent personally by President Eisenhower and Prime Minister Nehru. Ill-conceived, at any rate, was his sardonic remark in Parliament at Ottawa that the era had ended when the supermen of Europe could govern the whole world. For with this taunt—a throwback to Ottawa's own semi-isolationist period—much that Britain had done in underpinning a free world order was decried.

It is not unusual for Canada or other members of the Commonwealth to express dissent from a current British policy. Unforeseen in London was the possibility that Canada might be more at odds with Britain than with the United States at so decisive a juncture. And this would be no laughing matter. When the United States took Britain's place as leader of the West, Canada had also risen in rank. Among independent countries of the Commonwealth, she was one of the few whose oversea communications were no longer served by the British power structure. To maintain this structure she had, nevertheless, twice rallied to the British cause; in two world wars she had from the outset evinced a swifter, broader grasp of joint world tasks than her American neighbor. Since World War II, moreover, Canada had been a Commonwealth partner and Atlantic ally that employed her new, higher stature as a corrective against whatever in American coalition leadership tended towards the self-willed and unilateral. Now, however, Canada stood closer to the United States than to Britain.

* The Canadian External Affairs Minister, Lester Pearson, did not, however, exclude military sanctions as a last resort when the NATO Council met on September 5. See Eden, *op. cit.*, p. 511.

The British Prime Minister, Sir Anthony Eden, had been reduced to despair by the vagaries of Eisenhower and Dulles, and Ottawa's censorious attitude must have come as a further shock. At home in Canada, some months later, it may have speeded up the swing of the electoral pendulum. Meanwhile, when Britain and France were opposed at the United Nations by the United States, Canada tried to restore the situation. As distinguished from NATO, where authority must rest with its strongest members, the world body gives extra scope to a Middle Power like Canada. The General Assembly adopted the Canadian proposal that a United Nations Emergency Force be sent to the scene of hostilities—a contingent that would be commanded by a Canadian officer, and one to which the Canadian contribution would otherwise be large.

What distressed Ottawa was plain. Like most of the General Assembly, it, too, felt that the Charter had been violated. But it also had its own catalogue of complaints. In Anglo-American friendship, Canada is a third component, and that relationship had been jeopardized. Two inner Commonwealth features of the Suez episode had, besides, exasperated the St. Laurent government. The first was the fact that London had been remiss in telling it when force was finally decided upon; the second was the extent to which Asian partners might be alienated. Procedurally, in an uncoordinated Commonwealth, it has been through consultation between sovereign units that some measure of co-ordination could yet be attained. Downing Street had no time to inform friends, Sir Anthony Eden was afterwards to explain, before the die was cast.* But there was more to it than that. If Asian members or Washington had gotten wind of what was afoot, the Suez expedition would have been scuttled in advance. And so, rather than consult some Commonwealth partners but pass up others, the British ignored them all.

Little of this could be admitted. Then, too, President Eisenhower, as well as Prime Minister Nehru, would have held it against Louis St. Laurent if the Canadian Prime Minister, having been tipped off, did not relay his information. Ottawa was cut to the quick. Yet what allowance did it make for Washington's devious course?

Commonwealth consultation had broken down. But this collapse was preceded, during the summer and autumn of 1956, by a breakdown in consultation between the United States and Britain. For the two principal Western powers could not be es-

---

* Eden, *op. cit.*, p. 588. (On this point, see Chapter VII.)

tranged from each other without a loss of confidence spreading—
such now was the web of Anglo-American and Commonwealth
affinities—to other interrelated capitals.

Would its Asian members secede from the Commonwealth?
That this might be one outcome of the Suez expedition worried
Ottawa more than London. Other methods of dealing with Egypt
had been tried—by conferences in London and at the Security
Council in New York; during the crucial preliminary stage of the
Suez episode, New Delhi, Colombo, and Karachi were less eager
to have the interests of canal users protected than to let Cairo
have its own way. "Quit the Commonwealth!" was a cry that,
when the bombs fell and the guns roared, did arise in India,
Pakistan, and Ceylon. As Britain and France quickly desisted, it
soon faded away.

Ottawa, however, had been afraid that it would not. In the
Canadian Parliament, Lester Pearson declared later that, when
land fighting started at Port Said, the Commonwealth was on the
verge of dissolution; that it might not have stood the strain if, after
Egypt and Israel had acceded to the General Assembly's call for
a cease-fire, Britain and France had proceeded to occupy the
entire Suez Canal Zone. Among diverse pressures exercised at
London, this was not an aspect of the Anglo-French undertaking
on which Washington or Moscow would have laid stress; nor did
Ottawa have any electoral mandate to suggest that Canada's own
membership in the Commonwealth might likewise be imperiled.
What it could do, while imploring Britain to make one sort of
withdrawal, was beseech India, Pakistan, and Ceylon to refrain
from making another.

The story might have been different, in Asian capitals of
the Commonwealth as elsewhere, if negotiations with Egypt had
not interposed months of delay and if the Suez operations could
have been mounted earlier and carried out with more dispatch. Of
significance, afterwards, was the emphasis with which Asian
statesmen of the Commonwealth reasserted Commonwealth affilia-
tions. For these, it is evident, would have been severed with reluctance, and threats uttered in the heat of the moment are not
always put into effect.

A resilient Commonwealth had weathered the storm. It
was enabled to do so because, within it, varying national interests
still overlapped. Britain, nevertheless, was the only Commonwealth
member which shared most of these with others and fitted them
together; her capacity to do this could not be stultified without the
Commonwealth as a whole being throttled. For the question of

status in the Second Commonwealth has not merely been that posed by aspiring British dependencies. The problem of Britain's own status in world politics has likewise been implicit throughout.

It was, as a matter of fact, the centrality of Britain within the Commonwealth grouping that provoked the Commonwealth phase of the Suez crisis. Other members have had their feuds— India and Pakistan over Kashmir, the Afro-Asian wing with a racist Union of South Africa. But it is when Britain does something that a number of Commonwealth partners, rightly or wrongly, take amiss that the Commonwealth may, in its entirety, be shaken to the core.

No basic Commonwealth issue arose, however, during the summer of 1958 when, after the American landings in Lebanon, British paratroopers were flown to Jordan. And that was so for several reasons. The Middle Eastern episodes of 1956 and 1958 had similar root causes; their immediate circumstances were not the same. The initiative, moreover, had been assumed by the United States, and it was with Washington rather than London that fault must now principally be found.

India again disapproved. Pan-Arab–pro-Soviet influences in the Middle East still bothered her less than efforts made by Western powers to counteract them. Though she demanded the recall of American and British troops, she did not favor schemes for another international force under the aegis of the United Nations; employed in the Middle East, a stand-by force might also be employed in Kashmir. A faint cooling-off towards Moscow and Cairo could, nevertheless, be detected in New Delhi. What if Egypt's ambitions, which India herself had furthered, were ever to get out of bounds? Emboldened by Iraq's defection from the Baghdad Pact, Colonel Nasser might even vie with Jawaharlal Nehru for the leadership of the Bandung or Afro-Asian bloc. And that, too, is why Pakistan's alliance with the West is better for India than a pan-Islamic combine in which Pakistan and Egypt would, with others, be ranged against her. It was, at any rate, a straw in the wind when Prime Minister Nehru exhorted Arab countries to accept the existence of Israel.

But with Russia also, there had been disenchantment. India did not like the way neutralist Yugoslavia, with her own version of a Communist economy, had been treated; New Delhi's indignation was more spontaneous when Hungarian patriots were executed than it had been during Hungary's travail two years before. Soon, too, Russia had to prove her goodwill towards India by softening Chinese truculence on India's northern frontier. It was the West rather than the East that had done most to buoy up a sagging Five-Year Plan. While there was less in the Anglo-American intervention of 1958 to evoke an uproar against Britain, India's own mood may also have changed.

Nor did other Asian members of the Commonwealth put on a repeat performance. Ceylon, again in accord with India, did not expatiate with her former vehemence; with Turkey and Iran, Asian cosignatories of the Baghdad Pact, Pakistan acclaimed the Anglo-American landings. Meanwhile two new Commonwealth voices, one Asian and one African, had been raised, and neither sounded extreme. Malaya regretted the haste with which Washington and London had acted but, contrary to the tenets of Afro-Asian neutralism, expressed fresh satisfaction over her defense treaty with Britain. Nor was Ghana's view the same as India's. By favoring a United Nations force and the neutralization of Lebanon, she implied that the Middle East should not be abandoned to Egypt or to pro-Soviet–anti-Western influences but protected from them.

In the rest of the Commonwealth, on the other hand, three out of four oversea members reacted in 1958 as they had in 1956. Australia, with Robert Menzies as Prime Minister, supported Britain and France during the Suez episode; American intervention in Lebanon was greeted as a heartening sign of American leadership. New Zealand, with Walter Nash as Prime Minister, backed the United States and Britain as she had previously backed Britain and France. And on this topic the Union of South Africa again said nothing.

Less nervous than before was Canada's role. She expressed willingness to assist in the organization of another United Nations Emergency Force, one by which American troops in Lebanon and British troops in Jordan might be relieved; a new government under Prime Minister John Diefenbaker saw no alternative to Western intervention. To have it confined to Lebanon and Jordan was their objective; Canada hoped there would be no action that might involve other NATO members. But for the exercise of mediatory talents there was less opportunity. Differences in the Commonwealth had not deepened into a serious rift. On the Middle Eastern front, the United States and Britain were marching in step.

For Ottawa, above all, this was a significant change. During the Korean War and subsequent crises in the Far East, Canada, like Britain, toiled at Washington against any extension of conflict; during the Suez episode, Ottawa veered round and worked with Washington to restrain the British. However, when the Americans and the British co-operated, as they were currently doing in the Middle East, Canada could not demur. She may not have exulted over the Anglo-American landings. It is on Anglo-American solidarity rather than the activities of the United Nations or the preachments of New Delhi that she must ultimately depend.

To Anglo-American solidarity there has been no uniform Commonwealth response. And yet, some Commonwealth bonds may be facilitated by Anglo-American interaction. A number of Commonwealth countries have, for instance, entered into separate defense commitments with the United States; it is Anglo-American friendship that precludes any clash between them and prior Commonwealth ties. Intangibles of history and tangibles of power impinge on the American-Commonwealth relationship, and in it even unaligned members of the Commonwealth have a footing. So, too, the United States is not concerned only with Commonwealth allies as individual associates; in the perpetuation of the Commonwealth group she has, as leader of the West, a concurrent interest. Britain, moreover, is still its focus. And this again must suit the American purpose. For whatever enhances the stature of her chief ally will strengthen America's own hand.

The foundations of British power have been world-wide. And that is why the West would suffer from the conversion of Britain into an outer province of a federalized Europe. A century ago some mid-Victorians toyed with a Little England philosophy; for the British people, after wartime buffetings and postwar frustrations, oversea responsibilities may again lose their allure. By themselves, however, industrial skill and scientific progress would not be enough to provide the British welfare state with a rising standard of living or substantive rank. In an age of giant technologies, Britain is a small island with a relatively large population and few natural resources. But her key membership in the Commonwealth compensates for other deficiencies and buttresses her position in general world affairs.

That, moreover, is an aspect of the British role to which Americans have also had to adjust themselves. Traditionally it is from land power, huge, compact, visible, that their own strength flows; Britain's influence derives from a residuum of sea power that is at once palpable and impalpable. Then, too, though the American political system is less well co-ordinated than the British for leadership, the United States is internationally more self-contained. As leader of the West she may consult allies. Additional consultations with Commonwealth partners, among which neutrals as well as allies are numbered, must precede any British action.

A service is rendered, all the same, when powers that are disparate in view and dispersed in locale stay banded together. Britain was not the first to carve out an empire or combine with allies. None before her, however, let dependencies be transmuted into a Commonwealth or made an unwritten alliance more decisive than a written one. The United States has taken Britain's place as leader of the West; as pivot of the Commonwealth, Britain still occupies a place of her own. Through the Commonwealth she may, then, still play a great part. What she must ensure is the survival of that fellowship as a force for good.

Unique as an entity, it would have dissolved long ago if there were not in it more to attract than repel. Ambiguities may abound; overlapping interests do not only crisscross but mutually cohere. The Commonwealth may have no manifest potential for unity; tendencies by which it could be splintered are somehow overcome. And it helps to fortify a free world order by the mere fact that it persists.

VII

The Great Divergence

THE SUEZ CRISIS

Unity without unanimity had been achieved by the West in response to the challenge from the East. But in 1956, when President Nasser nationalized the Suez Canal Company, the United States quarreled with her British and French allies over how this step should be met; never, since primacy had shifted from Britain to the United States, had Anglo-American friendship, the very cornerstone of a free world order, been so jeopardized. During the Korean War, when the United States acted in the Far East as chief local agent of the United Nations, there was no tendency to treat that organization as a substitute for alignments by which the general peace is maintained; during the Suez episode Washington gave it priority. Others shared interests in the Middle East that Britain and France strove to preserve; that is why the United States, as leader of the West, soon attempted to do what she had prevented them from doing. Stopgaps could be devised. No commentary on the misjudgments of 1956 was more eloquent than the course on which the United States herself subsequently embarked.

Years must elapse before the archives of governments and the memoirs of statesmen yield missing pieces for the Suez puzzle. One feature, nevertheless, was evident from the start. Upside-down language had, early in the cold war, typified Russian pronouncements on foreign affairs. But, then, as though it had spread from one side of the East–West contest to the other, the topsy-turvy even bedeviled international relations within the West.

To joint effort in furthering the continuance of a free world order, the English-speaking peoples were wedded. And that was a corrective which arrested Anglo-American divergence before it went too far. Not for the first time, in accordance with historic imperatives, were the United States and Britain to be reconciled by a dialectical process that brought them together again after they had been driven apart. And yet, one aspect of the great divergence over the Suez venture marked it off from other divisive incidents. What had previously been questioned by many in Britain was the nature of American leadership, but never American goodwill. A direct misunderstanding was to raise doubts about both.

A common global front with regional diversification: that —until the Suez crisis—might have been regarded as a general Allied objective. In Western Europe, the British, the French and the Americans had their North Atlantic commitment. But with East Asia, the British were less concerned than the United States, and the French, after they retired from Indochina, less concerned than the British—though none could be unconcerned about a sphere where, under the strategic interlock, a forward policy by the United States might embroil them all. Britain and France were African powers; in the Middle East, Britain still clung to remnants of a vanished predominance—oil concessions, treaties, air bases, dependencies that were part of her oversea communications structure. But the influence of France had also been strong in the area. And after the British Army terminated French mandates over Syria and Lebanon during World War II, it took the anti-Western intrigues of the Egyptian dictator, Colonel Gamal Abdel Nasser, to draw London and Paris together.

Then also, after World War II, Britain and the United States agreed about some Middle Eastern trends and disagreed about others. Palestine had been under a British mandate and in that territory President Truman backed the emergence of Israel. Britain, however, did not, and the complaisance of Ernest Bevin, the British Foreign Secretary, towards Charter-breaking Arab invaders has been pointed out by Trygve Lie, first Secretary-General of the United Nations.* A number of British public servants had become the early patrons of that pan-Arab lawlessness whose ultimate anti-Western target was, as foreseen, Britain's own oversea realm.

On both sides of the Atlantic there have been those who were willing to condone Arab anarchy as long as oil gushed from Arab wells. Not that oil-producing territories can always blackmail the West: Iran discovered under Mossadegh, and Arab rulers found out during the Suez crisis, how costly it was for them to impede the flow of oil. Western countries are the only ones that can provide transportation, marketing facilities, and the larger markets. Unless they sell oil, the oil lands of the Middle East will

---

* Truman, *op. cit.*, II, pp. 132-169; and Trygve Lie, *In the Cause of Peace* (New York: The Macmillan Co., 1954), pp. 174-186.

have no revenue to finance programs of economic and social reform.

But these were lessons that had yet to be learned. Before the Suez episode, Britain had one set of Arab friends and the United States another: Egypt and the oil domain of Saudi Arabia had been cultivated by Washington; Iraq, Egypt's rival, and oil principalities in the Persian Gulf were, with Jordan, the chief British protégés. Probably, too, the international oil companies cannot tell the degree to which they themselves are competitors or partners. And when Western defense against Soviet expansion required the establishment of Allied air fields on Arab soil, a strategic pattern was superimposed on oil politics.

For the great divergence of 1956 there had been a number of dress rehearsals. The first of these occurred when Iran confiscated British oil property in 1951. As Foreign Secretary in the last Churchill government, Sir Anthony Eden retrieved much of that investment by suggesting a share for American oil companies (one that amounted to forty per cent) in a new international consortium. But, before agreement was reached in 1954, London had with difficulty persuaded Washington that Communist domination was not the sole alternative to rule by the clownish Mossadegh.*

Less gratifying was the inability of London and Washington to concert a joint approach towards Egypt. Even when their differences were transitory, like those over the disposition of the Sudan, they were symptomatic. For when Egypt abrogated her alliance with Britain in 1951, she also repudiated the treaty on which reposed the Anglo-Egyptian condominium for the Sudan. The British now renegotiated their rights. They might have extracted concessions in the Suez Canal Zone if they had recognized King Farouk as King of the Sudan. But this London refused to do —and despite Washington's desire that the Egyptian monarch be given such recognition. Farouk himself abdicated in 1952; Egyptian pretensions could, after that, scarcely be regal ones.† But in the light of American anticolonial attitudes, then and later, the situation verged on the grotesque. Britain, an imperial power, had been grooming the Sudanese people for self-government. The subjugation of the Sudan to Egyptian imperialism was, however, what the United States sought to further.

Nor in the purely strategic phase of the Anglo-Egyptian negotiations did the British get much help from their American ally. The Suez Canal Zone had been the bulwark of Western power

* Eden, *op. cit.*, pp. 222-224; see also pp. 212-243 and 647.
† *Ibid.*, pp. 253-274.

in the Middle East. For a while, early in 1953, it looked as though the United States would deal jointly with Britain at Cairo; things might have worked out differently, Sir Anthony Eden was afterwards to remark, if she had done so. But Washington would not ask for Egyptian assent to any such Anglo-American collaboration. American reluctance was ascribed to anticolonial sentiment and the desire to maintain popularity with Egypt's new republican regime. More disquieting, in terms of American leadership and Anglo-American solidarity, was another element that Sir Anthony Eden detected. Even in an area where the primary responsibility was not theirs, the American government was disinclined to take second place.*

Under the Anglo-Egyptian agreement of 1954, the British consented to evacuate the Suez Canal Zone; they were to reoccupy it only if an attack were launched on Turkey or the Arab states. The fact was that, until Russia began to brandish rockets during the Sinai-Suez hostilities of 1956, her threat in the Middle East had been a covert rather than an overt one. Nasser, however, subordinated the Arab League to his own ambitions and when Iraq, by joining the Baghdad Pact, edged towards the West, Egypt reacted by moving towards the East.

In July, 1955, when President Eisenhower attended the Big Four conference at Geneva, Western chancelleries had received word of the pending sale of arms by the Soviet bloc to Egypt. Rather than spoil the false harmony of the proceedings, the Western leaders did not mention this ominous development to Bulganin and Khrushchev. If Colonel Nasser had purchased weapons from the United States, he would have been precluded from using them against Israel; nor could he procure more of them from Britain unless his antagonism towards the Baghdad Pact were dropped. But when he sold Egyptian cotton to Communist countries and purchased Czechoslovakian arms, he not only flung his door open to Soviet influences but afforded Russia, foiled for two hundred years, the chance to buy her way down into the Middle East rather than fight for it. And in so epoch-making a penetration, there was a certain malevolent logic: Russia and Egypt were dictatorships whose single-minded antipathy towards the West overrode other barriers, economic and religious.

Until the Anglo-American factor replaced it in the twentieth century, the *Pax Britannica,* coupled with a favorable European equipoise, had underpinned a free world order. And one of its safeguards was British ascendancy in the Middle East. Tsarist

* Eden, *op. cit.,* pp. 280-281 and 284-285; see also pp. 274-290.

Russia, pushing out from land-locked confines to warm-water ports, had been kept at bay. As a signatory of the Nazi-Soviet Pact, Molotov was to inform Ribbentrop that Soviet aspirations were directed, in the area south of Batum and Baku, towards the Persian Gulf—an aim that would have deflected Russian imperialism from Finland and the Balkans, territories long coveted by Germany for herself. During World War I, Britain and other Britannic countries defended the Middle East against both Germans and Turks, and during World War II held it against Italians and Germans. Spheres of influence in Persia had been demarcated by Britain and Russia before World War I; after World War II, the Soviet Union did not keep a wartime engagement to evacuate the Iranian province of Azjerbaijan until Washington and London —the matter having been aired in the Security Council—insisted that it do so. The Truman Doctrine, supplemented with Greek-Turkish aid, signalized the voluntary transference of a Mediterranean burden from Britain to the United States. An involuntary transference was the sequel to Sinai-Suez diplomacy.

President Eisenhower and Secretary Dulles deemed it more nuisance than menace when a Cairo-Moscow axis first cast its shadow across the British lifeline. In outlying theaters, Britain often thought Americans unduly alarmist; in the Middle East it was Washington which saw no need for that closer Anglo-American co-operation that London now proposed They did agree, nevertheless, to provide funds for the construction of a high dam at Aswan, so that Egypt might be enticed from Muscovite clutches. But upon mature reflection even that idea had to be shelved.

Anglo-American support of the Aswan project would have been mistaken on a number of counts. Sir Anthony Eden has described how hard it was to deal with Nasser when Russian overtures for the contract had turned his head; nor was the investment a sound one when Cairo had mortgaged the Egyptian economy to pay for arms from the Soviet bloc.* President Nasser's other ties with the East were, besides, scarcely a recommendation. He had welcomed advisers as well as arms from the Soviet bloc; by choosing that moment to recognize Peking, he mocked Washington while requesting it to bolster him financially. Then, too, if the United States and Britain backed the huge Egyptian undertaking they would have been doing more for Egypt than for Iraq, an Arab country allied to Britain, or for most other underdeveloped

---

* Eden, *op. cit.,* pp. 467-470; and John Robinson Beal, *John Foster Dulles* (New York: Harper & Brothers, 1957), pp. 255-261; see also pp. 262-288.

countries—a point that New Delhi seemed to miss. Credits that Russia granted several years later for building the Aswan Dam were in keeping with all that had gone before.

There was opposition, moreover, in the American Senate. Some of this might have been inspired by the State Department; much of it came from spokesmen for the southern states. The Nile Valley competed with the American South in the export of cotton; southern states did not want their own country to help finance an irrigation project that would increase the size of Egyptian crops—especially when Egypt was on cordial terms with the Russian adversary. A brusque rejection of the Aswan undertaking by Secretary Dulles is supposed to have hurt Egyptian feelings and gained sympathy for Cairo in the Afro-Asian camp. Though Nasser retorted by nationalizing the Suez Canal, the timing of his coup was determined by two other circumstances.

A move like Nasser's had to be carefully planned, and this one must have been in preparation for a year or more beforehand. So also Hitler's successive prewar forays were arranged long ahead of time; for making them at a convenient moment a pretext could always be found. And it was the departure of British troops from the Canal Zone, in accordance with the Anglo-Egyptian agreement of 1954, that now rendered the Egyptian coup opportune. American support of the Aswan Dam project was cancelled on July 19, 1956; Colonel Nasser would never have been able to seize the Suez Canal on July 26 if the Canal Zone had not finally been evacuated on June 13. Nor could he justify retaliation against the United States by breaking a series of treaties with quite other powers.

What, then, stirred up a furore was no ordinary confiscation of foreign property. The British government possessed forty per cent of the canal company's stock; the remainder was held by French investors—the enterprise itself being French in its inception and administration. Under the Constantinople Convention of 1888, the waterway was to be kept open to the ships of all nations in war and peace alike. Ownership of the Canal would devolve upon Egypt in 1968. But was a regime that seized it twelve years too soon, one whose leanings were at once pan-Arab and pro-Soviet, likely to be a reliable trustee? The master of Suez would be the master of interests far transcending local property investments or the sovereign rights of the land through which the Canal had been dug.

Should the Suez Canal Zone be reoccupied? Any such riposte to the Egyptian maneuver would have to be delivered at once, before Russia or others could intercede. Though the British, French, and Americans deemed it inadvisable to begin with a reference to the Security Council, London and Paris were resolved to submit the question to the United Nations before employing force as a last resort.*

Military precautions were taken by Britain in her Middle East Command. But it would have been impracticable for her to bring force to bear instantaneously. On Cyprus, springboard for the return to Suez, Cypriote insurrectionaries were being tracked down; as that island had no deep water harbor, troops and equipment for the expedition also had to be mounted at Malta, which was six days journey from Egypt by sea. British military services had been organized since World War II for the defense of Europe against Soviet attack. Mobile forces required for disciplinary action on a lesser scale were not available.†

Nor did Washington and a number of oversea Commonwealth capitals—Ottawa, New Delhi, Karachi, Colombo—want force to be used. Sir Anthony Eden, the British Prime Minister, could not disregard their pleas. The Eisenhower Administration hoped Nasser might be persuaded to relent under moral pressure. This did not mean that in the early weeks of the Suez crisis the United States excluded the use of force as a last resort. The Secretary of State told Prime Minister Eden that the American government understood the purpose of the British military preparations and thought that they had had a good effect. "A way had to be found," said John Foster Dulles to the British and French Foreign Secretaries, "to make Nasser disgorge."‡ And through that search, the United States, as leader of the West, procured a breathing-space during which any resort to force might be headed off—a respite during which a suitable alternative should have been, but was not, devised.

The chief user powers met in London from August 16 to August 22 and adopted an American proposal for an international board to operate the Suez Canal. India had sponsored a plan under which, with an advisory group from other nations, the management of the waterway would be left to Egypt; Russia, denouncing the majority scheme as an imperialist plot, sought to obstruct any sort of agreement. The London proposal was submitted to President Nasser by a mission that had the Prime Minister of Australia, Robert Gordon Menzies, as its spokesman. But in

---

* Eden, *op. cit.*, pp. 475 and 478-479.
† Eden, *op. cit.*, pp. 479-480; see also pp. 596-598.
‡ Eden, *op. cit.*, pp. 486-488; see also pp. 482, 484, and 497-498.

London and Paris there were rumblings against Washington already: canal tolls were being paid by American shipowners to the nationalized Egyptian company; and the Menzies mission was undercut by a willingness to compromise that President Eisenhower in the White House, and his Ambassador in Cairo, Henry Byroade, had been evincing. With Moscow on his side and with Washington not fully against him, President Nasser was encouraged to stand fast.

There was, moreover, a flaw in the case that the West propounded. Egypt had been able to bar Israeli ships while the British were still in occupation of the Canal Zone. Britain, France, and the United States were thus setting themselves up as monitors of treaties at whose violation they themselves, apart from routine protests in the Security Council, had winked. Nor had they insisted upon the free passage to which Israel was entitled through the Gulf of Aqaba. Yet what all this meant in terms of the rule of law was that Egypt had perpetrated not one but two acts of force—that against Israel as well as another against the canal company—and that lawless force would reign if there were neither collective redress nor some remedial counterforce.

Meanwhile, thanks to Nasser's intrigues against France in North Africa, the government of Guy Mollet had an unusually solid backing for strong measures. Though heavily engaged in Algeria, French troops joined their British comrades in Cyprus on August 28. Doubts over the propriety of a firm hand had, however, assailed the Labour Party and a large segment of the British people. The Menzies mission got nowhere. A second American attempt to divert Britain and France from the reoccupation of the Suez Canal Zone had therefore to be undertaken.

Nasser may have been stiffened by aid and comfort from Moscow and New Delhi. But to embolden him, there was also the zig-zag course that Washington then pursued. General Eisenhower had swept the polls four years before with his pledge to bring the Korean War to a conclusion. In November, 1956, he made his second bid for office and, if the image of Eisenhower the peacemaker was to be as overwhelmingly sustained, warlike gestures against Egypt must be discountenanced.

Did London exaggerate the danger of a Soviet breakthrough in the Middle East? Washington must have thought so. The Truman Administration had been raked fore and aft for complacency towards the growing peril of Communism in postwar China. Their successors were, nevertheless, to minimize the Russian threat to the Levant during the summer and autumn of 1956.

The Rhineland, when Hitler marched into it twenty years before, was as much in German territory as the Suez Canal was in Egyptian. His right to smash a treaty system upon which the European equilibrium reposed appeared as plausible as Nasser's latter-day act of force. And just as prewar Britain held back the French, so in 1956 Washington served as a damper on London and Paris. Nasser, to be sure, was no Hitler; but Nasser plus Moscow could be a formidable combination, one that should be forestalled before it was too late. Recalling the misjudgments of the nineteen-thirties, the British Prime Minister pointed out to President Eisenhower how, as the transit of oil through the Suez Canal is obstructed, Western Europe could be held to ransom by Egypt "acting at Russia's behest," while all Arab lands were made subject to Nasser.* Sir Anthony Eden acquired fame on the eve of World War II by demanding, with others, that Axis dictators be stopped before they got out of hand. The prewar outlook of men who were now Presidential coadjutors had, however, not been the same as his and, with them, parallels cited by Eden might not have gone down very well.

It was ironical, nevertheless, that the Secretary of State should have ignored them. For two years before, when Dulles himself had compared the situation in Indochina to the prewar invasion of Manchuria by Japan and to Hitler's reoccupation of the Rhineland, Churchill and Eden were the ones who balked. But as the Soviet Union might have backed its Chinese ally in 1954, the steps that Washington was then considering may have widened the war.† This time, however, her Egyptian protégé could not similarly involve Russia. There was no treaty of mutual assistance between Moscow and Cairo. Western interests in the Middle East could therefore be preserved and Soviet penetration curbed without serious global risks being run. If, moreover, analogies with the 1930's had been suggested with conviction by Dulles in 1954, he would not have deemed them inapposite in 1956.

There were, besides, personality conflicts that, in themselves, tended to make Washington unreceptive. A President whose wartime services had earned the esteem of the British people depended on a Secretary of State whom they had less reason to admire. When John Foster Dulles negotiated the Japanese Peace Treaty on behalf of the Truman Administration, he had not been entirely forthright with the Foreign Office. Nor had it been Secre-

---

† Eden, *op. cit.*, pp. 518-521; see also pp. 480-481, 493, 511, 568, 578, 608, and 626.

† Eden, *op. cit.*, pp. 104-108.

tary Dulles but Sir Anthony Eden who, at the Geneva Conference of 1954, arranged an armistice in Indochina—a matter that may have nettled him. During the negotiations conducted by Sir Anthony Eden that culminated in West Germany's admission to NATO, John Foster Dulles could have upset the applecart. Unintelligible to Eden was Washington's coolness towards that Baghdad Pact which it had, in part, originated. It sometimes seemed, Eden was to observe later, as if Dulles, a preacher in a world of politics, had little regard for the consequence of his words.* Custodians of Anglo-American friendship lacked the fullest confidence in each other. The ground was thus laid for a crisis of confidence.

London and Paris did not, at any rate, merely differ from Washington in their estimate of future contingencies. Negotiations were ruined by American pronouncements. Dulles had stated in London that Nasser must be made to "disgorge," and expressed approval of British military preparations. Eden, nevertheless, heard from Eisenhower on September 3 that American public opinion had rejected the use of force even as a last resort.† Already, at a press conference on the eve of the Menzies mission, President Eisenhower had so restricted any possible resort to force that President Nasser, who should have been kept guessing, was relieved of anxiety on that score. Some days later, when Secretary Dulles said that the United States would not shoot her way through the canal, Cairo knew that it could thumb its nose at a divided West with impunity.

American leadership had been predicated upon the concept of peace by power. Its application to the Suez dispute was repudiated. But American diplomacy could not divest its own side of bargaining weapons without making it more likely that weapons of war would in the end be employed.

So as to restrain Britain and France, Secretary Dulles next suggested a users' association. This device was approved at a second London conference in September. If the United States footed the bill, oil tankers and other traffic could be rerouted around the Cape of Good Hope and Western Europe might import dollar oil from the Western Hemisphere. But American funds were not forthcoming and, with other seafaring nations, the United States

---

* Eden, *op. cit.*, pp. 20-22, 70-71, and 177-178; see also pp. 179-194.

† Eden, *op. cit.*, pp. 517-518. During October, Dulles thought the use of force would be mistaken because he felt Nasser's position was deteriorating. Apparently, however, the Secretary of State still did not deem it wrong in principle a few weeks before operations against Egypt began. *Ibid.*, p. 561.

herself was reluctant to by-pass the Suez Canal or compel American ships that sailed under the Panamanian and Liberian flags to withhold canal fees.

Teeth were thus removed from the Dulles scheme before it could be set going. But its prospects were dim from the moment the Secretary of State disclaimed any intention of falling back on the use of force. French and British Ministers regarded the idea of a users' association as a stratagem to postpone a showdown with Nasser. Sir Anthony Eden was willing to try it, however, because, as he afterwards recollected, Anglo-American co-operation had been a guiding principle throughout his political life. This, he felt, would be destroyed by the kind of "cynicism" that Dulles exhibited. "Parting, or a master and vassal relationship" might then be the choice before allies.*

The matter was, nevertheless, submitted to the Security Council where the Western powers were to have one last chance for harmonizing respective policies and for ascertaining how far the United Nations could enforce that rule of law to which, under the Charter, it had been dedicated. Little was accomplished. On October 13 the Security Council did adopt six requirements, one of which stipulated that the operation of the Suez Canal should be insulated from the politics of any country—a stipulation that even Egypt accepted. But the Russian veto had excised any reference, as specified by the London proposals, to international regulation. And anyway, before the six requirements could be carried out, or the users' association implemented, there would have to be full co-operation by the United States with Britain and France. Of this there was no sign. British opinion had been rent over the question of using force; hoping that domestic pressure would check Sir Anthony Eden, the Eisenhower Administration played for time. But no alternative to coercion could be improvised when Washington itself did more to hinder than help.

Nor did the United States and Britain diverge only over the modalities of common action. A more far-reaching discrepancy had opened up. President Eisenhower and Secretary Dulles had, by their neopacifist–no-force utterances, conveyed to the Egyptian dictator that the West's bark would be worse than its bite. Still more serious was it on October 2, when Secretary Dulles adverted to other, fundamental, differences in the approach of the three Atlantic allies to the Suez problem. The United States stood with Britain and France in NATO areas where she was bound to them by treaty. But where, as over Suez, the colonial problem

* Eden, *op. cit.,* pp. 534-540.

arose, the American role had, he said, to be a somewhat independent one. To London and Paris, it seemed incredible that the Secretary of State could draw such a distinction at such a time. His remarks were a portent.

Colonialism had not been and would not be the issue. Nobody intended to reimpose a colonial regime upon Egypt. What might be enforced was the observance of contracts on which neutral as well as allied economies depended. And when the United States distorted that crucial fact, she played up to a pan-Asian gallery of which the larger part had been neither pro-Western nor pro-American. NATO, it is true, did not extend to the Middle East—though it had its contacts, through Britain and Turkey, with the Baghdad Pact. But leadership must be impelled by a comprehensive view, and this it did not get.

NATO, as the West's major grouping, cannot be cut off from whatever happens elsewhere. Washington might try to divorce it from a vital outlying interest of Britain's; this could be done only by ignoring the global foundations upon which a key regional edifice reposed. Under the primacy of the United States, a strategic interlock enabled the West to establish against the East a world-wide counterpoise. But in that counterpoise the British component has been sustained by a world-wide power structure of its own. American and British interests were not identical at every point of the compass; the interaction between them was unremitting, subtle, and profound. Washington overlooked that. And a narrow, arid legalism served lawlessness rather than law.

At the end of October, 1956, a counterattack, mounted by Israel in the desultory war which Egypt had been waging against that country, brought the Suez crisis to a head. For, as the Israelis swooped across the Sinai Peninsula, they moved down towards the Suez Canal Zone in little more than four days. The Anglo-French intervention ensued. It may be that President Eisenhower would have been in a less censorious mood after the American elections at the beginning of November;* the Sinai campaign forced Sir Anthony's hand. A decision about Suez could not in any case have been postponed much longer. British reservists had been called up, and discontent among them made it difficult to keep them idle indefinitely. To have demobilized them would have been to notify Nasser that, as negotiations with user powers were spun out, he had nothing to fear from Britain. But action against him required an objective that a divided public, Commonwealth

* Randolph S. Churchill, *The Rise and Fall of Sir Anthony Eden* (London: Macgibbon & Kee, 1959), pp. 294-297.

partners, the American ally, even some Arab associates could, presumably, accept. When the Israelis lashed out, the British and French governments announced that they must protect the Suez waterway from hostilities and, by separating belligerents, prevent other powers from being drawn in.

Ostensibly a balance could thus be achieved between Israel and Egypt. This, however, was a British rather than a French policy. Against pan-Arab pretensions, France saw in Israel a natural ally; the British were torn between the need to chastise Nasser and to keep unscathed their oil and other interests in Arab lands. Treated nonchalantly by the West, the Israeli republic was regarded by the Orient as a salient of Western imperialism. It had proclaimed its independence in 1948 after the General Assembly adopted a plan for the partition of Palestine; against Israel, five Arab countries plunged immediately into war. But the United Nations sealed the right of Israel to exist when it admitted her to membership in its ranks. The armistice of 1949, which forbade warlike threats and action, stipulated that a peace treaty was to be arranged. Sworn to avenge the Arab defeat, Egypt would not negotiate one.

In 1951, the state of war that she maintained was deemed invalid by the Security Council. The United States and Britain let her invoke it, all the same, when Egypt barred Israeli ships from the Suez Canal and the Gulf of Aqaba; when Arab rulers organized an economic boycott and land blockade against Israel; when attacks by guerrilla or Fedayeen bands enlarged the scale of irregular warfare. In 1950 Britain, France, and the United States had said that they would take preventive action if boundaries and armistice lines were about to be violated. But Arab hopes of getting Israeli territory were revived by a speech that Sir Anthony Eden delivered at the Guildhall in November, 1955; as the Tripartite Declaration of 1950 was strengthened, Israel's minute territory might be further reduced.* There were the truces that the United Nations had brought about and a truce machinery to give them effect. There would be no peace.

When the Arab states invaded Israel in 1948, they induced Arab kinsmen to flee from that country and then insisted afterwards that Israel permit them to return. The Charter bans threats as well as acts of war. Remorselessly, nevertheless, the Cairo radio and the Arab press incited Arab peoples against the young Israeli republic. The frontiers of Israel, as Sir Winston Churchill noted, flickered with murder and armed raids.

* Eden, *op. cit.,* pp. 368-369 and 372-373; see also pp. 574-575.

When Israel struck back on October 29, 1956, this signified no unprovoked aggression but the renewal of a war that Egypt refused to terminate. There had been unrest in Communist Poland; on October 23, the Hungarians uprose against their Russian overlords; and the United States was in the last throes of her Presidential campaign. Did Jerusalem think that the Washington administration would be influenced by their quest for Jewish votes? That was a theory against which, at the request of President Eisenhower, Secretary Dulles may have warned the Israeli Ambassador. But Jerusalem must have had other things to worry about.

For Israel, time was running out. If the United States and Britain could differ over Suez, they might be even less disposed to co-operate on her behalf when Israel had again to fight for her life. Would the Israelis break out of the trap that was being set? Despite the Moscow-Cairo arms deal and the sale of Western arms to other Arab states, Israel could not obtain delivery of an adequate arms supply for her own defense; not only Russian technicians but former servitors of the Nazi Reich were busy in Egypt. And then, in October, Egypt, Syria, and Jordan established a joint command against their Israeli neighbor. Israel could either move at once or await her doom at the convenience of her enemies. She moved at once.

But Israel's swift lunge down the Sinai Peninsula also set in motion the Suez venture of Britain and France. The French had been in touch with the Israelis; Prime Minister David Ben-Gurion paid a secret visit to Premier Guy Mollet, and London heard of his intentions from Paris. The United Kingdom had a treaty obligation to defend Jordan; on October 16, Sir Anthony Eden therefore requested the French to suggest that the Israeli counterattack should be mounted on Egypt rather than on Britain's own Arab client state. If, nevertheless, Jordan now came to the support of Egypt, she could still drag in Britain against Israel—and on Egypt's side. That is why an Anglo-French intervention that drew a line between the two belligerents might have been justified even if free transit through the Suez Canal did not have to be protected from hostilities in the area.

Nor could there be consultations with Washington and oversea capitals of the Commonwealth. More "palavers" of the kind against which London and Paris had been chafing since July would, on the eve of action, have been intolerable to contemplate.*

Towards the last, moreover, Israel had procured military aircraft and weapons from France. During the brief Sinai cam-

* Eden, *op. cit.,* pp. 571-574 and 586-588.

paign the French dropped supplies, provided naval support on the Mediterranean coast of Israel, and maintained an air cover for Israeli cities.* Land conflict was, besides, confined to her southern frontier; before other members of the Arab League could gird their loins, Egypt had again been trounced. The Anglo-French ultimatum—that they withdraw forces ten miles back from the Suez Canal—was accepted by Jerusalem on October 30 and rejected by Cairo early on October 31. An Israeli vanguard could, however, have taken most of the zone and held it for Allied airborne troops before resistance at Port Said stiffened. That was not allowed.

London, Paris, and Washington concurred at an early stage that the Arab-Israeli dispute and the future of the Suez Canal should be treated as separate matters. Any direct liaison between the two expeditions against Egypt had therefore been ruled out by London from the start. What the British authorities had been planning was to support Jordan against Israel;† they still hankered for the cession of Israeli territory to Arab countries. As go-betweens, the French did their best. But their assault upon the Suez Canal might not have wound up so ignominiously if British and French troops could have co-operated with Israeli forces in the vicinity. For all military objectives might have been attained before a cease-fire was ordered.

Not that combined operations would have been to Israel's liking. A singlehanded victory was what she needed rather than one gained in conjunction with others; after another display of her prowess, Arab states might have resigned themselves to a peaceful settlement with her. And yet the concatenation of the Suez with the Sinai undertaking was fortunate for Israel. Without this the French might not have been on hand to give covert military assistance; there would have been no destruction of Egyptian airfields to ensure that Israeli cities were saved from air attack. Diplomatically, too, the sequence of events was such as to protect Israel from hidden pitfalls. If she had stood alone in the United Nations, crippling sanctions would have been decreed; and, by collective duress, a pan-Arab solution of Arab-Israeli disputes might now also have been imposed. From so cruel an undoing the young republic was preserved by vetoes which Britain

* Merry and Serge Bromberger, *Secrets of Suez* (London: Pan Books, Ltd., 1957), pp. 11-12, 14, 21, 24-25, 39-45, 83-84, and 87-88.

† Eden, *op. cit.,* p. 486; Bromberger, *op. cit.,* pp. 15, 16, 32, 37, 40; and General Sir Charles F. Keightley, in *The London Gazette* (Supplement), Sept. 12, 1957, p. 5327.

and France cast in the Security Council on October 30. Never before had they thus voted against an American proposal; with their own Suez expedition in train, they could do nothing else. For, during the first decisive hours and days of the Sinai campaign, the Anglo-French coercion of Egypt was to deflect wrath and thus be Israel's lightning rod.

But the Anglo-French venture fell short when it failed to generate the same kind of speed. American and Commonwealth dissent required that Western interests be reasserted by a *fait accompli;* the logistics of the Suez expedition militated against one. An amphibious operation, it was slowed up by poor loading facilities at Cyprus, in the Eastern Mediterranean. From Malta, where commandos and armor were located, it took landing craft six days to travel to Port Said. Nor was the Anglo-French armada allowed to make an early start; shunning any semblance of collaboration with Israel, Sir Anthony Eden would not let it sail before ultimata had been dispatched to both Jerusalem and Cairo on October 30. Meanwhile, there was to be no deployment of airborne troops—this was not permitted until November 5 when seaborne forces were about to arrive at Port Said and could, as they did next day, go to the support of the paratroopers. Egyptian airfields and military targets had been under air attack since October 31; but that alone did not suffice to make Egypt capitulate when succor by diplomacy seemed near. And on the coercing powers, American pressure bordered on the coercive.

During the height of the Suez and Hungarian crises, especially when the Soviet Union shook its fist, the American Navy and the Strategic Air Command everywhere were put in a state of readiness. Yet the one clash that would be risked was not with adversaries of the United States but with a seaborne contingent of her own principal allies. By its patrol of the Mediterranean, the Sixth Fleet is an arm of Western power that has strategic access both to Eastern Europe and the Middle East. And, from an expedition to which the American government objected, it might be expected to hold itself studiously aloof. Instead it did much to harass the British and French naval forces psychologically and thus to impede them in the fulfillment of their mission.

Controversy between major Atlantic capitals was reflected on the scene of operations. The United States had left Britain and France with no alternative but a resort to force; yet this, too, might have been sabotaged if plans for the coercion of Egypt had been divulged to Washington in advance—if there had not been what Dulles described to Eisenhower as a blackout on news.

Heedless of the distrust they had incurred during the previous three months, the Eisenhower Administration now regarded itself as the injured party. And to even up the score, the United States treated her allies in the Eastern Mediterranean as they had treated her.

The Sixth Fleet was stationed in the operating area from October 31 to November 4/5. American military authorities had been kept in the dark by their British and French colleagues; the latter were not told the exact dispositions of the Sixth Fleet. More ugly still was a rumor without parallel since the rise of Anglo-American friendship at the turn of the century: as the British and French convoys moved in from Malta and Algiers, the report circulated that the American government had considered interposing the Sixth Fleet between them and the Egyptian coast.

To it, moreover, credence might have been lent by the manner in which the Sixth Fleet comported itself. During the bombardment of Egyptian airfields, American naval units entered the harbor of Alexandria to evacuate American citizens from Egypt; Egyptian destroyers were preserved by their presence from rocket attack. American naval aircraft buzzed a French warship which assisted the Israelis in the Sinai campaign; when they flew in the Cyprus air and over the Anglo-French convoys, they interfered with the expedition's radar. On the approach of the armada to Port Said, moreover, an alert was caused by submarines that were neither Soviet nor Egyptian but American. Sir Charles Keightley, Commander in Chief of the Allied forces, reported afterwards upon the anxiety, difficulties, and great inconvenience that resulted from the activities of the Sixth Fleet.* It had been ordered by Washington not to "take any guff from anyone." Yet none would be offered.

The navies of Atlantic allies had been earmarked for common global tasks but in the Mediterranean they were at cross-purposes. An inglorious conjuncture, it was one over which the Western coalition touched bottom. It contrasted, moreover, with the posture of affairs during the Spanish-American War when, ushering in Anglo-American friendship, the predominant seapower of Britain had been put to a creative use. Britain did not only hold the ring oceanically for the United States against European intervention; as Manila was about to fall, British ships were so deployed that the German naval commander, whose

---

* Bromberger, *op. cit.,* pp. 93, 111, and 162-163; and Keightley, in *The London Gazette* (Supplement), Sept. 12, 1957, p. 5331.

attitude had been antagonistic, would have been unable to trespass. By November, 1956, American sea power was predominant. Its demeanor, however, recalled no historic debt but a more ancient grudge.

Coalition policies were, besides, not the only ones to which damage was done during the Anglo-American divergence. When the United States endeavored to have the Suez expedition halted in its tracks, she set regional precedents that might eventually recoil against her. For what she then did ran counter to her position, past and present, as paramount power in the Caribbean. And the degree to which this is menaced was subsequently made clear when, as tutelary angel of Castro's Cuba, Premier Khrushchev proclaimed the demise of the Monroe Doctrine.

About the Middle Eastern diplomacy of the United States there may have been a Wilsonian aura. But here, too, Eisenhower and Dulles should have pondered the facts of history. Woodrow Wilson and contemporary Allied statesmen might have formulated epoch-making precepts of world settlement; before that, nevertheless, the President had been goaded into an attack on Mexico, as Israel, four decades later, was to be goaded into an attack on Egypt. Since those days, to be sure, the Covenant, the Charter (and, hemispherically, the inter-American treaties) have set forth a new code under which nations are enjoined against taking the law into their own hands. In 1956, however, few believed that the United States would forbear, as she exhorted Britain and France to forbear, if the site of danger were the Panama rather than the Suez Canal. And that she would not have done so under his Presidency, Harry Truman was frank to confess.

To Britain in particular this question was a piquant one. It may have been forgotten how, at the turn of the century, she had, for the sake of her modern friendship with the United States, forfeited equal rights in the projected isthmian waterway; how, some years later, President Woodrow Wilson appealed against the discriminatory tolls that, in contravention of the Hay-Pauncefote Treaty, Congress had levied. Yet, in 1956, an anti-colonial refrain over such an issue could scarcely have been more incongruous; for when Theodore Roosevelt acquired the Panama Canal Zone, classic imperialism was at its most unabashed. In the Suez venture, moreover, Britain and France did not envisage a permanent occupation. Unlike the United States at Panama, they were actuated by no long-range national design but by a global exigency that was unforeseen.

One argument, above all, should not have been omitted from any well-grounded calculation of American policy. Legalistically, in their London talks, American spokesmen tried to distinguish between the Suez Canal as an international waterway and the Panama Canal as an American waterway leased in perpetuity to the United States.* But the international character of the Suez Canal was precisely what substantiated the Anglo-French contention that the remedy at Suez ought to be an international rather than a self-regarding Egyptian one.

During the Potsdam Conference of 1945, President Truman had suggested that such international arteries as Suez and Panama be internationalized. The East–West contest soon dissipated the spirit which evoked that proposal. Nationalization rather than internationalization of the Central American waterway is, furthermore, what Panama desires. It is, in addition, highly improbable that Egypt would follow the American example if the United States entrusted the management of the Panama Canal to some international or hemispheric organization; Cairo is more rather than less nationalistic than ever. That the United States will willingly relinquish jurisdiction over the Panama Canal is, as a matter of fact, inconceivable at the present time. But her case has been weakened by the attitude she adopted during the Suez crisis of 1956. For when she deferred to Egypt over the nationalization of the Suez Canal, she herself yielded a point to Panamanian and other opponents of her own isthmian holdings.

Two years before, moreover, the United States and Britain had concurred over the measures to be taken against Communist inroads in the environs of the Panama Canal. The Eisenhower Administration may or may not have furnished arms and supplies to Colonel Carlos Castillo Armas when he invaded Guatemala from Honduras and unseated a pro-Soviet regime in that Caribbean country; whatever other backing the United States could give him was given. And prior to that, in 1953, a pro-Soviet regime had been curbed on the north shore of South America when Britain pared down British Guiana's right of self-government. Against this exercise of imperial power, not a murmur was heard from Washington. And yet, over what they had done in British Guiana and Guatemala, the British and American governments were, by the strict tenets of anticolonialism, both seriously at fault. But the colonial issue was not only irrelevant when the United States dwelt upon it in 1956. Anglo-American

* Eden, *op. cit.*, p. 485; see also p. 557.

divergence is unavoidable if Washington takes one line when American regional interests have to be protected, another when the vital outlying interests of its own chief allies are menaced.

Nor was anticolonialism the only principle to whose application an air of expediency had been given. United Nations procedures were anticipated, waited upon, or sidetracked in the same erratic manner. In June, 1950, President Truman ordered American forces to support South Korea before the Security Council could meet and legitimize what had been done. So also, by stationing the Seventh Fleet in the Formosan Straits, he may have consolidated the American defense perimeter in the Western Pacific; when the United States thus intervened on one side in the Chinese civil war, she did not ask for United Nations approval but acted on her own.* In 1954, however, London and Washington had agreed to evade Soviet tirades in the Security Council and an anticolonial outburst in the General Assembly by keeping the world organization out of the Guatemalan picture entirely; matters were allowed to take their course through the inter-American system. There was discomfort in Britain about this. But in the reckoning of the Churchill government, Anglo-American solidarity came first.†

And now, unlike the treatment accorded the Guatemalan problem, the Sinai campaign and the Suez expedition were not allowed to take their course. President Eisenhower and Secretary Dulles put these items on the agenda of the United Nations with the utmost speed. For the question of recourse to the world body depends on whose ox is gored.

And there, during the autumn of 1956, the great divergence became a public spectacle. Britain and France vetoed the Dulles proposal for sanctions against Israel on October 30, and then, as the Suez venture also began, the whole dispute was transferred from the Security Council to the General Assembly. But that organ had no authority to prescribe sanctions against any of the coercing powers; it could only urge them to cease fire and withdraw—something which it did in the early hours of November 2. Canada thereupon suggested that a United Nations Emergency Force be dispatched for service in the Sinai Peninsula and the Suez Canal Zone. The Canal itself was, moreover, blocked

---

* Truman, *op. cit.,* II, pp. 334-338.

† Eden, *op. cit.,* pp. 150-155 and 634. London also promised to maintain an embargo on the shipment of arms to Guatemala. International law forbids the search of ships on the high seas, but Secretary Dulles had threatened to violate this if necessary.

by Egypt, and arrangements for clearing it had to be negotiated. But the lesson of that event went undigested: that by its mastery of a major thoroughfare, so backward a country was enabled to levy blackmail on a number of advanced ones.

A still broader issue was, however, to make an indelible impression. On an American resolution, the United States had been aligned with the Soviet and Afro-Asian blocs against her own British and French allies. The West was split and the East, stamping out the Hungarian revolt, must have gloated. For this was no routine question over which polemics in the West were relatively innocuous; Britain's global status, major French interests, the power foundations of a free world order were affected by it. A higher loyalty, according to Washington, was owed to the principles of the United Nations. But even of these, as a vengeful Anglophobia burst forth, no calm, equitable interpretation was permitted. Arab lawlessness would have been curbed long before if there had been an authentic rule of law. And when those who had done least to observe it voted with the United States against those who had done so much to maintain it, the American course itself should have been re-examined.

Fresh emphasis was laid instead on outworn clichés. Since the shift of primacy from one to the other, it had been incumbent on the United States to respect the narrow margin of power within which her own British ally operated. Yet on November 2, when Vice-President Nixon rejoiced over a second declaration of independence from colonialism, two important coalition associates were, at a hazardous moment, hit below the belt. They could not do without the United States; while she cultivated Afro-Asian goodwill, it looked, for a delusive interval, as though she might be willing to do without them. When the United States moved fast in the United Nations, she stole a march on the Russians. But as this had to be done at the expense of Britain and France, it was scarcely worth doing.

News from the Sinai Peninsula was, moreover, to put the American initiative in a strange light. For when Israel crushed armored divisions poised against her, she also unearthed emplacements and stockpiles of a magnitude suited to Russian rather than Egyptian designs in the Middle East.

The British people themselves would long differ over the rights and wrongs of the Suez venture. It may be that Britain had neither currency reserves nor proper armament for an expedition of that kind. But none of this will acquit the United States of sabotaging proposals that might have averted the use of force or of doing her utmost to nullify operations after they began. The chronology of the Suez venture suggests that if Washington had not bristled up, even Moscow would have been circumspect. As ally of Britain and leader of the West, the United States could express disapprobation; an effort to humiliate the British was inexcusable. Until the Suez Canal Zone had, at least, been reoccupied, the Eisenhower Administration might well have marked time. So feverish was the haste to have the Suez expedition curtailed, that the procedures of the General Assembly were telescoped.

The rush to rescue Egypt from condign punishment contrasted, moreover, with procrastination over Hungary's cry of anguish. That hapless land had been seething with revolt for six days when Israel, having struck back in Sinai, touched off the Suez venture. Yet, after a preliminary debate in the Security Council on October 28, the United Nations paid little heed, and the United States took no steps until after Britain, France, and Israel had, with the help of Soviet votes, been collectively rebuked.

One hidden motive for delay should be noted. The American representative privately accused London and Paris of attempting to exploit the plight of the Hungarian people so as to divert attention from the Suez venture.* But Moscow could not be brought to book; only from London, Paris, and Jerusalem was any success for the United Nations to be wrested. Politics were being played with great issues. Measures taken against the Soviet imperium might plunge mankind into nuclear war. No such danger would attend anything done against Britain, France and Israel. The Western coalition had alone provided the non-Communist world with the necessary safeguards. But as Washington upgraded the United Nations, it downgraded its own alliances.

Pique, too, became an instrument of policy. There had been no consultations before the resort to force because, after being so unco-operative, Washington might nip the whole enterprise in the bud. But there was an imputation of bad faith here which a President, who had never been renowned for a placid temper, did not take with good grace. And Mr. Eisenhower, whose Presidency was about to be re-endorsed at the polls, now had the plaudits of new Asian admirers to supplant those transAtlantic ones which had but lately resounded in his ears.

Stern was the demand from Washington that London accept the cease-fire at once. And if there was no direct threat of American oil sanctions, these figured indirectly in developments

* Eden, *op. cit.*, p. 609.

throughout. Visiting allied Cabinet Ministers could not, moreover, get in to see the President; the Secretary of State underwent surgery; at the General Assembly the American representative, Henry Cabot Lodge, Jr., would not talk with Selwyn Lloyd, the British Foreign Secretary. The French public had, besides, not reacted to the Suez expedition in the same way as the British. On the attempt to overthrow Nasser, the French nation, usually so divided, had seldom been so united. But the use of force against Egypt was, irrespective of party, repugnant to large sections of British opinion. American policy was praised in Parliament by elements that, since World War II, had done most to malign it. Protests from infuriated Commonwealth capitals—Ottawa, New Delhi, Karachi, and Colombo—merged with American censure and political tumult at home.

Then, too, there was a threat of Soviet intervention. Prime Minister Eden had warned Bulganin and Khrushchev, when they visited England in April, that Britain would fight to maintain her oil supply; when they attended the first London conference in August "as watchdogs for Nasser," Soviet representatives seemed to recognize British interests in the Middle East; in correspondence with Sir Anthony Eden during September and October, Marshal Bulganin sounded querulous but comparatively restrained.* Russia, however, could not let her role as patron of the pan-Arab cause go by default; and then, in November, other vistas appeared. The Western coalition had cracked open; unbelievably, a new configuration in world politics might be feasible—one of which the Kremlin had dreamed ever since the primacy of the West had shifted from Britain to the United States during World War II. Hitler aspired to a planetary deal between prewar Britain and the Third Reich. For that kind of global duumvirate between the United States and Russia the time might, at last, be ripe.

Washington was the one capital in which Soviet diplomacy overreached itself. Yet the American attitude was what had emboldened it. Unlike the Security Council, the General Assembly could only request a cease-fire and a withdrawal of invading armies. Teeth might, however, be put in its resolution if Russia and the United States imposed it on Britain, France, and Israel conjointly; if, uninvited, they were to undertake enforcement measures together. A prerogative that neither could permit the other to exert by itself they would thus arrogate to themselves in unison.

---

* Eden, *op. cit.*, pp. 401, 494-495, 503, and 543-544; see also pp. 555-556.

The Charter does not provide for any such delegation of authority; in its name Washington and Moscow would themselves be *ultra vires*. But at that possibility, so enraged was it by the Sinai campaign and the Suez venture, the General Assembly might not have boggled.

In the end what Russia achieved was the effect of a unilateral intervention without the risk. To have done more than she did would have been foolhardy. Between the NATO area and the Middle East, the United States may have wanted to segregate treaty obligations from general coalition interests; there could, in any final emergency, be no compartmentalization of that sort. The West's legal commitments may have been limited ones; its defense was more ramified. Nor could Moscow, unlike Washington, deceive itself about this. The Sino-Soviet grouping had been immobilized on the global front by the countervailing strategy of the West; by its own dissensions the West might presently be self-immobilized. Meanwhile, it was not by opposing the United States but by collaborating with her that Russia could, with safety, meddle still further in the Middle East.

In a war of nerves, Soviet diplomacy did not confine its activities to the dispatch of notes. Russian troop movements seemed larger than the unrest in Poland and the uprising in Hungary warranted; fresh supplies of Soviet aircraft and war matériel were reported as being en route to Egypt and Syria. Messages from the Kremlin to Britain and France proved somewhat less bellicose in their text than they sounded when first broadcast late on November 5. Bismarck had precipitated the Franco-Prussian War by re-editing the Ems telegram. A similar ruse, made possible by mass media, helped curb Anglo-French operations against Egypt.

There was, at any rate, ambiguity in the Soviet resolve to have so-called aggressors crushed. Nobody could be sure whether Russia had threatened to intervene by herself or whether the Kremlin, by mentioning the United States and the United Nations, did not mean to toss the ball, after an ominous feint, back to others. The fact was, nevertheless, that, in his note to Sir Anthony Eden, Premier Bulganin referred to the prospect of rocket warfare against the British Isles; and, in his letter to Mr. David Ben-Gurion, the Russian Prime Minister warned that Israel's national existence might be jeopardized. Soviet rocket diplomacy had begun. And yet it did not do so until there had been a grave split in the West—one on which Russia would try to capitalize in collaboration with the United States rather than against her.

Only Port Said had been occupied when London and Paris accepted the cease-fire and consented, on November 6, to evacuate their expeditionary force from the Suez Canal Zone. They did this, according to Sir Anthony Eden, because when fighting stopped in Sinai, the British and French had accomplished their mission: there was no longer any danger that conflict between Israel and Egypt would spread. Then, too, there had been a heavy run on the pound—speculation against sterling, largely, he observed, in the American market or on American account.* In his memoirs, Sir Anthony Eden is silent about specific pressure, at this climactic hour, from Washington and oversea capitals of the Commonwealth. To most people, it looked as though Moscow had tipped the beam. There would, however, be no Soviet-American directorate to reorder world affairs, and here the Kremlin's overtures were repulsed.

"Unthinkable" was how President Eisenhower dismissed Moscow's proposal for close Soviet-American co-operation against Britain, France, and Israel. No other answer, unless all need for the collective defense of a free world order had vanished, could have been given. The President reminded Premier Bulganin that Russia herself, in keeping with a request by the General Assembly, had troops of her own to withdraw from Hungary. The American Navy and the Strategic Air Command were, moreover, on the alert; the United States would not be taken unawares if Russia, unable to enlist active American support, intervened with rockets or "volunteers," and a global showdown should ensue. Trends in the White House were further clarified on November 13 when General Alfred Gruenther, an intimate of the President's and the retiring Supreme Commander of NATO, stated that if the Soviet bloc attacked the West, it would be destroyed.

But no time for a concerted resistance by the Western coalition could have been more unpropitious. Until the eve of the first Anglo-French landings, the Sixth Fleet hovered about the Anglo-French armada—as disposed to collide with its chief allies as to fight at their side. There had been a rising chorus of dissent in Britain as well as in Washington and some oversea capitals of the Commonwealth. And while President Eisenhower reacted with vigor to Soviet blasts, these may not have been wholly inopportune. His own efforts to make Britain and France desist were thus reinforced.

Nor was Israel's compliance to be long delayed. Russia might hector and bully; it was not only in pro-Soviet or Afro-Asian quarters that sanctions against Israel, then and later, would

* Eden, *op. cit.,* pp. 622-624; see also pp. 588 and 620-622.

have been a popular move. On November 7, Jerusalem had been warned by Washington that, because of Israel's refusal to withdraw from the Sinai Peninsula, the world stood on the brink of general war; American economic aid would stop if she were obdurate and Israel might be expelled from the United Nations. On November 9, Israel agreed to a withdrawal of troops from Egyptian territory. Unlike Britain and France, she had attained immediate military objectives. The question was whether more satisfactory border arrangements could be made before troop withdrawals were complete.

And as with the Sinai campaign, so also with the Suez venture, disputes over its liquidation prolonged Western cleavages. In the Middle East, the field was thus left open to pro-Soviet–pan-Arab influences. At Washington, it is true, the Russians had been snubbed for their pains; and yet Washington itself had furnished ample grounds for the Soviet *démarche*. After Nasser's coup in nationalizing the Canal, only a basic reorientation could explain American indifference towards British and French interests; in Washington and New York, as the Suez venture reached its climax, all signs pointed to an irreparable breach. It is significant that rocket diplomacy was first accompanied by a bid for Soviet-American hegemony. Against them both, nevertheless, coalition strategy prevailed.

This latter had, as a matter of fact, governed the whole course of events. The great divergence may have shaken the Western coalition to its depths; peace by power is the broad concept on which it rests, and that held sway. Over a particular regional application, the quarrel between Western allies was bitter. In general, when the United States stood firm against Russian intervention, she bore up an East–West equilibrium to which British and French power also contributed.

But something else might likewise have been implied: the East was not only warded off; the global stalemate would have enabled the coercion of Egypt to be concluded without a wider conflict being provoked. During the Korean War the danger was that of a clash between Chinese and American forces across the Manchurian frontier or in the Manchurian air, one that could not be localized if China turned for assistance to her Russian ally. But during Sinai-Suez operations, neither Russia, China, nor the United States was to be territorially involved or directly engaged. Such danger as there was in 1956 arose from Moscow's belief that, if Russia intervened against Britain and France, the United States would not come to the defense of her principal

allies. And to disabuse the Kremlin of that illusion was to preserve the peace.

Not that the idea of joint rule by Russia and the United
States had been abandoned. So patent are its attractions, strategic
and ideological, to the Soviet mind that it was bound to recur.
The countervailing alliances of the West would, first of all, be
wrecked by any such global realignment; and if the two colossi
were to face each other alone, an isolated America could be
preyed upon with greater ease. Their dual hegemony would therefore be but a step towards Russia's own domination—though
the emergence of Communist China may both quicken and modify
the Soviet quest.

It is, at any rate, natural enough for the Kremlin to conceive of leadership, with or against America, with or without
China, along dictatorial lines. What must baffle it is the perverse
way it mends rifts in the West by trying to exploit them. For
with their rigid view of history, the dialecticians of Moscow can
never comprehend the kind of dialectical process that underlies
Anglo-American friendship. Again, as so often before, a rival of
the West had set limits to Anglo-American divergence by striving
to maximize it. At a low as at a high point in Anglo-American
friendship, the overriding interest of the English-speaking peoples
in the continuance of a free world order was to be reaffirmed.
The American rebuff to Moscow had been unequivocal: the
United States would not combine with Russia to intimidate Britain
and France. But Washington was, nevertheless, still resolved to
bend them to the American will.

AFTER THE CEASE-FIRE

After the cease-fire sounded on November 6, arrangements had to be made for occupying troops to hand over Port
Said and the Sinai Peninsula to the United Nations Emergency
Force. Then, too, Britain, France, and Israel were loath to withdraw unconditionally. Ostensibly it was to the United Nations
that Egypt owed her deliverance. It would have been in consonance
with the purposes of that body if a termination of her state of
war with Israel were first procured, together with a renunciation
of her demand for exclusive control over the Suez waterway. But
Colonel Nasser was regarded as more sinned against than sinning
by his Soviet and Afro-Asian supporters; by Dag Hammarskjold,
the Secretary General, to whom had been entrusted negotiations
with Egypt over the Emergency Force and the clearance of the

canal; and by American policymakers that were in tune with them. Washington, besides, was eager to have the Emergency Force take over and occupation troops depart before Russian "volunteers" were dispatched to Egypt and Syria—an eventuality which, in the Bulganin-Eisenhower exchanges, the United States had warned she would oppose. With sympathy from the United Nations and with backing from Washington, the vanquished Nasser could therefore extort a victor's terms.

Against her British and French allies the United States now exercised two kinds of pressure, one personal, the other economic. Sir Anthony Eden thought her attitude was harsher after the cease-fire than before. President Eisenhower might have dissipated his new-born popularity among Afro-Asian peoples if a meeting were held in the White House with Sir Anthony Eden and Premier Guy Mollet; such a visit was deferred until after Allied troops had been withdrawn from Egypt.* Herbert Hoover, Jr., was Acting Secretary of State and he may have been the one to advise that any top-level meeting of the Western Big Three be countermanded. Oil sanctions were in the offing. The franc and pound sterling had weakened; oil from the Persian Gulf could not be transported through a waterway which Egypt had blocked. Syria, moreover, had cut some pipelines and might yet cut others; further sales of Saudi Arabian oil to Britain and France were barred. The economy of Western Europe would be crippled if the flow of oil from the Middle East were not sustained or if the United States, out of her own abundant resources, did not come to the rescue. For the purchase of dollar oil and for the organization of an adequate supply, Britain and France needed direct American assistance. This, as the American Treasury made plain, they could not get without the prior evacuation of the Suez Canal Zone.†

Vast must have been the East's unearned increment if the West had disabled itself. That European prosperity was a brace of American security had, throughout a decade of postwar American leadership, been axiomatic. British loans, the Marshall Plan, NATO were all pillars of the same defensive edifice. But Western countries that had had nothing to do with the Suez expedition might also be penalized. During the previous summer, moreover, the user powers had discussed how to lessen dependence on the Suez bottleneck: the United States was to finance the extra cost of dollar oil and of rerouting Middle Eastern oil shipments around

---

* Eden, *op. cit.,* pp. 628-631; see also pp. 633-635 and 640.
† Eden, *op. cit.,* p. 641.

the tip of Africa. Plans for drawing upon American oil supplies had been drafted. And so that American oil companies could pool their efforts, it was agreed to suspend the Sherman Antitrust Act.

Nothing, however, had been done to carry out this program, and a resort to force ensued. One of its objectives was to maintain free access to Middle Eastern oil; what nobody could have anticipated was that the United States would even withhold alternative oil supplies. Before the Suez landings, the Sixth Fleet had raised the specter of American obstruction; that, though in an economic rather than naval guise, was what Britain and France were again confronting. After building up the Western coalition, the United States herself might thus undermine it; and though this seemed to be done on behalf of the United Nations, it would actually be one of those excursions into the unilateral by which her allies have periodically been discomfited. The United States had not been, could not be, asked by the General Assembly to extract compliance with its decrees. A right that does not exist under the Charter she would enforce anyway.

No all-out compulsion was set on foot. Under private American auspices there had been a substantial increase in the flow of oil to Western Europe; surreptitiously, as though to keep the news from Cairo and New Delhi, even government oil tankers were provided. On the whole, nevertheless, the economic life of Western Europe could be throttled by punitive measures. Britain and France rationed petrol. Then, towards the end of November, with venom rather than zeal impelling executants of Executive policy, other corrective influences from within the American political system made themselves felt.

The turning-point came after the United States voted in the General Assembly, on November 24, for an Afro-Asian resolution which brusquely demanded that the British, French, and Israelis withdraw from Port Said and the Sinai Peninsula forthwith. It ignored the fact that some of their occupation troops had already been evacuated and that in any case the United Nations Emergency Force was just taking shape. A milder resolution had, moreover, been proposed by M. Paul-Henri Spaak of Belgium. But among those to whom Afro-Asian goodwill meant more than friendship with Britain, France, and Israel, the American representative, Henry Cabot Lodge, Jr., was conspicuous; and on this occasion he employed a discretionary power to align the United States again with the Soviet and Afro-Asian blocs. Perhaps, if the President had known, this would not have been done; it was, all the same, a logical manifestation of the policy that Eisenhower and Dulles had pursued from the outset. A further blow to the interests of the Western coalition, it did, however, have one salutary result. Senators attached to the American delegation at the General Assembly awoke at last to what had been happening and proceeded to put their feet down.

New friends, the State Department was told by Senator Hubert Humphrey, could not be won at the expense of old ones. The emergency oil program had been pigeonholed and, if the British and French reiterated their intention to go on withdrawing occupation troops, this should be implemented at once. Democratic copartisans on the Senate Foreign Relations Committee endorsed these views; so did Senator William Knowland, delegation colleague and Republican floor leader. The latter was one of those who urged sanctions against Britain, France, and Israel; it had, however, been an eye-opener for him when Indian and other pro-Egyptian spokesmen assailed these countries but disregarded Russian wrong-doing in Hungary. Until then, the Democrats hesitated to bestir themselves against a Republican Administration that had just won a resounding victory at the polls and had, moreover, stolen their own anticolonial thunder. But now a bipartisan revolt was brewing.

Normally it is the task of the Executive branch to define and assert the national interest. The situation was, however, an abnormal one; and when everything else had been topsy-turvy, so, within the American system, was the transposition of political forces. Key legislators of both parties might resign from the American delegation; the charge against the Eisenhower Administration would be that it had lined up with neutrals and the Soviet bloc against traditional allies longer than the issues justified. The President's own re-election earlier that month had coincided with hostilities in the Middle East and the Hungarian uprising—with an hour of crisis, that is, when a mass electorate shrank from change and before the full import of current policies was to be widely understood. If Ministers had been answerable to Parliament, they could still have been called to account. Under the American system, where there are both divided powers and fixed terms, not even adverse midterm Congressional returns can affect the Administration's second four-year tenure. The Senate might, nevertheless, have a Democratic majority, and in foreign affairs a Republican President would have to lean on it for support. In their Suez diplomacy, the White House and the State Department therefore beat a hasty retreat—a performance that would be repeated some months later when sanctions against Israel were again contemplated.

Muted as an incident, its implications were dramatic. When so much else was upside down, it was typical of the time that legislators should have to save from the Executive branch, rather than the Executive from legislators, the American leadership of the West.

Three steps tended to restore the coalition front. And as far as these were related, they also showed how unrealistic in a global contest was Washington's attempt to keep its West European and Middle Eastern policies entirely separate from each other. Some weeks before, when the United States had urged acceptance of the cease-fire, she reminded Britain and France that, under the North Atlantic Alliance, she would not be obliged to assist them against a Russian attack at Cyprus or Suez. But after the cease-fire was accepted, and after the Russians were rebuffed, President Eisenhower had been constrained by this same Middle Eastern crisis to assure London and Paris that against Russian threats he would, in general, stand by them. During the next three weeks, Washington tried to elicit compliance with withdrawal undertakings. Then, on November 27, as Senators interceded, a statement by President Eisenhower not only renewed old ties with Britain and France; a far-reaching divergence over the Middle East made it essential to re-endorse NATO as a basic and indispensable element in American defense. The great bonds that long joined the United States with the United Kingdom, France, and other allies had, said the President, not been weakened or disrupted by recent differences.

But these occurred over the Middle East, and there, too, a reconvergence of American and British policies was foreshadowed. Despite the objections of cosignatories to her Suez venture, Britain still belonged to the Baghdad Pact, and Washington reiterated its support of that treaty on November 29; any threat to the territorial integrity or political independence of Iraq, Iran, Turkey, and Pakistan would, it was declared, be viewed by the United States with the utmost gravity. From Moscow there had been a barrage of invective against Iraq as well as against Israel, Britain, and France; Soviet arms were being delivered to Syria and in that country, as in Egypt, they might be employed by Russian "volunteers." Soviet designs may have been foiled for the moment when Israel captured Egyptian armament in Sinai and when Anglo-French bombings demolished a number of Egyptian aircraft. Yet, with a footing in Syria, Russia could encircle Turkey, a member of NATO and the main bastion of the West in the Middle East, and would also be entrenched on Israel's northern frontier.

Israel, however, did not figure in the American statement of November 29. She had undertaken to evacuate occupying troops from conquered Egyptian territory. But she first wanted to ensure that her right of self-preservation would not be deemed less valid than Egyptian contumacy in waging war. Here Israel obtained little satisfaction, and Washington did all it could during the next few months to make her conform.

Meanwhile, as leader of the West, the United States also took remedial action in the economic sphere. On November 30, the emergency oil plan was authorized at last. London and Paris had informed Washington beforehand that the evacuation of occupation troops would be phased with the arrival at Port Said of the United Nations Emergency Force. And on December 3, when the British and French governments announced early withdrawals, they could maintain the pretense of acting voluntarily, of not having bowed to inexorable economic pressure. But neither had the West retained—though there would still be Israeli detachments in the Gaza strip and on the Gulf of Aqaba—a lever for pressure on Colonel Nasser. Much in the life of Europe and the strength of Britain depended on the Suez artery. The net effect of American diplomacy had been, and would be, to confirm Egypt in unrestricted control.

To win her point the United States had utilized economic weapons. But Anglo-American friendship might be renewed through economic cooperation. Britain is banker for almost half of the world's trade: it would be in American as well as British interest if a run on the pound sterling, started by Anglo-American divergence over Suez, were brought to a halt. The British Exchequer did not have to use all of the loans and credits with which the Export-Import Bank of the United States and the International Monetary Fund in Washington were now prepared to tide it over. On the money marts of the world the mere fact that these were available sufficed to work its magic. And to the same end, the American and Canadian governments waived interest payments on British postwar loans.*

---

* Britain repaid the Export-Import Bank loan in the autumn of 1959, five years ahead of schedule, and dollar imports were now also allowed freer entry. This was done to help the United States meet a deficit in her balance of payments. British recovery owed much to postwar American economic aid and it was gratifying for Britain thus to return the compliment.

Transit through the Suez Canal was, all the same, still
to be by sufferance rather than right. Dollars were scarce; Britain
therefore could not look to North America as a permanent source
of oil supplies. It might, however, pay to transport oil from the
Persian Gulf around the Cape of Good Hope if supertankers were
built; new pipelines could also be constructed through Turkey
and Israel. But oil discoveries in North Africa and atomic energy
developments can do the most to relieve some European economies of dependence on the oil of the Middle East, and thus parry
an Arab penchant for political blackmail.

As for the British, they had become inured to a shrinkage
in their overseas power structure. During the Suez episode, however, it was an American ally and a number of Commonwealth
partners who had accelerated a further decline in status—and
that rankled. Britain was thwarted in an area long considered vital.
And yet the United States, as leader of the West, had only added
to her own troubles. For she would have to shoulder burdens
that she had compelled Britain, in association with France, to
drop.

Not that error was likely to be acknowledged. But a more
adequate statecraft would not have had to backtrack at once.
During the great divergence, the United Nations outranked the
Western coalition as an instrument of American policy. This, then,
was also a testing-time for it. For the preservation of a free world
order, would it yet reveal unsuspected capacities? American
policymakers were not the only ones that, focussing attention on
the Sinai campaign and the Suez venture, dallied at first over
censure of Russian misdeeds in Hungary; Dag Hammarskjold, the
Secretary-General, did the same. There was, of course, no way,
short of an East–West nuclear holocaust, to bring Russia to heel.
The Middle East offered the United Nations a more promising
terrain. This meant, nevertheless, that Charter rules were no
longer universal in effect; powers that flouted them least were
the only ones against which they could seriously be invoked. The
United Nations might act in the name of principle where it was
expedient, but not where it was inexpedient, to do so. Charter
rules had been invoked selectively. Would they be applied at
least with an even hand?

To cope with vague directives from the General Assembly,
the discretionary powers of the Secretary-General were enlarged.
Over the coercion of Egypt, he and Washington were in accord;
the American government could therefore sit back while terms
were discussed with Colonel Nasser under which the Emergency

Force would function, the Suez Canal be cleared, occupation troops be withdrawn. Soon the United States herself was to take up the cudgels for the West in the Middle East, and she then reverted to more traditional instruments of policy. She insisted that the United Nations handle the vital concerns of her allies. Her own interventions in the Middle East were, however, to by-pass the world body.

The Egyptian dictator had every reason to do business with the Secretary-General. Negotiations were inspired by the hypothesis that the evildoer was a victim and victims evildoers; on them, moreover, Moscow as well as Washington had bestowed its blessing. Without this joint benediction Secretary-General Hammarskjold could scarcely have proceeded as he did. From time to time he might differ in turn with various aspects of Russian and American foreign policy; he could never afford to disagree simultaneously with both. Trygve Lie, his predecessor, had incurred the Kremlin's wrath by espousing Charter enforcement in Korea; the widening of the East–West contest and the emergence of the Afro-Asian bloc called for a more complex diplomacy. Among candidates for the post of Secretary-General, it was only upon a Swedish neutral that all factions were able to concur. But it was not the neutrals who had created and defended a free world order; over the years none had been more unneutral than the British, the French and, historically, the Israelis. Between their mentality and that of the Secretary-General there may have been a deeper chasm than any of them appreciated.

The receding empires of the West have offered an easier target than the expanding empires of the East. But the United Nations can also breed a moral imperialism of its own. Achievement in the Middle East might have dimmed impotence over Hungary. Yet the world body could do no good when it abased countries from which its own progressive doctrine is derived; when it condoned the aggrandizement of those, in the Levant and Eastern Europe alike, which have treated the principles of the Charter with scorn. Other pressures on London, Paris, and Jerusalem were the decisive ones; the United Nations was, however, to receive credit for obtaining the cease-fire and the withdrawal of occupation troops. No other agency could have rendered the service which the quick establishment of the Emergency Force provided; and a precedent had been set for another Emergency Force which was sent even more expeditiously to the former Belgian territory of the Congo four years later. But administrative success cannot eclipse political failure; and, in 1956–57, the

United Nations failed to resurrect international rights in the Suez waterway or to make peace in the Middle East. It boasted of short-run accomplishments. The long-run problems of the area were given a new lease of life.

Nor has the pattern of achievement changed since then. From Suez in 1956 to the Congo in 1960, it was within the strategic bailiwick of the West that the United Nations operated. When wrong was done in the East's sphere of influence, the claims of the world body, from Hungary in 1956 to Tibet in 1959, were more modest.

The limitations under which the world body labors have long been familiar. But, in 1956, fresh questions about it were posed by the very nature of its success. During the previous year, when sixteen new members were admitted and the Afro-Asian bloc augmented, the balance of power within the General Assembly was altered. Ottawa promoted this move in collaboration with New Delhi—a fact that should be recalled when students of the Commonwealth analyze Canada's dissent from Britain over the Suez venture. In 1955 the United States had been less than enthusiastic about the so-called package deal; a year later she endeavored to profit by it.

These matters were, at any rate, no trivial ones in a world body where a two-thirds majority is required before a resolution can be adopted. By its possession of more than a third of the votes, the Afro-Asian bloc may either hold up a Western initiative or strike bargains with other voting groups whose consequences might be pan-Asian, pro-Soviet, anti-Western. The Security Council has been reduced to futility by the Russian veto. Will the Afro-Asian bloc have a similar veto in the General Assembly? By pandering to the susceptibilities of the Afro-Asian bloc, the United States may have tried, during the Suez episode, to forestall a division of the world along lines of race and leap ahead of the Soviet Union as a champion of the colored multitudes. But Washington was soon to make an about-face in the Levant, one that confirmed that there would have been more to gain and less to lose by a middle course.

The United Nations is, above all, a vehicle of politics rather than a court of law. In it, as in every representative institution, the crass and noble commingle unremittingly. But analogies between the General Assembly and democratic legislatures are deceptive and, despite outward procedural resemblances, raise undue expectations. The United Nations is not designed for world statehood; its task is to improve relations between sovereign countries rather than abolish national sovereignty. And the manner in which this is done must determine the extent to which the peoples of the West put their faith in the world body. Most of its founding members subscribed to the historic postulates of a free world order. But if those that spurn these should acquire control, they will change the character of the organization. And from it the West must thereupon turn away.

Not that the issue is one of democracies versus dictatorships. If it were, everything might be ideologically more simple: it would, in strict logic, debar treaty arrangements such as Britain has with Arab sheikdoms and the United States has with Franco Spain. Among NATO powers, Portugal and Turkey can scarcely be listed as paragons of democratic virtue; still less may all members of the Central Treaty Organization, the Southeast Asian Security Pact, or the Organization of American States. But freedom is served when the independence of their signatories is bolstered. The West has therefore co-operated with others on the basis of common interests that transcend its own ideology. Whether the East can do the same remains to be seen.

Universality of membership might, by the same token, be of practical value to the United Nations. But this is also self-inhibiting. Many of its members are governed by regimes whose despotism varies from the barbaric to the relatively benevolent; Communist China, when she enters, will hardly rank as an apostle of sweetness and light. Not all peoples represented in the United Nations are free to speak for themselves. How, then, can the world organization speak authentically and irrefutably for mankind?

Useful work may still be done. The utility of the United Nations is considerable when delegates from East and West, plus neutrals of one sort or another, foregather under a single roof. And yet the very circumstances that produce these groupings narrow the organization's scope. Without a lower common denominator the United Nations could not exist. But, on a higher level, it is an inner consensus that enables men to coalesce in defense of that which they cherish most. Nor is this an abstract truth with no bearing on the conduct of affairs. The events of 1956 merely underscored what should never have been lost from sight.

Nevertheless, moral force was said by President Eisenhower to have carried the day. That is not how Sinai-Suez diplomacy could have appeared to London, Paris, and Jerusalem—nor, from another standpoint, to Moscow. But when the United States acted through the United Nations, she had to soft pedal such exercises of power as she undertook, unbidden, on its behalf. The founders of the world organization intended it to be something more than a sounding board for moral force; it will be something less if what it does is not scrupulously just. A principle of moral force that is invoked to reinstate a Nasser, while it acquiesces in some Communist iniquity, is a caricature of morality. Moral force did not save Hungary; what the United Nations meant by this, Israel did not mean, and she preserved herself accordingly. It is as a preceptor of force, and not as a substitute for it, that moral force has a mission to discharge. The weak are at their weakest when they depend on it alone; with it as a goad, the strong should know how to exert their strength. Power without purpose will triumph, if power that is morally purposeful does not prevail.

The English-speaking peoples would not have had to fight a second world war if they had grasped these realities after the first. And in the East–West contest, they were as valid as ever. But did inordinate stress on the United Nations, did an unwonted *rapprochement* with Asian neutrals, presage a new theory of leadership in Washington? London had had no inkling that one was in store. The American public itself was taken as much by surprise.

It may be that a Churchillian stroke like the Suez venture needed a Churchill to carry it off. But for his misreading of the official American mind it was scarcely fair to reproach Sir Anthony Eden. Ever since Pearl Harbor, the basic presupposition of American leadership has been Anglo-American friendship and coalition solidarity. Yet, in 1956, a President who leaned on his staff was surrounded by foreign-policy advisers whose prewar antecedents were isolationist, if not anti-British. Subconscious motivations can neither be proved nor disproved. Britain, however, was the symbol of a past that each of these individuals might have preferred to forget: to put her in the wrong would have been, subtly and yet potently, for them to get their own back.

Sir Anthony Eden argued that the way to treat Nasser, especially when Moscow lent Cairo its patronage, was the way he had wanted to have Adolf Hitler treated during prewar appeasement days. But the more he suggested similarities with the nineteen-thirties, the more he might have stirred up among Presidential advisers an unavowed sense of guilt. The most inadvertent reminder of their own imprescience is not relished by public men whose past misjudgments have had to be lived down.*

It was, at any rate, no ephemeral irritation but a deep-

---

* This point is dealt with more extensively in Chapter III.

seated rancor that moved Washington, week after week, to shelve the time-honored prerequisites of Western leadership. They were all, the makers and executants of Administration policy, internationalists now. But a brand of internationalism was purveyed wherein the Anglo-American factor and friendship with France no longer came first; one whereby the West might be preserved without the preservation of outlying interests on which it relies.

And on this perhaps President Eisenhower had stamped a preconception of his own. The British were dismayed when Vice-President Nixon and Secretary Dulles confused the Suez question with colonialism. Before that, these two American spokesmen had hardly been favorites of Indian or other Asian neutralists. But it may have been at the behest of the President himself that the American bid for Asian goodwill was couched in language so bluntly anticolonial.

On this topic a revealing opinion is expressed in his war memoirs. Discussing relations between the United States and Russia, General Eisenhower remarked that "both were free from the stigma of colonial empire building by force."* And it went without saying that Britain and France were not "free" from any such "stigma." As a comment on Russian and American expansion, this dictum may not hold water. Yet it could be illuminating as a clue to the President's own mental reflexes during the Suez venture.

But misjudgment in the present may not only have derived from the President's own misinterpretation of the past. The past of that most influential Secretary of State, John Foster Dulles, lent a certain irony to warnings from Sir Anthony Eden, a prewar foe of appeasement, against a repetition of prewar mistakes. For when the Churchills and Edens were sounding the alarm about Axis dictators, John Foster Dulles had been sedulously finding excuses for them.

These, at any rate, would have been the beneficiaries of that "peaceful change" to which, in his writings, he advised free peoples to surrender. What he then portrayed as "dynamic" forces were, during the epoch of America First, to be hailed by Lindbergh as "waves of the future." After Munich, as late as the seizure of Prague in 1939, John Foster Dulles scoffed at the notion that the defense of the United States might be bound up with the defense of other free peoples. So immune was she that only hysteria could, he declared, entertain the idea that Germany, Italy, or Japan contemplated war upon her. What worried him

---

* Dwight D. Eisenhower, *Crusade in Europe* (Garden City, N. Y.: Doubleday & Company, Inc., 1948), p. 457.

was not Axis domination but any American participation in the coming war that merely restored the "military domination" of Britain and France.* To maintain their European preponderance was, as he saw it, to prolong injustice. Justice would be done, in other words, when their power crumbled—a point that Nazi warlords might have savored without demur.

Thus error in high office may have had diverse roots. When Ministers are also members of Parliament they must stand on their own record as well as on that of the Cabinet as a whole; where, as in the American political system, Executive and Legislature are separated, they do not answer either to electors or the House, and it is mainly the President's reputation that counts. John Foster Dulles was later on to expound the verities of Western defense as though he had always served them. But, during the summer and autumn of 1956, the gods on Olympus must have laughed when the historical case against the appeasement of the Egyptian dictator seemed more cogent to Sir Anthony Eden than it did to Washington. That it had been sound throughout was indicated by the course that the Eisenhower Administration took afterwards in the Middle East. But there would be little solace in all this for Sir Anthony Eden.

Nor were ideological lags in the President and Secretary of State the only ones that might have sharpened the great divergence. Some may also have influenced Henry Cabot Lodge, Jr., permanent American representative at the United Nations, and Herbert Hoover, Jr., the Under-Secretary of State. The former, it will be remembered, voted on his own for the Afro-Asian resolution that demanded the withdrawal forthwith of British, French, and Israeli occupation troops from Egyptian territory; the latter, as Acting Secretary of State during the first illness of Secretary Dulles, sought, through oil sanctions, to tighten the screws on Atlantic allies. Both of these men had been isolationists. Both had family loyalties that may have colored personal attitudes more than they realized.

It was a sign of the changed American outlook when a grandson of Henry Cabot Lodge was appointed spokesman for the United States at the United Nations. A recent defense of his forebear by the younger Lodge may, however, also be noted: a denial of any disservice rendered the cause of peace when Henry Cabot Lodge did all he could to prevent the Senate from redeeming a security pledge made to war-ravaged France by Woodrow Wilson, and from ratifying, with the Treaty of Versailles, the

* Address at the Economic Club of New York, March 22, 1939.

Covenant of the League of Nations.* The ardor displayed by the grandson in wooing the Afro-Asian bloc would not have been to the taste of so consummate an American imperialist as his grandfather. Yet it was in the spirit of the clan when he snubbed fellow delegates from Britain and France. For one obstacle to the settlement of Anglo-American disputes at the turn of the century had been the Anglophobia of the elder Lodge.

And as with the Lodges, so with the Hoovers. Fortress America had been the ex-President's isolationist concept; the Under-Secretary of State may not have accepted his father's views in their entirety—though, when he was appointed, a Republican Senate fancied that he did.† But what could not be ascribed to filial piety was the viewpoint of an oil engineer for whom the protection of American oil investments might bulk large. In 1953–54, at any rate, Herbert Hoover, Jr., had been deemed anti-British when, after the Mossadegh nationalization of British oil property, he negotiated the Iranian oil consortium. The degree to which the great divergence stemmed from differing backgrounds must, to be sure, remain conjectural. But between London and Washington there had been no meeting of minds. And none are more apt to resent the lessons of history than those that might be discredited by them.

The visitors list at the White House highlighted new trends. Britain and France had to keep their Prime Ministers at home; however, a welcome mat was put out, in December, for Jawaharlal Nehru, the foremost exponent of Asian neutralism. On January 11, 1957, Sir Anthony Eden, slighted by the President and broken in health, was succeeded in office by Harold Macmillan. To the latter, an old wartime friend, President Eisenhower sent a message that indicated, at last, a willingness to let bygones be bygones. Too much was still in flux for top-level Anglo-American contacts to be resumed. The Suez Canal had not been cleared; Israel had not withdrawn from the Gaza strip or Aqaba strong-points; Congress had not yet debated the Eisenhower Doctrine. But Prime Minister Macmillan expressed his resolve to further Anglo-American friendship after references to "the traditional Anglo-American alliance" and the "abiding strength" of the Anglo-American partnership had been made by the President.

A visit to the White House by King Saud of Saudi Arabia

---

* John A. Garraty, *Henry Cabot Lodge* (New York: Alfred A. Knopf, 1953), notes by Henry Cabot Lodge, Jr., pp. 352-353, 358, 366-368, 379-382, and 401.

† Eden, *op. cit.,* p. 182. This was what Dulles told Eden at the time.

at the end of January, 1957, afforded some comic relief. It could be rationalized as a conventional exercise in power politics. Power politics, however, were what the Eisenhower Administration had, during the Middle Eastern crisis, professed to spurn.

London was quick to observe how Washington, steeped in anticolonialism, might entertain a desert imperialist whose tribesmen were engaged in constant forays against the Buraimi Oasis and other British oil protectorates in the Persian Gulf. But the vast productive oil fields of the Arabian-American Oil Company are situated in Saudi Arabian territory; Egyptian and Syrian intrigue against the West had thereby been subsidized through American oil royalties. It had distressed Sir Anthony Eden that these should be used to undermine the British position in the Middle East, and to play the Soviet game.* But for a brief spell, after Saud's American pilgrimage, the Saudis were detached from Nasser and dropped their family feud with the Husseini kings of Iraq and Jordan; a lease on the American base at Dhahran was also renewed. Christian chaplains and Jewish personnel were to be excluded from this Air Force installation.

It was therefore Mayor Wagner of New York, rather than the White House, who voiced national sentiment when he refused to accord civic honors to a slave-holding Moslem bigot, one who had sided with the Nazis during World War II. A revulsion from the character of the Arab regimes Washington had been courting, from the line it had taken during the Sinai-Suez episode, now set in.

WASHINGTON BACKTRACKS

Evidence of a fresh approach was provided when the Administration invited Congress to endorse a new general statement of American policy in the Middle East. The right to declare war rested with it. But, on January 5, 1957, President Eisenhower asked Congress to authorize the employment of American forces so that the United States might secure and protect the territorial integrity and political independence of Middle Eastern countries that requested aid against overt armed aggression from any nation controlled by international communism. An offer of economic assistance accompanied this program. No aid was suggested, however, against indirect aggression, pan-Arab as well as pro-Soviet, and that was the more immediate regional danger.

The Truman Doctrine, which applied to Greece and Tur-

---

* Eden, *op. cit.*, pp. 370, 373-374, 382-383, and 648-649.

key, might thus be extended within and beyond the Mediterranean basin. For any such further American intervention the President probably had no need of additional powers. And yet, as with a similar authorization in 1955 to defend the area around Formosa and the Pescadores, he could move more freely if the Congress were committed in advance. He did not elicit from it everything for which he asked. But when Congress resolved in March that the United States would act in the Middle East at the President's discretion, the change from the Sinai-Suez interlude was drastic.

Neither on Capitol Hill nor at Westminster was the reception accorded the Eisenhower Doctrine an exuberant one. So abrupt a *volte-face* on a major foreign policy issue would, under the British parliamentary system, have brought about the fall of the government. The threat against which the Administration now proposed to take measures, it had itself pooh-poohed for more than a year. Unlike the Truman Doctrine, the Eisenhower Doctrine did not arise from an Anglo-American concert; the great divergence had supervened. So as to keep the Afro-Asian bloc in good humor, the United States, though leader of the West, not only wanted to delimit the Western coalition regionally, she also sought to reject Anglo-American co-operation in a region where her own British ally had long been predominant.

"If," remarked Secretary Dulles with singular infelicity, "I were an American boy who had to fight in the Middle East, I'd rather not have a British soldier on my right hand and a French soldier on my left." The fact was that there might have been no need for the Eisenhower Doctrine if, so as to forestall Russia and prevent an adverse shift in the world balance, Britain and France had been allowed to proceed with their intervention; the United States proposed to fill unilaterally a power vacuum to which she herself had contributed. The Eisenhower Administration may have disseminated the notion that the United States was not going to take Britain's place in the Middle East; that in creating a place of her own, the American incentive would be more exalted than Britain's had been. But a vested interest in misjudgment is what had really been engendered, and that could only be rectified by events.

Stress on the United Nations as the main instrument of American policy in the Middle East had, all the same, already begun to dwindle. For liquidating the Sinai campaign and winding up the Suez venture, Washington still gave it precedence; nevertheless, the Eisenhower Doctrine would have been superfluous if, for the defense of the West in the Middle East, the world body sufficed. Barren, too, had been the experiment of squaring American leadership with Afro-Asian neutralism. During February, Jawaharlal Nehru, who deprecated the military aspects of the Eisenhower Doctrine, greeted with acclaim Moscow's counter-proposal: that non-interference by the powers in the Middle East would be a remedy for ills already aggravated by Russia's own interference. President Eisenhower and Secretary Dulles might commend moral force to the British, French, and Israelis. For the United States herself they advocated something more tangible.

Debate in the Senate over the Eisenhower Doctrine coincided with efforts by the United Nations to clear the Suez Canal and have Israeli withdrawals from conquered territory completed. Assigning unconditional control of the international waterway to Colonel Nasser, the United Nations Emergency Force advanced from Port Said to the Israeli lines where it served as a buffer between victor and vanquished. British and French salvage vessels were banned and others had to be fetched; Cairo, in any case, would not permit the canal to be reopened until Israel toed the mark. And this she was reluctant to do.

Vital interests were what Britain and France had striven to safeguard. But when the Israelis hit back at Egypt, it was to break a pan-Arab stranglehold on the very life of the nation. The General Assembly, nevertheless, still hewed to the thesis that Israel had never been entitled to the same belligerent rights as Egypt; that, under the Charter, lawlessness could be legalized and self-defense rendered illegal. Egypt had seized the Gaza strip in 1948, and guerrilla attacks on Israel were mounted from it year after year. So, also, Israeli traffic to the Israeli port of Elath had been interdicted by Egyptian gun emplacements at Sharm El Sheikh, a Sinai strongpoint that controlled exit and entry to the Gulf of Aqaba. Could guarantees against their misuse be procured? If these were forthcoming, the last of the Israeli occupation troops would be recalled.

Guarantees of that sort could not, however, be granted without Arab States and the Afro-Asian bloc taking umbrage. Rather than vex them, Washington backed their demand for the unconditional evacuation of the Gaza strip and the Sharm El Sheikh; if the General Assembly, exceeding its powers, voted sanctions against Israel, the United States would, moreover, be the one to enforce these on its behalf. And that was farther than even Secretary-General Hammarskjold, who toiled to reinstate Nasser, was prepared to go. In the end there would be no sanctions; but what saved Israel from American economic pressure was pressure against the Administration by Congress. British and French vetoes preserved her from a hostile decree by the Security Council when, in October, she had, momentarily, been the sole recusant. And then, some weeks later, oil sanctions against Britain and France were revoked when key Senators interceded at the State Department. In the winter of 1957, the Senate as a whole staged a sit-down strike.

The Administration was caught between two fires. Arab rulers were being persuaded to accept the Eisenhower Doctrine; this, however, Congress would not approve until Israel was treated less inequitably. Sunday school Machiavellis might consort with King Saud; dissatisfaction had been simmering over the American alignment with the Soviet and Afro-Asian blocs against British and French allies, and with the Israeli issue it came to a boil. Cynics at the United Nations murmured that Congress was looking over its shoulder at the Jewish vote; but, by persevering against heavy odds, Israel had evoked admiration in American quarters where the conventional forms of anti-Semitism were not unknown. Nor were Senators pleased with the way the Eisenhower Doctrine had been presented to them; accusations of bad faith voiced against Secretary Dulles were reminiscent of charges bruited about in London when the Suez venture took shape. Congress, unlike Parliament, had no means of driving a government out of office. But it could make the Administration climb down—and that is what it did.

Perhaps the White House and the State Department would have ridden less high if, before Britain and France capitulated, a well-timed opposition could have been mustered on Capitol Hill. This, at any rate, was the first chance the Legislative branch had had to pronounce upon policies pursued during the Sinai campaign and Suez venture. A non-Soviet world which left Hungary to her fate might now forbid Israelis to improve their defenses. Egypt was not only to go unpunished after a decade of bellicosity; by supporting Nasser, India reminded others of her own moral vulnerability over Kashmir. Throughout, in fact, there had been a distortion of values, and that the Senate could not stomach. Senator William Knowland, minority floor leader, had rebelled against his copartisan in the White House more than once; but it was with the assistance of Senator Lyndon Johnson, leader of the majority Democrats, that Executive bills were passed, and he, too, had turned against the Administration. On February 20, a radio address by the President missed the mark. Until Washington dismissed the idea of sanctions against Israel, action on the Eisenhower Doctrine was to be deferred.

In basic postwar initiatives, since the shift of primacy from Britain to the United States, bipartisanship had mitigated that struggle for and against co-ordination which is endemic in the American political system. At this juncture, however, a new species of bipartisanship had cropped up. For it did not cut across parties to support the President but to withhold support from him. Against the Executive, when it seemed willing to adopt sanctions against Israel, the Legislature adopted its own brand of sanctions.

Nor were tergiversations that the Senate deplored likely to get applause elsewhere in the West. British opinion may have been divided over the merits of the Suez venture, but it was as one in regarding with repugnance the possibility of sanctions against Israel; in backing her the Quai d'Orsay and the French public did not waver; and, to the General Assembly, Canada had submitted a compromise proposal. Only in the Congress, however, did President Eisenhower and Secretary Dulles meet their match. Late in February they had to discard the idea of sanctions and give Jerusalem, instead, the assurances for which it pleaded. On March 1, 1957, Israel informed the General Assembly that her troops were about to be evacuated from the Gaza strip and the Sharm El Sheikh.

Not that the Administration revised its attitude ungrudgingly. The United Nations Emergency Force took up its vigil at the mouth of the Gulf of Aqaba. But Israel also assumed that the United Nations would govern the Gaza strip until a peace settlement, or some less provisional arrangement, was concluded with Egypt; and that her right to use the Suez Canal would be sustained by the United States. At the General Assembly, Ambassador Lodge watered down these "hopes and expectations." Revalidated in a letter from President Eisenhower to Prime Minister Ben-Gurion, they were modified again by Secretary Dulles. And Israeli forebodings were swiftly fulfilled.

Jerusalem withdrew the rest of its troops on March 6–7. The Egyptians, flouting assurances tendered Israel in Washington, and brushing aside United Nations officials, thereupon reoccupied the Gaza strip. Israel, moreover, was still denied the right to use the Suez Canal. And yet her Sinai counterstroke had not been entirely fruitless. Time must elapse before the Soviet Union would rearm the Egyptians; Israel, once more, had proven her mettle. The pan-Arab and Russian camps might still deem her expendable.

But, after the Sinai campaign, few in the West would be inclined to do so.

Meanwhile, as the revolt of Congress restored confidence in the caliber of American leadership, free peoples again took heart. The sequence of events was significant. An understanding between Washington and Jerusalem was announced on March 1. As soon as the shadow of sanctions against Israel had been lifted, the Senate resumed debate on the Eisenhower Doctrine—the Congressional resolution was signed on March 9. Amending and temporizing, the Senate compelled the most popular idol of American democracy to yield. Traditionally, the separation of powers has hampered the exercise of American power abroad. But on two critical occasions in 1956–57, it had been members of the Legislative rather than the Executive branch who spoke for America.

Schism in the West had ranged American power alongside that of others whose aim was to bring it low. But it was not only the promulgation of the Eisenhower Doctrine that paved the way for a full renewal of coalition diplomacy; notice had been served on the Eisenhower Administration that it would have to reckon with the Senate if any further deviations from established friendships were attempted. Defense matters were discussed between Washington and London in February; as a White House visitor, Guy Mollet, the French Premier, had mediated between Washington and Jerusalem when the latest crisis over sanctions was acute. However, it was British rather than French responsibility for the Suez venture that had done most to anger the Eisenhower Administration. To the special role of the Anglo-American factor a special gesture bore witness: so that conversations with Prime Minister Macmillan could be held on British soil, President Eisenhower traveled to Bermuda.

They conferred from March 21 to March 23, and the fact that they had thus met was more important than any decision taken. Nevertheless, two earlier decisions were disclosed and both had some bearing on issues raised during and after the great divergence. From Bermuda it was announced that the United States, though not a signatory of the Baghdad Pact, would join its military committee. In the Middle East, that is, the American approach might be neither as unilateral nor as dissociated from Britain as the Eisenhower Doctrine implied.

Then, too, as her chief ally, Britain would be the first to receive intermediate-range ballistic missiles from the United States, and this step, also, was announced at Bermuda. Russia had threatened the British Isles with rocket warfare during the Suez episode; Britain might presently be able to retort in kind. A fillip to the reinforcement of the key NATO area was thus given by a dispute which arose elsewhere and whose connection with NATO affairs Washington itself tried to evade. Moreover, the Eisenhower-Macmillan communiqué observed that, in the absence of an East-West arms agreement, the security of the free world still depended to a marked degree upon the nuclear deterrent. Limited atomic warfare may or may not be feasible. A strategic interlock which could spread war might, through the East-West equilibrium that results, also ward it off. And here the United States and Britain were to be involved with each other as much as ever.

No grand inquest on the state of Anglo-American friendship after the Suez episode could be undertaken at Bermuda. Seeking to co-ordinate foreign policies, President Eisenhower and Prime Minister Macmillan reported that they had talked "with the freedom and frankness permitted to old friends in a world of growing interdependence." Trends were more eloquent than words. Disparities of power between the United States and Britain had been exhibited during the Suez débâcle; the latter, as after World War II, might again retrench and retract. But in conjunction with the United States, Britain still had a crucial part to play, and that would have to be acted out on a world stage—or not at all.

Reconciliation followed divergence as the inner correctives of the Anglo-American dialectic took hold. Their stake in the continuance of a free world order had been imperiled when the United States and Britain swerved apart. On Britain's global status, on the position of the West in the Middle East, the damage wrought was irreparable. But as Washington and London swung together again they could make a fresh start.

The rehabilitation of Nasser had, in the meantime, proceeded apace. After the last Israeli withdrawals, shipping began to pass through the Suez Canal again; the terms upon which that route might now be used were divulged by Cairo in April. The General Assembly concurred when the United States suggested that these be given a trial; at the United Nations the arbitrary Egyptian statement was registered as an international engagement. In May, London and Paris rescinded their ban on the use of the canal by British and French vessels. Ostensibly, the Constantinople Convention of 1888 was still valid; but on the pretext of a state of war with Israel, one which the Security Council had rejected, Egypt still barred Israeli shipping. Current Egyptian transgressions were not only condoned. Whoever may be pulling strings in Cairo henceforth will have all Canal traffic at his mercy.*

Finishing touches on the appeasement of Nasser were still incomplete when the United States herself exposed one of the consequences of misjudgment. On April 26, the Security Council acknowledged that there was to be a wholly national Egyptian control over the international Suez waterway; on April 24, however, the Sixth Fleet had been ordered by Washington to the Eastern Mediterranean to buttress against Egypt and Syria the independence and territorial integrity of the Kingdom of Jordan. A dramatic stroke, it ran counter to American policies which, during the autumn of 1956, had caused the great divergence. The Suez expedition could have demonstrated the power of the West at a relatively small price; Jordan was being held together by no inner cohesion but simply by the fear of others over what would happen if she fell apart.

Arab rulers were at daggers-drawn. A Saudi feud with the Hashemite royal houses of Iraq and Jordan had, nevertheless, been terminated after King Saud's visit to Washington. During April, 1957, when a pro-Egyptian palace revolution flared up in Jordan against the youthful King Hussein, Feisal and Saud rallied to the side of their fellow monarch. Saudi, Iraqi and Syrian contingents had moved across the borders of Jordan either to checkmate each other or, should that hapless kingdom disintegrate, to snatch a goodly portion for themselves. It would, however, scarcely have paid Syria, an adjunct of the Cairo-Moscow axis, to march far into Jordan while Turkish troops lowered along her own northern frontier.

Then, too, during the Jordanian crisis, Israel again sought to maintain against Soviet-Egyptian inroads the Middle Eastern *status quo*. Jerusalem urged Washington to take the action it was to take. For on Israel, if Jordan were dismembered, the pan-Arab vise would tighten once more. As a measure of self-defense, her own perforated frontiers might have to be advanced to the River Jordan. This was territory that Jordan had taken during the war

---

* Nor was American shipping to be unaffected by the policies that Eisenhower and Dulles had pursued during the Sinai-Suez episode. American seamen organized a counterblockade in 1960 against a pan-Arab blacklist of American ships that touched Israeli ports. The United States had been subsidizing these practices fortuitously through her Mutual Security Program. In 1960, Congress therefore sought to have economic aid withheld until Egypt permitted unrestricted use of the Suez Canal as an international waterway.

of 1948; but Israel exhibited no desire to annex it. The large Arab population of the area, native and refugee, was anti-Hussein and pro-Nasser; disaffected in Jordan, it was not likely to be any less restive when Israel absorbed it. At any rate, the Israeli army, with laurels still fresh from the Sinai campaign, stood between Egypt and her Jordanian prey. Nor was Syria, daunted by Turkey in the north, thirsting for an encounter on southern borders with Israel. In an unstable region, the Israeli Army had become a stabilizing element.

An American show of force, however, did most to frustrate Egypt. Under the Eisenhower Doctrine, Middle Eastern countries were to be protected from overt pro-Communist aggression rather than indirect aggression or pan-Arub intrigue. It was the latter that menaced Jordan; nevertheless, her independence was declared vital to the national interest of the United States. The Sixth Fleet, as it sped to the Eastern Mediterranean, had an airlift ready to deposit troops in Jordan; eighteen hundred marines were landed at Beirut. Pressure on Hussein from Cairo and Damascus relaxed. Thus, too, had Britain's place in the Middle East been taken over. And when the United States acted against Nasser rather than for him, there was also a switch in the role of the Sixth Fleet, as the British Admiralty may have observed.

Both moral force and the United Nations had been extolled by Washington at the expense of Britain, France, and Israel. These were now ignored. Yet nobody asked the Eisenhower Administration to eat its words. In the American system of representative democracy, the Executive does not have to answer for alternating certitudes; as for Britain, she must have preferred a change for the better rather than no change at all. Washington did, however, still want to keep its anti-imperialist credentials unsullied; it therefore intimated that the American course in the Middle East was not the same as any that the British had pursued. Methods might vary. But American disclaimers could not banish the realities of power, or the resemblances which they imposed.

The United States and Britain have differed in power structures, not in the ends which Anglo-American power must serve. And yet the United States has her own oversea fulcra in the Caribbean and Pacific. Protectorates, colonies, mandates had been an apparatus of power which enabled Britain to defend the Middle Eastern crossroads. The floating air bases of the Sixth Fleet may be a substitute for it. Yesterday, the techniques of power in the Middle East called for sea power plus territorial footings; today, from its outskirts, a patrol of the region may be attempted through the massive deployment of sea-air power. Even this cannot do without land moorings—friendly ports in the Mediterranean, supplementary British airfields on Cyprus, and NATO bases in Turkey. All the same, at a time when Britain is no longer predominant in the Middle East, the levers of power have also been recast. But their function has not altered, nor the manner in which, at rock bottom, they might still have to be employed.

The recrudescence of Russian ambitions in the Middle East is accompanied, moreover, by fresh Russian naval activity in the Mediterranean. Soviet war vessels have been traversing it; in the Russian satellite of Albania, where a missile launching site may be established, there is an Adriatic base for Soviet torpedo boats and submarines. Russia has, besides, supplied Egypt with submarines; and her own, presumably, can use Egyptian and Syrian ports. Sea power is, at any rate, again a link between European and Middle Eastern affairs. During the epoch of British predominance, the politics of southern Europe were influenced by the near presence of the British Mediterranean Fleet; the sea-air power of the American Sixth Fleet is within striking distance of Russian captive states and southern Russia itself. The buildup of a Mediterranean naval force, surface and submarine, has therefore been an aspect of Russian home defense as well as a concomitant of the new Russian thrust towards the Middle East.

Will the Soviet Union again demand that the Montreux Convention be revised so as to permit freedom of transit through the Bosporus gateway for the Black Sea Fleet? The Russians and the British, threatened by Austro-German domination, had settled their differences on the eve of World War I; both, during the conflict of 1914–18, fought the Turks. Before that, however, there was a constant duel over the Russian drive towards warm-water ports; so as to sustain Turkey's vigil at the Straits, Britain had propped up "the Sick Man of Europe." And the problem recurs. The Dardanelles would have been included in the proposal made at Potsdam by President Truman, with the approval of Prime Minister Attlee, for the internationalization of key waterways. But Egypt is not likely to internationalize that Suez artery whose nationalization rocked the chancellories in 1956, and the East–West contest scarcely disposes the United States to loosen her hold on the Panama Canal. Whatever course Russia favors will, moreover, have her own control of the Straits as its inveterate aim.

Against such a contingency, now that the sea-air power of the United States is predominant in the Mediterranean, the

Western lead must be an American one. Yet elsewhere in the Middle East there is still a substantial British position—and of this Washington must also take note.

What that entails was illustrated in 1957–58 when a rebellion occurred against Britain's ally, the Sultan of Muscat and Oman, and British forces went to his support during those years and again in 1959. For the Sultanate is situated at the mouth of the Persian Gulf, in a British sphere which stretches from Iraq and Iran to Aden, and which contains the three major oil principalities of Kuwait, Qatar, and Bahrein. The latter is claimed by Iran which, with Britain, is a signatory of CENTO, the former Baghdad Pact; dollar revenues from the oil of Kuwait have been the largest in the sterling area and constitute the London capital market's biggest source of investment. The fact is that if Egypt could sink her talons into these oil-rich sheikdoms, she would get the means to finance the extravagant pan-Arab designs which she has nourished. Britain, on the other hand, would be less dependent on fields at the head of the Persian Gulf if Oman and Muscat were to yield oil in sufficient quantities.

Egyptian intrigue might have been behind the Omani insurrection. But so, also, was the desire of King Saud to filch the Buraimi Oasis from Oman and Muscat and one of her lesser neighbors. Here Saudi Arabia, which gets her arms from the United States, has been on bad terms with Britain. For the land which the one covets, the other is obliged by treaty to protect.

What should concern the United States is that these British arrangements not be altered to the detriment of the West. Access to the oil of the Persian Gulf and its sale on world markets will be essential if her British ally is to remain solvent. Then, too, American oil enterprise has been sheltered by local British commitments. Aramco might prosper when Saudi Arabia expands; mostly, however, British and American companies tend to co-operate. Iraq Petroleum, which is British, presides over a consortium in Muscat and Oman; half of Kuwait's fabulous oil output and all of Bahrein's belongs to American firms. Not only Britain but the United States, France, and the Netherlands derive profit from the oil principalities of the Persian Gulf. And whether their security should be underwritten by Britain alone has, under the new circumstances, been a moot point.

The existing state of affairs in the vicinity of the Persian Gulf redounds, moreover, to the advantage of India and Pakistan. It might not be hard for Pakistan, as a signatory of CENTO, to admit this; India, with her particular amalgam of neutralism and anticolonialism, may be more reticent. A charge of imperialism was levied by Cairo and the Arab League when Britain backed the Sultan of Muscat and Oman; it is improbable, nevertheless, that a change of regime would make India more comfortable. Muscat and Oman lies across the Arabian Sea from Bombay as well as Karachi. As long as pan-Arabism looked in other directions, India might cheer it on. But she herself may not want to have it ensconced on an outer flank of the Indian subcontinent.

It was, after all, from Delhi that, before the age of oil diplomacy, Britain kept watch over the Persian Gulf. India still trades there and a special Indian rupee has been issued for the area. Two objectives were accomplished when, during her days of primacy, Britain established her sphere in the Persian Gulf. First, it was interposed between India and any plan that Russians or Germans, breaking through Persia and the Ottoman Empire, harbored for the conquest of the Indian subcontinent; second, by its propinquity to the sea lanes between the Orient and the Occident, it helped to reinforce the British oversea power structure. That structure is not so strong as it was; since the Suez episode, when Washington and New Delhi gave Pan-Arab pretensions a green light, it has been weaker than ever. But in so far as it preserves a peripheral *status quo* both India and Pakistan have more reason to be glad than sorry.

Elsewhere in the Middle East, however, the United States had become the West's main champion and she again took the lead when, during the summer and autumn of 1957, the struggle for Jordan was extended to Syria. A pro-Soviet junta collared the government of that country, Egypt's closest ally, after an American plot against it had been alleged. Their Turkish neighbors infuriated them by offering anti-Communist opponents a haven; they aroused the Turks by their intimacy with Russia. Soviet arms and technicians were arriving in Syria. It seemed as though she might be converted into the sort of prestocked Russian forward base that the Israelis had uncovered in the Sinai Peninsula.

But the Turks were not going to be caught unawares between the two jaws of a Soviet-Syrian nutcracker. When Jordan was saved during the spring, the movements of Turkish divisions on the Syrian frontier coincided with those of the Sixth Fleet; now there were Turkish autumn maneuvers. But these in turn sparked Soviet maneuvers in Transcaucasia, above Turkey's frontier with Russia. On September 11, Moscow warned Ankara against an attack on Syria incited by the United States; the Russians sounded even more truculent in October when, by lifting the first earth satellite, they displayed their skill in the new war technology. In Soviet utterances there was henceforth a menacing note.

At the end of October, nevertheless, the Turkish-Syrian crisis petered out. Marshal Zhukov, whom Nikita Khrushchev dubbed a would-be Bonaparte, may or may not have contributed to it; his demotion was, at any rate, what preoccupied the Kremlin. In the eyes of Arab capitals, moreover, Russia's support of Syria had been overdone; lest Damascus become a cat's-paw of Moscow rather than Cairo, President Nasser sent to Syria a detachment of Egyptian troops. And soon there were other signs of Soviet-Egyptian friction within the Cairo-Moscow axis. The Turks learned on October 29 that the Kremlin would desist. Before that, however, they had received firm backing in the West.

Nor did this only emanate from Washington. The unilateral in American efforts had been supplemented by a broader Anglo-American approach. The Sixth Fleet was dispatched once more to the waters of the Eastern Mediterranean; an airlift of American arms to Jordan and a reaffirmation of the Eisenhower Doctrine in September were commended by the British government. Twice before the United States had co-operated with Britain and France to reject a Soviet bid for recognition of the Soviet role in the Middle East. On September 24, she did the same again.

Turkey, however, is a member of NATO, and the re-enunciation of the Eisenhower Doctrine in the Levant was combined with a re-enunciation of the North Atlantic Treaty against Russia. After allies had been consulted, an American statement of October 10 coupled together American obligations under NATO and American policy under the Eisenhower Doctrine. Then, too, American warships did not merely put in to Turkish ports during October; NATO forces held sea and air exercises in the Aegean. On October 16, Secretary Dulles said that the United States would not stick to the defensive, that Soviet territory could not be treated as a privileged sanctuary if Russia attacked Turkey. And later that month, when Prime Minister Macmillan visited President Eisenhower, their communiqué pointed out that, under the North Atlantic Treaty, an assault on Turkey must be considered an assault on all other NATO members.

Moscow relented. And it had not only caused Washington

to reassert the Eisenhower Doctrine. The United States was tending to collaborate with Britain in that Middle Eastern region where she had sought recently to proceed alone.

Their co-operation became still more explicit when American and British landings were staged in Lebanon and Jordan during the summer of 1958. Revolution in Iraq was to provoke these, but they had been preceded by other regional changes. On February 1, rather than subject themselves to outright Communist rule, the pro-Soviet camarilla in Damascus engineered a union between Syria and Egypt—one in which Cairo was to have the upper hand. Egypt might not be equipped to govern a province that was more progressive than herself; nevertheless, so as to retain Syria in his own pan-Arab orbit, President Nasser had to forestall his Russian patrons at once. Yet when he did this he also took another forward stride in his contention with the West. Oil from the Middle East to Western Europe could either be shipped through the Suez Canal or flow to Mediterranean ports through Syrian pipelines; the latter, too, were now under Nasser's control. A single Egyptian command over northern and southern fronts might, moreover, confront Israel with new peril. But the inclusion of Jordan in the ring forged by the United Arab Republic was less likely than it had been.

As proponents of Arab nationalism, Cairo and Baghdad had long vied with each other. On February 14, Iraq and Jordan tried to bolster themselves against Egypt's bid for pan-Arab supremacy by proclaiming an Arab Union of their own. Then it was announced on March 2 that Yemen was going to join up with Egypt and Syria—a grouping to be known as the United Arab States. Through Yemen, with her Sino-Soviet armaments and pan-Arab affinities, the United Arab Republic might thus nudge the British strategic outpost of Aden, a crucial vantage point in the oceanic communications of the Commonwealth and of the Western coalition. And on Saudi Arabia also the advent of the United Arab Republic was to cast a shadow. With all his oil riches, King Saud could not prevent its formation; until December, 1960, full authority was assigned to Crown Prince Feisal and other anti-Western, pro-Nasser elements. Saud's subsidy to Jordan had already been curtailed, and now Washington's brief reliance on him fizzled out. Nasser's recovery from defeat in Sinai and at Suez had been rapid.

An Iraqi revolution which promised at first to broaden his sway served, however, to check it. For this not only prompted an Anglo-American attempt to maintain the political independence and territorial integrity of Lebanon and Jordan; in Baghdad, the old rivalry between Iraq and Egypt flared up again under what seemed to be pro-Soviet rather than pro-Western auspices. During the spring of 1958, it looked as though Lebanon would be next on Nasser's list. The conversion of Syria into a province of the United Arab Republic made her a more convenient terrain for subversive activities against her Lebanese neighbor. In Lebanon, half-Christian and half-Moslem, dissension anyway was always rife. What fanned it in May, 1958, was talk of an amendment to the Lebanese Constitution that, by allowing President Camille Chamoun to have a second term of office, would have prolonged a pro-Western regime.

It may be that when his own Syrian adherents supplied Lebanese insurrectionaries with men and munitions, they forced the pace for Nasser himself. But there were also inflammatory broadcasts by the Cairo, Damascus, and Soviet radio to spur them on. The Lebanese Army, moreover, did little to arrest the Lebanese civil war. Torn between two segments, one Christian and pro-Western, the other Moslem and anti-Western, its divisions were in microcosm those of wider conflicts which cut across existing frontiers.

On June 11, the Security Council agreed to dispatch to Lebanon a corps of observers. Though United Nations officers were barred from numerous border areas, they differed from Western intelligence and discounted the degree of infiltration. Reports that absolved the Egyptian dictator of complicity might, however, have been to the liking of the Secretary-General, Dag Hammarskjold; to admit Nasser's capacity for mischief, in 1958, would be to cast doubt on the wisdom of efforts by which the Cairo regime had been salvaged during the Suez venture. But on that previous occasion the Secretary-General had had the United States behind him. This time he did not.

A policy of hands-off impelled the West at first. But this only emboldened its foes on the spot. The Russian veto in the Security Council provided cover; with a plot being hatched in Iraq, the sole Arab country with Western commitments, there was little to interfere. King Feisal and the Crown Prince, Abdul Illah, were assassinated on July 14; Nuri es-Said, the architect of alliance with the West, shortly thereafter. The blow inflicted on London and Washington was a heavy one.

It would have been heavier still if a pan-Arab–pro-Soviet conspiracy reached into other Arab capitals. President Camille Chamoun of Lebanon, and King Hussein of Jordan, begged the

West for assistance. Their pleas were answered by an American landing in Lebanon, on July 15, and a British landing in Jordan, on July 17; from those two countries, moreover, the Western contingents could have made a further advance into Iraq. But universal acclaim was not likely to greet steps such as these. From Cairo and New Delhi, Moscow and Peking, the usual anti-imperialist chorus was audible. Yet many in the West had also been indignant.

Did the Anglo-American landings violate international law? The right of a government to call for military succor might be abused if it could be employed on behalf of usurpers or against the will of the nation. Then, too, the Eisenhower Doctrine had cleared the path for American intervention in the Middle East, but at this juncture it had not even been cited. What President Eisenhower did invoke was the Charter right of self-defense, individual and collective, against armed attack—a right, however, which might not apply to "indirect aggression from without" wherein the Cairo-Moscow axis had specialized of late.

The United Nations could not, in fact, measure up to its responsibilities. Britain, France, and Israel by-passed it in 1956; now it had to be by-passed again. The legal warrant for the Anglo-American landings may be disputed. One truth is plain. To have construed international law so that the Middle East would have been abandoned to Nasser—to some blend of the pan-Arab with the pro-Soviet—was not to further the reign of law. Lawlessness, instead, would have been sanctified.

And yet, but for the misjudgments of 1956, there might have been no need for any Western intervention in 1958. Not that Secretary Dulles ever admitted past error. The case against Britain, France, and Israel was, according to him, that they had tried to coerce a recognized government; recognized governments, however, had called for the Anglo-American landings. But the distinction thus drawn between the events of 1956 and 1958 was not an adequate one. It is only in a larger political and strategic context that these can be properly compared.*

---

* In 1960, it was a Congolese "recognized government" which invited the United Nations to maintain order in the former Belgian territory. But, unlike Hungary or Tibet, that mid-African zone was still strategically beyond the Sino-Soviet pale; the United Nations could, therefore, attempt to preclude a Russian or pro-Russian occupation.

The Congolese Republic was, as Metternich described Italy, less a unified state than a geographical expression. However, lest the eligibility of other members be questioned, nobody questioned the Congo's right to belong to the world body.

It required more than the legitimacy of an appeal from Beirut and Amman to bring about the Anglo-American landings. Nobody, after all, had lifted a finger to assist Premier Imre Nagy eighteen months before. Hungary belongs to the Russian sphere; to have intervened there might only have been to precipitate nuclear war. But in the Middle East, it is the West rather than the East which possesses vital interests; and it was to preserve these that the United States and Britain made their joint response. Differences between the Western undertakings of 1956 and 1958 might, technically, have been vast; local circumstances were not the same. Counteraction had, nevertheless, been evoked by the same underlying contingency.

The one big change was in the American attitude. Legal grounds for the Sinai campaign and the Suez expedition had been controverted by the Eisenhower Administration in 1956; in 1958 some were to question the legalities of their own Middle Eastern venture. Noteworthy was the fact that unilateralism had then been dispelled, and when the United States took a lead she did so in conjunction with Britain. What they did may have perturbed many. The pattern of power in the Middle East was to be a co-operative one and, after the great divergence, that, at least, should have been gratifying.

A number of objectives were attained by the Anglo-American landings. A temporary occupation of Lebanon and Jordan did not only retard the Nasserist onrush; Moscow perceived that Western interests in the Middle East would not be relinquished lightly. As Iraq reoriented herself, she might turn her back on former associates in the Baghdad Pact; coalition strategy had been deprived of the British air base at Habbaniya. But safeguards were renewed for those oil supplies from the Persian Gulf on which the British economy depended; rulers of oil protectorates saw that Britain would uphold her obligations to them and that behind her stood the United States. Sighs of relief were heaved by Turkey, Iran, and Pakistan, three Asian members of the Baghdad Pact. At the same time Turkey could be dissuaded from taking action across her own Syrian or Iraqi borders—a move which would have given Russia a pretext for sending "volunteers" or for meddling somehow.

Then, too, King Hussein had to be restrained from trying to stamp out the Iraqi revolt or from asserting an authority, inherited from his murdered cousin, over the short-lived union of Iraq and Jordan. Nor would it be necessary for Israel, so long as Jordan could be preserved from dismemberment by other

Arab states, to round out her own menaced frontiers. But what also enabled Washington and London to calm the atmosphere was the fact that the new Iraqi regime, though neutralist and anti-Western, was as yet beholden to neither Cairo nor Moscow. It enjoyed wide popular approval; any endeavor to overthrow it would heighten unrest in the Middle East just when this was being reduced. Anglo-American landings, therefore, went no further than Lebanon and Jordan. But on the region as a whole they did, for an interval, exert a sobering effect.

They were, besides, followed by an effort to strengthen the Baghdad Pact—an instrument which, after Iraq stepped out, was renamed the Central Treaty Organization. On July 28, the United States pledged herself to collaborate with its members for their security and defense. Some of its signatories wanted her support against non-Communist enemies. Defense against Communist aggression was, however, what the Eisenhower Doctrine envisaged; and it was in consonance with the authorization which Congress had provided that separate bilateral agreements were signed on March 5, 1959, with Iran, Pakistan, and Turkey. Britain, moreover, was the one non-Asian member of the Central Treaty Organization and, when the United States thus verged on a commitment to it, another seal was affixed to their common regional alignment.

Anglo-American intervention presupposed Anglo-American unity. In other respects, nevertheless, the diplomatic lineup of 1958 resembled that of the great divergence in 1956. Washington and London had to reckon with the dissent of allies, with denunciation by Asian and European neutrals, with the Kremlin's minatory tactics. But when the United States herself took the lead, none of this could be pressed as far.

Not that European allies such as France and West Germany nourished the same grievances. The French lamented the premature termination of the Suez venture; they were irked by their exclusion from the Anglo-American landings. All Arab peoples were, however, in favor of the Algerian rebels, and the Lebanese government had ruled out Paris as one of the capitals to which it might appeal. West Germany, on the other hand, was afraid of being identified with a proceeding at which she looked entirely askance. For, while Britain, France, and the United States incurred Arab ill will, the West Germans were busy drumming up Arab trade. What worried Bonn was that its Arab friends might be offended by the use of American troops and aircraft stationed in West Germany. For it had interests of its own to maintain when the United States and Britain were endeavoring to preserve in the Middle East the general interests of the West.

To what extent did Moscow influence the course of events? When the Kremlin threatened counterintervention in 1956, the United States had been arrayed diplomatically against her British and French allies; in 1958, however, there could be no Soviet counterintervention which did not risk a showdown between the Russian and American colossi themselves. Soviet aims were the same. Russia possessed ample oil reserves of her own but, if Britain and Western Europe were denied access to Middle Eastern oil, her global designs could be furthered commensurately. Through subservient Arab regimes she might seat herself upon the Indian Ocean. The Middle East is the crossroads of Europe, Asia, and Africa, and it could be transformed into a platform for the Russian control of southern Asia and the African continent. A goal of world dominance might, at any rate, be less distant if the West recognized the Soviet claim to an equal voice in Middle Eastern affairs. And that is why Western policymakers hesitated to concede this. So as to hold the inner citadels of the West, its outer ramparts had to be watched.

A series of moves that might net such recognition was undertaken. Revolutionaries in Baghdad had burnt down the British embassy; in Moscow there were mob demonstrations against both the British and American embassies. Nor was sympathy with any Arab upsurge against the West all that the Kremlin evinced; it had the territorial defenses of the Soviet Union to consider. The American landing in Lebanon and the British landing in Jordan aroused it because they were heralded as a prelude to the allied occupation of Iraq, a country within easy reach of Soviet borderlands. On July 16 and 18, Moscow demanded the withdrawal of Allied forces from areas adjacent to Russia's own frontiers. Annual maneuvers in the military districts of Turkestan and Transcaucasia, together with exercises of the Black Sea Fleet, were announced; Soviet airborne troops were dispatched to Bulgaria. But President Nasser, frightened by the danger of a global holocaust, hastened to Moscow; Anglo-American landings in Lebanon and Jordan were not counterbalanced by a Soviet landing in the Syrian province of the United Arab Republic. A warning of serious Russian countermeasures against an Allied advance into Iraq may have been conveyed privately to Washington. The occupation of that country was, however, no longer contemplated.

Most Iraqis welcomed the downfall of the old regime;

and the new one, despite its anti-Western posture, did not grovel before Cairo. Though American and British troops had still to be withdrawn from Lebanon and Jordan, London and Washington recognized the new government in Baghdad. In Washington, moreover, Soviet irascibility had been anticipated. The Atlantic and Pacific Fleets, together with the Strategic Air Command, were put on the alert at once. The Far East and the line of the Iron Curtain across Central Europe were familiar sectors of the East–West contest. The Middle East would tend henceforth to be numbered among them.

Tension mounted, as armed forces marched and countermarched, until a meeting of the powers was proposed. Rockets figured in Soviet diplomacy during the Suez crisis and Russian weapons were mentioned on July 19 when Premier Nikita Khrushchev again suggested a summit conference—one which was to include Prime Minister Nehru of India. As in 1955, so now, British public opinion did most to insist upon such a meeting. Russia's claim to a voice in Middle Eastern affairs would have been acknowledged by holding with her an *ad hoc* conference to discuss them; there would, on the other hand, be no formal recognition of this if, under established procedures, heads of government foregathered at the Security Council. Washington had been reluctant; willingness to attend, however, was expressed by President Eisenhower and Prime Minister Macmillan on July 22. Formerly there were British misgivings when American domestic politics determined the conduct of American foreign policy. British domestic politics were, nevertheless, now putting their impress on British policy.

But all this annoyed France. What she wanted was a summit conference which steered clear of the United Nations and met in Geneva rather than New York. The Soviet Premier would, moreover, have been reined in or outvoted under the rules of the Security Council. With his original suggestion, to which he had reverted on July 28, he could still make no headway in Washington and London; on August 5, Mr. Khrushchev therefore proposed that Middle Eastern issues be submitted to the General Assembly—an expedient which Washington itself had broached. Perhaps, too, his Chinese ally frowned upon a summit conference in which India rather than Communist China was to speak for Asia—while, in its Security Council version, Formosa rather than Peking still represented China. A renewed bombardment of the Chinese offshore islands may also have made it advisable for the Russian Premier to pipe down over the Middle

Eastern situation. Nor were Washington and London broken-hearted when the idea of a summit conference on the Middle East was dropped. There would be no public skirmishes between President Eisenhower and Premier Khrushchev; no offense would be given Asian allies and Commonwealth partners by singling out neutralist India. And at the emergency session of the General Assembly Russia was to overplay her hand.

Meanwhile, Anglo-American landings were not all that had stopped the spread of violence. Israel was situated between the two segments of the United Arab Republic; before pan-Arab ambitions could be fulfilled, she would have to be overrun. As a progressive social democracy, she had a role in the Middle East that was unique; but the prowess she exhibited during the Suez campaign also did much to steady the region—an item which Washington, London, and Paris could now add to the power calculus of the West. If other Arab states attempted to carve up Jordan, Israel might have to protect her own narrow waist by occupying that kingdom's west bank; fear of the Israeli army thus helped to preserve her enemy in Amman from her enemies in Cairo, Damascus, and Baghdad. A large populace of hostile Arabs can, as a matter of fact, only be annexed by Israel as a last resort. Nor was Nasser, with Syria proving a somewhat indigestible morsel, as eager as he had been to swallow Jordan or Jordanians.

The Israeli presence complemented the Anglo-American landings. The logistics of the British intervention were, nevertheless, to create a problem for Israel. A supply and transport route by sea through the Gulf of Aqaba to Jordan was not so good as an air route from Cyprus across Israeli territory. Yet when Israel allowed the Allies to utilize her air space she found not only that she had been involved, though obliquely, in the Anglo-American undertaking but that there were no compensatory safeguards if she got herself into trouble as a result.

A sharp note from the Kremlin on August 1 exposed her predicament. The Anglo-American airlift came to a stop within the next ten days. Soviet patronage of the pan-Arab cause was, however, not the sole reason for the Israeli ban. Objections had been raised by Afro-Asian friends and by neutralist parties at home. The arms that were being conveyed across Israel's own air space might, moreover, be employed by Jordan against her. And so cogent was her case that London as well as Paris, with a smaller amount provided by the United States, now expedited arms deliveries to Israel.

A *rapprochement* between Britain and Israel had always

been in the common interest. When Iraq, a British ward, defected from the West, this seemed more likely to materialize. But Israel also wanted security guarantees; the tripartite declaration which the United States, Britain, and France made in 1950 needed to be reinvigorated after Soviet penetration of the Middle East, the expansion of Egypt, and revolution in Iraq.

Early withdrawals from Lebanon and Jordan had been sought. But Anglo-American terms stipulated that Arab states must first turn over a new leaf. Pledges to do so, as extracted at the emergency session of the General Assembly, might not prove immutable in the long run. They meant, in the short run, that there would be none of those unconditional withdrawals that Moscow and New Delhi were, typically, demanding.

Not that the proposals made by President Eisenhower on August 13 were, apart from the idea of an Arab development institution, to win assent. A permanent international force might, for instance, take over in Hungary or Kashmir. To the American suggestion neither Russia nor India acceded. (In 1960, however, a Soviet disarmament plan incorporated the idea of an international force. United Nations forces in the Middle East and the Congo were not mustered on a permanent basis.)

Less and less able to devise political settlements, the United Nations at least made itself useful again in the brokerage of diplomacy. Until other Arabs agreed to leave Lebanese and Jordanians alone, the Anglo-American landings would not be terminated; their Russian and Indian mentors, meanwhile, became more pan-Arab in vociferation than Arab states themselves. Interference in each other's affairs was renounced by an Arab resolution which the General Assembly adopted on August 21. And for carrying out this self-denying ordinance, arrangements were entrusted to the Secretary-General.

As during the Sinai campaign and Suez venture, the United Nations served to register and implement what, basically, was decided elsewhere. The world organization had been established to curb the thrust and counterthrust of power; all it could do, on a more secondary plane, was regulate and administer. And it could not have done that much if other forces, American, British, Israeli, had not been in play—if these had not renewed for the Middle East an uneasy regional equilibrium.

Such a lull might not last long but it did give Lebanon and Jordan a chance to pull themselves together. The transition from the Presidency of Camille Chamoun to that of General Fuad Chehab was accomplished without the Lebanese civil war intensifying; after a neutralist government had been installed, pan-Arab turmoil died away. And in Jordan, King Hussein still clung to his throne.

Nor was President Nasser likely to find the subversion of Jordan, from within or without, an unmixed blessing. The acquisition of Jordan might give him control of adjacent Arab oil lands and, with their oil revenues, the means to finance that country and replenish his own coffers. But he not only had to discourage an Israeli occupation of the left bank, a Jordanian territory which Jerusalem thought the United Nations should rule as an international enclave; the Iraqi revolution, as far as Egypt was concerned, had gone sour. Cairo assumed that Baghdad would now bow low before it. There was a danger, instead, that Iraq might grab Jordan for herself and lure Syria into a pan-Arab constellation stronger than any centered on Cairo.

Still willing to wound, the Egyptian dictator had grown afraid to strike. And when a local stalemate also tended to pacify, Anglo-American forces could be withdrawn. By October 25, 1958, American troops had departed from Lebanon; the British evacuation of Jordan was to be completed within the next few weeks.

A new phase had begun and now the question was whether Nasser, having played the East against the West, would show the same dexterity in playing the West against the East. Not even among Arab countries did he fare so well as expected after the summer of 1958. An army regime in the Sudan was correct rather than compliant; relations with Saudi Arabia improved, but not with President Bourguiba of Tunisia. Worst of all, Iraq not only purveyed her own brand of Arab nationalism; a Moscow-Baghdad axis was difficult to square with the Cairo-Moscow axis. The Communists might be among the political parties that Nasser proscribed in the United Arab Republic; Nasserist conspiracies, nevertheless, impelled the Iraqi Premier, General Abdel Karim el-Kassem, to lean on the Iraqi Communists. But, essentially, the problem which these rival Arab rulers faced was the same. Each made his way with Russian patronage and yet it was from Moscow that each had most to fear.

Nor did it take long for this dilemma to emerge. An opportunity to exploit the natural resources of Egypt, Syria, and Yemen was awarded Russia when she offered, during the autumn of 1958, to finance the first stage of the Aswan Dam, build airfields and factories, and lend Egypt other industrial assistance. But when efforts to sever the union of Egypt and Syria were divulged, President Nasser accused Syrian Communists.

So, too, Iraq might be visited by missions from the Soviet bloc and procure arms from Russia. However, when the Kurds, who live in oil-rich Iraqi areas, are stirred up against her, it is the minions of Moscow who jeopardize her territorial integrity and financial solvency. A separate Kurdistan may be carved out of Kurdish districts in Iran and Turkey to furnish Russia with a corridor to Iraq—one which would ensure Soviet domination of regional oil fields, Soviet access to the British sphere in the Persian Gulf and, thence, to the Indian Ocean. And whatever promotes disunity in Iraq will bring Russia nearer her goal.

It was Nasser who brought Soviet influence into the Middle East and much of Africa. Can he and Kassem take what Russia has to give but withstand Soviet encroachments? So far as they will maintain the independence of their countries, Washington and London have been willing to help them. The United States agreed in 1959 to furnish Egypt again with economic aid and technical assistance. So also, Britain, which had previously armed her, resumed the sale of arms to Iraq. The British market Iraqi oil; for economic as well as strategic reasons, it is the aim of Britain to prevent Iraq's total dependence on the Soviet Union and to bolster such Army elements as may be neither Communist nor Nasserist. There might be Arab blackmail in all this; as they balance East against West and West against East, Arab states may only outsmart themselves. The United States and Britain were, all the same, working at Cairo and Baghdad along parallel lines.

It is a precarious situation. Such are the nature of Arab nationalism and Soviet designs that the West will be lucky if vital Western interests can be defended by a regional holding action. Irreparable loss was suffered when, during the fateful summer and autumn of 1956, the British and the Americans diverged. The loss would have been still greater if, as leader of the West, the United States had not subsequently changed her course.

And four years later a harsh, retributive postscript was added to this United Nations phase of Middle Eastern diplomacy. In 1956–58, Dag Hammarskjold had been preoccupied with Afro-Asian shibboleths rather than with underlying power realities. But the Afro-Asian propensities of the Secretary-General were not the same as Moscow's and, when the United Nations intervened in the Congo, they had, from Moscow's standpoint, outlived their usefulness. Russia tried to unseat his successor as it had unseated Trygve Lie.

Communist and neutralist countries might be able to exert

administrative control if, as the Soviet Union proposed, three global blocs were represented in the Office of the Secretary-General. Soon, too, Mr. Hammarskjold was pilloried by some of the very Afro-Asian elements that he had befriended; and though her own lawbreaking was still unpurged, Egypt was even elected in 1960 to the Security Council. About the realities of power the United Nations could do little. For lowering the political standards of that organization, more than the East was to blame.

VIII

Interdependence in the Space Age

MISSILES AND MISSIVES

Never have the stakes of power been higher than they are today. For the East–West contest is not merely between two ways of life; life itself, should there be total war, might perish from the face of the earth. One grim paradox by which Britain, in her days of primacy, had not been plagued, brooded over the era of American leadership: the weapons with which, and against which, the West now defended itself might also wipe out all that it defended. Everything is magnified in scale. Multitudes can be enslaved as well as emancipated by techniques of bigness. Improving the human lot, they may destroy humanity.

As long as the United States held air-atomic supremacy, the West had a respite. But with the dawn of the space age came the danger that preponderance might pass to the East. It had been to her technological superior that Britain relinquished the leadership of the West. Yet, during the second half of 1957, Russia tested successfully an intercontinental ballistic missile and put the first earth satellite in orbit. If she should prove more adept than the United States in the latest war technology, she might, short of countervailing Western progress, confront a free world order with the hideous alternatives of surrender or extinction. Will the United States keep abreast in the weapons race so as to deter fierce rivals? What, in diplomacy and strategy, is the future of the Western coalition to be? Familiar questions recur. Fresh ones appear. All would have to be reassessed.

The core of Western defense, at grave turning-points in the twentieth century, had been the Anglo-American factor— and it will be so again. Not that the United States and Britain now attain perfect concord; but the continuance of a free world order is a joint and abiding interest which, in accordance with a traditional Anglo-American dialectic, overrides the most stubborn of differences. They may, within their own battered framework of ultimate solidarity, still diverge. They diverge less from each other than, standing together, they diverge from such major allies as France and the Bonn Republic. And on coalition diplomacy that crucial fact leaves its mark.

Coalition strategy is, in essence, the same. Soviet power stretches from the Elbe to the Pacific and, by shuttling back and forth on inner Eurasian lines, can operate at will in a number of distant theaters. To hold it at bay, the West devised a worldwide system of alliances out of which a surrounding chain of military installations has been formed, before it can dictate to the West, the East would have to expunge that counteracting chain. But what effect on the East-West stalemate are the new weapons likely to have? Until the United States produces an adequate supply of intercontinental ballistic missiles, she may gird the West with ballistic missiles of intermediate range, the launching ramps of which are stationed on the territory of European allies. These can, for the moment, supplement rather than supersede manned bombers. However, they superimpose vexed new problems upon others that the strategic interlock had begot.

Control of nuclear warheads remains in American hands. Who, in an emergency, will have the right to pull the trigger? An American lag in building intercontinental missiles may imperil the entire West by leaving it open to Soviet blackmail. But will the United States, when intercontinental ballistic missiles are available, still require her European ramparts? Will her own North American bases not meet all her defensive needs?

It is inconceivable that a war of Titans could be waged without other countries being dragged in—even if there were no strategic interlock to engulf them. And yet the American leader of the West might pay less heed to the views of allies if, with the advent of intercontinental weapons, an overarching isolationism should take hold. As a matter of fact, a variety of weapons is needed. And as long as medium-range bombers can still be used, the countries in which they are based must be defended.

Once, however, all American forces have been withdrawn from Western Europe, the United States might be loath to fight a total war on its behalf. That region would, consequently, be tempted to accept terms that Moscow lays down—and the balance of power will then have moved from West to East. It is not enough, therefore, for the United States to build intercontinental missiles that will match the Russian armory. She must, in her own interest, still honor a NATO commitment which underwrites the European balance. For, in general, the obligations of American leadership have not altered.

Some of the conditions of primacy have, all the same, undergone a change. Hitherto, it was Western Europe which had been in the danger zone; the United States and Canada were henceforth to be there also. The United States and Russia could, furthermore, employ long-range aircraft against each other; but it was chiefly the West which had forward bases wherefrom medium bombers might also be used. What, however, would be the retaliatory value of launching sites and bomber bases on which Soviet ballistic missiles could be trained? The West has its counteracting weapons similarly poised, and the armed truce is thus prolonged.

For maintaining coalition strategy, other means than European launching sites may, in addition, be feasible. Nor is it beyond Western ingenuity to make them, and host countries, relatively less vulnerable. The devices envisaged are underground missile sites, mobile launching platforms, bombers that carry ballistic missiles, antimissile missiles. Britain and other West European countries will offer fewer targets to draw Russian missile fire as the number of fixed launching sites is reduced. A peripheral strategy can be exploited by the sea-air power of the West and, if it is, the advantage with which inner lines endows the East might again be equalized.

Not that Russia is incapable of making herself felt in that sphere, too. Possessing the largest of submarine fleets, she plans to paralyze NATO by cutting off supplies to Britain and other European allies from the United States and Canada. Missiles launched from Soviet underwater craft will, moreover, menace both the coastal cities and inland industry of North America and Western Europe. Under an American lead, nevertheless, the West otherwise still commands the seas. Nor is the East itself as invulnerable as it once was to maritime assault. The frozen wastes of the Arctic are no barrier to the atom-powered submarines of the United States; and, by equipping these with ballistic missiles, she brings Russia's own industrial heartland within range. Also to be preyed upon are industrial centers on the coast of Communist China. For the air-land stalemate now has its sea-air counterpart.

In the West, nevertheless, global deterrents have been self-deterring. When the Korean War broke out, Britain and other allies feared that, through the backlash of the strategic interlock, they might be more widely involved by their American leader without due cause. Will the growing importance of sea-missile power give coalition strategy a degree of mobility it had not previously enjoyed? It may. Britain and Western Europe will, at any rate, breathe more easily if, in combat operations, it is roving maritime sites rather than fixed territorial ones with which the enemy has to grapple.

In greater recourse to them, there would, besides, be a touch of the historically piquant. Land power and land-air power have, during the twentieth century, seemed to be the decisive strategic element. Yet it had been sea power that upheld a free world order in the era of British primacy. Though an indispensable auxiliary in two world wars, it could not call the turns. Vessels equipped with ballistic missiles might, under American auspices, bring it into its own again.

Nor can there be stress on sea power without some of its Anglo-American aspects being re-emphasized. Russian warships will have at their disposal nothing like the communications sector of the British overseas power structure. Then, too, while much smaller, the Royal Navy still offers traditional skills in naval seamanship. And recent major innovations in aircraft carriers have stemmed from British technical inventiveness.

But the ability of the West to withstand the East in war technology cannot disguise the fact that the Soviet Union is pressing it hard. When Russia set the first earth satellite in orbit, it looked as though she might overtake America and achieve world supremacy after all. A crisis in confidence among allies of the United States ensued. For them, however, this one was not the same as others that had preceded it. Previously, the security partners of the United States had been worried over how she would exercise her vast power. Now they wondered whether levers of American power, the tools of leadership in the military and political sphere, sufficed for safety.

Not that Eisenhower's America was to err as grievously as, on the eve of World War II, had Chamberlain's Britain. Businessmen in Cabinet posts again tried to put budget balancing ahead of the global balance; but on this occasion the fundamental issue was not entirely misconceived. And yet, for strong remedial initiatives, the American political system calls for a strong President. These initiatives were not forthcoming.

Steps taken to reassert American leadership were, nevertheless, in consonance with established patterns of Anglo-American friendship and coalition diplomacy. What had to be countered were familiar Soviet objectives as adapted to the space age. Flaunt-

ing her missile capacity, Russia sought to have the Western coalition dissolved before it could be reinforced. The American goal
was, contrariwise, to reinforce it before it was demoralized or
rendered obsolete by Russian advances. If allies could be induced
to desert the United States, North America would be split from
Western Europe, and the defense of the West undermined; Russia
might thus acquire piecemeal what could not be procured all at
once. Washington's retort was, instead, to reforge ties with London
and refurbish NATO.

A fusillade of missives from the Kremlin to West European
capitals warned of rocket vengeance by Russia if they accepted
tactical nuclear weapons from the United States or built launching
sites for intermediate-range ballistic missiles. Protection against
surprise attack was to be discussed in conference at Geneva; there,
too, nuclear powers conferred upon the abolition of those nuclear
and thermonuclear tests which had contaminated the atmosphere.
During the next few years, East and West also conferred over
proposals for total and partial disarmament. The deterrent effect
of coalition strategy was implied by the Soviet endeavor to have
it liquidated.

The West first responded to the latest Soviet challenge by
reaffirming the Anglo-American factor. There were talks at the
White House between President Eisenhower and Prime Minister
Macmillan towards the end of October, 1957. Queen Elizabeth II
and Prince Philip had just paid state visits to Ottawa and Washington; the Middle East was in the throes of another Russian war
scare; boasts and billingsgate accompanied Soviet feats in launching earth satellites. Technologically, and, therefore, politically, the
prestige of the United States had suffered; Britain, as her closest
ally, wished to ensure that nothing imprudent was done. All would
be embroiled in an East–West showdown if Washington forced
the issue before the latest Russian weapons were produced in
large quantities. Though morally repugnant, a preventive war had
been strategically feasible before the United States lost her atomic
monopoly. Now it would be catastrophic on every ground.

But one alternative could be the Soviet-American deal
which Moscow had long sought. And it would be by renewing
their support of the United States that her chief allies might stave
off such a global realignment. For at the expense of their most
vital interests, and of her own national security, the United States
could, in the short run, thus always buy time.

Eisenhower and Macmillan were, in fact, to put the accent
on interdependence—a coalition principle which they reiterated

when both attended the next Paris meeting of the NATO Council. And they made its meaning clear by a number of joint undertakings that followed their October conversations.

All this, moreover, was a far cry from the great divergence. A year before, when Russian intrusion in the Middle East might still have been checked, the United States had aligned herself with those who wanted to outflank the West by crippling the British oversea power structure; twelve months later, when progress in Russian missile technology had to be counteracted, the United States and Britain were on the best of terms once more. During and after the Korean War, her allies restrained the United States in the Far East; now her own capacity for discharging the responsibilities of leadership had to be renewed. Washington downgraded the Anglo-American factor in 1956. By 1957, that crucial friendship was again, in accordance with the processes of history and the realities of power, a prime requisite of American primacy.

A series of decisions taken in the realm of preparedness spelled out the Anglo-American phase of interdependence. It had been announced in March, 1957, when President Eisenhower and Prime Minister Macmillan started their post-Suez *rapprochement* at Bermuda, that ballistic missiles would be supplied Britain by the United States. They met once more in October, and, in February, 1958, their two governments agreed upon the establishment in the British Isles of four bases for ballistic missiles of intermediate range.

Agreement about atomic secrets came next. Here, over the years, there had been a wasteful duplication of effort; and only when Russia demonstrated how little she needed to glean from the West in war technology, was the United States more willing than she had been to share nuclear information with her British ally. Congress insisted that the atomic warheads of ballistic missiles, when stockpiled in Britain, were still to be in American custody; but so that she might more easily produce her own nuclear weapons, Britain was now to have the advantage of American designs and fissionable materials. In June, 1958, when Congress amended the Atomic Energy Act, and a year later, when new agreements took effect, Britain was the sole ally thus favored.

Early in 1960, President Eisenhower restated his desire to have the law made more liberal and not treat allies as junior members of a firm that are seen but not heard. Denied the necessary materials and data, France tried all the harder to become a nuclear power. But the United States and Britain had, with

Canada, been nuclear partners during World War II; each could furnish knowledge and materials that the other did not possess. Between them, too, there had been discord over the civil use of atomic energy, but in that field, likewise, information could be exchanged more freely.

Dialectical as ever was the character of Anglo-American collaboration. And the British provided evidence of this on two levels: those of domestic party politics and long-run national policy. There were dissidents in the ranks of both the Conservative and Labour parties; yet between Government and Opposition the importance of Anglo-American friendship was, on the whole, common ground. What it entailed in the light of the new weapons has, however, engendered acrimonious disputes. In Western Europe and the Middle East, the British were more exposed than their American ally to immediate danger. Many on the Left assumed, nevertheless, that American dependence on Britain now exceeded British dependence on the United States. Missile installations should, they argued, await the outcome of another East–West summit conference.

The British public was alarmed, moreover, when it learned that American bombers stationed in the British Isles carried nuclear and thermonuclear weapons with them on training missions. Permission to do this had been granted by a Labour Prime Minister, Clement Attlee, and endorsed by his Conservative successor, Sir Winston Churchill. All the same, one segment of British opinion called for the removal of American bases; another for a ban on the transport of hydrogen bombs by American bombers in British skies—though such a restriction must, logically, also apply to British aircraft armed with Britain's own nuclear and thermonuclear weapons.

American bases in Britain cannot be utilized for military operations without the consent of the British government. So, also, though nuclear warheads may stay in American custody, missile ramps are manned by the Royal Air Force, and it is only under joint orders by the British and American governments that they can be employed. But a better liaison over the use of American bases was arranged during the summer of 1960, after the Russians had shot down, over the high seas, an American reconnaissance plane which had been based on Britain.

Nothing less than the will to survive is what fans the current preoccupation of the British people with the nature of American leadership. Americans, in the days of British primacy, might have twisted the Lion's tail; when the British pluck the

Eagle's feathers, the issues involved are infinitely more grave. Allies on both sides of the Atlantic might be engulfed by an apparatus of defense that imperils as it preserves. Ultimate controls may not, however, be shared.

Can the exigencies of interdependence be coupled with a more independent status? British statesmen have thought so. Coalition strategy is Britain's over-all safeguard. But what has also been sought is a larger voice in its management, the means to act even when an American leader refrains from action. And the symbol of this quest is Britain's own production of the hydrogen bomb. A country whose industrial pre-eminence once rested upon coal, she has been to the fore in the non-military use of nuclear energy; the Suez crisis of 1956 showed that she must rely less on oil imports, and her program for generating electricity from atomic energy was tripled. But that should pay for itself; expenditure on nuclear and thermonuclear weapons is an unprofitable drain. Heavy bombers and intermediate-range ballistic missiles are the vehicles by which major weapons may be delivered. The British found, however, that they could not afford to manufacture those particular missiles. Less vulnerable, too, will be types that are based on mobile (manned aircraft and nuclear submarines) rather than fixed launching ramps. The United States can furnish those. In April, 1960, it was announced that intermediate-range ballistic missiles would not be made at home but would, instead, be bought by Britain from her American ally.

The British have wanted to supplement coalition strategy with an independent role of their own. This is not likely to be enhanced by their dependence on American delivery systems for major weapons. Part of the role she originally devised for herself Britain can, however, still pursue, as long as she produces her own nuclear warheads and keeps on hand a sufficient number of American intermediate-range ballistic missiles. But what if the supply of additional missiles from across the Atlantic should, when most needed, be curtailed? Britain may not be counting on these. They would be required if her own war plans envisaged a prolonged strategic counteroffensive. Yet, under the circumstances of the time, would that be practicable? Britain might best contribute to deterrence by preparing for a quick all-out stroke. Existing rather than future capacity is the threat she may pose—what, therefore, can lend substance, here and now, to British diplomacy.

Instruments of power that help to deter rivals might wrest extra attention from friends. In her association with the American leader of the West, and as a solid prop of the East–West equilibrium, Britain shuns a secondary role. She embarked upon her own nuclear program after her wartime atomic partnership with the United States and Canada had terminated; consistent with this was Sir Winston Churchill's decision in 1952 to persevere with the making of a hydrogen bomb. Nor did London merely expect more diplomatic influence to accrue at Washington. A wider margin of operational latitude was also forecast.

The United States and Britain diverged, during and after the Korean War, when the danger arose that, under the strategic interlock, the British people might be plunged into a nuclear holocaust over an outlying issue. Now the boot is on the other foot. Intercontinental bombers and intercontinental ballistic missiles, together with missiles discharged by Soviet submarines in coastal waters, would bring North America itself into the line of fire. At one time the Strategic Air Command might have assailed Russian targets without provoking Soviet reprisals on the cities and industries of North America. Such immunity has vanished, however. What London has to consider is not that the United States will be too rash, but too cautious; that, by holding back the over-all deterrent, the defense of Britain may be undercut.

Not that isolationism in the classic American style is again conceivable. The United States must prevent the Soviet Union from organizing the rest of the world against North America; for the United States to seclude herself again would only be to play into Communist hands. But it is one thing to uphold the NATO shield in Western Europe; it is another to unsheathe a two-edged sword that is not wielded by NATO. The unpredictable in American policy was exemplified during the Suez episode; what the British fear is that it might be unpredictably timid as well as unpredictably bold. The possession of major weapons may, at any rate, give the British a capacity to stand firm which they would not otherwise have. And these are not produced overnight. They are intended to bolster the status of Britain as the main security partner of the United States. They might also ensure that, in the worst of emergencies, she will not be caught short. Not that she could ever face Russia alone. But the stronger she is, the less will anyone, friend or foe, wish to disregard her.

Did concentration on one aspect of British security detract from others? A fresh effort had to be made to strike a balance between resources and burdens; it could only be done, however, in the light of American leadership and its effect on British interests. A drastic adaptation of British defense plans to the new war technology was first announced in April, 1957, when the Suez divergence still rankled; and yet the Strategic Air Command provided a screen of global deterrence so that it could be carried out unmolested. As international banker, Britain has to protect the pound sterling; as world trader, she cannot allocate a disproportionate amount of productive skill to preparedness; as a welfare state, her standard of living is sustained by costly social services. A straitened, overtaxed economy has its commitments to home defense, and to NATO in and around Western Europe; the communications sector and distant key points of the British oversea power structure cannot be neglected; Britain must be ready to discharge regional obligations under SEATO and the Central Treaty Organization. In over-all strategy, she refused to play a more subordinate part. She therefore tried to retrench elsewhere.

A revamped military establishment with reduced personnel would have more firepower and be more mobile. Politically and operationally, nevertheless, a Pandora's box had been opened up. At a time, for example, when French forces were diverted to North Africa, a cut in the British Army of the Rhine might have left to the United States and West Germany the onus of NATO defense. This would have been an ironic sequel to the Anglo-American liberation of Western Europe from the Nazi Reich. The Bonn Republic had vied with Britain on world markets and accumulated its gold surplus by delaying its rearmament. But the future of West Germany as a component of Western defense is an uncertain one.* When, therefore, the continental strength of a NATO bulwark such as Britain is diminished, the West as a whole is less secure. The British seek more influence at Washington and Moscow in the sphere of global deterrence. Yet Britain must also pull her weight in the home theater of Western Europe if her world position is not to be impaired.

British military reforms were bound up with the nature of American leadership in another respect. Democracies are averse to large standing armies; by adopting missiles and tactical nuclear weapons, they plan to offset the numerical preponderance which Communist dictatorships can muster. But the adoption of these devices raised more problems than it solved. Would the West be handicapped if situations arose in which only conventional arms were employed? Russia, after all, has a twofold capacity—a conventional as well as an atomic one. Deterred by the prospect of total war, the Sino-Soviet bloc may either sap the military strength of peripheral territories or, through its pawns, outflank the West.

* For comment on the German question, see pp. 317 ff.

Will the West be as able to supply menaced countries with conventional arms or be as capable of intervening in minor wars? What will Britain do in oversea areas where Western interests are still British rather than American? To cope with emergencies at more distant points, mobile forces have been formed.

In the East–West contest, however, Europe is still the makeweight, and there the West might only hamper itself if, while gaining technical mobility, it were to become politically more inert. Possession of Western Europe would do the most to turn the world scales to the East; but it has to be acquired as a going concern and not as a desolate radioactive shell. Russia may therefore not merely be daunted by what the latest weapons can do to her; it will not pay her to employ them tactically on land against NATO. She might, nevertheless, deem the overnuclearized defense of Western Europe a psychological boon. For, rather than provoke her into the reciprocal use of tactical nuclear weapons, the stoutest of West Europeans may quail at employing their own or at permitting Anglo-American forces to employ any on their soil. Nor can anybody guarantee that, once tactical nuclear arms have been thrown into battle, the major strategic ones will be withheld. Are there absolute distinctions between categories? In a desperate hour will these be observed? Outside Europe there may be limited wars; inside Europe, will not a limited war tend, nowadays, to become an unlimited one? There would be fewer palsying doubts among NATO allies if they, like the Russians, also retained an adequate complement of conventional weapons. Yet that cannot be done, there can be no such versatility in defense, without sacrifice by leader and led. The debate proceeds.

In making the changeover to tactical nuclear weapons, the British have gone along with their American allies. But one vocal group argues that Britain would be safer if she abandoned nuclear and thermonuclear weapons unilaterally. Some of this pacifist, unilateralist, neutralist agitation is anti-American. The more pronounced it becomes, however, the less is the likelihood of the Left winning an election and attaining office.

Would an independent NATO nuclear force (one composed especially of missile-firing submarines) help solve coalition differences in this sphere? It would appeal to West Germany. It would also enable France, after President de Gaulle passes from the scene, and if the load must be lightened, to relinquish nuclear and thermonuclear aspirations. But it is improbable that the British would be willing to forfeit the nuclear and thermonuclear status that they have achieved.

It is evident, all the same, that Britain might have met other military needs with less strain if her outlay on hydrogen bombs could have been stopped. And this would have had as its outcome a division of labor in the common defense between the United States and Britain: the former putting the emphasis on the more expensive weapons; the latter, with traditional interests in Western Europe and her oversea power structure, deploying a larger capacity in conventional ones. But the British clung to their share in the over-all deterrent. Influence at Washington and elsewhere may not only be determined by thermonuclear power; through it, Britain takes early precautions against a last-minute divergence from her own chief ally. For in Anglo-American interaction, the positive and negative are ceaselessly at work. And the English-speaking powers are denied full unison by the character of modern war technology itself.

THE FAR EAST AGAIN

Recently, moreover, there had been a reminder of the negative elements that inhere in coalition strategy. These exhibited themselves first during the Korean War and later, in the summer of 1958, when, the Chinese Communists having resumed their heavy bombardment of the Chinese offshore islands, East Asia again became the cynosure of all eyes. Calm had scarcely been restored to the Middle East by the Anglo-American landings in Lebanon and Jordan.* Much in Downing Street's attitude towards the new Far Eastern crisis was affected by events in the Levant.

Not that anybody knew whether this Chinese exploit signified harmony or friction between Moscow and Peking. Communist China was about to start her massive, brutal experiment in peasant communes, and an external issue might provide timely distraction; perhaps, too, industrial output could be speeded up under the whiplash of patriotism. Communist China had, moreover, been debarred from the United Nations and excluded from Soviet proposals for a summit meeting; it was surmised, after a visit paid by Premier Khrushchev to Peking, that she wanted to reassert her status as a great power, not only against the West but against her own Russian ally. What had been shown was the geographic capacity of the East to switch, in its harassment of the West, from one regional theater to another. The United States

---

* For the Anglo-American intervention in the Middle East, see Chapter VII.

and Britain could no longer be driven apart in the Middle East. Did the Far East offer a better opportunity for making mischief between them?

Washington itself had provided fresh grounds for Anglo-American divergence. An American defense perimeter which stretched from the Aleutians down the western Pacific to Australia, included Formosa. As an outpost of American power, that island served to reassure Asian friends and allies that dwelt under the lengthening shadow of Communist China—especially when their own Chinese inhabitants were tending to cast ever fonder glances at Peking. But the islands of Quemoy and Matsu belonged, geographically, to the Chinese mainland. To the protection of Formosa, which is more than a hundred miles away, they contributed little. Their value to an American defense perimeter, of which the Formosan bastion is part, was equally scant. The United States would, as a matter of fact, be weaker rather than stronger, if she overextended herself. And under the strategic interlock she could not be overextended in the Pacific without putting her Atlantic associates on tenterhooks. When it backed Chiang Kai-shek, Washington preserved the jurisdiction of its Formosan protégé over the offshore islands. But one test of leadership was the degree to which the United States could retain control over her own commitments.

About this Washington appeared unconcerned. The battle for the offshore islands was the last protracted campaign of the Chinese civil war; during the flare-up of 1954–55, the United States steered clear of it. Since then, nevertheless, President Chiang Kai-shek has been allowed to entrench about a third of his army on Quemoy and Matsu. Nor could he take seriously such unenforced protests as Washington registered: the move had been made with the advice and assistance of the American armed services. Not that the offshore islands were a good springboard for the invasion of the Chinese mainland; the topography of the adjacent Fukien coast was too inhospitable. Formosa, nevertheless, increased offshore garrisons.

These maneuvers implicated the United States more than Congress or the American people realized or had ever approved. For if there were an amphibious assault from the mainland, she would have to rush to the rescue. The United States could not let Chiang lose so large a fraction of his army. His regime on Formosa might collapse and be supplanted by one less opposed to Peking.

Would Chiang be supported on Matsu and Quemoy at the

risk of an East-West conflict? His aims were intelligible if the Chinese masses, rising at an early date against Communist taskmasters, were likely to turn to him; they were intolerable if, having trapped his American patron, he could set the world aflame. Chiang's ambitions were no secret. What nobody had anticipated was the complaisance of the Eisenhower Administration.

On this occasion, American public opinion was almost as adverse as that of allies and neutrals. In the end, Washington had to be firm with Chiang as well as with Peking and Moscow; but it tried, at first, to support him unconditionally. Mainland shore batteries opened up again on August 23, 1958, and not only was the American Seventh Fleet reinforced at once; President Eisenhower remarked four days later that, for the defense of Formosa, the offshore islands were more important now than they had been in 1954–55. In January, 1955, Congress had authorized operations on other friendly territory if the President deemed this necessary for implementing the defense treaty with Formosa. Did Mr. Eisenhower now intend to avail himself of that authorization? Somewhat cryptically, it was suggested on September 4 that he might. On September 7, rather than let Quemoy and Matsu be starved into submission, the Seventh Fleet began to convoy supplies as far as the three-mile limit.

There were, at the same time, ominous rumblings from Moscow. President Eisenhower had been warned by Premier Khrushchev that the Soviet Union stood behind Communist China; a note of September 19 was so rude that it was returned as unacceptable. Before that, nevertheless, Washington's stern demeanor impelled Peking to propose, on September 6, that perfunctory Sino-American talks, held in Geneva, should be resumed. Transferred to Warsaw, they were again entered into. But, on September 11, the President broadcast another one of those appeals for unity that had, at home and abroad, the opposite effect.

The United States, said the President, would not be lured or frightened into an appeasement of Communist China. There was, however, no comparison between the call for prudence in the Formosan Strait and the misjudgments of the 1930's when the independence of European democracies, and of areas vital to the defense of the West, were betrayed to Hitler. On neither side of the Atlantic did so inapt an analogy allay dissent. Appeasement, moreover, had been Washington's own policy during the Suez crisis of 1956. But was the caution that Mr. Eisenhower previously displayed in East Asian affairs about to be thrown to the winds? He inveighed against the Communist use of force; from the offshore islands, all the same, mainland ports were blockaded and minor raids conducted. Dismay was widespread over a concept of leadership that, by giving Chiang Kai-shek a free rein, let him be an arbiter of American, and therefore of Western, destiny.

Peking, nevertheless, desisted while Washington itself bowed to domestic and coalition pressure. Late in September, when the Nationalists were helped to run the counterblockade, there was no further need for American escort vessels to expose themselves to mainland guns. The offshore islands could thus hold out while a Sino-American collision was averted; a halter might next be put on Chiang himself. On September 30, Secretary Dulles admitted that the inordinate build-up of Nationalist forces on Quemoy and Matsu was rather foolish; and that to maintain it, if there were a *de facto* armistice, would be unwise— views which the President endorsed a day later. What this meant was that the offshore islands were, after all, not as important for the defense of Formosa as had been averred. It also implied that Chiang would have no unconditional American backing for whatever he did on them.

But neither was Moscow, presumably, any more disposed than Washington to let its ally run loose. It would only intervene, observed Premier Khrushchev on October 5, if the United States did so; even neutrals that advocated Peking's entry into the United Nations were discomfited when it again reverted to the use of force. The Chinese Communists failed to achieve their goal by artillery attack; in air combat, moreover, Nationalist pilots, armed with American missiles, had come out best. From October 6, Peking ordered a somewhat fitful suspension of its barrage if the American convoys were also stopped; and while a new series of bombardments began on October 25, this was scheduled for alternate days. The offshore islands might thus be supplied without Washington getting the period of calm which it desired. And by a gesture of mock generosity, Peking hoped to wean its Formosan brethren from their American patron.

The crisis had abated and, on October 23, Secretary Dulles persuaded Chiang himself to declare against the use of force as a principal means of liberating the Chinese mainland. The smaller his offshore garrison, moreover, the less chance there was of embroiling the United States and all who were aligned with her. Chiang might thin it out in return for American weapons with greater firepower; but, while force had been renounced as a principal means of liberation, it had not been totally abjured. Henceforth, nevertheless, Chiang's activities were to be more restricted. In fact, if not in theory, Washington had adopted the idea of two Chinas.

Peking, however, claimed Formosa as obstinately as ever. Its arms establishment on the mainland coast was not only improved but augmented. It had, besides, weapons of intrigue and propaganda. Nor did a lull dispose of the Formosan dispute. In any effort to reach an East-West accommodation, it was sure to be a contentious topic.

That topic can, furthermore, still divide the West itself. Alarm was widespread during the flare-up of 1958 when Washington seemed to be backing Chiang unconditionally; in Britain, the government was assailed for not speaking out against the danger of indirect involvement through the United States. But while Downing Street urged restraint at Washington, Peking, and Moscow, its own utterances were also restrained.

In no other fashion, as a matter of fact, could a variety of British objectives be served. Forward policies by the United States in Eastern Asia had been frowned upon ever since the Korean War; under a strategic interlock whose backlash might jeopardize the existence of the British Isles, it was only for the most momentous of issues that all-out war could be risked. Britain, moreover, had recognized Peking before the Korean War; its title to the offshore islands was acknowledged by Sir Anthony Eden in 1955. Then, too, London had persuaded Washington to let the ban on trade with Communist China be relaxed; there had been intervals when, but for American disapprobation, Britain and Canada might have voted for superseding the Chinese Nationalists by the Peking regime in the United Nations. The Crown Colony of Hong Kong was, in addition, highly vulnerable, and there had been recent threats against it. Did Anglo-American interaction now render that exposed British holding more secure— or less so?

In 1958, the Macmillan government stressed not disagreements with the United States but points of agreement. Conservative Ministers reiterated the American argument against Peking's use of force; to this, however, the Labour Party could retort that Communist China had been prevented by force from getting possession of what, in British eyes, was her own property. On September 12, the Prime Minister said that Washington had neither sought nor received promises of British support in the Formosa area; but he refused to tie his hands for the future. The

Eisenhower Administration had dissociated itself from Britain when, through the Suez venture, she tried to preserve vital interests in the Middle East. And yet, when American power was rashly overextended in the Far East, the Macmillan Government did not break ranks.

Between the British and American approaches to the Far East, there were still serious divergences. Downing Street attempted, nevertheless, to soft-pedal these so that the fullest accord with Washington might be maintained elsewhere. At the dawn of the space age, Eisenhower and Macmillan had reaffirmed the general Anglo-American principle of interdependence; in the Middle East, where they had had a post-Suez *rapprochement,* the United States and Britain were now collaborating against pan-Arab–pro-Soviet elements. And when British troops had yet to be evacuated from Jordan, it would be playing the Sino-Soviet game for London to quarrel with Washington about Chiang.

Politically, however, the Macmillan Government might have been naked to its enemies if the Eisenhower Administration had not altered its course. The strain on Anglo-American friendship was relieved. But its dialectical character had again been revealed. When primacy had shifted across the Atlantic, the United States could not have led the West without extending her power. But when American power is overextended, her closest associate will bring corrective pressure to bear. For the defense of a free world order, American leadership has been indispensable. The all-engulfing scope of coalition strategy enjoins that it be directed with care.

The new war technology aggravated Anglo-American differences in the Far East. It might also assuage them. There can, at any rate, be no satisfactory East-West arms agreement from which Communist China is excluded; and Peking may stipulate acceptance by the United States as one of its terms. Communist China is growing industrially by leaps and bounds; if the Soviet Union does not furnish her with nuclear weapons, she might soon produce her own. As long, too, as Moscow and Peking are allied, there must be safeguards against any Russian evasion of test bans on Chinese soil. But will Communist China permit inspection posts to be installed? She may first demand a favorable settlement of such thorny issues as Formosa, China's seat on the Security Council, recognition by the United States, and attendance at summit conferences. Nor is Peking in a hurry. Bombardment of the offshore islands, chronic war in the Formosan Strait, may

have deepened American entanglements. Communist China antici-
pates, all the same, that, after Chiang's demise, Formosa will fall
into her lap like a ripe fruit.

Over these matters Russia may be more inscrutable than
China. Does the Soviet Union want its Chinese ally to become
a nuclear power? Russian disarmament plans would seem to indicate that it does not. Peking and Moscow have both proposed
atom-free zones in Europe and the Pacific basin. The retraction
of American power in the Pacific as well as from non-Soviet
Europe could thus be obtained. But so, also, might Russia freeze
her superiority over her Chinese ally in the most advanced
weapons. To maintain primacy in the West has been no simple
task for the United States. To stay ahead in the East, Russia
may be confronted with difficulties that are still more onerous.
And much will depend on how well the West turns them to
account.

What price, then, is to be paid for a halt to the East-West
arms race? The Chinese problem has not only been an irritant
between London and Washington but also between the United
States and other members of the Commonwealth, allied and
neutral. Australia, however, has been more sympathetic towards
the Far Eastern policy of the United States. And yet, even Canberra moved ahead of Washington to ask for the inclusion of
Communist China in any East-West arms agreement. For such a
step may deflect a giant southward push. It would also signify
that Communist China had been admitted to the comity of nations
at last.

On the morale of free Asia, nevertheless, Peking's diplomatic victory might have a shattering effect. When the West deals
with Communist China, it will be hard to discourage oversea
Chinese in Malaya, Singapore, and Hong Kong from doing the
same. Along her southern and southeastern frontiers, from Ladakh
in Indian Kashmir to Laos and South Vietnam, will Communist
China be more disposed to respect the rights of weaker neighbors? That is a question upon which the signatories of SEATO,
Asian and non-Asian, must deliberate. Then, too, apart from
Formosa, the United States has special ties with the Philippines,
Japan, and South Korea. Would American concessions to Peking
so dispirit them that a switch from one camp to the other might
ensue?

There is no easy choice. Hazard will lurk in whatever is
done. A bargain may be struck, but only because that is where

the balance of advantage seems to lie. And over terms of settlement, there might again be Anglo-American divergence. Neither Washington nor London can permit it to get out of hand.

The Far East is, moreover, but one theater in a larger global contest. It has been in non-Soviet Europe that the East-West equilibrium could be turned most decisively against the West. Developments in France and the future of West Germany raise coalition issues that do not affect only American primacy. They shed light on the degree to which leadership must still be exercised in conjunction with Britain.

THE POSITION OF FRANCE

Foes of the West have always striven to pry the English-speaking powers loose from each other. Yet even so illustrious a custodian of Western values as France has been disgruntled by the part which the Anglo-American factor plays. History explains why the English-speaking peoples, after pulling away from each other, perennially band together; though her liberation in 1944–45 made her a beneficiary of this dialectical process, it is disliked by France. Not that she caviled at the need for leadership in NATO and the Western coalition. But she has tended to confound the underlying imperatives of Anglo-American friendship with an Anglo-American duumvirate.

Can there be a Western triumvirate in which, as a global power, France should be included? That was the objective of General Charles de Gaulle when he ushered in the Fifth Republic. However, Bonn, Rome, Ottawa, and other North Atlantic capitals shrugged it off. To Anglo-American friendship they had long been accustomed. But neither wartime experience nor the postwar distribution of power seemed to warrant a special place for France. Nor were they likely to accept her as a spokesman for Western Europe or as leader of a Third Force which might function as a check within the West upon American leadership or upon Anglo-American initiatives. For General de Gaulle reappeared in an hour of disarray, and it was her own house that France first had to set in order.

In French recovery, the attitude of her English-speaking allies has been an important element. France joined with Britain in that Suez venture which the United States condemned; subsequently, however, there was dissension between her and the two English-speaking powers. In the wake of the Indochinese débâcle, the Algerian revolution had been sapping the strength of France;

a dispute over North African affairs with Washington and London attended the last days of the Fourth Republic. Paris feared that arms which they had supplied Premier Habib Bourguiba of Tunisia would reach Algerian insurrectionaries. The United States and Britain, on the other hand, wanted to bolster an Arab regime, which was anti-Nasser and pro-Western, in a Mediterranean sector the West could ill afford to lose. After the Suez fiasco, moreover, France pinned her hopes on the oil of the Sahara. But it was suspected that the United States wished to develop the untapped natural resources of that region and to oust the French from it. When, too, the Algerian issue came up in the General Assembly, Washington, with a glance at the Afro-Asian bloc, tried to hedge.

Wherever they looked, the French felt they were being treated cavalierly. About the Anglo-American landings in Lebanon and Jordan they had been given little prior notice; on the Chinese offshore islands, Washington acted by itself and London was taciturn. As one of three Western powers with extensive oversea interests, France did have a genuine claim for more systematic consultation; events in the Middle East and Far East had exhibited the fallacy of attempting to keep NATO consultations within the strict geographic confines of that instrument. But on this question the British were silenced by their own post-Suez *rapprochement* with the United States. Consultation *à trois* improved, however, after the breakdown of the Paris summit conference in 1960.

Over anything, as a matter of fact, that regenerates their French ally, the English-speaking peoples will rejoice. Among reforms that accompanied the birth of the Fifth Republic they were cheered, above all, by economic and fiscal changes at home, and by the advent of a progressive new French Community between France and her oversea territories. In other respects a somewhat unco-operative posture did not bode well. President de Gaulle was intent upon restoring the grandeur of France. But this national *mystique* might impel her to diverge more basically from English-speaking partners than they normally allowed themselves to diverge from each other. Dialectical habits borrowed from domestic politics may be a clue to what is unique in Anglo-American interaction. And, while French democracy is served by a similar dialectic, is it schooled to observe similar limits?

The constitution of the Fifth Republic must, at any rate, prolong uncertainty in Washington and London about the course that France will follow. In 1958 General de Gaulle preserved his country from civil war, took a restive army in hand and, firm yet enlightened, mended the tattered fabric of national unity. But a representative system refashioned to suit the idiosyncrasies of a particular individual might be misused by a successor. For France has swung from the executive debility of the Third and Fourth Republics to a Presidential quasi-dictatorship, when it is between those two poles that some lasting equipoise is to be attained. Will authoritarian innovations ever be revised without bloodshed? Those who work with their French ally may yet be reminded that the quest of French democracy for stable institutions is still under way.

As the unfinished business of France, its implications are not merely political. Much of the infrastructure for the defense of Western Europe rests on her soil. Havoc might be wrought by civil strife, by a neo-Pétainist regime on the Right which turns its back on the West, or by a popular front government on the Left which gazes to the East; Moscow is always ready to revive, at the expense of other French alignments, the old Franco-Russian alliance. And the military consequences of any such *bouleversement* will be evident. The Western coalition may do without French air bases; to its advanced land bases it might reroute supply lines through Belgium, the Netherlands, West Germany, and Italy. NATO armies would, nevertheless, be unable to maneuver freely if the French hinterland were not at their disposal. And what has disquieted allies is the tendency of France to step back from NATO just when a higher global rank is demanded.

Not that others have done their utmost. Thirty divisions were prescribed for NATO; it does not possess that many. Nor did Britain, in paring down the British Army of the Rhine, set a good example. The fact is, nevertheless, that by diverting the bulk of her land forces to Algeria, France left the protection of hearth and home to NATO allies. She might thus maintain access to those riches of the Sahara which are to be the sinews of her new status; thus, too, she can hold the North African flank of Western Europe against neutralist, Nasserist, pro-Communist inroads. But, unduly protracted, the pacification of Algeria could be as bad a drain as Indochina was—one that would lower rather than raise her rank. A solution that is fair to all may be found. Without it, however, France could default on her European defenses while the German component of NATO becomes regionally predominant—an eventuality which, in three wars, millions of Frenchmen have died to prevent, and one which the nascent amity between Paris and Bonn might not fully mitigate.

It is the aim of France to be strong on all fronts simultaneously. But she will not need to be so if an East-West arms agreement is attained. Meanwhile, her bid for equal status with Britain at Washington has been capped by the manufacture of nuclear weapons. Through such production, forbidden West Germany, France may be able to compensate for the smaller size of her continental forces. But it will take a number of years for her to build up a nuclear arsenal and acquire the requisite delivery systems. Politically and strategically her motives may be the same as Britain's; others have doubted, however, whether she was in the same position to make the attempt. Britain reciprocates for nuclear secrets which she now gets from the United States. More information, as far as the edicts of Congress allow, may be given France. But here, again, France will have done less than Britain did to achieve her goal.

Nor were the methods that France employed likely to enhance confidence in her among her principal allies. She hesitated to install intermediate-range ballistic missiles unless she was accorded complete control over them and, despite the enactments of Congress, over stockpiles of nuclear warheads. The French may have felt that, as targets, launching sites only made their country more vulnerable—and without fortifying the over-all deterrent; Britain, facing the same risk and sharing control with the United States, took American ballistic missiles at once. The British but not the French assigned fighter aircraft to NATO command; it was divulged during the Berlin crisis that French warships, previously earmarked for joint NATO operations, were to be withheld in wartime. Then, too, American fighter bombers had to be moved in 1959 from French bases to Britain and West Germany, where American custody of nuclear weapons was permitted.

The picture was not all dark. French troops stationed in West Germany were allowed during 1960 to accept weapons with a nuclear capability, and Paris agreed to an integrated NATO command in the air from which most of the territory of France was excepted but to which part of the French Air Force could belong. Supply depots, land and air training bases on French soil were, moreover, conceded the Bonn Republic that same year— a move that came only two decades after the last German invasion of France. For NATO, nevertheless, the French attitude was still a serious handicap.

It was, looking backward as well as forward, an odd situation. World War II might have been averted if the United States had not reneged on guarantees of French security which were to underwrite the treaty settlement of 1919; now, however, France herself may impede the implementation of American support. Co-operation with NATO was desired; yet NATO would be subject to operational disabilities if it did not meet the terms that France laid down. What Paris wanted was the right to be consulted by Washington before nuclear weapons were used anywhere in the world—other, that is, than for the defense of American soil. During Far Eastern crises, the operational veto that the British sought was an informal one. A formal one, like that which France envisaged, was more than Washington could grant.

Consultative procedures have been improved, and France may thus be mollified. Her malaise might last, however, as long as the East-West contest itself. For English-speaking allies cannot reverse the historic circumstances under which primacy shifted from Britain to the United States; and it is against these, at bottom, that France has rebelled. She might have asked Washington for a formalized parity of command. The British, after 1945, could do without one. They had other consolations.

Disparities between Britain and the United States were patent. But these were redressed by the sort of bonds that conduced to reconciliation after divergence. For Britain's decline in status was eased by a Commonwealth partnership and an Anglo-American solidarity of which each is *sui generis;* with them the French Community and ancient French ties with the United States are not quite comparable. An inner circle is what France perceives; she overlooks a process of politics that Anglo-American policymakers express but did not create. And it is not out of prejudice or by premeditation that France is excluded from this. She is self-excluded by her own individual patrimony.

Perhaps if Anglo-American friendship were less uneven in its course, the French could resign themselves more readily to its peculiarities. But over a major problem like the reconstruction of Europe it is with them rather than the British that the United States has been in accord. Ever since the European Recovery Program of the Truman Administration, Washington has done what it could to promote the unification of Western Europe.

In the Council of Europe and organizations for European economic co-operation, the sovereign powers of member states have been undisturbed. But the European Coal and Steel Community, the European Economic Community, and the European Atomic Energy Community point towards a supranational unity, and of these projects France has been the main architect.

Under General de Gaulle the French may shrink from that integration of Europe which is the ultimate political consequence of their own handiwork. No state within a federal union can have its own outside connections. That is why full participation is incompatible with interests that sustain Britain's rank in both European and global affairs—as the pivot of an oversea power structure, as the center of Commonwealth and Imperial trade preferences, and as the principal ally of the United States. And because her role is many-sided, the damage would be widespread if British exports were debarred from the Common Market which six West European nations—France, the Bonn Republic, Italy, Belgium, the Netherlands, and Luxembourg—have established. Other forms of Western unity might suffer. In the Outer Seven, Britain has a European trading bloc of her own. But will she be as able or as disposed to maintain the British Army of the Rhine when France and West Germany are the foremost constituents of a tariff zone that penalizes the British economy? And if she is not, will France herself be as safe as she has been?

With all of these questions the United States, as leader of the West, must also conjure. But in the Common Market she has seen the inception of a federal union like her own; a United States of Europe in which the rising productivity of a semicontinental region will bolster against the East the West's most crucial theater. Analogies between North American and West European conditions can, however, be overdone. London and Paris might bicker; a major British contribution to continental defense is still a premise of French security. And this may be impaired if Britain is constrained to choose between two sets of ties, a European and a non-European. For it is by combining both that she has been a bulwark of the West.

Nor are the French as unaware as Americans of such axiomatic realities. They have put Britain in a quandary because they themselves have been ensnared in one. In the new era of American primacy, few decisions were more far-reaching than that by which the Western segment of German power was resurrected. But with Russian forces seated on the Elbe, the North Atlantic area had to be reinforced. Can West German power be canalized in a westward rather than an eastward direction? France is compelled to assume that it can.

It is the East-West contest which has lent impetus to the drive for integrating European economies. During World War II, General de Gaulle renewed the old Franco-Russian alliance as an offset to a German revival; Communist penetration of France and Italy, Soviet political designs in the two Germanies were, after World War II, to render that traditional remedy worse than the disease. The alternative for France has been so to rivet the Bonn Republic to the West that the East could never lure it away. First, however, Franco-German antagonism would have to be ameliorated. France relinquished the Saar; a Rhine-Moselle waterway, facilitating the reciprocal use of coal and iron ore, was to be built; West German capital may invest in the Eurafrican undertakings which France has visualized. But what would happen to France if, as during the 1930's, German intentions had again been misjudged?

Burned into the consciousness of France is the recollection of how her defeat in World War II might have been avoided if, after World War I, French sacrifices had not been slurred over and the English-speaking peoples had not been the willing dupes of German propaganda. A Franco-German *rapprochement* betokens an effort by France to ensure that a German resurgence, which her own English-speaking allies have again fostered, will be kept within the Western fold. But what if Moscow ever offers Bonn more potent inducements to switch sides?

In reasserting herself France relies on her partnership with the West German Republic. She will, as a matter of fact, only be safe as long as Germany is divided. France would be swamped economically, a greater Germany would dominate the Common Market, if East Germany could ever be reunited with West Germany on Western terms; a reunification of the two Germanies on Russian terms will, on the other hand, spell the end of the Common Market and imperil the French politically. To the ill-starred European Defense Community, with its federalizing measures, Britain could not adhere, and France, rather than subject herself to West German preponderance, rejected it in 1954. The problem remains. It may be expedient for Paris to echo Washington and London in calling for the reunification of Germany. *Au fond* the French must pray that the existing equipoise within wider European projects will be perpetuated.

There is, at any rate, little in the position of France to suggest a more sure-footed role. A redefinition of her status within Anglo-American and NATO councils may be sought; it will be well if, at home and abroad, she can hold her own. President de Gaulle was to get the support of Chancellor Adenauer in the controversy with Britain over the Common Market, and Chancellor Adenauer obtained his support during the East-West crisis over Berlin. The result was that, after the breakdown of the

Paris summit conference in 1960, some American officials even bestowed on the French President the accolade of Western leadership. In coalition affairs, however, France still dragged her feet. On the other hand, ever since the coal-steel pool was first broached, French and Germans have been burying outworn enmities; and a tragic chapter in modern annals might thus be closed. Yet economic bonds and treaty obligations may not avail to close it. A moral commitment by West Germans to the West is also needed.

But that is something which they themselves cannot guarantee. Forging elaborate ties with the Bonn Republic, France does not dispense with safeguards against it; resenting her English-speaking allies, she depends on them for her ultimate reinsurance. And that is another reason why a Franco-German partnership may not burgeon into a neutralist Third Force; as an integral portion of the West, France cannot cut herself adrift from it for long. The Franco-German *rapprochement* is a progressive move; it might, if Bonn stays in the Western camp, prove to be one of those contingencies, dear to the French mind, in which the provisional becomes permanent. But, hidden and unavowed, there must still be a Watch on the Rhine. It is the alignment of France with English-speaking allies by which, despite ruffled French susceptibilities, she is chiefly protected.

GERMANY BETWEEN EAST AND WEST

On such issues, however, it is not merely the French who have been equivocal. Proposing that the German *status quo* be altered, the United States and Britain have likewise had a paramount interest in its preservation. To restore the major segment of German power was to reanimate German national impulses. Washington and London hoped that these might be harnessed for the defense of the West. But it is only under circumstances inimical to the West that they can be fulfilled entirely. Washington presupposed that Russia would somehow relinquish her grip on East Germany; however, Moscow's prerequisite for the reunion of the two Germanies has always been the detachment of the Bonn Republic from the West. For Germany is to Western Europe what Western Europe is to the global balance—a makeweight that can, geographically and technologically, turn the scales.

And that is why a reunified Germany which may belong to the West, despite all that American and British statesmen said and did, was never in the cards. Moscow's bargaining advantage has been perfectly clear from the outset. The West, having rebuilt it and released it from postwar servitudes, ceded to the Bonn Republic freedom to choose between East and West. But Russia grants her German vassal no such option. She can thereby preclude German reunification on Western terms: it must either come about as she stipulates or not at all. The existing equilibrium, for English-speaking allies as well as for France, is the one viable alternative.

A divided Germany was, it so happens, what the Big Three contemplated during World War II. What they could not foresee was the way that land would be polarized between them in any postwar contest of their own. Germany consisted of a cluster of smaller states before Bismarck unified them. If she were again dissected, would recurrent German wars be averted? Roosevelt, Churchill, and Stalin discussed this notion at the Teheran and Yalta conferences. The Morgenthau Plan, which would have reduced the German economy to pastoral and agricultural pursuits, was to be an extreme version of earlier moderate proposals. Contrariwise, when the United States financed Europe's postwar comeback, she did not discriminate between evildoer and victims. For this the West Germans have chiefly Russian intransigence to thank.

Decentralizing trends were reversed, at any rate, as soon as President Truman took office. Berlin and the rest of conquered Germany had, for occupation purposes, been carved up into separate zones; wartime projects for internationalizing the Ruhr were, however, rejected at Potsdam. The vast economic and military potential of that industrial basin might thus be of use to the West. But, conversely, its resources would accrue to the East if Russia could get her terms for German reunification accepted.

Anguish over systematic German iniquities had, meanwhile, been deflected by the callous Russian subjugation of Baltic, East European, and Balkan peoples. Czechoslovakia passed, after a brief interval, from Nazi to Soviet clutches; and, three years after Berliners had been engaged in bombing London, an Anglo-American airlift rescued them from blockade by Russia. In the administration of occupied German zones the Americans, British, and French were to find the Soviet Union recalcitrant; Communism might batten on economic distress. But this had been alleviated when American authorities reformed German currency and, as Marshall aid poured in, the Bonn Republic was established. Allied zones in Berlin were, nevertheless, surrounded by East German territory and there the Soviet Union retained its ability to obstruct. If Churchill's wartime advice had been heeded, Anglo-American forces would have done their utmost to take the former Reich capital before Russian armies reached it. Washington was to rue the day that it had overruled the great British war minister.

What accelerated the rehabilitation of West Germany was the outbreak of the Korean War. She might not only stand on her own feet; in helping to defend herself she would, as East-West antagonism deepened, also help defend the West. Secretary Acheson persuaded the British to consent to her rearmament;* the French, however, did not concur until 1954 when the Bonn Republic entered NATO and the Western European Union. In proposing these arrangements, Sir Anthony Eden sought to keep the Bonn Republic out of Russia's grasp and to dispel the danger of any reversion to isolationism in the American Congress.† The Soviet Union had remilitarized East Germany, but this could not match the strength which West Germany might now lend to the West. And to subtract all German strength from the West rather than let more be added to it was the Russian aim. Russia could not forget, as Sir Anthony Eden discerned at the Geneva summit conference of 1955, the havoc wrought by invading Germans.‡ Until the Bonn Republic can be enticed from the West, the Russians will perpetuate the division of Germany.

Another hazardous phase of American leadership and coalition diplomacy had thus begun. A unified Germany which leans towards the West was the objective that Washington and London, Paris, and Bonn were to pursue. National goals were sought by West Germany in association with the West. But what if the Bonn Republic's association with the West were to render these goals unattainable? Would West Germans then react against the West? East Germans cannot dissever their moorings with the East; West Germans, however, are free agents. Will they always refuse to pay Moscow's price for reunification?

They are, after all, not in the same category as the French. France has been discontented with American leadership and the part that the Anglo-American factor plays; but in the German mind—such has been the German heritage—there may be mental reservations about the West as a whole. The Germanies missed those seventeenth- and eighteenth-century revolutions, English, American, and French, by which democracy was furthered; it was

---

* Truman, *op. cit.*, I, pp. 236-237, 306, 327, 389, and 406; and II, pp. 254-257.

† Eden, *op. cit.*, pp. 32-52, 63-65, and 169-194.

‡ Eden, *op. cit.*, pp. 334-335; see also pp. 323-324 and 327-339.

a German counterrevolutionary tradition that, in two world wars, undermined a free world order and gave other illiberal forces their chance. The Bonn Republic, like its feeble Weimar predecessor, is an offshoot of defeat. No product of stout indigenous principle, it was ushered in with Anglo-American bayonets. Would the desire for reunification and the experiment in democracy tally with each other or conflict?

To achieve reunification on Russian terms it may not be necessary for the Bonn Republic to go Communist. A neutralized, unified Germany could still attempt to govern itself as a representative democracy. But when Bismarck conducted a self-regarding policy, imperial Germany was a semiabsolutism. Economic and military ties will not link the Bonn Republic irrevocably to the West unless, in the imponderables of politics, there is also a Western orientation.

Today, all the same, it is by the *status quo* that West Germany likewise profits. Vigor has been acquired under Anglo-American auspices and this she must have if she is ever to negotiate with Moscow from strength. Nor does the economic outlook call for change. It is not required for trade with Russia and China. Much more lucrative have been the opportunities that the Bonn Republic has enjoyed, overseas and nearer home, in non-Soviet lands; others, through the Common Market, should open up. Nor do the industrial districts of the Bonn Republic need the agricultural areas of East Germany; farm products can be procured more cheaply elsewhere. There has, besides, been apathy among West Germans towards the plight of East German kinsmen; here there are differences in religion and politics which may be noted: West Germans are largely Catholic and liberal-conservative, East Germans Protestant and Socialist. A divided Germany might suit them better than many in Bonn and Washington have supposed.

One point about current trends among the French and the West Germans can be made: in the decisive theater of Western Europe there are elements of incertitude against which Anglo-American friendship shines by contrast. France, inspired by Charles de Gaulle, may be loath to cut her coat according to her cloth; with the Bonn Republic, care must be taken lest, prone to the frustrations of irredentism, it yet leave its French partner and other Western allies in the lurch. Between the wars, when the Treaty of Versailles symbolized the defeat that a greater, unified Germany brought upon herself, it was the West at which

German nationalists railed. Once more, if they were to recapture their place in the sun, they would have to turn away from the West.

Communism may be abhorred; not for the first time would doctrinal antipathies have been overlooked. After World War I, the German Right strove to reverse the verdict of 1918 by dealing with Moscow; before the verdict of 1945 can be reversed a Soviet veto must be removed. Chancellor Adenauer renounced a concept of national interest that runs from Tauroggen through the diplomacy of Bismarck to the Rapallo and Nazi-Soviet pacts. But the reunification of the two Germanies has also been Bonn's objective, and only with Moscow's assent can this be achieved.

The predicament of the West will be evident, and to it, alas, there is no watertight solution. It was a united Germany which, in recurrent German wars, demolished the European balance of power and destroyed ramparts against any counter-thrust from the East; it is access to a divided Germany that has enabled the United States, Britain, and Canada to combine with continental allies in shoring up a key sector of a global equilibrium. The Bonn Republic emerged under the shelter of that equilibrium and, as long as they need it for their security, West Germans themselves must boggle at any one-sided modification of the German *status quo*. But if the time should ever come when they want reunification more than other things, the defense of the West will suffer.

Unsettling, too, has been the impact of the arms race on the Bonn Republic. In any East-West clash, that country, with its borders on the Soviet imperium and with allied forces stationed on its soil, is destined to be a battleground. Would the Bonn Republic be devastated less if the NATO plan were one of holding a line at the Elbe rather than of giving way towards the Rhine and then lunging back? What, in NATO strategy, is the relation of land defense to the over-all deterrent by air? Would not local havoc be irreparable if tactical nuclear weapons were used? Can atomic and hydrogen weapons be banned altogether?

So as to maintain the NATO vigil in West Germany, American and British troops have been equipped with tactical nuclear weapons. These questions are therefore of the most immediate concern. It is with tactical nuclear weapons that the numerical superiority of Russian garrisons across the Elbe may be withstood. Will they also be assigned to the new *Bundeswehr*? What concessions will Moscow offer if, as it insists, they should be withheld?

A variety of schemes for disengagement and a more tolerable *modus vivendi* have been suggested. The arms race is, however, but a symptom of a deeper political malaise: only when the one is arrested can the other be fully curtailed. The continental framework of East-West power might be revamped. It will only be safe if an existing equilibrium is reproduced within it. To grant Soviet demands that NATO bases be dismantled would mean, of course, that the West European sector of coalition strategy must immobilize itself; the countervailing defenses of the West would contract, while Soviet power again expands unopposed. And among their political foundations is the German *status quo*.

It is far from ideal. Yet it does preserve an existing equilibrium and is therefore the one practicable alternative to Russian predominance. Some in the West have favored the idea of reunifying Germany through neutralization; the two separated German sovereignties should, according to Moscow, be neutralized and disarmed. But American, British, and Canadian forces have NATO obligations to carry out; either proposal would handicap them. For the neutralization of Germany, as a whole or in part, entails the withdrawal of NATO and Soviet troops from German territory. The Soviet imperium gives ample space in which Russian divisions that have been pulled back from East Germany can be wheeled about and sped westward again. However, troops from extracontinental NATO allies would have to be concentrated in the relatively narrow coastal fringe of France and the Low Countries; lacking room for deployment, they might be more exposed to assault, manned and missile, from the air. So, too, bases for supporting NATO aircraft would have to be crowded together when they should be scattered.

The West European sector of coalition strategy will have been impaired. But what if Anglo-American forces, rather than be thus jeopardized, are evacuated beforehand from the European continent? That is what Moscow has always sought: should Yankees go home, it would be dominant at last from the Pacific to the Atlantic.

And, from the Anglo-American standpoint, there is yet another military consideration. East and West would have to furnish guarantees of any German neutralization. That, however, cannot be done when the English-speaking powers have lost a tenable

foothold on the European continent. For the military consequences of German neutralization may be such as to render the
West less able to enforce it.

If the two Germanies could be unified in alliance with
the West, this thorny problem would not arise. But they cannot be; and it is through the Bonn Republic that NATO front
lines have been drawn. A reunited Germany may be the aim
that Western statesmen profess. It is upon a divided Germany
that Western defense is predicated.

Meanwhile Russia, like the West, must also prefer the
German *status quo* to any other arrangement that her rivals can
accept. "My cousin Charles and I are perfectly agreed," said
King Francis I during his campaigns against the Emperor Charles
V: "We both want Milan." To detach West Germany from the
West is still the Russian objective; but, until that proves feasible,
the consolidation of Communist rule in East Germany will best
serve the Soviet interest. During the second Berlin crisis, Premier Khrushchev demanded an allied withdrawal from West Berlin. The intention, however, was not to revise the German *status
quo* but to maintain it with less difficulty.

The gist of Russian policy is in that confederation of the
two Germanies which Moscow has advocated—a project whereby
the sundered halves of the former Reich may negotiate between
themselves for any further unity, but one, also, by which East
Germany will retain her Communist character. And yet, not
even a loose grouping can be approved that requires West Germany to sever her ties with the West or enables the Communist
component of a German confederation to act, within its walls, as a
Trojan Horse. What this means will be clear. The only safe
measures are those which, by pressure and counterpressure, redu-
plicate the German *status quo* in a new form.

Is it a peril to peace? The United States and Britain
have been dogged by their wartime failure to extract from Russia a postwar land corridor to West Berlin. In other respects,
nevertheless, the German *status quo* has not been as unstable
as many believe. In June, 1953, when East Germans uprose
against the local Communist regime, the Bonn Republic had not
yet been rearmed. But would regular or irregular troops from
West Germany now back another insurrection and thus embroil
with the East the entire NATO alliance? They might. For the
liberation of East German kinsmen, West Germans have displayed no great ardor; apprehensive over their own involvements
in the nuclear-missile age, they do not seem bent on military

adventure. Reunification may be negotiated one day—if not through the West, then with the East. West Germans are not likely to fight for it.

As for East Germany, since 1953 there has been a steady exodus from that totalitarian state, and it may be those least compliant, the ringleaders of any future revolution, that have fled. Nor do Germans, East or West, resemble the mercurial Poles and Hungarians; it is with the more submissive Czechoslovaks that they should, on the record, be compared. The Bonn Republic might yet prove itself steeped in democracy and welded to the West. Little about it has suggested quixotry as a distinguishing trait.

The East-West contest is, moreover, not all that freezes the German *status quo*. Moscow must also reckon with the nature of the Soviet imperium—a realm which is adapted economically, ideologically, and politically to the existing equilibrium. East Germany furnishes uranium; her heavy industry imports raw materials from other Soviet client states, from Communist China, and from Russia herself; to them she exports chemicals, fertilizers, and metal products. With a unified Germany which is not only neutralized but oriented towards the East, trade might be still more voluminous. In lieu of that, a maximum development of available resources has been undertaken.

Then, too, from the standpoint of Communist discipline, the German *status quo* is not devoid of merit. There has been serious disaffection in East Germany, as in Poland and Hungary. The latter, however, belong to Russia's own defense belt; non-German satrapies would be harder to cope with if the two Germanies were reunited. East-West disengagement might deprive Soviet forces of an East German springboard for a sudden leap against NATO defenses towards the Rhine. But as long as East Germany is kept relatively docile, she may also constitute an ideological buffer between provocative Western influences and the remainder of the Soviet imperium.

A divided Germany is, furthermore, what other captive nations wish their Russian overlord to maintain. Between two recent invaders, the German and the Russian, they still regard the Russian as the lesser evil; it is by fending off the apparition of another strong Germany that Moscow elicits from them a modicum of unenforced obedience, even consent. If Soviet forces were pulled back, Poland, for one, might gain more autonomy. But her project for East-West disengagement was of a piece with Moscow's scheme for a confederation of two disarmed, neutralized German states. She may hope that there will be less constraint in the Russian sphere. It is from the prospect of a German sphere that Poland recoils most.

Her attitude is, moreover, a natural one. During World War II, the Soviet Union redrew the boundaries of occupied German and Polish territory; their final disposition, it was decided at Potsdam in 1945, would have to await a German peace treaty. In addition to East Prussia, Russia filched a large slice of eastern Poland, and compensated Poland with Pomerania and Silesia, former German provinces to which she clings fiercely. In the surrender of these Oder-Neisse lands, the Communist regime of East Germany has had to acquiesce. The Bonn Republic, however, has been less amenable.

It may have withheld its assent as a trump card to be played when reunification is negotiated; but there have also been refugees who agitate for a return to lost territories. Warsaw, at any rate, has suspected that Bonn's real objective is the reunion of the two Germanies within prewar (1937) boundaries. President de Gaulle recognized that there could be no retrocession of the Oder-Neisse lands, and his candor annoyed West Germans. The upshot is that, in Russia's sway over East Germany, Poland sees a guarantee of her own postwar frontier.

Not that she is without anxiety on this score: what if Moscow were to offer the Oder-Neisse lands to the irredentists of Bonn as a bribe? It is at Poland's expense that a German reunification on Russian terms may be expedited.

Nor is it an imaginary bogy that frightens her. From Frederick the Great to the Nazi-Soviet Pact, the partition of Poland has always been the outcome of Russo-German agreements. It is the sight of a divided Germany that now helps Poles to accept their own harsh fate. In the Soviet imperium, moreover, Poland is not the only one that speaks from tragic experience. Czechoslovakia is afraid that Sudeten areas might, as at Munich, again be stolen by a greater Germany. On the West, a staggering blow will be inflicted globally if the two Germanies are reunified on Russian terms. But such a reunification would also be anathema locally to Soviet captive states.

That is another reason why the Western powers may be served best by the existing equilibrium. The British and French were to join the United States in sponsoring the idea of reunification. But none of them can neglect the cause of those who languish under a Soviet yoke. The West has welcomed the fact that Poland is neither as oppressed nor as oppressive as she was; nothing could so swiftly drive her back into Moscow's protective embrace as the rebirth of a greater Germany. Captive peoples lose heart whenever the Bonn Republic is courted. For their ordeal, the West often expresses sympathy. Yet, solicitude for them and Western efforts to reunify Germany have implicitly been at odds.

It is, moreover, not only East Europeans that have been haunted by the specter of another Russo-German accord. Generalissimo Stalin treated as a scrap of paper the agreement about Eastern Europe which he had reached with Roosevelt and Churchill at Yalta in 1945; but the clue to Western policy at Yalta may have been the dread of a second Nazi-Soviet Pact before victory over Hitler was clinched. No Russo-German alliance will materialize as long as the Bonn Republic wishes to remain aligned with the West; in that alignment the German *status quo* is presupposed. For it is a crowning irony that the United States, Britain, and France should endeavor to change an equilibrium that, from the standpoint of the West, is best left unchanged.

In West Berlin, nevertheless, they had given a hostage to fortune. When Premier Khrushchev threatened, from 1958 onward, to undermine Berlin's four-power rule, he could therefore no longer be denied the top-level talks he desired. More than others in the West, British statesmen and the British people had again been to the fore in urging that meetings at the summit be reconvened. Prime Minister Harold Macmillan, eager to head off an East-West conflict, hastened to Moscow; Foreign Ministers conferred at Geneva; President Eisenhower made a trip to India and visited his allies in Bonn, London, and Paris; so as to remove the sting from the Berlin crisis, the United States played host, in 1959, to Premier Khrushchev. Nor could less American reluctance to resume contacts with Russia at the highest level be attributed to the death of Secretary Dulles. Recent Soviet advances in war technology shaped policy inexorably.

To defend the independence of a city that is marooned like an island in an East German sea had always been an arduous task. Could Premier Khrushchev be convinced that he would precipitate all-out war if he pressed his advantage against the West in the former German capital? Since the blockade of Berlin in 1948–49, the major East-West crises had occurred in the Far East and the Middle East; between the United States and Russia there had been no direct confrontation. Now it was imperative to avert one.

And here coalition diplomacy underwent another strain. Immured in their small domain on the North Sea, the British differed from American, French, and West German allies with respect to the circumstances under which a summit conference should be held; ever since the Korean War first revealed the dangers latent in the strategic interlock, they had searched with more assiduity than others for ways and means to stave off nuclear war. Then, too, with their dependence on Middle Eastern oil the British were also exposed to a Russian squeeze through Iraq. Yet nothing said or done by the French or West Germans could diminish the British role.

As a preliminary to any Big Four conference at the summit, Mr. Eisenhower had visited European capitals in 1959. Worth noting in his London telecast with Mr. Macmillan and in his farewell statement was the President's testimony to the value of Anglo-American friendship; for while this gratified the British, it served no less to rap others on the knuckles. The British structure of oversea power not only rated high in American global estimates. Over-all deterrents preserved Europe from conflict, and it was still principally in conjunction with Britain that, as leader of the West, the United States maintained them.

Not that this was a point the British themselves were disposed to emphasize. Explorations for an East-West *détente* were more to their liking. But that did not make the Bonn Republic, as would be averred in some American quarters, the strongest ally of the United States—much less the most trustworthy. The fact was that if a showdown occurred over West Berlin, neither the French nor the West Germans had forces available that might have enabled them to bear on land, in the air, and at sea, as big a share of the load as Britain. Gaullist France had not been strengthening but weakening NATO; and the more the cause of German reunification is promoted, the less firm is the ultimate identification of the Bonn Republic with the West. All the same, a typical exercise in Anglo-American dialectic ensued. The United States and Britain diverged over how any new phase in East-West relations should be treated. Their solidarity was attested, nevertheless, by plans now mooted for dispersal, interchange, and joint use of bases by the Bomber Command of the Royal Air Force and the Strategic Air Command of the United States, and by permission granted American nuclear missile-firing submarines to use a British port.* For, at bottom, the principal English-speaking countries stood closer to each other than either stood to other major allies.

Over the underlying realities of the East-West contest there was no Anglo-American divergence. Russia might try to divide the Western powers—Britain from the United States,

---

* No less typical was a public misunderstanding, soon cleared up, over the degree of prior consultation that would be feasible before missiles were launched from American submarines based on the British Isles.

France from her English-speaking allies and from West Germany. Unlike Paris and Bonn, London had not been afraid that President Eisenhower and Premier Khrushchev would endeavor to carve up the world between them; the safeguards of interdependence were too profoundly in accord with the American national interest. Ever since the defeat of Nazi Germany and imperial Japan, the Kremlin has aspired to a bilateral settlement of global affairs between the United States and the Soviet Union. But that would detach the United States from her allies and leave her to cope alone with predatory rivals. A consolidation of the *status quo* may figure in the Soviet blueprint for the future. Yet Russia might still be tempted by her own ebullience to make a final bid for global hegemony, and against that contingency it is coalition strategy on which the West must, as ever, rely.

Meanwhile the mood of the West over Berlin, as the Eisenhower Presidency drew to a close, was a less pliable one than the East had anticipated. Mr. Khrushchev seemed to have been discomfited by that before May, 1960, when Washington mishandled the Premier's announcement that an American photo-reconnaissance plane had been shot down over Russian territory. Then, too, the fact that there had been such breaches of Russian air-defenses could only be acknowledged with the utmost chagrin. There were, besides, some in the Sino-Soviet camp who had long been opposed to the policy of an East-West *détente*: remnants of Stalinism among the Kremlin oligarchs, disgruntled elements in the High Command of the Soviet Army, the Peking regime with its more impassioned anti-Westernism. The Russians cancelled a return visit which President Eisenhower was to pay them and, in a series of diatribes resembling those that Adolf Hitler used to unloose, Premier Khrushchev made it impossible for the Big Four, all of whom had convened in Paris, to proceed with their meeting at the summit. Berlin, however, lay at Russia's mercy, and blows over it had still to be parried.

All the same, the inner lines of the East have been offset and its expansion checked by the encircling chain of air bases and missile ramps which the West has established. Devices that are less vulnerable may now have to supplement or supplant them. But when the Khrushchev plan for total disarmament was revised in 1960, Russia, by proposing the initial liquidation of coalition instrumentalities, again revealed her desire to gain a free hand in Europe and elsewhere. It was to prevent this that the countervailing defenses of the West were first organized. And only as the East takes a new course can they be dismantled.

THE WORLD BALANCE

The nature of any East West standstill will determine the sort of counteracting strategy that the West must retain. But to what extent would an armed truce be rendered unstable by the energies which the Communist system generates? In one respect, this is a problem for the West. In another, it could hamper the East. Under an American lead, the West has one common interest—the perpetuation of a free world order—which overrides differences and divergences. Does an equivalent goal in the East, that of a Communist world order, ensure that Russia and China will always be similarly compelled to get along with each other?

A rift between them would, it is evident, transform the entire scene. After strenuous efforts to drive wedges between others, Moscow and Peking greet with derision the idea that they, too, can be parted. They have used ideology as an instrument of power. The question is whether they will not have their own conflicts of power; whether these may not lie deeper than any ideological affinity.

China's alliance with Russia saved her from condign punishment during the Korean War and enabled her to dig her claws into neighboring territories. It also made the conditions of American primacy strategically more intricate and thus had a lasting impact on the coalition diplomacy of the West. Yet the amount of economic aid that Russia can furnish has been limited by the requirements of captive nations in Eastern Europe; assistance bestowed on other underdeveloped Afro-Asian countries; and competition, within the Soviet Union's own maturing economy, between domestic and military demands.

Communist China feels, however, that her ideological orthodoxy entitles her to more consideration than seed-beds of heresy like Eastern Europe. She wants all the assistance that Russia can spare; at the same time she has been vying with her own Soviet benefactor in proffering economic aid to Asian lands in a region where she herself means to be paramount. Perhaps, with a more plentiful supply of capital from Russia, there might have been less forced labor and the Chinese peasantry would not have been penned up in their hive-like communes. But whether this was so or not, other post-Stalinist regimes did not approve of what Peking had done. A fresh discrepancy in doctrine between Communist countries was visible.

A Communist world order may be the common objective of Russia and China—but is it, for each of them, the supreme national interest? Or are other more traditional ones still likely to come first? Russia has been the senior partner—a status to which, as the Chinese economy matures, Peking might aspire. Anglo-American friendship facilitated a shift in the primacy of the West from Britain to the United States. But their purposes are protective; though they diverge, they do not collide. A common ideology might also curb Sino-Soviet dissension. However, when two allies as expansionist as Russia and China must live cheek by jowl, this may be of less avail.

Tsarist Russia was the chief miscreant at the turn of the century, when it seemed that the Chinese Empire might be dismembered by foreign powers. China herself, by the end of the century, may be the one that menaces her own Soviet neighbor. Only the most grandiose of aims could incite so furious an industrialization. Great natural resources and a more ample supply of foodstuffs for the largest of populations are needed for that. Deficiencies can be made up, however, if, by sheer force of numbers, the Chinese spill over into the borderlands of Soviet Central Asia, into Outer Mongolia, and into Siberia as well.

For contention over *Lebensraum,* the time is scarcely ripe. Yet in the sphere of nuclear and thermonuclear weapons, the East-West equilibrium can be affected by Sino-Soviet differences at an early date. China may soon emerge as an atomic power; it is in the civilian use of atomic energy that the Soviet Union has assisted her. Russia has proposed various schemes of disarmament to the West. But no agreement is feasible that does not also deprive her Chinese ally of nuclear and thermonuclear weapons. Moscow has supported Chinese operations in the Formosan Strait as an internal matter; should Communist China become an atomic power, she may be more headstrong. There has been periodic alarm in Britain over the danger that, under the strategic interlock, an American quarrel with Communist China will involve others. Russia may be as eager to avoid an involvement with her Chinese ally against the United States.

The fact is that in their encounters with the West, Moscow and Peking have had axes of their own to grind. The Soviet Union may seek co-existence by bullying and blustering in the Russian interest; China's undue militancy might, however, jeopardize all that Russia hopes to obtain without a nuclear cataclysm. An East-West lull has been the Soviet goal. Yet, without global tension it will be harder for the Peking regime to whiplash its own people and wring from Moscow additional economic support. Russia may want to overtake the United States productively. She must beware, nevertheless, lest she be overtaken within her own camp. Her lead in the East is immense. But, as leader of the West, the United States faces no similar dilemma.

Does Russia have a Frankenstein's monster on her hands? In providing shelter, the Sino-Soviet alliance did for Communist China what the Royal Navy once did for the young American republic. What Russia herself gains is a freedom of action she did not previously possess. There was little to distract her, after the defeat of Germany and Japan, from imposing her will on Eastern Europe. On the Pacific, however, the United States had become predominant in the Japanese sphere. Narrow waters divide Siberia from Alaska, but below that a Communized China furnishes Russian territory with a buffer zone. An unanticipated boon, its consequences have been far-reaching. To a considerable extent, the rear of the Soviet Union has been covered, while forward policies are pursued in the Middle East and while, with the dawn of the missile age, wider intimidations may be attempted.

But whatever is eruptive in this same Chinese ally must, more recently, have ruffled the Kremlin. As a step toward the fulfilment of Soviet ambitions, Moscow may have toyed with the idea of a bilateral accord between the American and Russian titans; yet, such an idea would also relegate China to a lower rather than higher rank, and one, therefore, that Peking will not accept supinely. Even Moscow's program for consolidating the *status quo* in Eastern Europe may derive from its preoccupation with the development of Siberia; from an effort to erect economic barricades at the opposite extremity of the Soviet imperium. For Russia herself would be a handy victim if the Communist evangel serves to awaken, among a people as fecund and virile as the Chinese, immemorial hatreds of all that is alien to them.

No such contingency is imminent. Russia may, nevertheless, have to follow a double course: she will do her utmost to maintain the Sino-Soviet alliance; by a modus vivendi with the West she may also reinsure herself against her own intractable ally. Diplomacy by threat might reflect the overweening self-confidence of technological parvenus. It could also spring from a desire to achieve an East-West compromise on convenient terms before misdirected Chinese strength compels Moscow to take what it can get.

A Sino-Soviet cleavage would, to be sure, redress the world balance in favor of the West. But that is precisely why Moscow and Peking must fight one off as long as possible. The detachment of Communist China from the Soviet Union was an endeavor which London urged on Washington. The Russian attitude has tended to change instead. Nor is this only due to evolution in the Communist economy at home; some initial precautions against Chinese megalomania could thus also be taken abroad. Can Russia, for purposes of negotiation with the West, drop the leadership of the East? This might be done more easily in form than in substance. For leadership is a function of power and, while Russia is vexed by her ties with China, she would be much weaker without them.

As a coalition, at any rate, the East may no longer have the edge in maneuverability over the West. For now there are tugs in opposing directions which might also separate its components from each other. Inwardly so disciplined and outwardly so unruly, her Chinese ally can harass Russia in the Orient; in Eastern Europe, captive nations would turn against her if major hostilities broke out. But American problems are different. Free peoples have welcomed American leadership; it is the conditions of American primacy that trouble them—the fact that they have had to delegate to another country responsibilities which, by every principle of democracy, they should keep for themselves. Never in human annals has there been a more tragic paradox: a coalition strategy which entails grave risks is what also wards danger off.

And that is a truth which should never be ignored. Global mastery eludes the Kremlin when it fulminates against the West; its aim might be achieved if, by an East-West lull, the West were induced to lower its guard. A wise statesmanship in the West will adjust itself to the political realities of a split world; the means of guaranteeing any East-West accord must also be retained. For, if the two rival camps could trust each other, they would not spar in so deadly a manner; when there is no trust, it is the availability of counteracting sanctions by which agreements must be underwritten. In an era of bigness, the scale of preparedness by the West is necessarily world-wide. But, whatever augments that, extends grounds for divergence.

These, however, will be pushed into the shade if the East-West contest alters. The game for ascendancy between two concepts of world order—a free one and a Communist one—would then be played with non-military counters. Nevertheless, in quest of the over-all prize, it is coalition strategy which ensures that more lethal weapons are not employed; that, despite the intoxications of rocket diplomacy, the Soviet Union does not go too far. The alternative to defense is surrender. But the one rule under which freedom may be preserved without a major war is peace by power.

The accent might therefore still be on ideological and economic competition—a topic to which the last chapter of this book will be devoted—as East and West battle for supremacy. In the last analysis, it is a blend of military and non-military elements that gives strength. And power for peace will be exerted through interdependence.

IX

Sources of Strength

In the first decade of the postwar crisis, the United States, as leader of the West, had to renew friendships, build alliances, and ensure that uncommitted nations did not join the other side. But soon a second phase began. For with fresh prowess in war technology and political warfare, the Soviet dictatorship does not merely threaten that coalition strategy of which the Anglo-American factor has been the core; the challenge to our form of society is more formidable than any of which imperial German warlords or Nazi upstarts had ever dreamed. Not every nation enlisted in the defense of a free world order is a simon-pure democracy. But the interests of the West are upheld when any that wish thereby to preserve their own independence are aligned with it.

Other conflicts of principle have been as intense as the East-West contest. Its sweep is what makes it so all-encompassing and, therefore, so grim. The pages of history are studded with ideologies that have been set to work as implements of power; never before has there been an interplay of power and ideology which is at once so intrusive and so far-reaching. Nazism, with its Teutonic self-idolatry, narrowed its own scope; in universality of appeal, Communism has outshone it. And trends that two world wars had accelerated have come to a climax in collective efforts to fend off a third one. For an era of bigness in which the scale of human endeavor is enlarged not only widens the possible range of combat and extends the organization of deterrents but more and more obscures any dividing line between the military and non-military segments of the national being.

Coalition strategy has fostered a global stalemate between East and West. But this may be broken if the East is spurred on by a more potent dynamic; if it can yet summon up a force which, fusing tangibles with intangibles, seems irresistible. And that is why concrete military measures for the defense of the West are not enough; why it must also re-examine other, more impalpable, sources of strength.

Do these serve American power as well as they might? When primacy first shifted from Britain to the United States, it was the American political system which, with its pristine struggle for and against co-ordination, had to show what it could do; now, it is the American way of life, as a whole, which must pass muster. For American leadership cannot be sustained, the West will be outpaced in industry, in technology, in applied science, if Russia brings intellectual energies to bear with greater diligence than her adversaries. If young Americans are poorly trained at home and in school, if mass media induce mental sloth, if conformity spells mediocrity in the corporate and institutional sectors of the American economy, an easygoing American materialism will be surpassed by a more Spartan variant.

Not that there is anything new about such defects. They took root during formative years under the rubric of isolationism. For the security that the United States enjoyed while Britain was leader of the West not only permitted the American people to concentrate on their own affairs without serious distraction from outside; they did not then have to match wits with foreign rivals who were geographically less well endowed. It took skill for the British, much of whose oversea power structure rested on imponderables, to stand first in an increasingly competitive world. Americans, with their own ample backyard as the foundation of power, had chiefly to compete with each other. From the American Civil War to the economic depression of the 1930's, they did not have to pay abroad for mistakes they made at home, or pay at home for mistakes they made abroad. Britain, however, is a small island in the North Sea with no comparable reserves of physical strength. When she appeased Nazi Germany she exceeded her own margin for error, and, as a result, primacy in the West shifted across the Atlantic.

Little respite has been granted Americans to discover what their margin for error might be. National aptitudes were tested on the broadest front without delay. Coalition unity had to be maintained first of all; the most searching competition between free and totalitarian economies has also unfolded. Only through war could Western democracies hold their own in Hitler's day. Now the West is subject to the arbitrament of war—while staving it off.

It is, moreover, not the United States alone that must generate vigor in the non-military sphere. As an exemplar of bigness, she may be technologically pre eminent; in invention, it is her principal European allies that have been pioneers. Among them, too, mass living standards are on the rise; upon their ways of life it is not merely Americanization but also the East-West contest that has an impact. Certainly, it is through enterprise in science and industry alike that Britain, for one, can best keep a special place in world politics at the side of the United States. The tangibles and intangibles of power intermingle with her oversea ties, with the innate stability of her national character and public life, with the proven worth of her commitments to the West. Yet, she is no longer one of the colossi and, if she is still to make her mark, she must rely on gifts and qualities that mere size does not provide. More than for other important Western countries, resourcefulness may be her chief natural resource. But all are on trial.

And never has the issue been so complex. Inner directives, stemming from its deepest traditions and highest aspirations, may redeem the power of the West and govern the use to which it is put; the difficulty is that, as weapons, ideas are two-edged swords. With the English-speaking peoples in the van, the West may, over the years, have faltered and stumbled; its cause has been the cause of a free society in a free world order. It has stood for an upward revaluation of man; regimes that have devalued man it has opposed. Bigness has no ideology. However, it furnishes tools through which, as productivity is raised, the human lot may be bettered. But techniques that are employed by the West to emancipate can be utilized by the East to dragoon.

Germany was the first to demonstrate their dual capacity. Communist rulers of Russia and China have merely taken a sinister leaf from the German book. Nor is it an accident that, despite antipathies of race and doctrine, Germans and Russians should, in their revolt against the West, have followed a similar pattern: they had never been part of the Western political tradition.

Russians and Germans struck no lasting blows on their own behalf until reigning autocracies had been routed in war. The acquiescence of Germans in Nazi counterrevolution should have surprised nobody; it offered much that was congenial to the German soul. In Russia the Reds did not merely fight the Whites; proponents of representative democracy were also stamped out mercilessly. Repudiating the revolutionary ideals of the West, the Soviet dictatorship organized, on a large scale and in modern dress, its own brand of counterrevolution. And that is what it still purveys.

In the Occident it has had to bide its time. But more headway was made among the disinherited of the Orient. Colonizers like the British brought to Asia and Africa the rudiments of self-government; yet, against Communist propaganda, the peoples of the Orient have, on the whole, had no countervailing ideology of their own. It is not therefore incomprehensible that many among them should favor short-cuts to the conquest of poverty; and in this regard Russia and China have more to teach than the West. East and West vie with each other in giving aid to underdeveloped countries; the demand, however, will long out-run the supply. The Soviet Union and Communist China have accumulated capital by forced savings. Will the unprivileged peoples of the Orient be disposed to emulate them?

Asians and Africans might detest the cruel totalitarian methods to which Peking has resorted. Nor has esteem for China been enhanced by the rape of Tibet in 1959, or violations of the Indian and Laotian frontiers. But most Russian misdeeds have been more remote and, for those who were disenchanted by Chinese Communism, there was still its Soviet prototype to ad-mire. The fact is that without its particular moral code, the West might never have been free. But a concept of man's revaluation that derives from the Bible is, despite its Mediterranean origin, ideologically alien to much of the Orient. Not that the Occident accepts this in full; its own transgressions have been legion. In the democracies of the West, nevertheless, there has been an earnest attempt to overcome the illiberal use of technology. Only two Asian countries have also adopted it on a large scale and both have misused it.

Since 1945, Japan has been licking her wounds. Until then, however, she furnished a classic illustration of what happens when the industrial techniques of the West are borrowed before its political legacy has been assimilated. And as with her, so with China: for fifty years the industrialization of that land was deemed a liberal objective. But, under Communism, China has merely supplanted ancient evils with modern ones that are infinitely worse.

Nor have representative institutions flourished among all Asian and African members of an entity such as the Common-wealth. It is improbable that they will fare better among nations of the Orient which have not had the same kind of Western tutelage. And this is what makes so crucial India's herculean effort to emancipate, democratize, and modernize, concurrently. In her view of world order, she has registered dissent from the West. Yet she is also trying to recast her economy without sacri-ficing the rule of law and parliamentary government. If she suc-ceeds, a great Asian neutral will have done more than most to bolster a free world order. The danger remains that if she has to choose between democracy and technology, democracy will come off second-best.

But even dictatorship cannot bring quick results if Asian misery is self-perpetuating. The population explosion will nullify every effort to raise living standards. And, as a circumstance peculiar to our time, it again reveals the ambiguity that resides in twentieth-century techniques: the greater amount of harm, as well as of good, that they can do. Progress is at work when advances in medicine and sanitation lower the death rate; but, in underdeveloped countries, these have the Sisyphean effect of so multiplying the number of mouths to be fed that pressure on the means of subsistence may never be relieved. Together with Latin America, the Orient is caught in a vicious, Malthusian circle. Primitive peoples have been averse to birth control; instead of improved living standards arresting population growth, the latter drags down the entire economy. And when underdeveloped countries thus set themselves back, it is harder for East or West to lend a helping hand.

Can economic assistance be proffered them for its own sake, and as an end in itself? The East-West contest shapes international relations in the second half of the twentieth century, and little of global import can be done without reference to it. Very different, however, are the problems this question raises for the two rival camps.

In the past, private investment did what official economic assistance must also do today. As leader of the West, the United States is not as dependent as Britain was on oversea trade and finance; she does not therefore export so large a percentage of her gross national product. But now, too, the political instability of many underdeveloped countries may discourage private investment. At no previous time, nevertheless, was it deemed as essential to bridge an ever widening abyss between the "have" peoples and the "have nots." That is why a varied intergovernmental mechanism has been established to allocate loans, give credits, and make grants. The more recipients stand on their own feet, the less likely it is that they will succumb to the wiles of the East. And yet, as they are industrialized, their increase in output could embarrass the West. For they will have to have access to markets that, outside special groupings, Western nations do not open freely to each other.

These same issues could, however, embarrass the East even more. Russia, having furthered her own economic development, expects to utilize economic assistance as a means of further-ing the Communist cause elsewhere. But Western nations co-operate in this field; competing with the West, Russia and China also compete in the Orient with each other. To signalize an East-West truce, a joint project in economic assistance has been sug-gested. In such an undertaking Russia would take a front seat among the "haves." But China does not belong there with her. More suited to that company, industrially and politically, would be some of the captive nations of Eastern Europe.

A similar, if antagonistic, interest might impel the "haves" of East and West. What could realign them is a common threat. Satisfaction of their needs must constantly elude "have nots" whose population growth is excessive. But new levers of power might be employed to extort privilege and resources from those who possess them. Will "have nots" be emboldened by modern technology to band together against the "haves"? And if they are, will China, that most populous of states, put herself at their head? Colored races outnumber the white. Will they, under the aegis of Peking, be mobilized against it?

The portents are not all dark. For one thing, the interplay of power and ideology within the Orient itself may not, from the standpoint of the West, be wholly adverse. Pan-Asian incitements have lost their vogue. Domination by China would be at least as repugnant to her neighbors as was that of European empires. The West may be dismayed when the non-Communist countries of the Orient turn their backs on the processes of representative democracy; but some Asian regimes might also seek strength through dictatorship for defense purposes that coincide with those of the West. Diplomatically, at any rate, the Peking regime has been a poor salesman; against a backdrop of high-flown Chinese insolence, memories of white arrogance may fade. In 1959, when Communist China crushed the hapless Tibetans, a tremor of fear reverberated throughout southern and southeastern Asia. India, as a neutralist democracy, had, until then, discerned more virtue in Western values than in Western power. What she may now per-ceive is the extent to which these two elements intermix and sustain each other.

Nor is the Kremlin likely to observe new trends in the Orient with elation. Ultimate Chinese aims may not be for today or tomorrow; but the consequence of China's immediate designs might also be unpalatable. It is in the Orient that Russia has expected, ideologically as well as strategically, to outflank the West. There, however, her ties with China may already be a handicap. As leader of the West, the United States has been torn between NATO allies and their anticolonial critics. But her difficulties do not compare with the agility Moscow will have to display when it rides with Chinese hounds and yet hunts with Asian hares.

Meanwhile, it is the interplay of power and ideology within Russia herself that reinforces the Russian challenge and compels the West to reassess its own sources of strength. The captive nations of the Soviet imperium may be an Achilles' heel; but reforms that seem to relax its grip might yet ensconce the Communist regime more firmly at home than ever. Marshalling talent and directing labor, it can, as it combines bigness with despotism, canalize the collective effort, and thus devote to selected realms of war and space technology a higher proportion of the national product. If democracies did this, however, would they cease to be democratic?

Can free societies yet do by self-discipline what is achieved elsewhere by an imposed discipline? In 1914–18 and 1939–45, the productive feats of countries like Britain and the United States were as prodigious as any accomplished by an absolutism as technologically advanced as the German. But the East-West contest calls for wartime priorities without the goads of war.

Not that the fast rate of technological growth which the Soviet Union and Communist China exhibit is proof of doctrinal superiority. The British, French, German, American, and Japanese economies expanded as rapidly when they were undergoing industrialization. There is a point, nevertheless, at which its adversaries may catch up technologically with the West, if the United States and her principal allies do not do their utmost to stay ahead; if, above all, their economic capacity is not put to the best possible use. Nor is it only the American economy that will be tested. Tested also, from every angle, will be a potential for leadership on which the fate of a free world order depends.

Russia's ideological predicament is, nevertheless, quite as baffling. The belief is instilled as an article of the Marxist-Leninist faith that the West will collapse of its own inner contradictions. But those within the Soviet economy may be as sharply evoked if, while the West's rate of economic growth is speeded up, a countervailing strategy is still maintained. Science and technology are, for example, instruments of Russia's bid for global rule. Among her own populace, however, these generate pressure for change—for more of the national product to be transferred from military to non-military use. A law of diminishing returns is combated by allotting enough consumer goods to ensure productive efficiency, by offering limited incentives, and by providing, within an apparatus of constraint and relative deprivation, opportunities for self-advancement. Yet military preparedness must taper off if even these minimal needs are to be met. Nor can that be done if the emphasis in competition with the West does not move from the military to the non-military sphere.

But this also means that the state has, after all, not been in danger—that, with their Western allies, American capitalists are not out to overthrow it. The hypothesis by which a life of hardship has always been justified will, in other words, be outmoded. Russia may go on the warpath again when she can overtake her rivals in every category of industrial output, military and non-military. But the nation might, by then, be psychologically less malleable. There is, moreover, another reason why the Soviet Union may be slow to beat the tom-toms later on. To surpass the United States is the goal set before the people of Russia. Yet, as the Chinese shadow looms, despite Communist dogma, Western decrepitude might not be in the Russian national interest.

It is plain that a change in the pattern of Soviet politics would have wide repercussions. In tyrannies, the classic outlet for the wrath of the people has been war. But for Moscow, if not Peking, that formula is obsolete; the continuation of war by other means is, if Clausewitz may be so reversed, the substance of Russian policy. It is by diverting productive resources from the military to the non-military sector that the Kremlin might head off discontent. Sabres may be rattled and the world kept on tenterhooks as Soviet diplomacy exploits progress in Soviet war technology. But it is through measures short of war that the life expectancy of the Communist political system is prolonged.

This, however, cannot happen without another familiar postulate being disproved. During the middle years of the twentieth century, the English-speaking peoples usually assumed that there was an automatic correlation between abundance and democracy. But the Soviet Union may yet demonstrate that you can have the one without the other.

It has, at any rate, learned how to utilize energies which Western democracies have prided themselves on being best able to release. As the West reads history, the seeds of dissolution must sprout in every regimented society. And where, as in Franco Spain, the economy has not been transformed by techniques of bigness, that may still be true. But regimes that are politically retrograde could never have survived in modern industrial states if, willingly or unwillingly, educated classes had not served them.

Both German attempts to subdue a free world order owed much to the brains as well as the brawn on which German warmakers could draw. Before the Russian Revolution it was the Russian intelligentsia that spearheaded unrest against the Tsardom. Nowadays, they are not only cowed by a more repressive regime but, as pay for apolitical services, accept its highest rewards. The masses welcome slowly rising living standards; prosperity and prestige are garnered by intellectuals who have engineered the nation's forward surge. The Soviet Union has, moreover, become one of the two mightiest powers on earth; and, for this, Communist rule gets the credit. Perhaps minds will be opened by the kind of training and experience that more and more Russians must have if the economy is to remain buoyant. But, at the same time, there has been a broadening of the national base on which the entire system rests. Elements of change abound. Yet those who have a vested interest in the perpetuation of the Communist system are also more numerous.

In tapping Russian sources of strength, the present regime must, nevertheless, gamble heavily. It would lighten more trammels than it does, if that were not so. The risk it runs will be patent. Domestic forces which the regime itself has set in motion and strives to regulate may, as the economy matures, get out of control. Beneficiaries of the system might realize that their services would also be required under any other system; disparities in privilege may, as education spreads, vex many. And it is here that, in the East-West contest, the ideological advantage will lie with the West. For non-military competition with the West could make the Communist system less totalitarian. But insofar as competition with East will put the West on its mettle, free societies might be inwardly renewed.

The Western coalition is enriched by its diversity. The United States towers above her principal allies in mass production and war technology; yet, unlike Communist China, they crossed the threshold of industrialization long ago, and they have a good deal more to add to the common stock than Russia will ever elicit from the captive states of Eastern Europe. Not that they are on a par with the United States in the manufacture of major deterrents. In science and invention generally, however, they need take no back seat. The Anglo-American concept of interdependence is as relevant here as elsewhere.

And it is one which the British may well rub home on

their own behalf. Among the first to probe the atom, the compatriots of Sir Isaac Newton have always blazed trails in pure science; then, too, they brought out stainless steel and plastics, discovered penicillin and vitamins, pioneered television and turbojet engines. Among tangibles of power, the British may no longer be foremost. They still excel, nevertheless, among intangibles that can be transmuted into power. The past has given Britain a special place as center of the Commonwealth and as ally of the United States. But fresh achievement in non-political spheres must also uphold it.

And yet science is only one segment of the West's intellectual heritage. There is the lamp of the humanities to be tended. Nor is that task unrelated to the East-West contest. A free society is one in which man is revalued; non-material values give it its bearings. Nowadays, the emphasis may be on pure science or, more pragmatically, on its conversion into power, military and non-military. But care must be taken lest such pursuits become overspecialized and one-sided. When they did so in modern Germany they were, from the advent of Bismarck to the death of Hitler, a curse rather than a blessing. And under the Soviet dictatorship there has been a similar tendency. For an intellectual life that is overspecialized, and, therefore, one-sided, will always be easier to manipulate than a well-rounded one.

A totalitarian state makes the illustrious abject and the abject illustrious. Yet, it constricts some fields less than others. Scientific research, basking in a Kremlin glow, may break new ground; but, as tools of indoctrination, political thought and historical studies in the Soviet Union have been absurdly banal. Nor is there any mystery about this. Scientific research is, or can be rendered, ideologically safe; as far as political thought and historical scholarship consist of an unfettered search for truth, they must breed doubt about eternal Communist verities. Not that free expression in the West is beyond the reach of mass or group conformities; as a custodian of Western values, America, its own leader, has been prone to much that is anti-intellectual or intellectually one-sided. But here the mission of leadership is to defend a free world order in which there is a free flow of ideas; it is not also incumbent on the United States to assert intellectual primacy. Free societies borrow from each other. Russia, however, cannot allow an unpoliced exchange of ideas: what sustains democracy will subvert dictatorship. Unity among the tangibles of power is essential if the West is to persevere. Multiplicity among intangibles is a self-replenishing source of strength.

But it is not merely the interplay of power and ideology

within and between rival camps that governs the march of events. War technology has so altered the character of war that an armistice has had to precede rather than follow major hostilities. And it is this fact which differentiates the East-West contest from previous cleavages of a doctrinal nature. Peace did not come between Christian and Moslem, Catholic and Protestant, before it seemed likely that they would bleed themselves to death; for Hitler, there was no middle ground between destroying or being destroyed. But now the decivilizing potential of bigness overtakes a civilizing one, and what might otherwise be an irrepressible conflict must somehow be repressed. Under an American lead the countervailing strategy of the West has conveyed to the realists in the Kremlin the weightiest of messages: that modern weapons are ideologically indiscriminate; that, if the West is pulverized, the East will not be immune. The prizes of war may still be coveted. War itself would consume them—and much else besides.

The most awesome of contests was thus curbed before it ran its course, and the effect of that may be an unexpected one. Not that peaceful coexistence implies in the Russian political lexicon a willingness to live and let live; ascendancy over the West would merely be pursued in non-military rather than military spheres. But as this offensive proceeds, its initial impetus might wane. Communism, Fascism and Nazism were spread by failure and frustration; now the Soviet Union must learn to cope with success. After their defeat in World War I, the German people disclaimed war guilt and painted a compensatory self-portrait of modern Germany as a "have-not" power. Similar rancors against the West were nourished, moreover, by the Soviet Union during its early years—as an agreement between outlaws, the Nazi-Soviet Pact did, after all, have a certain evil logic of its own. But such grievances would be ludicrous from one of the principal victors of World War II, from a country which lords it over a domain vaster than that of the Romanoffs. And what the Kremlin must ask itself is whether others on which it harps may not soon be just as inapposite.

Will an outlook that served the purposes of Communist rulers up to this point go on doing so? Not that a less militant temper is an inevitable outcome of the favorable circumstances in which Russia, at last, finds herself. Prior to 1914, when Britain was leader of the West, the prosperity and possessions that the greater Reich enjoyed simply whetted the German appetite for more. But in those days, as again in 1939, Germans thought that they might conquer Europe before the United States intervened, and that the gains of war might still outweigh its losses. Today, however, Russia must not only employ non-military weapons to obtain the fruits of war: ascendancy over the West may cease to be a rational objective.

When Bismarck unified modern Germany he deemed her a sated power, and mankind would have been spared many ills if, under the Emperor William II, more heady liquors had not been quaffed. Now it is the Soviet Union which, like the United States, has come up in the world; and for her, as a satisfied power, the tactics of a dissatisfied one would, in the nuclear-missile age, be even more dangerous than they once were for imperial Germany. It is, in fact, the dissatisfactions of others and not her own that Russia must either exploit or protect herself against.

Moscow may allege that, so as to retrieve former Reich territory, the Bonn Republic will drag NATO allies into war against the East. Another Russo-German agreement is, actually, the one alternative to the German *status quo* which Russia herself would permit. And as in Europe, so in the Far East, it is against the Soviet Union's own Chinese ally and neighbor that the Far Eastern *status quo* must be maintained. Elsewhere—in the Middle East, in Africa, in Latin America—Russia may be at variance with "have" powers like Britain, France, and the United States. Yet she herself is a "have" power where, from the standpoint of her own immediate security, that consideration is all-important. Hitherto, the dynamic of a "have not" furthered the national interest. But such a dynamic is outdated by the new position that Russia herself has achieved.

Any dramatic acknowledgment of this is improbable. Russia's economic growth and technological progress have stimulated public self-scrutiny in the West; the question is whether, like post-war America, contemporary Russia would change her entire outlook on international affairs. To make her do so the West must hold its own ground throughout. And here, as leader of the West, the United States did not get off to so good a start as her British predecessor. A free world order was confronted by no serious challenge from the fall of Napoleon to the turn of the century. But the Soviet Union flung down its gauntlet as soon as America took Britain's place.

Not that this is the first time free societies have discovered how, in their interpretation of the past, treatment of the present, and hopes for the future, competing systems belong to different universes of discourse. A similar void yawned between Germans and the West when they let Hitler bewitch them. But now, under an American lead, there are the countervailing defenses of the West to ensure a reprieve from war. Free societies have, moreover, a capacity to outlast dictatorships—a capacity by which their power for peace may be renewed.

It is the genius of democracies that, amid the havoc of total war and short of utter cataclysm, they will rally and resume where they can. But a dictatorship can never be sure of its own subjects. Having seized the helm in one kind of chaos, it may expire in another; once its clasp is loosened, an authority dissolves which the submissive at home and the captive abroad will scarcely rush to restore. Even that sword of ideology which is brandished by the East with such bravado may thus be turned against it.

And these are truths that the firebrands of Peking as well as the sophisticates of the Kremlin will have to accept. If civilized society is shattered beyond repair, it will be no solace that democracies are better able than dictatorships to begin afresh. Yet the latter may shrink from ordeals that the former can face and endure because they, after all, have faith in themselves.

But democracies must also have faith in each other—enough, at least, to make the common defense workable. Sources of strength in a free world order are many and diverse; yet, unless they help leader and led to achieve unison voluntarily, the West may crumble and the East prevail. Coalition strategy, embodying the will to resist, demonstrates what the West is against. The reaffirmation of great imponderables proclaims what it is for.

And, at all that, few nowadays would carp. Gone, too, are interwar misjudgments by which, when they ascribed the plight of Europe to the peacemakers of 1919 rather than the warmakers of 1914, the English-speaking peoples paralyzed themselves. Even neutralists among them do not (as American isolationists and British appeasers once did) deny basic realities from which they would, if they could, escape. Peace by power is a doctrine it took two world wars to drive home. But disaster will again ensue if its safeguards are mismanaged.

Civilization was set back when Britain faltered in leadership. Still less, in the nuclear-missile age, can it afford some grave American error. Associates of the United States had long beseeched her to exert a directing hand; but what the conditions of primacy would be, only the circumstances of the time could reveal. Proud, self-governing peoples have had to preserve their freedom by entrusting to their American leader responsibilities that spell an abridgement of self-government. The allies of the United

States would have reacted against so harrowing a posture of affairs even if the American political system fostered the highest qualities of statecraft. There must be leverage for the United States if coalition strategy is to daunt adversaries of the West. But misgivings about it are bound to ensue.

These will persist as long as East-West tension lasts. They can, however, be allayed. Defects in American statecraft are projected, nowadays, on a screen as large as the Western coalition; and the more this is realized in the United States, the less will the strictures of allies be resented. Many of her critics are incapable of providing as high a standard of performance as they demand from her; a common peril is their warrant. Some admonitions by others in the West may spring from anti-American sentiment. Most signify that freedom of expression which is the prerogative of democracies and a source of strength that the United States herself must cherish.

Moreover, what is true of the West in general applies with special cogency to Anglo-American friendship. Two world wars and the East-West contest have tested it as they have tested no other factor in international affairs; a shift in primacy from Britain to the United States does not reduce its function as the chief bulwark of a free world order. And yet, as old divergences are overcome, new ones appear. Common interests will tell in the end. In one respect, nevertheless, the situation has altered. Britain's place was taken within a pre-established Anglo-American framework. But there is no power which can replace the United States and lead the West.

In another respect, however, history does repeat itself. As leader of the West, Britain did not always endear herself to those —the United States among them—who were beneficiaries of British primacy. Her backslidings dotted the map from Ireland to India. A free world order in which nations might attain or enlarge their freedom did, all the same, expand and flourish when Britain was pre-eminent. This world order the United States is now doing the most to uphold. Others, in varying degrees, share with her that cardinal task. And, if the West maintains unity, it may be for weal rather than woe that the supreme issues of the age will be decided.

Index

Index